VAT Planning for
Property Transactions

VAT Planning for Property Transactions

Seventh Edition

Patrick C Soares

LLB, LLM, FTII, Barrister

Sweet & Maxwell

Published by
Sweet & Maxwell Limited of
100 Avenue Road
London NW3 3PF
Set by Servis Filmsetting Ltd, Manchester
Printed in Great Britain by Biddles, Guildford

A CIP catalogue record for this book
is available from the British Library

ISBN 0–75200–588X

No natural forests were destroyed to make this product,
only naturally farmed timber was used and re-planted

Contents

Acknowledgments

The Customs and Excise Value Added Tax notices and leaflets reproduced herein are Crown copyright and are reprinted with the permission of the Controller of Her Majesty's Stationery Office.

The extracts from the *Yellow Tax Handbook* reproduced herein are the copyright of Butterworth & Co (Publishers) Ltd and are reproduced with their kind permission.

The extracts from the *Law Society's Gazette* reproduced herein are the copyright of the *Law Society's Gazette* and are reproduced with their kind permission.

The extract from *Taxation* reproduced herein is reproduced with the kind permission of Tolley Publishing Co Ltd.

Preface

This book examines the VAT provisions which apply to UK land transactions and related transactions. It also looks at the pitfall areas, as well as planning opportunities.

Since the last edition of this book major changes have occurred.

The provisions disapplying the election to waive exemption have been fundamentally altered. In relation to grants by developers the election to waive exemption will now be disapplied where there is an intention or expectation at the time of the grant that the land will become exempt. Chapter 19 deals exclusively with these new provisions which were introduced by the Finance Act 1997 and have effect on and from 19 March 1997.

Also since the last edition of this book major parts of the legislation dealing with the capital goods provisions have undergone fundamental changes with effect from 3 July 1997. These changes were introduced by the VAT (Amendment) (No 3) Regulations 1997.

The Customs have issued a new going concern relief notice—Notice 700/9/96—together with many examples of when the relief applies and does not apply.

There have been many cases which practitioners will have to get to grips with. One area of difficulty is the seeping effect of the European Court decision of *Lubbock Fine & Co v The Commissioners* [1994] STC 101 and there has been a recent VAT tribunal decision which confirms that the case has application where a tenant assigns a lease and pays a premium to the assignee (see *Cantor Fitzgerald International* (Decision 15070)).

The VAT treatment of many common transactions, such as the making of inducement payments etc, may have to be reconsidered in the light of the *Cantor Fitzgerald* decision and the true effect of the *Lubbock Fine* decision.

The law is stated as at 3 February 1998.

Table of Cases

Table of Statutes

Table of Statutory Instruments

Table of European Provisions

PART I

INTRODUCTION

Chapter 1

Basic features

Value added tax (VAT) is a tax chargeable on the supply of goods and services made in the United Kingdom.

It came into operation in the UK on 1 April 1973 and the principal provisions are in the EC Sixth Directive 77/388 of 17 May 1977, the Value Added Tax Act 1994 (VATA 1994), and the Value Added Tax Regulations 1995 (SI No 2518) (the 1995 Regulations).

The tax is administered by the Commissioners of Customs and Excise.

HOW VAT WORKS

Coming within the VAT regime

The prime charging provision is to be found in VATA 1994, s 4(1) which states:

> VAT shall be charged on any supply of goods or services made in the United Kingdom, where it is a taxable supply made by a taxable person in the course or furtherance of any business carried on by him.

The authority for that provision is in arts 2 and 4 of the EC Sixth Directive. Article 2 provides that VAT shall be charged on the supply of goods or services effected for consideration within the UK by a taxable person acting as such. Article 4 states that a taxable person shall be any person who independently carries out in any place any economic activity, whatever the purpose or results of that activity. Economic activities comprise all activities of producers, traders and persons supplying services including mining and agricultural activities, and activities of the professions. The exploitation of tangible or intangible property for the purpose of obtaining income therefrom on a continuing basis is also considered an economic activity.

The activities must be independently carried on, and this would exclude employed and other persons in so far as they are bound to an employer by a contract of employment, or by any other legal ties creating the relationship of employer and employee as regards working conditions, remuneration and the employer's liability.

Example—Employee/consultant

X Ltd employs Mr Y as a legal consultant. He charges X Ltd VAT on his services. Subsequently he becomes an employee of X Ltd. He must not charge VAT on his salary. PAYE will also be applicable and higher NICs will be payable.

Rate of VAT

The rate of VAT is 17.5 per cent (VATA 1994, s 2(1)). Certain supplies are taxable at nil per cent; other supplies are exempt from VAT (s 4(2)) and others are outside the scope of UK VAT. Some power supplies are taxed at 5 per cent (VATA 1994, s 2(1A)).

Input tax and output tax

The other critical feature of VAT relates to input tax and output tax.

When a taxpayer makes a vatable supply charged at 17.5 per cent, he will be liable to account to Customs for output tax (VATA 1994, s 24(2) and EC Sixth Directive, arts 10.1 and 12.1). The taxpayer could well have borne VAT on supplies made to him, and if the supplies made to him are to be used for the purposes of any business carried on, or to be carried on, by him, then the tax on those supplies is input tax. That input tax can be reclaimed by the taxpayer if he uses the supply made to him in making taxable supplies (ss 24(1) and 26(1) and (2), and EC Sixth Directive, arts 17.1 and 17.2).

Example

X Builder pays VAT on the acquisition of a parcel of land (the tax is input tax) and later sells the land, charging output tax. He must account to Customs for the output tax, but he can reclaim the input tax charged to him. That is the basic rule.

If a taxpayer incurs input tax but makes taxable and exempt supplies, then the 'partially exempt rules', which may restrict the amount of input tax he can reclaim, must be looked at (*see* p 79).

THE FIVE CONDITIONS

In order for VAT to be charged with respect to a transaction five conditions must be satisfied. There must be:

(a) a taxable supply,

(b) of goods or services,

(c) made by a taxable person,

(d) in the UK,

(e) in the course or furtherance of a business.

Condition 1: The supplies must be taxable supplies

A taxable supply is any supply of goods or services in the UK other than an exempt supply (VATA 1994, s 4(2)) or a supply which is ignored for VAT purposes or is outside the scope of VAT.

Most land supplies are exempt (*see* Chapter 8). But some are always taxable (*see* Chapters 8 and 10) and others may be taxable because the election to waive exemption has been exercised (*see* Chapter 18). Some are ignored for VAT purposes (*see* Chapter 3) and some are outside the scope of VAT (*see* Chapter 12).

Direct link required between supply and consideration

In the *Apple and Pear* case [1988] STC 221 the European Court held that a statutory body established to promote and improve the quality of apples and pears in England and Wales did not supply services to growers who had imposed on them a mandatory charge (the charge being imposed by the Apple and Pear Development Council Order 1980 (SI No 623). There was not a direct link between the services provided and the consideration received. This 'direct link' requirement is very important and comes up again and again in the VAT decisions and should not be overlooked.

The supplier will be chargeable to VAT on the consideration he receives for making the supply of goods or services (see page 21). To be vatable the consideration must be directly linked with the services provided.

In determining whether any consideration has been provided at all for the supply one has to look at all the surrounding circumstances (*Customs and Excise Commissioners v Professional Footballers' Association (Enterprises) Ltd* [1990] STC 742, Nolan J at 747j). If a taxpayer in a commercial environment claims that he provides services for no consideration this may be easier to claim than prove.

In *Cheshire Chimneys Ltd* (MAN/89/672 Decision 5112) [1990] STI 843 the appellant had been engaged to renovate properties purchased as an investment by F Ltd. The appellant invoiced F Ltd for the full amount of the work. F Ltd decided to sell the renovated properties; a director of F Ltd offered to split the net profit on the sale with the appellant and asked the appellant to renovate further property. The Commissioners considered that the payment of the share of profits represented consideration for supplies of building services by the appellant and raised an assessment to VAT. The appellant argued that the payment was gratuitous. Both parties accepted that there was no partnership or joint venture between the appellant and F Ltd. In the tribunal's view it was possible that the payment represented consideration for the appellant's undertaking to carry out further works for F Ltd. The appellant had not satisfied the tribunal that the payment was made otherwise than as consideration for the supply of services by the appellant in the course or furtherance of its business and the appeal was therefore dismissed.

If X makes a supply to Y and Y pays X by making to X an interest-free loan, the value of that benefit (and not the full amount of the money lent) will be assessed on X (*Exeter Golf and Country Club Ltd v The Commissioners* [1981] STC 211, *Pollok Golf Club* EDN/80/4 Decision 1044).

Figure 1.1:   Interest-free loans are vatable

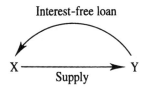

Interest-free loan

X ——————→ Y
       Supply

Identifying the person to whom the supply is made

There may be problems in discovering to whom a particular supply has been made.

The legislation states that 'supply' includes all forms of supply (VATA 1994, s 5(2)(*a*)).

The word 'supply' in its ordinary and natural sense means to furnish or serve (*Carlton Lodge Club v The Commissioners* [1974] STC 507). This indicates that there are two parties to the transaction—he who serves or furnishes and he who receives.

Supplies are not confined to sales (*Carlton Lodge Club v The Commissioners* [1974] STC 507).

It is important in land transactions to identify who is supplying what to whom. If the landlord grants a lease to a tenant the situation is clear: the landlord is making a supply of accommodation to the tenant.

If X has an onerous lease and pays Y £100,000 to take on that onerous lease, Y is making a supply to X of taking on the onerous lease (*see* p 335):

Figure 1.2:   Y is making a supply to X

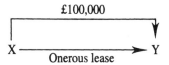

If A (landlord) pays B (prospective tenant) £100,000 to take up a lease of A's premises, B has made a supply to A of taking on the lease.

Figure 1.3:   B has made a supply to A

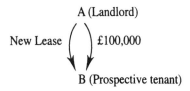

If a builder (B) carries out construction work for a developer (D), B is making a supply to D.

In *Ibstock Building Products Ltd v The Commissioners* (1987) VATTR 1, X (a limited company) bought hotel rights from The Measham Inn and allowed Mr Y and Mr Z to stay there. It was held that the hotel had made supplies to X, and X had made supplies to Y and Z. X reserved the accommodation rights in the hotel and the hotel thereby agreed with X to supply the accommodation to X. X, being a corporation, could in no circumstances use the accommodation personally. The accommodation was used by individuals nominated by X. Those individuals could be X's directors or employees or they might be others nominated by X. By nominating Y and Z to use the accommodation X transferred to them, ie supplied to them, the right to use the accommodation. The VAT supply line was therefore hotel owner to X then X to Y and Z.

Figure 1.4:   Buying hotel rights—who receives the supply?

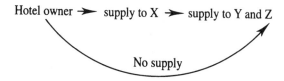

However, in the case of the *Institute of Purchasing & Supply v The Commissioners* (1987) VATTR 207, a lecturing institute arranged for a conference to be held at the London Tara Hotel and booked a hotel room for one of the lecturers. The institute paid the hotel fees. It was held on the facts that the hotel and not the institute had supplied the relevant services to the lecturer. The institute had merely paid the hotel fee.

In *The Commissioners v Battersea* [1992] STC 213 X sold property (Battersea Power Station) to Y for £1.5m and X agreed to pay £2.2m as a contribution to Y's costs of removing asbestos from the building. It was held that Y had made a vatable supply to X for £2.2m (*see* Figure 1.5).

Figure 1.5:   Contribution

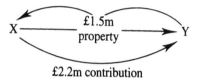

£2.2m contribution

Kerry J said the question was: what was done or to be done by Y which was directly linked to the payment being made by X? It was the service of removing the asbestos. Presumably, if the supply had been made by way of X paying a reverse premium of £0.7m to Y (£2.2m – £1.5m), VAT would have been paid only on the £0.7m. It is as if Mr X had a lease with positive values (eg rights to receive sub-rents) of £1m and negative values of £1.2m (eg obligations to pay superior rents), and he sold the positive elements of the lease for £1m and paid a reverse premium of £1.2m (vatable), instead of simply paying a reverse premium of £0.2m (vatable) (*see* Chapter 26).

General rule

Some projects can be very complex and one sometimes wonders who is making the supply to whom. It is safer to assume that if Mr X receives cash he is likely to be the person who has made the supply.

Buying off building obligations

A (a builder) may be under an obligation to build for B. A may pay C (another builder) £1m to build the building (*see* Figure 1.6). What is the VAT position? The answer to this question may lie in the doctors' surgery.

In *The Commissioners v Telemed Ltd* [1992] STC 89 the taxpayer company

Figure 1.6: Buying off building obligation

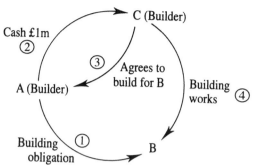

produced and distributed video tapes of programmes of medical interest interspersed with advertisements for pharmaceutical products. The tapes were distributed monthly to doctors free of charge, but charges were made by the taxpayer company to the advertisers, based on the duration and number of advertisements on the tape. The taxpayer company accounted for VAT on the advertisement revenue. The Commissioners considered that the supply of tapes to the doctors was a series of monthly gifts by the taxpayer company and decided that VAT was chargeable on the cost to the taxpayer company of producing the tapes under what is now VATA 1994, Sched 4, para 5(1). (Note that VATA 1983, Sched 2, para 5(1) is now VATA 1994, Sched 4, para 5(1) and Sched 4, para 7(*b*) was amended by the Finance (No 2) Act 1992, now to be found in VATA 1994, Sched 6, para 6(1)(*b*), so that VAT is now chargeable by reference broadly to market value rather than cost.)

The VAT tribunal allowed the taxpayer's appeal. Hodgson J in the High Court stated it was common ground that the supply of tapes to the doctors was a supply of goods under VATA 1983, Sched 2, para 5(1) (now VATA 1994, Sched 4, para 5(1)). The issue to be decided was whether the supply had been made otherwise than for a consideration. If it had, then the taxpayer company would be liable to account for VAT under VATA 1983, Sched 4, para 7(*b*) (the then relevant legislation) on the cost to it of producing the tapes. He held, however that no distinction could be drawn between the instant case and the case of *Customs and Excise Commissioners v Professional Footballers' Association (Enterprises)* [1990] STC 742. This required one to look at all the surrounding circumstances. Taking into account that case and the words of Lord Widgery in *The Commissioners v Scott* [1978] STC 191, which required one to take a common-sense view of any situation, it was clear that the taxpayer company was making supplies of goods to the doctors for the consideration paid by the advertisers, and that but for the consideration the supplies would not have been made. The appeal of the Commissioners was therefore dismissed.

Thus, if A pays C to do the building works for B the cases demonstrate that VAT would be payable on the monies paid by A to C, but there would be no VAT charge with respect to the supplies made by C to B (*see* Figure 1.6).

Agreeing to bear building costs in return for a land interest

The situation may arise where A grants a long lease, worth £1m, of Blackacre at a peppercorn rent to B in consideration of which B agrees to pay a builder to carry out £1m worth of work on A's land (Greenacre) which adjoins the land let to B. B will pay the builder the £1m for the works (*see* Figure 1.7).

The first supply (the grant of the long lease) will be an exempt supply by A to B in consideration of B agreeing to pay for the works. Assume the builder contracts with A to do the works direct for A with B paying the £1m. As mentioned, the supply by A to B will be exempt, but the supply by the builder to A (with the works of A being financed by B) will be a vatable supply, and the £1m will be the consideration paid to cover the building works (on which VAT will be charged by the builder to A).

Figure 1.7:   Building works in return for land

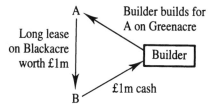

Intermediate plant scheme

Normally, of course, the payments will follow the supplies. Thus, if a landlord grants a lease to a tenant the tenant will pay rent to the landlord. The landlord has made the supply of the accommodation and the landlord has received the consideration.

It may happen that the landlord grants the undertenant of the tenant a lease of separate demised premises, having granted a lease of the common parts to the tenant who proposes to and does put plant and machinery into the common parts. The tenant will charge the undertenant a fee for the use of the machinery and may also exercise the election to waive exemption under Sched 10, para 2. This would enable the tenant to reclaim any VAT charged to him in connection with the installation of the machinery. The landlord will not exercise the election to waive exemption. This may save VAT. It is especially relevant if the occupiers are, for instance, insurance companies and the like.

It is important in a structure such as the above that the landlord makes a supply of the accommodation rights with respect to the demised premises and the appropriate part of the common parts and that the tenant makes the supply of the machinery rights which it installed in the common parts. That arrangement should succeed in its objectives but if, for instance, the landlord retained the rights with respect to the common parts and the right to receive rent with respect to any machinery installed therein, then all the supplies will have been made by the landlord to the tenant even though consideration may have been directed to be paid (in effect) to the tenant with respect to the machinery (*see* Figure. 1.8).

Figure 1.8:   Intermediate plant scheme

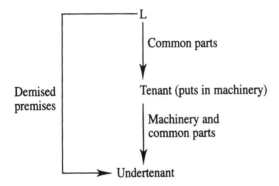

Finding the real service

It is not always easy to identify the real supply for which the relevant consideration was paid.

In *Harleyford Golf Club plc* [1996] STI 1764 (Decision 14466) a golf club wanted to carry out a major development and issued interest-free debentures (for at least 15 years of interest-free loan period) to individuals in return for becoming members of the club with full membership rights. If there was no debenture there could be no membership. The tribunal decided that the purchase of the debenture was non-monetary consideration for the supply of golf membership and there was a direct link between the two. The consideration could be expressed in money and one had to determine its subjective value (*Empire Stores* (C-33/93) [1994] STC 623 at 631).

The appellant received the free use of the purchase money until redemption of the debenture; the subjective value of that to the appellant was the avoidance of interest which it would otherwise have had to pay. In the absence of evidence as to the rates of interest at which the appellant could have borrowed the funds required for the development, the tribunal considered that the minimum lending rate was an appropriate measure of that value (*C & E Comrs v Exeter Golf and Country Club Ltd* [1891] STC 211 at p 217). The additional output tax would have to be calculated for each accounting period with specific adjustments for interest-rate fluctuations and membership changes as they occurred.

In the case of *Oldbus Ltd v The Commissioners* (LON/89/1657 Decision 5119) the question was whether monies invested in a company—which operated a flying club—by way of share capital derived from an exempt supply of a security (shares) by the company or a standard-rated supply of flying club facilities and advantages to the members of the flying club.

The tribunal stated:

> The correct approach, when this sort of question relates to a club, is to see what in reality the members are getting for their money. If in reality the member is getting the benefit of an exempt supply of shares, that concludes the matter but if in reality he is getting the benefits of membership the label given to the transaction will be disregarded.

The tribunal held in the particular case that the monies paid to the company by way of share subscription did not give to the subscribers any additional benefits or facilities as members of the flying club. The supply was thus an exempt supply.

In *Hinckley Golf Club Ltd* (MAN/91/1300 Decision 9527) [1993] STI 346 it was held that the only supply made by a golf company (a limited company) when it issued shares to shareholders was the exempt supply of shares in consideration for the purchase price of those shares.

In land transactions, if T has an onerous lease which he assigns to A with T paying A £x to take over the lease, A is providing T with the vatable service of taking over the onerous lease (*see* however Chapter 25).

Again if X transfers elected land to Y in return for shares Y will have made an exempt supply whilst X will have made a vatable supply equal to the value of the consideration X has received (ie the value of the shares).

Condition 2: There must be a supply of goods or services

Subject to exceptions, the general rule is that a supply takes place only if consideration is paid for the supply.

In many cases consideration is deemed to be paid where the supply is, for example, gratuitous.

If something is not a supply of goods but is done for a consideration (including, if so done, the grant, assignment or surrender of any right) then that will be treated as a supply of services. Thus if something is supplied and it is not a supply of goods and no consideration is paid, there is no supply at all; if consideration is paid then it is a supply of a service (VATA 1994, s 5(1)(2)).

There is contained in VATA 1994, Sched 4 a breakdown of various supplies into supplies of goods or services.

The general rule is that the transfer of the whole property in goods is a supply of goods. However, the transfer of any undivided share in the property or merely the possession of goods is a supply of services.

The supply of any form of heat, power, refrigeration or ventilation is a supply of goods.

The grant, assignment or surrender of a major interest in land is a supply of goods (Sched 4, para 4).

Is land goods?

It is often important to ascertain whether a particular item comprises goods (as opposed to ascertaining whether a *supply* of the same comprises a supply of goods). The general rule was that freehold land was not goods, although the grant assignment or of a major interest in land (freehold land or a lease of over 21 years) was (and still is) deemed to be a *supply* of goods.

However, a major change was made in the law by the Finance Act 1989, s 18 and Sched 3, paras 11 and 12, with effect from 1 August 1989. That legislation introduced a new para 8 to Sched 2 to VATA 1983. The present legislation is to be found in VATA 1994, Sched 4, para 9.

It would seem now that for nearly all relevant purposes land *comprises goods*. Land is deemed actually to comprise goods if it forms part of the assets of the business of the taxpayer, or it is sold, for instance, by an auctioneer, or it is held when a taxpayer ceases his business; and a supply of land interests (as a general rule) comprises a *supply of goods*.

However, that general rule is modified by Sched 4, para 9(3), which provides that, except in relation to a grant or assignment of a major interest or a grant or assignment otherwise than for a consideration (eg a gift), a supply of services shall be treated as having taken place rather than a supply of goods.

Special rules apply where assets are disposed of by, say, an auctioneer on behalf of another taxpayer (para 7) and where land is transferred as a going concern (para 8).

Example

X owns a freehold which forms part of the assets of his business. X sells the freehold. The freehold comprises goods. The sale is a supply of goods (Sched 4, para 9(3)(*a*)).

Example

X holds a lease which forms part of the assets of his business (the length of the term is not important). X gives the lease away for no consideration. The lease comprises goods. The gift is a supply of goods (Sched 4, para 9(3)(*b*)).

Example

X sells a lease which forms part of the assets of his business and which has five years to run. The lease comprises goods. The sale is a supply of services (Sched 4, para 9(3)).

Example

X has a freehold which forms part of the assets of his business. He grants a lease of 21 years or less than 21 years for a consideration (whether it is a market value consideration or not is not important). The lease comprises goods. The supply is a supply of services.

Condition 3: Supplies must be made by a taxable person

VAT registration

The taxpayer must register for VAT, broadly, at the end of any month if the value of his taxable supplies in the period of one year then ending has exceeded £49,000 or, at any time, if there are reasonable grounds for believing that the value of his taxable supplies in the period of 30 days then beginning will exceed £49,000 (the amount varies from time to time). If a taxpayer feels that he will not exceed the registration limit he may obtain intending trader registration. Customs feel they have a discretion to register such persons, but it may be that they are required to register them (*see* p 17).

Credit may be claimed for tax on expenditure incurred by a business before the effective date of registration in the following circumstances:

(a) in respect of goods purchased where these are held by the business or have been used to make other goods still held by the business at the date of registration; and

(b) in respect of services where these were supplied not more than six months before the date of registration (the 1995 Regulations, reg 111).

Tax invoices

A registered taxable person is obliged, when making a supply to a taxable person, to issue, unless Customs otherwise allow, an invoice or other document giving certain information (the 1995 Regulations, reg 13). This invoice or document is a tax invoice. The above is the general rule.

Regulation 14 contains a list of the information which must be included in the tax invoice to make it a valid tax invoice.

Ensuring no tax invoice is issued

In some property projects, the parties need to ensure that a particular certificate or document does not amount to a VAT invoice. In certain cases the position is clear. For instance, the valuation certificate issued by the quantity surveyor employed by the landowner, which is sent to the architect of the landowner, who in turn sends it to the landowner and the builder, would not be a VAT invoice. One would expect the builder to issue a VAT invoice to the employer in that case. However, there may be cases where it is important to make sure that a particular certificate cannot amount to a VAT invoice. Here it is normally important that no VAT number appears on the certificate, and it would be useful to have printed on it 'This is not a tax invoice'.

Obligation to issue invoice within 30 days

Under the 1995 Regulations, reg 13(5), the supplier is obliged to issue a tax invoice 'within 30 days after the time when the supply is treated as taking place'. The customer (the recipient of the service) can insist that an invoice be provided to show how much VAT should be paid by the supplier to Customs and Excise, and use that invoice, possibly, to obtain a VAT credit for offset against any VAT bill which the customer may have.

If an invoice is not issued on time, the customer, if he is able to show that he suffered damage, ie by not being able to reclaim VAT, may be able to sue for that loss. As far as Customs and Excise are concerned the position is governed by VATA 1994, s 69(1)(*d*), which provides penalties where any rules or regulations made under the VAT legislation are infringed. The penalty is contained in s 69(3), and could be £5 for each day the failure continues, up to a maximum of 100 days or, if greater, there is a penalty of £50. If there have been earlier infringements of the rules then instead of the £5 penalty there could be a £10 or £15 penalty per day, once again subject to a maximum of 100 days or, if greater, a penalty of £50.

In practice the Commissioners had often given a written warning to a person in breach. That practice had no statutory basis and could not be relied upon. However, FA 1988, s 19 (now VATA 1994, s 76(2)) states that there is a statutory condition that a penalty can be imposed only if the registered person has been given a written warning (which he has not heeded) in the two years preceding the date of assessment of the penalty.

The relevant provision reads thus:

> Where a person is liable to a penalty (under the relevant provision) for any failure to comply with such a requirement . . . no assessment shall be made . . . of the amount due by him by way of such penalty unless, within the period of 2 years preceding the assessment, the Commissioners have issued him with a written warning of the consequences of the continuing failure to comply with that requirement.

Issue of VAT invoice by landlord

If a landlord exercises his election to waive exemption, so that VAT becomes chargeable on the rent he receives, then it is important that the position with respect to the issue of tax invoices by the landlord is clarified between the parties.

Where property is let, the tax point will be the earlier of the following dates:

(a) whenever a part of the consideration is received; or

(b) whenever the supplier issues a tax invoice relating to the grant.

Thus in the normal case if the landlord is receiving rents and he exercises his election to waive exemption his tax point will be the date when he receives a particular rental payment (the 1995 Regulations, regs 85 and 90).

Regulation 13(5) of those regulations provides that within 30 days from the receipt of the rent the landlord must issue a tax invoice.

This can be rather an inconvenient procedure for a landlord, especially if his rent is paid by standing order.

Special arrangements for landlords

However, it is possible to rely on the special arrangements provided in regs 85(2) and 90(2). Under these, the landlord can issue an invoice at or about the beginning of any period not exceeding one year. The effect is that he will be treated as having made a vatable supply each time he receives or is entitled to receive his rent, so that the invoice does not bring forward the VAT liability date; nor does it enable the tenant to reclaim any tax earlier.

The tax invoice must contain the following particulars:

(a) the dates on which any parts of the consideration are to become due for payment in the period;

(b) the amount payable (excluding tax) on each such date; and

(c) the rate of tax in force at the time of the issue of the invoice and the amount of tax chargeable in accordance with that rate on each such payment.

If the rate of tax changes before particular payments are due, the new rates will apply to those payments, or at least the invoice shall cease to be treated as a tax invoice in respect of those payments (regs 85(3) and 90(3)).

Failure to register is not a pleasant experience

Failing to register while making taxable supplies is not a pleasant experience. The position of such a person is set out at V2.129 in De Voil, *Indirect Tax Service*, thus:

The situation of an unregistered taxable person is an unenviable one:

(1) registration is backdated to the date from which the supplier should have been registered (*Whitehead v The Commissioners* (1975) VATTR 152);

(2) he must account for output tax on taxable supplies made since that date;

(3) he appears to have no right to recover this tax from customers (*Franks & Collingwood v Gates* (21 September 1983 unreported));

(4) he is prohibited from issuing tax invoices while unregistered (VAT (General) Regulations 1985, Regulation 12(1) [now the 1995 Regulations, reg 13(1)] and he is liable to civil penalties if he does so; and

(5) he is liable to civil penalties by virtue of his failure to notify liability to registration by the due date.

Registering before business starts—it can be done

In certain cases, a taxpayer may not be obliged to register but may, nevertheless be entitled to register if he so decides.

Under VATA 1994, Sched 1, para 9 it is clear that a person who is not liable to be registered can, if he so requests, obtain registration from the Commissioners with effect from the day on which the request is made, or from such earlier date as may be agreed between the parties if he satisfies the Commissioners that:

(a) he makes taxable supplies; or

(b) he is carrying on a business and intends to make such supplies in the course or furtherance of that business.

This provision seems to be consistent with the Sixth Directive requirements—*see Rompelman v Minister Van Financiën* Case 268/83 [1985] ECR 655, [1985] 3 CMLR 202 and *Merseyside Cablevision Ltd v The Commissioners* (1987) VATTR 134. The earlier decisions of *Chapman & Chapman* (LON/81/213) No 1209 and *Cobbs Croft Service Station Ltd* (1976) VATTR 170 can be ignored.

In the *Rompelman* case itself the European Court held that, despite the restrictive wording of art 17 of the Sixth Directive (which seemed to imply that input tax can be reclaimed only if an actual taxable output was made with respect thereto), input tax can be reclaimed on a 'statement of intention' that a taxable supply would be made (page 211 of CMLR) although the legislation did not 'preclude the tax authorities from requiring the declared intention to be supported by objective evidence' (page 211 of CMLR).

The Customs issued the following Press Release on 25 September 1990 (reproduced in De Voil at V16.118):

VAT registration: intending traders—property owners and developers—objective evidence requirements (65/90)

Following representations from the accountancy profession and the trade, HM Customs & Excise have reviewed their objective evidence requirements in respect of property owners and developers who apply for VAT registration on the basis that they intend to make taxable supplies by way of business at a future date.

The evidential requirements will be relaxed with a view to reducing the burdens on business

—applicants will now only be required to state the nature of their intended supplies in order that local VAT office staff can confirm the liability of such supplies; in appropriate cases this may involve notification of their election to waive exemption for the relevant building or planned building;
—applicants will also be asked to confirm that they have commenced preparatory activites and the amounts of VAT that they have incurred to date; and
—the minimum evidence of preparatory activity that will be accepted is that an applicant has commissioned a feasibility study for which a consideration has, or will be, charged.

Further information regarding other types of acceptable evidence of preparatory activity is available from local VAT offices.

Prior to the review applicants had to produce copy documentation to show that they held title to the respective land or buildings, that full or outline planning permission had also been obtained, and firm arrangements had been made for the disposal of the property.

Notes
Under VATA 1983 Sch 1 para 5(*b*) [now VATA 1994, Sched 1, para 9(*b*)] a person who is not liable to be registered but who can satisfy HM Customs & Excise that he is carrying on a business and intends to make taxable supplies in the course or furtherance of that business is entitled to be registered on an 'intending trader basis'.

Prior to the changes in property liability introduced in FA 1989, many supplies in the field of property ownership and development could only be exempt. In order to satisfy Customs that taxable supplies were likely to be made, an applicant had to provide objective evidence to show that title was held to the respective land or buildings, that full or outline planning permission had been obtained, and firm arrangements had been made as regards the disposal of property.

Customs have decided to relax the above criteria following representations. The minimum evidence of preparatory activity that will be accepted is that an applicant has commissioned a feasibility study for which a consideration has, or will be, charged. Other types of acceptable evidence of preparatory activity are

—that the applicant holds title to land or buildings, or is currently negotiating to purchase, or holds an option to purchase;
—the applicant holds full or outline planning permission or is to apply for permission in the near future;
—the applicant has commissioned architect's services with a view to applying for planning permission or is to apply for permission, or legal or other professional services in connection with the intended sale or letting of the property;
—in respect of intended zero-rated sale or long lease of old people's homes, hospices and non-business charity buildings the applicant has obtained from his customers the certification required for zero-rating; and
—in respect of the intended zero-rated sale or long lease of substantially reconstructed protected buildings, the applicant has the listed building consent for conversion to residential use and, if necessary, the relevant certification from his customers.

Local VAT offices will now accept written statements from either the applicant or his professional adviser confirming that the above types of evidence are held. They will no longer have to produce copies of planning permission and legal documentation. More information about the election to waive exemption in respect of property transactions is in Notice 742B—Property ownership [now Notice 742].

The Customs subsequently amended that Press Release by a Business Brief of 17 May 1996 (8/96) which reads thus:

> The VAT (Building and Land Order) 1995 (SI No 279) has introduced the gradual abolition of the VAT self supply charge.
>
> This means that any development, where construction commenced on or after 1 March 1995, will not be liable to a taxable self supply charge. It is therefore no longer the case that a taxable supply will always be made of commercial property.
>
> This will only be the case if the developer intends to make a taxable freehold sale of a new property or the developer has opted to tax the property and intends to let it. This change means it is essential that Customs & Excise establishes the trader's intentions at an early stage.
>
> News Rlease 65/90 issued in September 1990 relaxed the evidential requirements necessary for securing intending trader registration. However, in view of this order, local VAT offices may require more detailed information before allowing intending trader registration. Notification of the option to tax is still required prior to registration being allowed.
>
> For further information traders and their advisers should contact their local VAT business advice centre listed under Customs & Excise in the telephone book.

Intending trader registration and sub-sales

Example

> X Ltd proposes to buy Blackacre from Vendor Ltd who has not elected to waive exemption. X Ltd intends immediately to sub-sell and complete the vesting of the property in Purchaser Ltd, and wants to ensure that all the VAT charged on the legal, accountancy and architect's fees relating to the property can be reclaimed. The contract of sub-sale will be completed straightaway. X Ltd should elect (and thus register as an intending trader) and notify Customs before acquiring any interest whatsoever in the land. There should be no difficulty in so electing (*see* Figure 1.9).

Omitting to charge VAT

The general rule is that if VAT is not mentioned and the contracts do not otherwise provide, the consideration paid for a supply is VAT inclusive and the supplier must meet and bear the VAT.

Figure 1.9: All at one moment

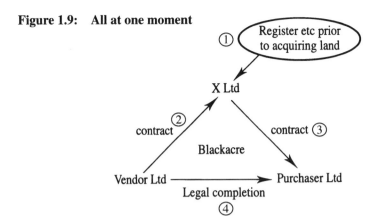

VATA 1994, s 19(2) states that if the supply is for a consideration in money its value shall be taken to be such amount as, with the addition of the tax chargeable, is equal to the consideration.

Thus it seems clear beyond argument that if X supplies widgets to Y for £100, X will be assessed to VAT and the value of the supply on which X will be assessed shall be taken to be such amount as, with the addition of the tax chargeable, is equal to the consideration. One multiplies the £100 by ⁷⁄₄₇ (known as the 'jumbo jet' fraction ('747')) to find the VAT payable by X: that VAT is £14.89. After paying that VAT, X is left with £85.11.

General rule: VAT lies where it falls

In the case *Love v Norman Wright Builders Ltd* [1944] 1 KB 484 neither party to a contract for sale had contemplated the incidence of purchase tax. Goddard LJ in the Court of Appeal, at p 490, stated:

> The plain fact is that the parties omitted to take purchase tax into consideration at all, and the incidence of the tax must lie where it falls. The plaintiff is accountable for it . . .

Contribution to tenant's shopfitting costs

In the case of *E S Poyser & Sons Ltd v Capital & Counties plc* in the Nottingham County Court, 24 January 1991, Case No 89/75411, Recorder Alexander Dawson dealt with the situation where a landlord paid the tenant £55,000 as a contribution to shopfitting costs. He held that the landlord agreed to contribute that sum to shopfitting costs (so that the tenant would receive a full £55,000 for use in defraying the shopfitting costs) and it could be necessarily implied from the wording of the contract (the landlord would 'contribute

£55,000 to [the tenant's] shopfitting costs') that that meant a net, after VAT, sum, ie the landlord agreed to make a net-of-VAT payment of £55,000. The tenant successfully sued the landlord for the VAT.

The judge distinguished the earlier case of *Franks & Collingwood v Gates* (1985) 1 Con LR 21 by holding that the relevant issue in that case concerned the relationship between Customs and Excise and the supplier, and that position was not altered by any contractual terms (although the *quantum* of the liability could be affected by the terms of such a contract).

In para 25 of the judgment, the recorder stated:

> In my judgment, however, the combined effect of ss 2(3) and 10(2) of the 1983 Act is to fix the liability for physical payment of the tax—ie to Customs and Excise—on one party to a given contract rather than on the other, and then to set a criteria for quantifying the liability where the contract is silent about its amount: as Judge Newey said in the case of *Franks & Collingwood v Gates* (1985) 1 Con LR 21 to which I have been referred in the Lexis version by both counsel, the Act may well be conclusive between the supplier and Customs and Excise, but as between the parties to a contract of supply it is only part of the background—and not definitive. So far as definition, is concerned, it seems to me that the words of the contract itself must primarily be definitive of the parties liabilities inter se.

The recorder said that it may become a practice in certain areas that VAT is assumed to be charged on top of the agreed fees—for example, if counsel mentions his fees to solicitors, there is an implied term established by custom that VAT can be added on top of the figure quoted. There is, however, no such custom in the case of landlords' contribution payments. Nevertheless, there was an implied term in the particular contract in dispute that the payment would be made net of VAT. The landlord, therefore, had to pay a further sum to the tenant to cover the VAT.

There are some curious parts in the judgment (against which there was no appeal) which can be questioned, but it is in line with principle, ie that the supplier must bear the VAT, but the parties (the supplier and customer) can contract between themselves to decide who shall ultimately bear that tax. What is difficult to see in this case is how the landlord agreed to pay the VAT on the £55,000 when the contract simply provided the landlord would 'contribute £55,000 to [the tenant's] shopfitting costs'. The result of this case, no doubt, will be that, where taxpayers have forgotten to charge VAT, the position will no longer be treated as clear cut (*see* Figure 1.10).

In *Jaymarke Developments v Elinacre Ltd (in liquidation)* [1992] STC 575, X sold land to Y and the purchase price was stated to be deemed to be inclusive of VAT. No VAT was charged because the supply was an exempt supply, but the purchaser sought to argue that the price should be reduced by the

Figure 1.10:

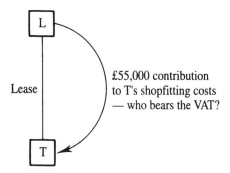

£55,000 contribution to T's shopfitting costs — who bears the VAT?

amount of VAT which would have been charged. The court held that the clause would be VAT inclusive if any VAT was payable, but none was payable and thus the purchaser's claim was unfounded.

Case study

X Ltd has contracted to sell land to Y for £1m *after* X Ltd had exercised its election to waive exemption. However, X Ltd omitted to increase the price to cover VAT. What can X Ltd do?

X Ltd should check to see if the election was validly made and notified.

It may argue that the Value Added Tax (Special Provisions) Order 1995 (SI No 1268) art 5 has application in an appropriate case (sale of going concern).

It could 'take on' s 19(2) (*see* p 20).

Condition 4: Supplies must be made in the UK

VAT is chargeable only on the supply of goods and services made in the UK.

If the supply of any *goods* does not involve their removal from or to the UK, they are treated as supplied in the UK if they are in the UK. Otherwise they are treated as supplied outside the UK and thus they will be outside the scope of VAT (VATA 1994, s 7(2)). Thus the sale of UK freehold land by a Frenchman to a German will result in a supply of goods in the UK, even though all the agreements and deeds may have been executed outside the UK and the parties never step foot in the UK.

If the supply of any goods involves their removal from the UK, they are treated as supplied in the UK. If a supply of any goods involves their removal to the UK they are treated as supplied outside the UK.

A supply of *services* is treated as made in the UK if the supplier belongs in the UK and in another country, and not in the UK if the supplier belongs in that other country (VATA 1994, s 7(10)).

The supplier of services is treated as belonging in a particular country (X) if:

(a) he has there (X) a business establishment or some other fixed establishment and no such establishment elsewhere (Y); or

(b) he has no such establishment there (X) or elsewhere (Y) but his usual place of residence is there (X); or

(c) he has such establishments both in that country (X) and elsewhere (Y) and the establishment which is most directly concerned with the supplies is there (X) (*see* VATA 1994, s 9(2)).

A person carrying on a business through a branch or agency in any country is treated as having a business establishment there, and the reference to the usual place of residence above in relation to a body corporate means the place where it is legally constituted (VATA 1994, s 9(5)).

Condition 5: Supplies must be in the course or furtherance of any business

Only goods and services supplied in the course or furtherance of a business can give rise to a charge to VAT (VATA 1994, s 4(1)) (note, however, the expression 'economic activities' dealt with below). 'Business' includes any trade, profession or vocation (s 94(1)). This is not an exhaustive definition of the term. Section 94(1) merely sets out a list of activities included or deemed to be included in the term.

The meaning of 'business'

The existence of a 'business' has been examined by the courts on many occasions. The taxation cases indicate that the expression 'business' tends to denote that one is dealing with:

(a) an activity (*IRC v Marine Steam Turbine* (1920) 12 TC 174 at 179), although there may be periods where not much is going on (*IRC v The Westleigh Estates Co Ltd* (1923) 12 TC 657 at 712); which is

(b) generally related to the commercial sphere (*Chandler (EA) v CCE* (LON/73/89), *Archer (RA) v CCE* (1974) VATTR 1, but *see CCE v Morrison's Academy Boarding House Association* [1978] STC 1);

(c) which exhibits a degree of continuity (*Marine Steam Turbine, above,* and *Morrison's Academy, above*); and which

(d) may create an entity which is distinct from its separate parts (*McGregor v Adcock* [1977] STC 206 at 209; assets are 'brought to life' by being used in a business). 'There is something organic about the whole which does not exist in its separate parts' (*Graham v Green* (1925) 9 TC 309 at 312 (Rowlatt J)); in addition some element of

(e) organisation, as in the case of a trade, may be necessary or, at least, a useful indication of the existence of a business (*Ransom v Higgs* [1974] STC 539 at 554).

In *Rael-Brook Ltd v Ministry of Housing and Local Government* [1967] 2 QB 65, it was held that a business tended to indicate the existence of a serious undertaking earnestly pursued.

The activities would generally have to be carried out for some consideration. Thus activities carried out without payment are unlikely to amount to business activities; for example the assignment of a lease, without payment, in accordance with the terms of a trust is unlikely to comprise a business transaction (*The Commissioners v Royal Exchange Theatre Trust* [1979] STC 728). Similarly, the receiving and distribution of monies in accordance with the terms of a trust without making and receiving goods or services in return would not comprise business activities.

The letting of three semi-detached houses may amount to a business even though the rent is investment income in the hands of the taxpayer (*Walker v CCE* (1976) VATTR 10). The same applies to the letting of 60 to 70 garages by two taxpayers jointly (*Williamson (R W and A A W) v CCE* (1978) VATTR 90).

In the *Williamson* case the taxpayers were actively concerned in the management of the garages and letting them to tenants for rent, not merely receiving rents therefrom. At p 100 of the decision it is stated:

> ... such activity is essentially a business activity of a very normal and usual kind: it is regular, conducted on sound and recognised business principles, with a structure which can be recognised as providing a familiar constitutional mechanism for carrying on a commercial undertaking and it has as its purpose the provision, for a consideration, of services which are of a type provided in the course of everyday life and commerce. In all these respects it competes in the market with other persons and concerns offering precisely similar services to the public at large.

Both the above cases (*Walker* and *Williamson*), however, involved the taxpayer carrying out some degree of control and management over what the tenants did, which went beyond the concept of mere investment. The mere holding of property even by a company was stated, in *Godlin Ltd* (LON/88/912Y Decision 4416), not to be a business.

In *National Society for the Prevention of Cruelty to Children* (LON/92/602) [1993] STI 275, it was held that the investment activities of a charity, although professionally managed, on a large scale and on a continuing basis, did not amount to a business or an economic activity. The mere investment of money and the purchase and sale of investments in pursuit of a normal investment management policy did not in themselves amount to a business or an economic activity.

In *J Prescott* (MAN/77/239 Decision 529) it was held that the letting of 12 houses by an individual amounted to a business. If the letting is left to an agent that does not prevent it being a business (*J W Wilcox v The Commissioners* (1978) VATTR 79).

In *Chandler (E A) v CCE* (LON/73/89) the appellant built on his land a house in which he intended to live. He intended to find another piece of land and sell the first house and perhaps carry through the same procedure again. It was held that he could not be registered for VAT because he was not carrying on a business. The same consequence would ensue even where the construction operations will result in an extension to a jointly owned property, or where planning permission has been applied for in connection with the erection of housing (*Foster v The Commissioners*, BIR/74/76, and *Nixon v The Commissioners*, CARH/75/184).

In *Archer (R A) v CCE* (1974) VATTR 1, the appellant (an Associate of the Royal Institution of Chartered Surveyors and employed as the projects officer of Essex University) was going to build a house for his own occupation on land which he owned. His application to be registered for VAT was turned down. The tribunal held that a degree of commercial activity was essential to the concept of carrying on a business.

In *David Ernest Sherwin v CCE* (MAN /86/171) the question was whether Mr X, who let a residential flat, was carrying on a business. The tribunal referred to *Walker v CCE* (1976) VATTR 10, *Coleman v CCE* (1976) VATTR 24, *CCE v Morrison's Academy Boarding Houses Assocation* [1978] STC 1, *Wilcox v CCE* (1978) VATTR 79, *Williamson v CCE* (1978) VATTR 90 and *CCE v Lord Fisher* [1981] STC 238. At p 4 of the decision it is stated that:

> ... it is clear that the question whether the activities of the property company amounted to merely investment or to a business is one of substance and degree. The property company may have had little to do in practice except to receive the rents and to pay the outgoings. In our judgment, however, the property company's function was not limited to those matters, but extended to managing the property and generally turning it to account, and in our judgment to describe the property company's role as a merely passive one would be inappropriate. In our judgment the property company's activities constituted a business.

The property in this case was beneficially owned not by a company, but by an individual.

In *The Trustees of the Mellerstain Trust v Commissioners of Customs and Excise* (1989) VATTR 223, X acquired assets by way of gift. It was held that if X then disposed of the assets there was no 'business' for the purposes of VAT. Thus VAT could not be charged unless it could be demonstrated that the proceeds of sale were to be used in carrying out a new business as opposed to, for instance, simply putting the money on deposit or investing in shares. This is because the sale of the assets would have been made in furtherance of the new business.

If an activity is carried out basically for pleasure or for social enjoyment there will be no business, even though the activity may be organised in a businesslike way. In *The Commissioners v Lord Fisher* [1981] STC 238 the appellant owned the shooting rights over the family estate and invited friends and relations to shoot there as family guests. He also carried out some business activities on the estate and was registered for VAT. In time the expenses of the shoots became onerous and guests made a specific contribution to costs. The contributions met about half the costs. Guests who accepted the invitations met at the mansion and were provided with refreshments, and they brought their own cartridges. Records of the receipts from the shoot and the expenses were kept as part of the estate records. Gibson J held that the running of the shoots did not amount to the carrying on of a business; the shoots were for pleasure and enjoyment, and the fact that they were run in a businesslike way, and that guests contributed towards the costs, did not turn the activity into a business for VAT purposes.

If a non-resident company sells a UK dwelling house, can VAT be chargeable? Often a non-resident company will buy a UK dwelling house for its shareholders to use and the question may be raised whether VAT must be charged on the sale thereof. No VAT it is felt will be in point because, *inter alia*, a dwelling house (this includes all fixtures but not loose items such as furniture) is being sold and the supply is therefore exempt (VATA 1994, Sched 9, Group 1). The present VAT registration limit is £49,000 (*see* VATA 1994, Sched 1, para 1(1)). If the furniture is sold at *market value* of, say, £45,000 no VAT will be in point. If it is sold for over £49,000 the vendor must register for VAT and charge VAT on the sale; the vendor is a company and is likely to be making a supply in the course of a business (VATA 1994, s 4).

Deemed business

For VAT purposes the following are deemed to be carrying on a business:

(a) the provision by a club, association or organisation (for a subscription or other consideration) of the facilities or advantages available to its members; and

(b) the admission, for a consideration, of persons to any premises (VATA 1994, s 94(2)).

Livery companies and the like may register for VAT so that they can reclaim input tax on extension works. However, they should be aware that, once registered, Customs can in many cases substitute market value when they make outputs for a consideration (eg subscription fees or dues) at less than the market value of the goods and services provided by them to their members.

Note also that whatever a company does is likely to amount to a business or economic activity.

Example

X Inc owns a flat in the UK which is used by its non-UK owner. It sells the flat for £3m and the furniture (eg chairs etc) therein for £70,000. VAT must be charged on the £70,000 unless exceptionally the company can successfully plead the application of the composite supply doctrine (*see* page 42).

Economic activity

Although VATA 1994, s 4(1) refers to a 'business', the expression which should have been used in s 4(1) is 'economic activity'. That expression is found in the EC Sixth Directive, art 4(1) and (2), and is a wider concept than business and is to be given 'a very wide scope' and be 'broadly interpreted' (*Van Tiem v SVF* (Case C-186/89) [1993] STC 91 at 100). This may be of particular importance if the taxpayer waives the exemption under VATA 1994, Sched 10, para 2 with regard to the letting of a property. The relevant terminology must be that contained in the Sixth Directive. The UK legislature has invented its own term and, if it conflicts with the directive, it will be overridden by the directive. There are many cases on the meaning of 'business' which have come before the VAT tribunals (*see* pp 24–7 *above*). Those cases may be irrelevant if they have not been (and few have been) construed in accordance with the requirements of the Sixth Directive and they conflict with the directive. The Sixth Directive, art 4(2) provides:

> The exploitation of tangible or intangible property for the purpose of obtaining income therefrom on a continuing basis shall also be considered an economic activity.

If that definition is applied, then if Mr X lets property, albeit on a tenant's full repairing lease, Mr X will be carrying on an economic activity and is in a position to exercise the election to waive exemption under Sched 10, para 2. Customs may (though this is unlikely) argue that Mr X is merely holding an investment and is not carrying on a business, and therefore cannot exercise the option. If they were to raise such an argument, they should be referred to the Sixth Directive.

If Mr X, on the other hand, wishes to sell a piece of his back garden, this is unlikely to comprise a business or an economic activity, so that he could not effectively waive exemption. Much may depend, however, on the particular facts of the case, eg he may apply for planning permission and enter into a joint venture agreement with a builder, and that may amount to a business or an economic activity.

If Mr Y surrenders the lease of his flat, which is his residence, that is unlikely to amount to a business or an economic activity.

Note that anything a company does is very likely to be done in the course or furtherance of a business or an economic activity, but not always.

If a family trust lets property, that is likely to amount to a business and an economic activity.

Example

X family trust—it could be a discretionary trust or one where property is held for A for life and then B absolutely—buys property and exercises the election to waive exemption. The exercise should be effective as the trustees would be carrying on a business and an economic activity.

If the taxpayer buys and sells a parcel of land without having developed or redeveloped it, and that amounts to a trading transaction, he will have carried on a business (s 94(1)) and an economic activity.

If the taxpayer buys and sells a parcel of land without having developed or redeveloped it, and this does not amount to a trading transaction, the position is borderline, although the author feels it is likely to amount to a business and an economic activity.

However, one should note the following statement in one VAT case which dealt with a one-off transaction:

The expression a person who makes taxable supplies, with its use of the present tense and the plural number, seems to us to denote at least some degree of continuity or regularity; we do not think that it will apply, for instance, to a person who has only ever made one taxable supply and has no immediate prospect of making another (*Merseyside Cablevision v The Commissioners* (1987) VATTR 134).

There is some European law guidance in this area. In *DA Rompelman and EA Rompleman-Van Deeden v Minister van Financiën* (Case 268/83) [1985] ECR 655 it was held the acquisition of a right to the title in a building under construction with a view to subsequent letting was on economic activity. The European Court in *Van Tiem v SVF* (Case C-186/89), 4 December 1990, [1993] STC 91, held that the grant by X to Y of the right to use development property (*droit de superficie*) for 18 years for an annual consideration amounted to an economic activity. There was thus a VAT supply by X.

RATE OF VAT AND HOW IT IS CHARGED

The standard rate of VAT is 17.5 per cent and is charged on the supply of goods or services by reference to the value of the supply (s 2(1)).

If the supply is for a consideration in money, its value shall be taken to be such amount as, with the addition of the VAT chargeable, is equal to the consideration (s 19(2)).

Example

X Ltd makes a supply of elected land to Y Ltd for £100,000. X Ltd has to pay £14,893.62 in VAT (ie 7/47ths of £100,000).

If the supply is for a consideration not consisting or not wholly consisting of money, its value shall be taken to be such amount in money as, with the addition of the VAT chargeable, is equivalent to the consideration (s 19(3)).

Example

X Ltd makes a supply of elected land (Blackacre) to Y Ltd for £100,000-worth of land (Greenacre). X Ltd has to pay VAT of £14,893.62 (ie 7/47ths of the value of Greenacre) (*see* page 385).

The test to be applied in valuing Greenacre in the above example has a surprisingly subjective element. In *Cumbernauld* (EDN/96/92; Decision 14630) the Cumbernauld Development Corporation (CDC) spent a considerable sum of money on developing land as part of a land exchange deal with Dullatur Golf Club (DGC) (*see* Figure 1.11 *below*).

The tribunal held one had to ignore the fact the parties put in nil consideration for the exchange (p 11). The correct test is to find the consideration

Figure 1.11:   Consideration in the form of a land interest

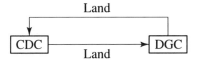

obtained by CDC (being the land obtained from DGC) and its value must be 'calculated subjectively by determining the value attributed by CDC to what they obtained' (p 13).

The relevant provisions are in the EC Sixth Directive, art 11(a) and VATA 1994, s 19(3) and a curious subjective element (presumably a *bona fide* subjective element) has crept in.

Practitioners should always seek to agree the exchange figures; if reasonable the Customs are unlikely to get over-concerned, depending on the precise circumstances of the case.

Changes in VAT rates between contracts and supplies

The general rule is if a taxpayer omits to refer to VAT in his contract then the supply is VAT inclusive. He is liable for VAT and cannot demand further sums from the purchaser/lessee to cover that VAT (*see* p 20).

Where, after the making of a contract for the supply of goods or services but before the goods or services are supplied, there is a 'change' in the tax charged on the supply, then, unless the contract otherwise provides, VAT can be added to the amount otherwise chargeable (s 89(1)).

References to a 'change' above include a change because the supplier has exercised his option to waive exemption (s 89(3)).

Example

> L granted a lease many years ago to T. The rent is £1m. No reference to VAT and the like is made in the lease. L exercises its option to waive exemption on 1 August 1989. T must pay the additional standard rate VAT on top of the £1m. The same applies whenever the lease is granted provided there are no specific terms in the lease preventing VAT being added to the rent otherwise chargeable (*see* p 33).

If X has exercised the election with regard to a particular property and thereafter contracts to sell the same the VAT is inclusive, ie he cannot add VAT on top of the agreed sale price (unless the contract so provides).

Position if VAT were to become compulsorily chargeable on rents

The question is often raised as to what the VAT position would be if, in future, VAT becomes chargeable on all commercial lettings. No problems will arise with respect to lettings after the change as a taxpayer would ensure that there is an appropriate clause in the lease enabling the landlord to charge VAT in addition to the rent. But what of leases granted before the change in the law?

The position may have been specifically anticipated by the landlord and the tenant and dealt with in the lease, the rent being either VAT inclusive or exclusive. If, on the other hand, the lease simply reserves a rent without any reference to VAT, the author feels that the situation is likely to be governed by VATA 1994, s 89. Section 89 provides that where, after the making of a contract for the supply of goods or services and before the goods or services are supplied, there is a change in the VAT charged on the supply then VAT can be charged in addition to the consideration for the supply. This provision specifically applies to a tenancy or lease, and references in the provision to a contract are deemed to be references to a tenancy or lease.

If there are no particular clauses in the tenancy or lease dealing with VAT the landlord can add the VAT on top of the rent; on present rates, if the rent is £100, the landlord can charge £100 plus £17.50 VAT. However, to exclude that provision from applying, for example, to make the rent VAT inclusive, it is important that the clause specifically refers to VAT or to VATA 1994, s 89. It is not sufficient to refer to taxes in general as that is not a specific reference to VAT. Thus, if the clause specifically provides that if VAT becomes chargeable on the rent then any VAT would be included in the rent figure, or if VATA 1994, s 89 is specifically referred to and its provisions excluded, then this should ensure that the rent is VAT inclusive.

Omitting to collect VAT at completion

If at legal completion the vendor is entitled to a further sum for VAT by virtue of VATA 1994, s 89, but does not claim it because he was not aware of the VAT position, but soon thereafter recognises his oversight, there is nothing to prevent him suing the purchaser for the further sum to cover the VAT. It is unlikely that the purchaser can rely on the Misrepresentation Act 1967 to defeat the vendor's claim (*see Chitty on Contracts*, 27th edn, Vol 1, 6–004 *et seq* and *Brekom Investments Ltd v Seaford* [1981] 1 WLR 863; *Beesly v Hallwood Estates Ltd* [1960] 1 WLR 549; *Smith v Chadwick* (1884) 9 App Cas 187; and *Seddon v North Eastern Salt Co Ltd* [1905] 1 Ch 326. *See also Hedley Byrne v Heller and Partners* [1964] AC 465 and *Caparo plc v*

Dickman [1992] AC 605). Ideally, of course, the vendor should collect the money at completion! The vendor should also supply the purchaser with a VAT invoice (the 1995 Regulations, reg 13(1): a person making a taxable supply must always, subject to certain exceptions, supply another taxable person with a VAT invoice).

If X has let his freehold property to Y and VAT is not mentioned in the lease, and X subsequently exercises the election to waive exemption, VAT can be added to the rent. If, subsequently, Y surrenders the lease or it expires and a lease on similar terms (ie not mentioning VAT) is granted by X, the rent is VAT inclusive (*see* VATA 1994, s 42). This trap is to be avoided at all costs.

TAX CLAUSE IN A BUSINESS LEASE

A business lease may contain a clause covering rates and taxes, for example:

Rates, taxes, etc

The tenant is to pay and discharge all general rates, water rates and all existing and future rates, taxes, charges, assessments, impositions and outgoings whatsoever (whether parliamentary municipal parochial or otherwise) which are now or may at any time hereafter be payable charged or assessed on or in respect of the demised premises during the said term except tax assessable on the landlord in respect of rents and other payments arising under this lease or any superior lease.

This clause will not prevent the landlord from exercising his election to waive exemption so as to add VAT on the rents, even though it may be claimed that the VAT is assessable on the landlord in respect of the rents and other payments arising under the lease. The VAT will be added on top of the rents and other sums payable by the tenant under the lease. This is because of VATA 1994, s 89.

Section 89(1) provides:

Where, after the making of a contract for a supply of goods or services and before the goods or services are supplied, there is a change in the tax charged on the supply, then unless the contract otherwise provided, there shall be added to or deducted from the consideration for the supply an amount equal to the change.

Section 89(2) provides that s 89(1) shall apply:

... in relation to a lease or tenancy as it applies in relation to a contract except that a term of a tenancy or lease shall not be taken to provide that the rule contained in that subsection is not to apply in the case of tenancy or lease if the term does not [refer] specifically to value added tax or [to s 89].

Finally, it is provided in s 89(3) that:

> References . . . to a change in the VAT charged on a supply include refer-
> ences to a change to or from no tax being charged on the supply (includ-
> ing a change attributable to the making of an election under para 2 of Sched
> 10).

Would such a clause in the lease (effectively) prevent the landlord from electing to waive exemption with respect to the property or ensure that such an election results in a VAT inclusive charge?

Such a clause will not prevent the landlord from electing to waive exemption and would enable the landlord to add VAT on top of the monies otherwise payable under the lease for the following reasons:

(1) Section 89 of VATA 1994 is not referred to in the clause and there is *no specific reference to value added tax*. There is only a general reference to tax. The use of the word 'VAT' in the VAT legislation is a reference only to VAT (*see* VATA 1994, s 96) and in the Income and Corporation Taxes Act 1988 a reference to 'tax' generally means income tax and corporation tax (Income and Corporation Taxes Act 1988, s 832(3)). Even if the technical meaning of the word 'VAT' is implicitly incorporated into the clause in the lease it cannot be said that there is a specific reference to value added tax.

(2) There has to be a provision in the lease providing that tax cannot be added to the rent or other sums payable to the landlord. The above lease clause does not provide that tax assessable on the landlord in respect of rents or other payments shall not be paid by the tenant; it simply provides that other taxes (eg rates) shall be paid by the tenant, excluding from that express obligation any tax assessable in respect of the rent and other payments. The tenant does not have to pay any taxes assessable on the rent because there is no provision saying that the tax referable to rents and other payments shall be paid by the tenant.

Thus not only does such a clause not refer specifically to VAT or VATA 1994, s 89, but the contract does not provide that tax assessed on the lessor in respect of rents and other payments shall not be paid by the tenant; there is simply no provision enabling the landlord to claim such tax.

PENALTIES

The VAT penalties are a 'tax' which the government has introduced by the back door. The 'tax' can be avoided by complying with the rules.

Penalties may be imposed if a taxpayer does not register for VAT in time, or Customs do not receive the return, or the return has been received but the tax not paid.

If the taxpayer makes serious mistakes (eg underdeclares (broadly) 30 per cent or more of the tax payable) he can be liable to pay 15 per cent of the VAT as a penalty (VATA 1994, s 63(2)), or if he persistently makes smaller underdeclarations he can be liable for a penalty of 15 per cent of the underdeclarations (VATA 1994, s 64).

Default interest on any outstanding VAT is also payable (VATA 1994, s 74).

Example

A Ltd sells a new commercial building to B Ltd. A forgets to charge VAT and treats the sale as if it were an exempt sale. Customs may seek to charge the various penalties and interest.

The taxpayer, of course, will be liable to account for the VAT which he had not paid. Interest will be payable at the prescribed rate on the unpaid tax until it is paid. The serious misdeclaration charge may be exigible; this could equal up to 15 per cent of the true amount of tax for the period.

The interest payment and the serious misdeclaration payment are not deductible for corporation tax purposes (ICTA 1988, s 827).

SCOTTISH LAW

Scottish property laws and conveyancing procedures are different from those which apply in England and Wales (and Northern Ireland):

(1) References to Scottish heritable property are to (1) land and buildings and fixtures and (2) interests in land and buildings and fixtures including leases.

(2) References to the *dominium utile* can generally be taken to denote references to the equivalent to the freehold of England.

(3) References to leases in both countries are more or less references to the same thing.

(4) References to contracts to dispose of land can generally be taken to be references to missives in Scotland.

However, whereas a contract to sell land may create an equitable interest (which is clearly an interest in land) in England, no such interest is created in Scotland: the missives (contracts) create a personal right and if, for instance, the vendor wanted to sell the land and only missives had been entered into in favour of the proposed purchaser, the proposed purchaser could not prevent the sale of the land by the vendor to a third party. The proposed purchaser merely has a *jus crediti* (*see Gibson and Hunter Home Designs Ltd* 1976 SC 23, SLT 96, SC 27).

Completion of a land transaction in Scotland takes the form of the delivery of the deed known as the disposition which is more or less equivalent to the delivery of the transfer or conveyance in the case of land in England. In Scotland deeds are registered in a public register known as the Register of Sasines and a simplified system of registration of title (as opposed to the recording of deeds) is gradually being introduced throughout Scotland under the Land Registration (Scotland) Act 1979.

The following should be noted with respect to VAT:

(a) 'fee simple', in relation to Scotland, means the estate or interest of the proprietor of the *dominium utile* or, in the case of land not held on feudal tenure, the estate or interest of the owner;

(b) 'major interest', in relation to land, means the fee simple or a tenancy for a term certain exceeding 21 years, and in relation to Scotland means:

   (i)   the estate or interest of the proprietor of the *dominium utile*, or
   (ii) in the case of land not held on feudal tenure, the estate or interest of the owner, or the lessee's interest under a lease for a period exceeding 21 years.

A 'restrictive covenant' equates in Scotland with a 'servitude'. A release of a restrictive covenant is achieved by a 'minute of waiver'.

Section 8 of the Land Tenure Reform (Scotland) Act 1974 provides that it is a condition of every long lease executed after the commencement of that Act that no part of the property which is subject to the lease shall be used as or as part of a private dwelling house (other than ancilliary use). A long lease is one of a duration which could extend for more than 20 years, or one which either party is obliged to extend to more than 20 years. Breach of this condition does not make the lease void or unenforceable but gives the landlord power to require the tenant to terminate the offending use within 28 days. If the landlord approves of the offending use the right to terminate the use is limited.

Planning which involves granting a long lease of a dwelling house (for example where it is necessary to grant a major interest) must be read with this provision in mind.

Under Scots law a partnership is recognised as a legal entity in its own right, separate and distinct from the individual partners. The Partnership Act 1890, s 4(2) expressly preserves this treatment. If the separate personality is to be ignored for tax purposes, it must be specifically provided for in the relevant tax legislation. In the absence of such a provision in VATA 1994, a Scottish partnership should be treated as a separate person for VAT purposes. It is much less difficult, therefore, to treat a partnership as the person for VAT purposes in Scotland.

The equivalent of a stakeholder account in Scotland is a joint deposit account in which sums are deposited in the names of both the parties. Normally the consent of both parties is required for the monies to be released.

In the case of compensation payments for agricultural tenancies, the relevant statute is the Agricultural Holdings (Scotland) Act 1991 which came into effect on 25 September 1991.

Although the term 'mortgage' is known in Scotland, the only form of heritable security which may be validly created under Scots law is a standard security. Any reference to a mortgage should therefore be read as a reference to a standard security in Scotland.

The legal/equitable distinction is not known to Scots law in the context of mortgages, the only heritable security being the standard security mentioned above.

Chapter 2

Time limitations, estoppel, Community law and composite supply

---

If a taxpayer is assessed to VAT he should also always check to see whether any one or more of the following basic defences are available:

(1) Is the assessment out of time?

(2) Are Customs estopped from raising an assessment because of the 'Sheldon doctrine'?

(3) Do the provisions of community law substantially contained in the EC Sixth Directive override the provisions of the VAT legislation, the statutory instruments made thereunder and the Customs' booklets because they are in conflict?

(4) Does the composite supply doctrine effectively redesignate a supply which is, for example, standard-rated to one which is zero-rated?

TIME LIMITATIONS—ARE THE CUSTOMS OUT OF TIME?

Before taxpayers agree to pay under assessments made by Customs they should see whether the assessments are out of time.

VATA 1994, s 83 states that an appeal shall lie to a VAT tribunal against the decision of the Commissioners with respect to a number of matters. One of these matters is set out in s 83, namely an assessment made under s 73(1) or (2) or the amount of any such an assessment.

VATA 1994, s 73(1) provides that where a person has failed to make any returns required under the Act or to keep any document and afford the facilities necessary to verify such returns, or where it appears to the Commissioners that such returns are incomplete or incorrect, they may assess the amount of tax due from him to the best of their judgement and notify it to him.

Section 73(6) provides that an assessment under that provision of an amount of tax due for any prescribed accounting period cannot be made after the later of the following:

(a) two years after the end of the prescribed accounting period; or

(b) one year after evidence of facts, sufficient in the opinion of the Commissioners to justify the making of the assessment, comes to their knowledge.

Where Customs make a control visit and take away the books, the one-year period is likely to run from the time when they take away the books.

If Customs overrun the one-year period and the control visit (as it often is) is made after the two-year period, the assessment will be out of time.

However, in the extraordinary decision of *Harish Roy Babber t/a Ram Parkash Sunderdass* (1992) VATTR 268 (Decision 5958) the tribunal held that an assessment was made not when the trader's copy of the assessment was date stamped, but when the Customs officer had signed an internal certificate setting out the amount of the assessment.

In addition to the above time limits no assessment (in the absence of fraud, where the time limit is 20 years) can be made more than three years after the end of the accounting period in which the relevant supply took place (VATA 1994, s 77(1)).

ESTOPPEL—HAVE YOU ESTOPPED THE CUSTOMS?

Customs have agreed to a self-imposed estoppel, ie they will not go back on decisions or directions which they have unambiguously given to taxpayers (*see* Practice Note (1978) VATTR 278). Customs have agreed the following:

PRACTICE NOTE

Assessment contrary to previous ruling by Commissioners

The following is the text of a written question and answer in the House of Commons (*Hansard*, vol 161, 21 July 1978, col 426):

Mr Peter Rees asked the Chancellor of the Exchequer whether it is the policy of the Commissioners of Her Majesty's Customs and Excise to assess a registered person to value added tax contrary to advice previously given by them.

Mr Robert Sheldon: When it is established that an officer of Customs and Excise, with the full facts before him, has given a clear and unequivocal ruling on VAT in writing; or it is established that an officer knowing the full facts has misled a trader to his detriment, the Commissioners of Customs and Excise would only raise an assessment based on the correct ruling from the date the error was brought to the attention of the registered person concerned.

The statement is now contained in the Customs booklet on extra-statutory concessions (Notice 748) and reads:

11 Misdirection

If a Customs and Excise officer, with the full facts before him, has given a clear and unequivocal ruling on VAT in writing or, knowing the full facts, has misled a registered person to his detriment, any assessment of VAT due will be based on the correct ruling from the date the error was brought to the registered person's attention.

Paragraph 10 of Notice 748 may also be useful:

10 Misunderstanding by a VAT trader

VAT undercharged by a registered trader on account of a bona fide misunderstanding may be remitted provided all the following conditions are fulfilled—

    (a) there is no reason to believe that tax has been knowingly evaded;

    (b) there is no evidence of negligence;

    (c) the misunderstanding does not concern an aspect of the tax clearly covered in general guidance published by Customs and Excise or in specific instructions to the trader concerned; and

    (d) the tax due was not charged, could not now reasonably be expected to be charged to customers, and will not be charged.

Where, at the time the misunderstanding comes to light, there are unfulfilled firm orders from customers, for which the price quoted has been based mistakenly on the assumption that no VAT, or less VAT than properly due, would be chargeable, VAT undercharged may be remitted in respect of such orders provided conditions (a)–(d) above are met.

Note also it is open to the taxpayer to report the Customs to the Adjudicator for Customs and Excise whose adjudication on a point is nearly always accepted by the Customs and Excise; it is a cheaper route than taking out judicial review proceedings in the High Court.

COMMUNITY LAW

The Treaty of Rome which established the European Economic Community provided, by art 2, that the Community shall:

> have as its task, by establishing a common market and progressively approximating economic policies of Member States, to promote throughout the Community a harmonious development of economic activities . . .

Article 3 of the Treaty indicated various activities that the Community was to carry out to achieve the purpose set out above. Included amongst these specific activities was:

> the approximation of the laws of Member States to the extent required for the proper functioning of the Common Market (*see* art 3(*h*)).

These provisions made it clear that the method to be adopted was the bringing closer together or 'approximation' of economic policies and the laws of the member states. Later this approach was taken a stage further when art 8(*a*) was added to the Treaty and provided that the Community should adopt measures with the aim of progressively establishing the internal market, that is an area without internal frontiers and in which the free movement of goods, persons, services and capital was to be assured. This was to be achieved, *inter alia*, in accordance with the provisions of art 99 of the Treaty which, so far as relevant, was in these terms:

> The Council shall . . . adopt provisions for the harmonisation of legislation concerning turnover taxes, excise duties and other forms of indirect taxation to the extent that such harmonisation is necessary to ensure the establishment and the functioning of the internal market . . .

So once again it was by harmonising the tax laws of the member states that progress towards the internal market was to be achieved. It was in pursuance of these objectives that the First and Second, and later the Sixth, Directives were issued. Reading the various articles of the Sixth Directive, it becomes clear that though certain fundamental features of the law, such as its scope (art 2) and territorial application (art 3), are laid down in categorical terms, many of the provisions relating to the detailed application of the tax leave the member states some discretion as to how the provisions are to be implemented.

This method of moving towards the internal market is in line with the well-known proposition that Council directives are to be binding as to the results to be achieved but the precise method of achieving the results is left to the member states. In other words, the tax laws of all the member states are not necessarily to be precisely the same but are required, by the chosen methods, to achieve the same ends.

It is quite clear from a number of decisions that a VAT directive of the Community is binding on the UK government and must be fully implemented in domestic law. Even when the contents of a directive have not been fully implemented into domestic law the directive is still binding and has direct effect.

The first important judgment was in the High Court in *Yoga for Health Foundation v The Commissioners* [1984] STC 630 where Nolan J allowed exemption from VAT on welfare services permitted by the terms of the Sixth Directive when no such exemption had been legislated in the UK. He stated:

> . . . it is now common ground that Article 13A of the Sixth Directive can be directly invoked by the appellants if these provisions are applicable.

The position was put simply by the chairman in *Merseyside Cablevision Ltd* (1987) VATTR 134 thus:

> We start with the law of the European Economic Community which prevails over any contrary provision in national law: *Amministrazione delle Finanze dello Stato v Simmenthal SpA* [1978] ECR 629.

In an Italian case it was held that a member state which had failed to implement the relevant directive provision could not rely on the directive against individuals (*Pubblico Ministero v Ratti* CJEC [1979] ECR 1629; [1980] 1 CMLR 96).

Reference should also be made to the cases of *Direct Cosmetics Ltd* [1985] STC 479, *EC v United Kingdom* [1988] STC 251, *EC v United Kingdom* [1988] STC 456, and *W Emmett & Son Ltd* (LON/90/1316Z Decision 6516).

Thus if a taxpayer is having problems obtaining relief from VAT under domestic law—VATA 1994 and the various regulations—he should see whether the EC Sixth Directive will assist him by overriding the UK law.

COMPOSITE SUPPLIES

This doctrine may prove to be the taxpayer's saviour in many cases.

The leading case is *BRB v The Commissioners* [1977] STC 221, especially *see* p 224. From that case it is clear the correct test is: what did the taxpayer supply to the purchaser in consideration of the monies it received from the purchaser? It may be that a taxpayer has supplied a number of things. It is necessary, however, to ascertain what may be called the main thrust of the supply or the main supply. Once that has been done, then any other supplies by the taxpayer which are related to the main supply take on the same character as the main supply. To an extent, of course, that still begs the question, what is the main thrust or the main supply.

Guidance can be obtained from the case of *The Commissioners v Scott* [1978] STC 191, especially at p 194. Thus if X undertook, for payment, to look after the horse of Y on X's land, a necessary component of that supply is the supply of accommodation, the supply of food (grass) and the supply of skilled care. Such supplies could not be broken up (for VAT purposes) and they will take on the nature of the main supply (taking care of the house: this is a taxable supply). Such supplies are known as composite supplies. The court indicated that the answer was largely a matter of first impression and a degree of common sense was required.

Equally, if a landlord pays an insurance premium to the insurance company to cover fire or damage and the tenant reimburses the premium, that reimbursement should take on the character of rent, especially if it is reimbursed as 'additional rent' (*see* p 298). Thus if the option to waive exemption has been exercised by the landlord, VAT must be charged on the reimbursement of the premium. Also, if X plc sells property with fixed machinery therein, the machinery will take on the same VAT nature as the bricks and mortar.

If it cannot be said that the supplies are incidental, etc to the main supply (so as to take on the character of the main supply) then the supplies must be dealt with under the VAT legislation as if they were separate supplies; exempt and vatable as the case may be (*The Commissioners v The Automobile Association* [1974] STC 192). Such separate supplies are called multiple supplies.

It is quite clear that if a supply comprises a composite supply, as opposed to a multiple supply, the fact that the taxpayer charges separately for items comprised in a composite supply will not cause the otherwise composite supply to be a multiple supply (*The Commissioners v Scott*). The supply of separate invoices, however, may be significant in marginal cases. Separate invoices may tend to indicate that the supply is capable of division and should probably be treated as a separate supply of multiple services and/or goods (*see Lylybet Dishwaters (UK) Ltd v The Commissioners* (LON/79/244)).

In *Domestic Service Care Ltd* (MAN/93/163 Decision 11,869) [1994] STI 654, domestic central heating engineers offered clients for an annual fee an annual service plus insurance against mechanical breakdown. It was held the fee must be broken up for VAT purposes between the supply of exempt insurance services and vatable (at 17.5 per cent) maintenance services. Note, in an appropriate case Insurance Premium Tax can be relevant (FA 1994, Part III).

In *Hazelwood Caravans and Chalets Ltd v The Commissioners* (1985) VATTR 179 the appellant company provided self-catering holiday accommodation in chalets and caravans at an all-inclusive price. The price covered the use of a furnished chalet or caravan and all gas and electricity used during the period of occupation. According to the brochure issued by the appellant company £10 per week of the all-inclusive weekly price for a chalet or caravan was for gas and electricity and the supply was zero-rated. The appellant company then accounted for tax to the Commissioners on the basis that it made supplies of gas and electricity which were zero-rated for £10 per week. The tribunal held that the appellant company did not make separate or severable supplies of gas and electricity but a composite supply of holiday accommodation which was chargeable to tax at the standard rate.

In *British Airways plc v The Commissioners* [1989] STC 182, Otton J held that it was not possible to dissect the price of an airline ticket between the part which related to transport (zero-rated) and the part which related to in-flight catering (taxable at the standard rate). At 191 the judge stated:

> In my judgment, the correct test to be distilled from the authorities is as follows: in substance and in reality, was the in-flight catering an integral part of the transport; or, put another way, an integrant of the transport or a component of the transport? At one stage in the argument, it was suggested the question should be: can it be said it was a separate but subservient supply which is nonetheless integral with the main supply? I find that unnecessarily complicated and prefer my formulation.
>
> . . . Assuming, as I do, that the question is one of law, I would answer it in the affirmative. Bearing in mind what Cumming-Bruce LJ said, it seems to me that the answer is one of common sense. In substance and reality catering was an integral part of the transport or an integrant of the transport or a component of the transport. There was only one price of the ticket. There was no contractual obligation to provide. It would have been impractical to identify the specific consideration. I was also attracted by the phrase used by the court in the case of *Mander* (*see Mander Laundries v Customs and Excise Commissioners* (1973) VATTR 136), which was concerned with the supply of services in a launderette: Was the supply (of soap powder) an adjunct to the facility? It seems to me that the providing of in-flight catering is an adjunct to the facility of transport. Thus if it is open to me to answer the question, I would answer it in favour of the taxpayer.

In the Court of Appeal [1990] STC 643, the Commissioners' appeal was dismissed and it was held that in-flight catering was part of, and integral to, the supply of air transportation. Lord Donaldson MR at p 647 C–J stated:

> Although the tribunal stated the right question, viz, 'was the supply of food and beverages incidental ["integral" might perhaps be a better word] to the air transportation?', this passage shows that it was in fact answering a different question, viz, 'was the supply of food and beverages a necessary or essential adjunct of the air transportation?', the answer to which was clearly that it was not. Until commercial pressures built up, there was no in-flight catering on these domestic services. This is not, however, the right question.

The reality is that transportation by air can be of different classes or qualities. Air carriers can and do provide alternative services which give the passengers the bare minimum of space both laterally and longitudinally or a great deal of space. They can and do provide the passengers with seats which do not recline at all, which recline to a limited extent or which, albeit only on long-haul services, recline to a point at which they are virtually beds. They could have provided and have in the past provided transportation without any in-flight catering and at the present time they can and do provide it on greatly varying scales and with different degrees of luxury ranging from plastic containers adorned by a cup of tea or coffee and a biscuit to, at least on long-haul services, a multi-course dinner served on china with high quality cutlery which would not disgrace a five-star hotel. The air passenger chooses from what is on offer, and pays for, whichever degree of luxury or lack of it he requires, but the choice is between grades of air transportation, not between grades of transportation and separate grades of in-flight catering.

This is to be contrasted with domestic rail travel, where the service is one of transportation coupled, on some trains, with the availability of a catering supply to those who wish to use and pay for it. The passenger selects his grade of transportation and whilst in transit can decide whether to take a supply of catering services, if such be available, and, if he has a choice, the grade of service (restaurant or buffet car). The two do not go together. They are distinct and separate supplies. If, as used to be the case with Canadian National Railways, the passenger bought his ticket and was supplied with all meals free of charge for as long as the journey lasted (which might vary considerably due to climatic and operational obstacles), the situation would be different and it could have been said that there was only one supply.

The answer to the question which we have to consider—was there one supply or two—may well be one of first impression, but for my part, despite the persuasiveness of counsel for the Commissioners, it has proved a lasting and indeed indelible impression. There is a single supply and it is of air transportation. I would dismiss the appeal.

In *Industrial Brushes (Leicester) Ltd* (LON/91/604 Decision 7409) [1992] STI 589 the taxpayer was having a factory built on its land. While the factory was in the course of construction a contract to sell it was made. The taxpayer sought to argue that the transaction involved two supplies. The tribunal held there was a single exempt supply.

The decision of *British Airways plc v The Commissioners* [1990] STC 643 was applied in *The Commissioners v United Biscuits (UK) Ltd* [1992] STC 325. In that case the taxpayer sold biscuits in high-quality tins which represented 55 per cent of the total cost of the products sold. The tins have a useful afterlife as containers.

The court applied the *British Airways* test and held that in essence what was supplied was biscuits in a biscuit tin, rather than a general-purpose container with biscuits in it. The tin was incidental to the biscuits rather than the biscuits being incidental to the tin. The tin was integral to the biscuits not merely in the sense that it was the container in which they were packaged, but further in the sense that it served the supply of those biscuits to a restricted quality market as well as prolonging their shelf life in keeping them in better condition once consumption had begun. Accordingly it was held that there was a single zero-rated supply of biscuits and not a mixed standard rate supply of tins and a zero-rated supply of biscuits.

Figure 2.1:

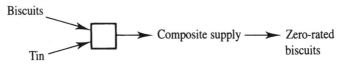

In *Rayner & Keeler Ltd* (LON/92/306 Decision 9349) a contractor carried out refurbishment and refitting works for a retail optician. In the invoices the supply was divided between the supply of the goods which were fitted and the supply of the services attributable thereto. The tribunal concluded that the provision of the goods and the installation of them were integral components of one entire transaction. The fact that it would have been possible for the contractor to issue separate invoices in respect of the supply of the various items and the fitting of them merely indicated that the obligations of the contractor were capable of being separately identified; it did not follow that those obligations were necessarily separate components of compound supplies rather than integral parts of a single supply. It was unrealistic to separate the obligation to provide an item from the obligation to fit it and to classify them as two different supplies. It was held that there had been a single supply of services.

Exclusions

The composite supply doctrine is specifically excluded by the legislation in particular cases. One case concerns protected buildings.

Protected buildings

Under the protected buildings provisions in Sched 8, Group 6, works of repair or maintenance and any incidental alterations to the fabric of a building which result from carrying out repairs or maintenance are excluded from the expression 'approved alterations' and thus such works of repair or maintenance will always be vatable (*see* Note (6)). Further, Note (9) to that Group specifically states that where a service is supplied in part in relation to approved alterations and in part for other purposes an apportionment shall be made. That is the safest course for Parliament to adopt if the composite supply doctrine is to be excluded, ie,

(a) to state what services are taxable and what are not; and

(b) to specifically provide that an apportionment shall be made between the two services.

College libraries

A university may make exempt supplies. If it constructed a new library the composite supply doctrine could prevent an input tax reclaim even though book-lending is, in principle, zero-rated (*see Leighton Park School v The Commissioners* (LON/91/1673Z Decision 9130)).

This is because of the composite supply doctrine, which is very tenacious (*BA plc v The Commissioners* [1990] STC 643). Recently, in *Virgin Atlantic Airways v The Commissioners* [1995] STC 34, it resulted in the limousine service to the airport (generally taxable at 17.5 per cent) being treated as an integral part of the flight (zero-rated) and so resulting in the entire cost being zero-rated. The limousine service was offered as part of the flight package to passengers.

To overcome the problem, the college could let the property on which the library is to be built to a new charity which would charge zero-rated (under present law) library fees to the students (*see* Figure 2.3(a)). This is similar to a 'design and build' contract for land (*see* Figure 2.2(a)) if one person carries out both functions the composite supply doctrine should apply (*see* Figures 2.2(b) and 2.3(b)).

Figure 2.2:   Design and build

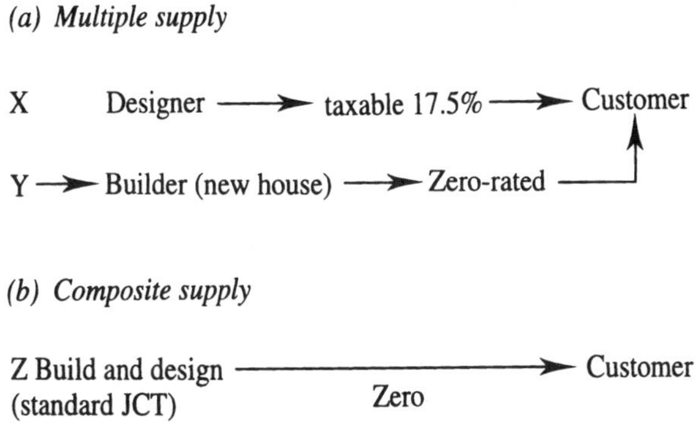

(a) Multiple supply

X   Designer ———➤ taxable 17.5% ———➤ Customer

Y ➤ Builder (new house) ——➤ Zero-rated ——⌐

(b) Composite supply

Z Build and design ————————————➤ Customer
(standard JCT)   Zero

Figure 2.3:   College libraries

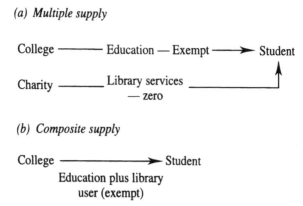

(a) Multiple supply

(b) Composite supply

General schemes to split the composite supply

It is clear that Customs would have great difficulty in applying the composite supply doctrine where two companies, even though within the same VAT group, make supplies to a customer.

In *Thorn EMI plc* (LON/91/2317) and *Granada plc* (LON/92/316 Decision 9782) the appellant hired TV sets to customers and charged a hire fee on which VAT was charged. To mitigate VAT, an insurance subsidiary was set up and insurance contracts to cover repairs (if and when needed) were entered into with customers. The appellants contended that there were two separate supplies to each customer; hiring out of TV sets and insurance.

Customs contended that although there were genuine contracts with the two companies there were single composite supplies comprising the renting out and maintenance of TV sets.

There is no reason why an insurance company should not satisfy claims by providing services instead of paying cash (*Department of Trade and Industry v St Christopher Motorists Association Ltd* [1974] 1 All ER 395 and *Medical Defence Union v Department of Trade* [1980] Ch 82, 94).

Mr Theodore Wallace, the Tribunal Chairman in the *Thorn EMI* case, at p 20 stated:

> Once the agreements are analysed and their legal effect is determined it is clear that in the present cases hiring supplies are made by the rental companies and insurance supplies by the insurance companies. In my judgment a supply cannot be characterised without reference to the supplier. It seems to me that it is impossible as a matter of law for one supply to be made by two different persons . . . In my opinion the fact that an insurance company is part of the same VAT group as the rental company cannot have the effect that

the supplies made by it can be treated as made by the hiring company. While s 29 has the effect of excluding supplies within the group from the charge to tax, it cannot have the effect of altering the character of the supply made to a person outside the group.

Both appeals were, therefore, allowed and the taxpayer succeeded in his contention that the composite supply doctrine could not apply. Note, in an appropriate case, Insurance Premium Tax can be relevant (FA 1994, Part III).

Figure 2.4:

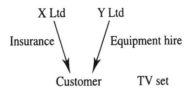

Supplies to demised premises and composite supplies

If supplies are made to demised premises they should be split up. In *Richard Haynes Associates v Customs and Excise Commissioners*, LON/92/2594 (Decision 12300) the taxpayer built a flat and sought to reclaim input tax on the basis he would be making exempt supplies (rent) and vatable supplies of laundry, shopping and secretarial services. There have been a number of cases dealing with this area: *Sovereign Street Workspace Ltd*, MAN/91/403; *Clovelley Estate Co Ltd*, LON/91/1356X; and *Business Enterprises (UK) Ltd*, LON/89/90. In Notice 742 the Customs allow apportionment of services such as heating, lighting and cleaning to demised premises from the rent. The tribunal held the services had to be divided from the rent and thus the amount of input tax reclaimed had to be calculated on that basis following *Customs and Excise Commissioners v Briararch* [1992] STC 732.

In *First Base Properties Ltd* (December 11598) the landlord let furnished office accommodation to tenants and charged £15 per square foot for rent and £40 per square foot for services (eg telephone, fax, copying, use of furniture). The tribunal held the supplies were separate: there was no composite supply.

Chapter 3

VAT groups

Forming groups for VAT purposes is very common and a very important area of VAT. The EC Sixth Directive, art 4.4 provides that after due consultation

> each Member State may treat as a single taxable person persons established in the territory of the country who, while legally independent, are closely bound to one another by financial, economic and organisational links.

The UK provisions providing for the grouping of companies for VAT purposes are to be found in VATA 1994, s 43, but there are a considerable number of anti-avoidance provisions which practitioners must take into account.

The basic aim of VAT group registration is to reduce the burden on businesses of keeping separate records for each company and accounting for supplies between two companies or more which for all intents and purposes should be treated as one entity.

GROUP REGISTRATION

Companies under common control can be included in one VAT group registration provided each is resident or has an established place of business in the UK (VATA 1994, s 43(3)).

Applications must be made to the Customs for group registration and one of the companies must be the representative member. The Customs can refuse the application for group registration, but they shall not refuse it unless it appears to them necessary to do so for the protection of the revenue (s 43(4)). Practitioners must, therefore, not assume they will gain group registration.

Where any bodies corporate are treated as members of a group and an application to that effect is made to the Commissioners, then, from the beginning of a prescribed accounting period:

(a) a further body eligible to be so treated shall be included among the bodies so treated; or

(b) a body corporate should be excluded from the bodies so treated; or

(c) another member of the group shall be the representative member in place of the original representative member; or

(d) the bodies corporate shall no longer be treated as members of the group.

The Customs do retain powers to refuse such applications (see s 43(5A)).

ATTRACTIONS OF GROUP TREATMENT

Group treatment results in the creation of a single taxable person for VAT (*see Customs and Excise Commissioners v Kingfisher plc* [1994] STC 63, but note also FA 1997, s 40). The general rule is that any supply of goods or services by one member of the group to another member of the group shall be disregarded and any other supplies made by a member of the group shall be treated as a supply by the representative member.

Example

A, B and C are members of a VAT group. A is the representative member. A makes a supply of goods and services to B. That supply is disregarded. C makes a supply to X who is not a member of the VAT group. That supply by C is treated as having been made by A, the representative member.

The only person who has any *locus standi* in any appeal is the representative member (*Davis Advertising Services Ltd* (1973) VATTR 16), although all members of the VAT group are jointly and severally liable for any VAT due from the representative member (s 43(1)).

ANTI-AVOIDANCE PROVISIONS AND GROUPS (VATA 1994, SCHED 9A)

With effect from 29 April 1996, but in relation to events occurring after 28 November 1995, FA 1996, s 31 and Sched 4 insert a new Sched 9A in VATA 1994. The new Schedule enables the Customs to give directions that:

(a) particular supplies between VAT group members shall be subject to VAT as if made between ungrouped companies;

(b) a particular company shall be assumed not to be within the VAT group for particular periods;

(c) a particular company (which will have been eligible to be a member of the VAT group) shall be assumed to be within the VAT group for particular periods.

These powers are potent and are intended to give the Customs wide powers to prevent the use of groups to mitigate VAT.

The power to give a direction (which is subject to a six-year time limit (*see* Sched 9A, para 4)) only applies if the following conditions are satisfied.

First, there must be a 'relevant event' which has occurred after 28 November 1995. A relevant event occurs when a body corporate begins to be or ceases to be treated as a member of a VAT group or enters into any 'transaction'. The word 'transaction' is capable of a very wide interpretation in the contexts of this legislation; entering into a lease, for example, would clearly be a transaction.

Secondly, there must have been, or will be, or may be a taxable supply on which VAT has been, or will be, or may be charged otherwise than by reference to the supply's full value (Sched 9A, para 1(3)(*a*)). The reference to 'full value' is curious, but it is felt it can reasonably be taken to mean that only if there is a VAT charge on the full value of the items supplied will this condition be avoided. If group registration, for example, prevents a VAT charge on the supply of goods from A to B (both within the same VAT group) then this condition will be satisfied.

The third condition is that there is at least a part of the supply which is not or, as the case may be, would not, be zero-rated.

Fourthly, the charging of VAT on the supply (otherwise than by reference to its full value) must give rise or, as the case may be, would give rise to a tax advantage because a person has become entitled to credit for input tax attributable to that supply or part of it.

There is an overall caveat that the Customs must not give a direction if they are satisfied that the change in the treatment of the body corporate or the transaction in question had its main purpose or, as the case may be, has each of its main purposes a genuine commercial purpose unconnected with VAT avoidance.

The initial instigation behind the new anti-avoidance provisions in Sched 9A was the VAT Tribunal decision of *Thorn Materials Supply Ltd and Thorn Resources Ltd* (Decision 12914), although curiously that case was reversed by the Court of Appeal which held that the particular arrangements never did work to avoid VAT ([1996] STC 1490). Nevertheless the anti-avoidance provisions are on the statute books.

In the *Thorn Materials Supply* case, B agreed to supply goods to C within the same VAT group and C prepaid 90 per cent of the price of the goods. No VAT was due on the prepayment. B then left the VAT group, purchased the goods on which VAT was charged (the purchase was from a non-VAT group company) and onward supplied the goods to C. C paid the remaining 10 per cent of the purchase price plus VAT (which C could not recover). B was in a position to reclaim all the input tax on the purchase of the goods as attributable to his onward supply to C. The case succeeded (for the taxpayer) before the VAT Tribunal, although the Customs convinced the Court of Appeal that all of the output tax, and not just 10 per cent of it, was due when the goods were delivered to C. The scheme, therefore, did not succeed.

One can see that this scheme would clearly be caught by Sched 6A. The relevant event will be B leaving the VAT group or even the payment of the 10 per cent of the purchase price. The Customs could counter the tax avoidance by treating the 90 per cent of the purchase price as having been paid when the parties were not members of the same group (by treating C and B as not being members of the same group). Alternatively one or other of the two parties could be deemed to be in the VAT group or out of the VAT group as the Customs considered appropriate.

Practitioners must be fully aware of these anti-avoidance provisions, although in many respects their relevance has been substantially reduced by the new disapplication of the election to waive exemption provisions introduced by the Finance Act 1997, s 37 which substantially amended the provisions in VATA 1994, Sched 10, para 2 (see p 243).

Chapter 4

Local authorities—the VAT havens

The VAT position of local authorities is often clouded in mystery. Developers making supplies to local authorities are often concerned about whether the local authorities can reclaim the VAT. Questions are often asked whether local authorities which let property or make other lands supplies can or should charge VAT on rents and other receipts.

What then is the VAT position of local authorities?

The governing provision in the EC Sixth Directive is art 4.5 where it is provided:

> States, regional and local government authorities and other bodies governed by public law shall not be considered taxable persons in respect of the activities or transactions in which they engage as public authorities, even where they collect dues, fees, contributions or payments in connection with these activities or transactions. However where they are engaged in such activities or transactions, they shall be considered taxable persons in respect of these activities or transactions where treatment as non-taxable persons would lead to significant distortions of competition.

The European law is reflected in UK law by VATA 1994, ss 33 and 42 and various Treasury orders made under s 33(3).

BUSINESS AND NON-BUSINESS ACTIVITIES OF LOCAL AUTHORITIES

The general rule is activities by local authorities which are in competition with the private sector are business activities. The local authority must charge VAT on such business activities.

Where the local authority provides services under statutory obligation and which are not carried out in competition with the private sector, such activities are non-business activities. The distinction between the two is critical. This is because any VAT incurred by the local authority in carrying out the non-business activities can be reclaimed in full under VATA 1994, s 33.

The general rule applies that any input tax incurred in making exempt suppliers is not recoverable. However local authorities are allowed to recover such input tax where in the opinion of the Customs an insignificant portion of the total tax incurred is attributable to the exempt activities.

In order for all the input tax to be reclaimed by a local authority in full, the input tax referable to the exempt supplies must be:

(a) not more than £625 per month on average (ie not more than £7,500 per annum); or

(b) less than 5 per cent of the total VAT incurred on all purchases in a year, including those on non-business activities.

Where the amount of input tax directly attributable to exempt suppliers exceeds both those amounts, then none of it may be recovered.

An annual calculation must be made for each financial year and any adjustments accounted for on the next VAT return.

The reason why the formula can prove attractive in many cases is that the following supplies are not to be treated as attributed to exempt supplies:

(1) VAT incurred on general administrative overheads or support services costs.

(2) VAT on goods and services that will be used to make supplies that are not exclusively exempt.

(3) VAT incurred on purchases related to exempt supplies which partly exempt businesses outside the financial sector can ignore when working out whether they can be treated as fully taxable.

The second heading is, of course, particularly attractive but it is subject to a caveat contained in para 4.5 of the Customs Notice 749 which states:

> Where a local authority or similar body has incurred VAT on purchases or acquisitions for supplies, that will be of mixed liability (eg non-business and exempt) it may be excluded from the calculation of the 5%.
>
> Where however such purchases will result in the making of exempt supplies and are of the type of value that their exclusion could be distortive of competition (ie capital projects with a cost greater than £1 million) advice should be sought from the VAT office at the earliest opportunity.

Thus, although local authorities may find themselves in the attractive position of being able to reclaim VAT on a commercial project without having elected to waive exemption because it satisfies the 5 per cent of input tax requirement, one must be aware of this Customs' caveat in para 4.5: if the project could be distortive of competition with developers in the private sector and the project costs more than £1m, then the local authority must take the position up with the Customs.

If a local authority makes taxable supplies, then of course it must account to the Customs for VAT on those taxable supplies whether or not a reclaim for input tax has been made. This applies whether the customer is a private individual, a trader or a government department or another public body or local authority. It must not, however, charge VAT on non-taxable supplies.

Thus, if a local authority elects to waive exemption with respect to a commercial building, it must charge VAT on the rents as that would be a business activity which would give rise to VAT on the supplies.

There is contained in Notice 749A a list of transactions relating to land and property which gives rise to non-business and business activities. The list is as follows:

2.5   Land and property

Supply/activity

(a)   Domestic accommodation and related activities

Provision of housing under the Housing Act 1985.	Non-business.
Provision of bed and breakfast accommodation to the homeless under the Housing (Homeless Persons) Act 1977 and the Housing Act 1985.	Non-business.
Sale of domestic accommodation under the 'right to buy' (Housing Act 1985).	Non-business.
Incentives paid to tenants to move out under the Housing Act 1988.	Non-business.
Sales of leases under the Leasehold Reform Act 1967.	Non-business.
Construction of domestic accommodation for sale.	Business.
Residents' parking permits.	Non-business.

Provision of allotments under the Allotments Acts 1908–1950 and the Allotment (Scotland) Acts 1922–1950.	Non-business.
Supply of central heating, double glazing, repairs and maintenance etc.	Non-business where tenant has no option or where supplied as part of a single supply of accommodation.
	Business where optional or at the request of the tenant—see Notice No 742 *Land and property.*
Service charges on local authority houses and flats sold leasehold.	Non-business.
Service charges on local authority houses sold freehold and, in Scotland, flats or houses held on feudal tenure.	Business—see Notice No 742 *Land and property.*
Provision of sites for gypsy encampments.	Business—see Notice No 742 *land and property.*
Repairs and maintenance carried out in connection with a control order issued under the Housing Act 1985.	Non-business.
Compensation.	Non-business but see Notice No 742 *Land and property*, for statutory payments and compulsory purchases.

(b) Commercial land and property transactions

Commercial property lease, sale, repair and maintenance.	Business—see Leaflet No 742 *Land and property.*
Sale or lease of land or property as a result of development funded by city challenge, safer city, derelict land grants etc.	Business—see Leaflet No 742 *Land and property.*
Grant of a licence to occupy land.	Business—see Notice No 742 *Land and property.*
Letting of sites and pitches for market stalls etc.	Business—see Notice No 742 *Land and property.*

Letting of leisure centres, halls, rooms, pavilions etc.	Business—see Notice No 742 *Land and property*.
Admissions to premises.	Business—see Notice No 700/22 *Admissions*.
Grant of mineral rights.	Business—see Notice No 742 *Land and property*.
Letting of cattle markets and small holdings.	Business—see Notice No 742 *Land and property*.
Rent of sites for kiosks, cafes etc eg at bus stations.	Business—see Notice No 742 *Land and property*.
Supply of the right for an independent operator to use a municipal bus station.	Business—see Notice No 742 *Land and property*.
Management of property.	Business.
Caretaking services.	Business.
Installation of fixtures and fittings in buildings.	Business—see Notice No 708 *Buildings and construction*.

(c)   Planning

Planning application fees.	Non-business.
Building regulation fees.	Non-business where local authorities retain a statutory monopoly—otherwise business.
Regularisation fees.	Non-business.
Listed building consent under the Planning (Listed Buildings and Conservation Areas) Act 1990.	Non-business.
Provision of information on unused and under-used land.	Non-business.

(d)   Miscellaneous

Default and emergency works carried out under specific legal provisions.	Non-business.
Renovation and other home improvement grants.	Outside the scope of VAT.

Recovery of costs from landlords for restoring disconnected utility supplies under the Local Government (Miscellaneous Provisions) Act 1976.	Business.
Contributions made by occupants towards exterior works of group repair schemes under the Local Government and Housing Act 1989, s 127.	Outside the scope for VAT.
Recovery of cost of acquisition and works to unoccupied listed buildings.	Non-business.
Charges made to third parties to recover the cost of repairing damage to local authority property.	Non-business.
Maintenance of closed churchyards in connection with an order served under the Local Government Act 1972.	Non-business.
Archaeological investigations carried out under the Ancient Monuments and Archaeological Areas Act 1979.	Non-business.

If one examines that list then under para 2.5(a) it is clear the construction of domestic accommodation for sale would be a business transaction, but it would be a zero-rated business transaction if new domestic accommodation was constructed and major interests granted.

If commercial property were let or sold (para 2.5(b)) then the transactions would be business transactions. This would give rise to exempt supplies unless the election waive exemption were exercised in which case vatable supplies would result.

Example

Z local authority has constructed a new commercial building. It does not elect a waive exemption and can reclaim all the VAT thereon because of the 5 per cent rule and because, although the capital project costs was greater than £1m, it can convince the Customs that the transaction does not have any distortive effect on competition. The transaction would be an exempt transaction.

Example

Y local authority has carried out a major development and the input tax referable thereto clearly exceeds the 5 per cent rule. The local authority decides to elect a waive exemption so that VAT is charged on the rent and with respect to any other supplies concerning the property. The transaction is a commercial transaction within para 2.5(b). The transaction is a business transaction. VAT is appropriately charged and the input tax position of the local authority is not adversely affected by the transaction. Overall the local authority has ensured that less than 5 per cent of the VAT incurred by it on all its activities will relate to exempt supplies (the supplies with respect to a particular project would not be exempt supplies).

VAT ON BUILDING REGULATION FEES IN ENGLAND AND WALES

The Customs in their Business Brief of 5/97 (5 March 1997) stated the following:

> From 13 January 1997 the possibility of competition exists across the whole range of building control work and VAT is therefore chargeable at the standard rate on all building control fees as from that date.
>
> New approved inspectors have been authorised by the Department of the Environment to provide building regulation services for commercial and mixed developments, as well as the residential and mixed developments for which NHBC (Building Control Services) Ltd was already authorised.
>
> The revised liability rulings apply to building regulation applications received on or after 13 January 1997. Applications received prior to this date should be treated as non-business by local authorities irrespective of when the work is actually carried out or invoices issued. This is because a local authority monopoly existed at the time the application was made and there is, therefore, no competition in respect of the supply of these particular services.
>
> We can also confirm that repayments of VAT paid in error in the past on building regulation fees will continue to be made. These are not caught by the three year capping provisions.
>
> This supplements and amends the guidance contained in Business Briefs 23/95 [see Simon's Weekly Tax Intelligence 1995 p 1663] and 26/95 [see Simon's Weekly Tax Intelligence 1995 p 2052]. For further information traders and their advisers should contact their local VAT business advice centre listed under Customs & Excise in the telephone book.

Chapter 5

Anti-avoidance

THE *RAMSAY* DOCTRINE

The *Ramsay* doctrine is a rule of interpretation (*Furniss v Dawson* [1994] STC 153 and *IRC v McGuckian* [1997] STC 908 at 916e) which excises or recharacterises steps introduced into transactions for the purpose solely of avoiding tax. Thus if A transfers a property to B who transfers it to C and the transfer to B is solely for the purposes of tax avoidance, that transaction can, for example, be excised and the transfer (for tax purposes) treated as taking place between A and C. One can make the following comments on this rule of interpretation:

The doctrine

In order for the doctrine to apply there must be a pre-ordained series of transactions with an intermediate step being inserted for no commercial purpose apart from the avoidance of the liability to tax. The doctrine requires the tax avoidance step to be ignored or recharacterised. Precisely how the end result will be taxed will depend on the terms of the taxing statute sought to be applied (*Furniss v Dawson* [1994] STC 153 at 166 (Lord Brightman); *IRC v McGuckian* [1997] STC 908 at 918a).

Inserted steps

Only inserted steps can be ignored: the end product cannot be ignored (*Furniss v Dawson* at 166h). However, if transactions are essentially circular the courts can actually alter the nature of a particular transaction. They can recharacterise the transaction. Thus if X is about to receive a dividend from his company and he sells the right for a capital sum to a connected party or to a person involved in the tax avoidance scheme, the capital receipt can be treated under *Ramsay* as an income receipt (effectively the dividend). This ability not just to ignore the tax avoidance step but recharacterise it was first formulated in *IRC v McGuckian* by Lord Cooke (at 919d) and Lord Clyde (at 922c) and should now be assumed to be a feature of the *Ramsay* doctrine.

Exclusive tax avoidance

Only an intermediate step entered into exclusively for tax avoidance purposes can be ignored or recharacterised (*Craven v White* [1988] STC 476 at 508(e) and *IRC v McGuckian* at 917f).

Pre-ordination

In order that the requirement of pre-ordination be satisfied the steps must be 'welded together to form part of a pre-planned continuum' (*Craven v White* at 509); or there must be 'no practical likelihood' that the transactions will not take place (at 508); or there must be no 'reasonable possibility' that they would not all be carried out (*Countess Fitzwilliam v IRC* [1993] STC 502 at 515).

Interruption

If there is a 'sensible and genuine interruption' between the various steps then the steps will not have been pre-ordained. Lord Oliver in *Craven v White* at 509 stated:

> A third identifying feature, at any rate in the *Dawson* type of transaction, is in my opinion that there should be no sensible and genuine interruption between the intermediate transaction and the disposal to an ultimate purchaser.
>
> If such an interruption occurs I cannot for my part see on what possible basis of statutory construction the intermediate transaction can, as it were, be held in limbo once it has been completed.

Alternative schemes

It is thus possible that, if a taxpayer sets up a scheme to sell assets to a purchaser and that scheme goes abortive because a purchaser does not continue with the scheme and a new person takes that purchaser's place, the doctrine will not apply as there will have been a sensible and genuine interruption in the sequence of transactions (*Craven v White* [1988] STC 476 at 509c).

Intellectual rewriting requirement

If a step is ignored, the non-ignored transactions must be capable of being analysed and the tax system applied in a realistic and intellectually defensible way. See *Piggott v Staines Investments* [1995] STC 114 at 140j; *Craven v White* at 508j and 509G; and *Fitzwilliam v IRC* [1993] STC 502 at 513, where Lord Keith at 513j stated:

> In the present case, therefore, the correct approach to a consideration of the four steps in the tax saving plan which the Crown says were ineffective for the purpose is to ask whether realistically they constituted an indivisible whole in which one or more of them was simply an element without independent effect and whether it is <u>intellectually possible</u> so to treat them (<u>author's underlining</u>).

Two normal alternatives

If there are two normal ways of doing a transaction the taxpayer is not compelled to take the most tax disadvantageous route (*Piggott v Staines* [1995] STC 114 at 142h).

APPLICABILITY OF THE DOCTRINE TO VAT

It was thought at one time that the doctrine might not apply to VAT. In *National Coal Board v CCE* [1982] STC 863, Woolf J at 865 stated:

> There is no suggestion in this case that, although their motive was a desire to avoid payment of tax, the alterations which were made to the mineworkers' scheme were not genuine or that since they were made the scheme, as amended, has not reflected the reality of how the scheme was operated and, in the circumstances of this case, it was wrong for the tribunal to have taken into account this alleged motive of the Board in coming to its decision. In these circumstances, the question of whether or not VAT is payable must be judged objectively having regard to the terms of the schemes and the activities performed by the Board.

That case was followed in the VAT tribunal case of *Spigot Lodge Ltd v CCE* (1983) VATTR 221, where the tribunal stated, at p 225, that they accepted the submission of counsel for the taxpayer 'that the objective test must be applied and that the motive to reduce (the taxpayer's) liability to tax should be ignored'.

In the High Court (*Spigot Lodge Ltd v CCE* [1985] STC 255) Hodgson J, at 259, stated: 'This motive (for the relevant tax avoidance transaction) it is accepted, is irrelevant.'

However, in the Court of Appeal decision of *CCE v Faith Construction Ltd* [1989] STC 539 it was not argued that the doctrine could not apply to VAT, although it was held on the facts of the particular case not to apply. Bingham LJ at p 547b seemed to indicate that it had not been established that *Ramsay* can apply to VAT, but:

> ... even if it be assumed that the *Furniss v Dawson* principle applies to VAT and that we are dealing with a preordained series of transactions as opposed to a single transaction (the case involved provocative payment up-front schemes) the argument in my view cannot succeed [on the particular facts of this case].

One must assume that the doctrine will apply to VAT planning arrangements. There is no reason in principle why it should not apply to VAT.

Chapter 6

Interaction of VAT with other taxes

GENERAL

It seems clear enough in law that just because a supply is, for instance, charge-able to income tax this does not preclude it from being chargeable to VAT, or just because a payment is treated as an emolument for Schedule E purposes that it must be treated as a payment by an employer to an employed person (such payments are excluded from VAT by the EC Sixth Directive, art 4.4) for VAT purposes.

Example

> T, having exercised the election to waive exemption, surrenders his lease to his landlord for £117,500. T will have to pay VAT of £17,500 and capital gains tax (at, say, 40 per cent) of £40,000 (£100,000 × 40 per cent).

In *RHM Bakeries (Northern) Ltd v The Commissioners* [1979] STC 72 Neill J dealt with a submission by counsel for the taxpayer that as a payment was taxable (income tax) as an emolument it fell outside the scope of VAT. He stated, at p 73:

> It seems to me, however, that this argument contains a basic fallacy . . . It is quite true that the payment of money by way of wages and salaries does not attract value added tax though such wages and salaries are taxable under the income tax legislation. It does not follow, however, that payments in kind and money will be treated in the same way under the value added tax legislation merely because such payments may constitute emoluments for the purposes of income tax. The two forms of taxation are not necessarily mutually exclusive. I therefore reject this submission.

However, in general, taxpayers must take particular care in this area of interaction. For example a taxpayer may have left an employment and received a considerable sum to enter into a restrictive covenant which could be assessed under Schedule E by virtue of the Income and Corporation Taxes Act 1988, s 313 (Taxation of consideration for certain restrictive undertakings).

The taxpayer may seek to avoid such a charge in an appropriate case by arguing that the sum is a capital payment within Schedule D Case I. If that argument is successful the taxpayer must take special care to ensure that no adverse VAT consequences may arise from such a success. That said, as mentioned in the *RHM Bakeries* case, each of the legislative provisions applicable to the particular taxes has to be examined independently.

The Inland Revenue has issued a number of statements of practice dealing with the interaction of VAT with other taxes.

INCOME TAX AND CORPORATION TAX ON INCOME

Statement of Practice SP/B1-A

This notice sets out the general principles which will be applied in dealing with VAT in the computation of liability to income tax and corporation tax. Further notes on practice will be published when it has become possible to identify where difficulties may arise. In the meantime, the local inspector of taxes should be consulted in any case of difficulty.

1   A person carrying on a business who is not a taxable person for VAT—

This broadly covers persons whose output is wholly exempt from VAT and those whose taxable output (including that which is zero-rated) does not exceed a certain limit each year. (This limit is increased periodically.)

Such persons will suffer VAT on much of their business expenditure. Where an item of expenditure is allowable as a deduction in computing income for income tax or corporation tax purposes, the VAT related to that expenditure will also be allowable. If the expenditure qualifies for capital allowances, these allowances will be based on the cost inclusive of the related VAT.

2   A taxable person for VAT whose output is wholly taxable (whether at the standard rate of VAT or zero-rated)—

There is no essential difference for this purpose between taxable and zero-rated output. It is expected that in general a VAT account will be kept on the lines recommended in the HM Customs and Excise Notice No 700 setting VAT on outputs against VAT on inputs and accounting for (or reclaiming) the difference.

In computing income for direct tax purposes in these circumstances it would be correct to take into account both income and expenditure exclusive of the related VAT.

VAT on inputs is set off whether it relates to capital or revenue expenditure and it would follow that capital allowances would be determined upon the cost exclusive of VAT.

There are certain categories of VAT on imports which are non-deductible—notably that relating to the cost of motor cars and entertaining. This VAT will no doubt be included in the accounts of the business as a part of the expenditure to which it relates. So far as the motor cars are concerned capital allowances will be computed on the cost inclusive of the VAT and the entertaining expenditure which is not allowed as a deduction for direct tax purposes will be the expenditure inclusive of VAT.

If a trading debt becomes bad it may well include the VAT related to the sale. As this tax will have been accounted for and cannot be recovered from HM Customs the full amount of the bad debt would be allowed as a trading expense for direct taxation purposes.

Where a trader does not maintain a separate VAT account the adjustments to be made in computing income and capital allowances for direct taxation purposes would be such as to achieve the corresponding result.

3   A partly exempt person—

As explained in HM Customs and Excise Notice No 706, a taxable person whose output is partly exempt and partly taxable may set off only part of his VAT on inputs against his VAT on outputs. In such a case the computation of income for direct tax purposes will follow the general principles set out in 1 and 2 above.

The VAT on inputs which cannot be set off may comprise two elements—

(*a*) that which is non-deductible because it relates to motor cars or to business entertainment, and

(*b*) that which is referable to the exempt output.

The treatment for direct tax purposes of non-deductible VAT on inputs under (*a*) will be the same as for a wholly taxable person, as explained above. VAT on inputs within (*b*) should be allocated to the categories of expenditure giving rise to it, and its treatment in computing income for direct tax purposes will be the same as the treatment of the expenditure to which it relates.

In many cases the extent to which a partly exempt person ultimately bears VAT on goods and services supplied to him will be determined in accordance with a working arrangement with HM Customs and Excise (such as the special schemes for retailers set out in Notice No 707). It follows that some approximation may be necessary in allocating the VAT ultimately borne to the various items of expenditure to which it was related. Inspectors of taxes will be prepared to consider any reasonable arrangements for allocation which follow the general principles set out above.

In certain circumstances traders may also decide that the cost of keeping records of some items of VAT on inputs is excessive in relation to the ultimate set-off to be obtained and will not make any claim. Where a trader ultimately bears additional VAT in consequence this may be treated as a part of the relevant expense or capital outlay for direct tax purposes.

CAPITAL GAINS TAX AND CORPORATION TAX ON CHARGEABLE GAINS

Statement of Practice SP/B1-B

This notice sets out the general principles which will be applied in dealing with VAT in the computation of liability to capital gains tax.

If VAT has been suffered on the purchase of an asset but that VAT is available for set-off in the purchaser's VAT account, the cost of the asset for capital gains tax purposes will be the cost exclusive of VAT. Where no VAT set-off is available, the cost will be inclusive of the VAT borne. Where an asset is disposed of, any VAT chargeable will be disregarded in computing the capital gain.

SCHEDULE E AND VAT

Statement of Practice SP/A6 and SP/A7

A6 Schedule E: value added tax

The introduction of VAT on 1 April 1973 will affect, in some instances, the amount of the emoluments chargeable to income tax under Schedule E, and the amount to which the PAYE procedure should be applied. The main circumstances in which this situation will arise are summarised below, and it is anticipated that all of the relevant information will be available to the employer in the records which he will maintain for general VAT purposes.

Expenses incurred by employees and reimbursed by their employer—

The amount to be entered by an employer on his return of expenses payments on Forms P 9D and P 11D, or by an employee when claiming a deduction for expenses, should include any amount paid in respect of VAT, which is reimbursed, whether or not the employer may subsequently recover all or part of that VAT by repayment or set-off.

Benefits—

Where the employer meets any pecuniary liability of an employee, etc the measure of the expenditure incurred by the employer should include any amounts payable in respect of VAT whether or not the employer may subsequently recover all or part of that VAT by repayment or set-off.

Where TA 1988, ss 153–168 apply (that is employees remunerated at the rate of £8,500 a year or more, and directors), and the employer incurs expenditure in providing a benefit (including the use of an asset) for an employee, in arriving at the amount of that benefit (or in determining the annual value of the use of that asset) only the VAT ultimately borne by the employer should be taken into account.

Sums paid for services to certain professional persons—

[VATA 1994, s 95(5)] provides that a person who, in the course of carrying on a trade, profession or vocation, accepts an office, other than a public office, is subject to VAT in respect of any services supplied by him as the holder of the office.

Where the emoluments payable to such a person are subject to Schedule E tax, deductible under PAYE, and also to VAT, the emoluments to which PAYE is applied should not include the VAT element of any payment.

A7 Benefits in kind and value added tax
The Revenue are now advised that where a director or employee is liable to income tax in respect of payments made to him or on his behalf by his employer or in respect of expenses incurred by the employer in providing him with a benefit the liability is on the full amount of the expenditure incurred, inclusive of VAT. This is so whether or not the employer may subsequently recover all or part of the VAT. The change in the basis of measuring benefits—from VAT exclusive to VAT inclusive—which is now required will apply to benefits received in 1974–75 and subsequent years.

THE SUB-CONTRACTOR PROVISIONS AND VAT

Under the Income and Corporation Taxes Act 1988, ss 559 to 567 a contractor is liable to deduct tax (at 23 per cent) from payments to his sub-contractor made under the terms of a contract relating to construction operations. An omission to deduct under these provisions can be devastating. The following points should be taken into account in respect of the sub-contractor provisions and VAT.

Where a payment by a contractor to a sub-contractor is subject to VAT the amount for the purposes of the deduction scheme is the payment excluding the amount of the VAT, ie it is not 23 per cent of the payment plus the VAT, it is only 23 per cent of the payment.

Example

Sub-contractor supplies services and charges contractor £100 plus £17.50 VAT (*see* Figure 6.1).

Figure 6.1:   Sub-contractors

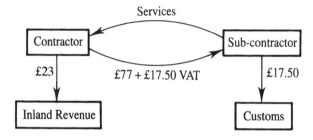

Where a payment by a contractor to a sub-contractor is subject to deduction, except to the extent that the payment represents the cost of materials, the amount that may be excluded from the payment before the deduction is calculated is the VAT exclusive cost of the materials.

STAMP DUTY

When taxpayers sell commercial properties (freehold and leasehold factories, offices and the like) or grant leases of such properties, they will be able to charge VAT on the sale proceeds and the rents and premiums if they exercise their options under Sched 10, para 2 of VATA 1994. This is also the case when a new freehold commercial building is sold within Sched 9, Group 1, Item 1(*a*).

Stamp duty on VAT—two axioms

The following points should be noted with respect to VAT and stamp duty:

1   VAT axiom

When a vendor or landlord makes a supply for a consideration in money he is charged to VAT on such an amount as, with the addition of the tax chargeable, is equal to the consideration (VATA 1994, s 19(2)). This is $\frac{7}{47}$ths of the consideration. The supplier is liable for VAT and he is required to pay this over in his normal returns; the charge is based on the consideration he receives. If he charges the purchaser or tenant sums to cover that VAT he has simply increased the consideration he would otherwise have charged. *He does not charge the purchaser or lessee VAT*. He has not the power to do that. Also, Customs do not charge the purchaser or lessee VAT. They have no power to do that. That is a basic feature of VAT law. What has happened is the vendor/lessor has simply passed the burden of the VAT on to the purchaser/lessee by contract between the parties. The purchaser/lessee may get a credit for the VAT assessed on the vendor/lessor but that is a different matter.

2   Stamp duty axiom

Under the stamp duty contingency principle, formulated in the cases of *Underground Electric Railways Company of London, Ltd and Glyns, Mills, Currie and Co v IRC* [1916] 1 KB 306, *ITA v IRC* [1961] AC 427 especially at 433 and *Coventry City Council v IRC* [1979] ChD 142, it is clear that if, at the time of the conveyance or lease or agreement to lease, further considera-tion may be payable by the purchaser or lessee or proposed lessee then that further consideration, if it is quantifiable or if FA 1994, s 242(1) applies is chargeable to stamp duty. The fact that it may never be paid is irrelevant.

The views of the Stamp Office are stated *below*. The old statement has been superseded by the new statement but is put in for completeness.

PRESS RELEASE [NOW REPLACED]

Inland Revenue   *22 July 1991*

Stamp duty—interaction with VAT

In response to a number of enquiries from practitioners, the Inland Revenue have today published a statement of practice (SP 6/91) explaining the interaction between stamp duty and VAT where a transaction gives rise to both these taxes. A copy of the statement is [reproduced below].

To comply with a European Court decision FA 1989 introduced, from 1 April 1989, a mandatory VAT charge on the sale of new commercial property. And from 1 August 1989 owners were given the option of charging VAT on sales of old com-mercial property, and on leases of old or new commercial property. The statement of practice explains the stamp duty implications of these changes. A change in the Stamp Office's practice will take effect from 1 August.

The statement also makes clear that there are no cases in which stamp duty is itself subject to VAT.

DETAILS

1   Where the VAT is compulsory, such as on sales of new commercial property, stamp duty is charged on the VAT-inclusive price.

2   VAT can be charged at the owner's option on:
 — sales of old commercial property
 — assignments of leases in old or new property
 — the creation of new leases in old or new property

In these cases stamp duty is charged on the VAT-inclusive price where the owner has opted to charge VAT. If the owner has not so opted at the time of the transaction, as from 1 August the amount on which stamp duty is charged will include the VAT that may arise later following an election by a vendor or lessor to waive his exemp-tion from VAT.

3   A formal notice of election by the vendor or lessor will not itself attract stamp duty.

4   In the case of new leases stamp duty applies separately to the premium and the rent. A premium attracts stamp duty in the same way as the price paid on a sale. Stamp duty is charged on VAT on rent whether or not the VAT is actually expressed to form part of the rent.

5   On a transfer of an interest in land the Stamp Office will need to know whether:
   (*a*) the property is commercial;
   (*b*) it is freehold or leasehold;
   (*c*) VAT has been charged on the payments referred to in the documents.
It will save time if this information is supplied in the first instance, in either the document itself or a covering letter.

NOTES
VAT charges introduced in 1989
1   FA 1989 s 18, Sched 3 applied the standard rate of VAT to non-domestic construction and to the freehold sale of new non-domestic buildings from 1 April 1989. In addition, owners of non-domestic property have had from 1 August 1989 the option of charging VAT on the price paid on sales of old buildings, and on leases of old and new buildings.

Stamp duty on VAT
2   Where VAT is payable on sales of businesses and business assets, it has always attracted stamp duty. But instances of interaction between the two taxes have become more common since the introduction of the new VAT charges.

The stamp duty charge on new leases
3   On the grant of a new lease, the premium attracts stamp duty at 1% as if it were the consideration for a sale. The £30,000 threshold for sales applies to the premium only where the rent does not exceed £300 per annum (so that the premium alone represents the bulk of the value of the lease).
4   Stamp duty on rent depends on the average annual rent and the term of the lease. The rate of duty increases with the term, from 1% for periods up to 7 years, to a maximum of 24% for leases of over 100 years.
5   Assignments of existing leases attract stamp duty on the price paid, in the same way as sales.

STATEMENT OF PRACTICE [NOW REPLACED]

SP 6/91   *22 July 1991*
               Stamp duty and value added tax (VAT)—interaction

Introduction
1   To comply with a judgment of the European Court of Justice in June 1988, standard rate UK VAT has been applied to non-residential construction with effect from 1 April 1989 (FA 1989, s 18). VAT is compulsory on sales of buildings treated as new for this purpose, which are mainly buildings under three years old that have been completed after March 1989. And owners of non-residential property were given the option from 1 August 1989 of charging VAT on sales of old buildings and on leases.
2   These new charges have prompted a number of enquiries about the relationship

between stamp duty and VAT where both taxes arise on a sale or lease of commercial property or, occasionally, other assets.

Sales of new non-domestic buildings

3   The Board are advised that for stamp duty purposes the amount or value of the consideration for a sale is the gross amount inclusive of VAT. Therefore where VAT is payable on the sale of new non-residential property, stamp duty is calculated on the VAT-inclusive consideration.

Other non-domestic transactions

4   Transactions in non-residential property other than sales of new buildings are exempt from VAT. These include:
— sales of old buildings
— the assignment of existing leases, or the creation of new leases, in old or new property.
However, the vendor or lessor can elect to waive the exemption.

5   The Board have received legal advice that stamp duty is chargeable on the purchase price, premium or rent including VAT, whether or not the vendor or lessor has elected to waive the exemption from VAT. The Board propose to follow this advice, which will result in a change of practice: hitherto, the Stamp Office have not sought to include the VAT element in the stamp duty charge in cases where the election to waive the exemption from VAT has not yet been exercised. In future, this approach will be restricted to cases where there is a binding agreement between the parties that such an election will not be made. The new practice will apply to documents presented on or after 1 August.

6   Neither a formal notice of election made to HM Customs & Excise, nor any notification to the purchaser or lessee that such an election has been made, will attract stamp duty.

Rent

7   Where VAT is charged on the rent under a lease, and is itself treated as rent under the lease, stamp duty at the appropriate rate according to the length of the term will be charged on the VAT-inclusive figure. If the lease provides for payment of VAT on the rent otherwise than as rent, duty will be charged on the VAT element as consideration payable periodically (Stamp Act 1891, s 56). In either case the rate of VAT in force at the date of execution of the lease will be used in the calculation.

8   In the case of a formal Deed of Variation of similar document varying the terms of the original lease so as to provide for payment of VAT by way of additional rent, further stamp duty may be payable (Stamp Act 1891, s 77(5)).

Agreements for leases

9   Paragraphs 4 to 8 above also apply to an agreement for lease if that is the instrument to be stamped (Stamp Act 1891, s 75).

Procedure

10   Applicants for stamping are requested to make clear, either in the conveyance or lease document itself, or in a covering letter to the Stamp Office, whether the property is commercial or residential.

11   Deeds of Variation etc (para 8 above) should be presented for adjudication together with a copy of the original lease.

No VAT on stamp duty

12   It is sometimes suggested that stamp duty might itself attract a charge to VAT. This is not the case. The value for VAT depends on the amount (consideration) obtained by the supplier from the purchaser, less the included VAT itself. Stamp duty is paid by the purchaser/lessee of property direct to the Inland Revenue and not to the supplier; it does not therefore form part of the consideration for VAT purposes.

PRESS RELEASES [LATEST STATEMENT]

Inland Revenue   *12 September 1991*

Stamp duty—interaction with value added tax (VAT)

The Inland Revenue have today published a statement of practice (SP 11/91) about the interaction between stamp duty and VAT. It *replaces* the statement of 22 July (SP 6/91 [see *Simon's Tax Intelligence* 1991 p 714]) on this subject. The new version has been issued in response to representations from practitioners for reconsideration and clarification of certain points.

A copy of the revised statement is [reproduced below].

DETAILS

1   The changes in the revised statement are confined to paras 6 and 7. There are two points.

2   First, the statement makes clear the effect for stamp duty purposes of a right to elect to waive exemption from VAT. VAT is not included in the charge to stamp duty where it is no longer possible to make an effective election to waive the exemption.

3   Secondly, the statement restricts the application of the change of practice to documents *executed* on or after 1 August 1991 instead of, as before, documents *presented* on or after that date. So documents executed before, but stamped after, 1 August will not be subject to the change of practice. Stamp duty paid on the earlier basis that is not due on the new basis will be refunded if the relevant documents are represented to the Stamp Allowance Section of the Stamp Office, at Ridgeworth House, Liverpool Gardens, Worthing, West Sussex BN11 1XP.

STATEMENT OF PRACTICE [LATEST STATEMENT]

SP 11/91   *12 September 1991*

Stamp duty and value added tax (VAT)—interaction

1   This statement is a revised version of the statement about stamp duty and VAT issued on 22 July 1991, and replaces it.

Introduction

2   To comply with a judgment of the European Court of Justice in June 1988, standard rate UK VAT has been applied to non-residential construction with effect from 1 April 1989 (FA 1989, s 18). VAT is compulsory on sales of buildings treated as new for this purpose, which are mainly buildings under three years old that have been completed after March 1989. And owners of non-residential property were given the option from 1 August 1989 of charging VAT on sales of old buildings and on leases.

3   These new charges have prompted a number of enquiries about the relationship between stamp duty and VAT where both taxes arise on a sale or lease of commercial property or, occasionally, other assets.

Sales of new non-domestic buildings

4   The Board are advised that for stamp duty purposes the amount or value of the consideration for a sale is the gross amount inclusive of VAT. Therefore where VAT is payable on the sale of new non-residential property, stamp duty is calculated on the VAT-inclusive consideration.

Other non-domestic transactions

5   Transactions in non-residential property other than sales of new buildings are exempt from VAT. These include—

— sales of old buildings

— the assignment of existing leases, or the creation of new leases, in old or new property.

However, the vendor or lessor can elect to waive the exemption.

6   The Board have received legal advice that where the election has already been exercised at the time of the transaction, stamp duty is chargeable on the purchase price, premium or rent including VAT. Where the election has not been exercised at that time, VAT should similarly be included in any payments to which an election could still apply which will depend on the facts of each case.

7   The Board propose to follow this advice, which will result in a change of practice. In the past, the Stamp Office did not seek to include the VAT element in the stamp duty charge in cases where an election to waive the exemption from VAT had not yet been exercised. The new practice applies to documents executed on or after 1 August 1991.

8   Neither a formal notice of election made to HM Customs & Excise, nor any notification to the purchaser or lessee that such an election has been made, will attract stamp duty.

Rent

9   Where VAT is charged on the rent under a lease, and is itself treated as rent under the lease, stamp duty at the appropriate rate according to the length of the term will be charged on the VAT-inclusive figure. If the lease provides for payment of VAT on the rent otherwise than as rent, duty will be charged on the VAT element as consideration payable periodically (Stamp Act 1891, s 56). In either case the rate of VAT in force at the date of execution of the lease will be used in the calculation.

10   In the case of a formal Deed of Variation or similar document varying the terms of the original lease so as to provide for payment of VAT by way of additional rent, further stamp duty may be payable (Stamp Act 1891, s 75).

Agreements for leases

11   Paragraphs 8 to 10 above also apply to an agreement for lease if that is the instrument to be stamped (Stamp Act 1891, s 75).

Procedure

12   Applicants for stamping are requested to make clear, either in the conveyance or lease documents itself, or in a covering letter to the Stamp Office, whether the property is commercial or residential.

13   Deeds of Variation etc (para 10 above) should be presented for adjudication together with a copy of the original lease.

No VAT on stamp duty

14   It is sometimes suggested that stamp duty might itself attract a charge to VAT. This is not the case. The value for VAT depends on the amount (consideration) obtained by the supplier from the purchaser, less the included VAT itself. Stamp duty is paid by the purchaser/lessee of property direct to the Inland Revenue and not to the supplier; it does not therefore form part of the consideration for VAT purposes.

The following appeared in the *Law Society's Gazette* on 4 March 1992, p 16.

Stamp duty and VAT

Following the publication of Statement of Practice SP 11/91 on the interaction between stamp duty and VAT (see *Simon's Tax Intelligence* 1991, p 818), the Law Society's revenue law committee raised a number of points of uncertainty in correspondence with the Inland Revenue. The Revenue's views on the points raised are noted below.

Amount on which stamp duty is payable

It has emerged from [the correspondence that the Revenue's] view, as a result of the legal advice it had received, and in the light of which SP 11/91 was published, is first that the contingency principle will apply to any transaction in respect of a property which could be affected by an election to waive exemption from VAT, where the election has not been exercised by a landlord at the time that a lease in entered into (and there is no contemporaneous or binding agreement between the parties to the lease that the election will not be exercised). Accordingly in calculating the duty payable VAT should therefore in the Revenue's view be added to any payments to be made by the purchaser or lessee to which an election could still apply.

Secondly, in the cases which deal with the so-called contingency principle it was held that stamp duty is chargeable on a *prima facie* sum regardless of whether that sum might increase or decrease depending on the occurrence of some contingency.

The Revenue considers that the calculation should be based on current rates of VAT, notwithstanding that there may be a fluctuation in the rate of VAT in the period which elapses between the date when the lease is granted and when any election is made.

Apart from the correspondence on the quantum of duty [the Law Society's revenue law committee reports that the correspondence to date has also established the Revenue's views on the following points].

Agreement by lessor not to elect to waive exemption

If, having entered into an agreement for a lease which made no reference to the intending lessor making an election to waive exemption from VAT, the intending lessor subsequently agreed that he or she would not make the election, on what basis would the agreement for lease be stamped, ie what would be the value of the consideration?

Review view   A binding undertaking by a lessor, after an agreement for lease is entered into but before it is stamped, not to exercise an option to charge VAT, would be effective to exclude any stamp duty on VAT that might otherwise be charged on that agreement.

Transfer of business as a going concern

[The revenue law committee] assume that where the transferor has elected to charge VAT in relation to land (so it will be necessary for the transferee to make a similar election), if the transfer is to be treated as a supply of neither goods nor services for VAT purposes, then conveyances or transfers will be stamped as if no VAT is due, provided the agreement itself or any covering letter to the local stamp office makes it clear that the parties expect such treatment to be available or can confirm that Customs & Excise will apply the transfers of going concerns provisions to the transaction. This would save having to delay submission of documents until it is clear (or has been confirmed post-transfer) that such treatment will apply. Could the Stamp Office confirm that this procedure would be adopted?

Review view   Yes. Such documents can be dealt with at any stamp office and do not need to be sent for adjudication on those grounds alone.

Groups of companies

Where a lease is made between two companies in a VAT group registration (and so the supply is to be ignored for VAT purposes) will the possibility of an election being made at a later date be ignored?

Review view   Yes.

Sub-sales

With sub-sales, is the additional amount that would be payable, had an election to charge VAT been made prior to A agreeing to transfer land to B, ignored in determining whether the consideration provided by C to B upon a sub-sale of the property was less than its value (Stamp Act 1891, s 58 (4) (*a*), (7))?

Review view   Yes.

Chapter 7

Reclaiming input tax and partial exemption

If a taxpayer has been charged VAT and wishes to reclaim that VAT, he must look at four matters:

(1) 'Input tax' properly so called: he must determine whether he has been charged input tax.

(2) Partial exemption: if he has been charged input tax, he must see whether he can reclaim that input tax by virtue of the 1995 Regulations, regs 99–111.

(3) Capital goods provisions—claw-back: he must see whether the input tax which may be deducted under the above regulations may be subject to adjustments in accordance with the capital goods provisions (1995 Regulations, regs 112–116).

(4) Blocked input tax: finally, even if the taxpayer is able to obtain a deduction by virtue of the above provisions, it may be that any input tax reclaim is specifically denied by the legislation. This is known as 'blocked input tax'.

'INPUT TAX' PROPERLY SO-CALLED—TWO-STEP PROCESS

The position with regard to input tax does require a two-step process and the steps should not be confused.

First step: is it input tax?

First, one must ascertain whether the taxpayer has suffered 'input tax'.

VAT charged to the taxpayer is only input tax if it is used or is to be used by the taxpayer for the purposes of any business carried on, or to be carried on, by him. Thus VAT charged to a taxpayer who is to use it for domestic purposes (ie private purposes) is not input tax at all and could never be the subject of a VAT reclaim.

If a taxpayer receives an input and is charged VAT and part of the supply relates to his business and part relates to other purposes, then there is an apportionment: only so much of the supply made to him as is referable to his business is counted as input tax.

Example

X Ltd is a registered taxable person. He pays input tax of £1,000 of which 30 per cent relates to a private non-business purpose, and 70 per cent relates to his business. The 70 per cent relating to his business is input tax.

Once one has ascertained the amount of input tax—£700 in the case of Mr X above—one must then go to step two (p 83) and if needs be the 1995 Regulations to see how much of that input tax can be credited (see p 84).

Private or business purposes

In *Rock Lambert* (LON/90/1544 Decision 6637) a partner in a business which produced books sold the house in which he lived, one room of which he used for the partnership business. The partnership did not have a lease or any other legal interest in the premises. The partnership was in financial difficulties and the property was sold to raise capital to pay off the partnership debts. The taxpayer sought to claim back VAT charged on the solicitors' and estate agents' fees in connection with the sale. The tribunal held that the partners owned and sold the assets as individuals. The supplies were not used for the purposes of a business carried on by the partnership.

In *GHJA Scott t/a Chancellor & Sons* (LON/90/1637 Decision 6922) an estate agent commissioned some urgent business works on behalf of a lessor for whom he acted, but the lessor refused to pay as he had no authority. To protect his reputation and avoid possible litigation the agent paid for the works and was charged VAT by the builder. It was held that he could reclaim the input tax charged to him as it was done for the purposes of his business.

In *Wheelcraft Centre/Original Homes* (LON/90/943 Decision 7150) the taxpayer carried out building works, intending to use them for his taxable business (the property was to be used as workshops and showrooms for skills associated with architectural techniques and house restoration). However, part was let exempt to various tenants. The tribunal made an appropriate apportionment for the amount of VAT claimable (relating to the taxable business user) and the amount not claimable (relating to the exempt letting).

In *David Grey Homes & Gardens Ltd* (LON/87/488: TP 1988 May 236) a barn was held to be used as to 50 per cent for business purposes and the balance as a family residence. Thus only 50 per cent of the inputs incurred on the refurbishment of the barn could be reclaimed.

In *D Dyball & Son* (LON/89/1449 Decision 4863) the appellant partnership ran three farms. They restored and renovated a derelict cottage on one of the farms. There were many possible uses to which the property could have been put, including use as a residence by one of the partners or even use as a holiday let. The tribunal, however, considered that, particularly having regard to the extent of diversification in farming businesses, it was normal for a farmer to renovate a building on his land for the purposes of the business without being committed to the precise use of the building until the renovation was complete (*Cobb's Croft Service Station Ltd* (1976) VATTR 170 distinguished). The tribunal was satisfied that the cottage had been renovated for use as a business asset of the partnership. The input tax on the renovation was, therefore, reclaimable.

In *Furness Vale Yacht Hire Ltd* (MAN/94/16 Decision 12628) [1994] STI 1320, the taxpayer purchased a yacht for business purposes but neglected to put it to business use for a considerable period. It was held that the input tax on acquisition was reclaimable as the business use had not been abandoned (the case of *Key Properties Ltd* (LON/92/2266) [1994] STI 575 was distinguished). The input tax was allowed pursuant to VATA 1983, s 14(3), now VATA 1994, s 26.

In *Warwest Holding Ltd* [1996] STI 1261 a property development company failed to reclaim input tax on the purchase of a yacht as there was no obvious or clear association between its business and the purchase (*Ian Flockton Devs Ltd v The Commissioners* [1987] STC 394). The evidence indicated the yacht was acquired for the directors' personal enjoyment.

It may be if the taxpayer incurs expenses (on which VAT is borne) for the benefit of others, he can still reclaim the VAT. This is a difficult area and there are cases either side. One case which is helpful to the taxpayers is *David Kelly and Doris Kelly v The Commissioners* (LON/87/173 Decision 2452). In that case the taxpayers provided their independent managers (they were self-employed) with the use of cars to carry out their tupperware distribution operations. The taxpayers incurred the expenditure in connection with the cars and Customs argued that the:

> ... cars provided ... had been provided to the managers for the use by such managers in the course of their businesses as managers. The cars had been driven around by the managers, not by (the taxpayers).

The tribunal rejected that argument and said that to ascertain whether the expenditure was laid out to serve the purposes of the taxpayer's business it was necessary to discover the taxpayer's object in making the expenditure.

At p 8 the tribunal concluded thus:

> Now it seems to me that the appellants' object in obtaining the supplies of the new motor cars under the Car Scheme was, in the first place, to reward their managers who had obtained 'Vanguard Status', in the second place to encourage and induce them to maintain and improve the sales of tupperware achieved by them and their units in obtaining 'Vanguard Status', in the third place to encourage and induce other managers and dealers to improve their sales and, in the fourth place, to assist their successful managers in transporting tupperware for display at parties and in delivering tupperware to hostesses and thereby tending to increase their own wholesales of tupperware to their managers and dealers and improving their commissions. The motivation effected by the provision of the new motor cars free of charge to the successful managers benefited not only those managers but also the appellants and the tupperware company. Accordingly, I consider the appellants used the new motor cars supplied to them by the tupperware company for the purposes of their business as distributors.

The European Court of Justice, in *Lennartz v Finanzamt Munchen III* (Case C 97/90) [1995] STC 564, ruled that a taxable person has the right to total and immediate input tax deduction on goods (not services) which are used partly for business and partly for private purposes.

This is because, when taxable persons use business assets for non-business purposes, they are making a supply of services and they must account for output tax on non-business use as and when it arises (under the Sixth Directive Articles 6(2)(*a*), 11A(1)(*c*)). Customs accept the decision (*see* Customs and Excise Press Notice No 1/92 dated 6 January 1992), and it is open to businesses either to continue using the UK method of apportioning the amount of input tax between business and non-business uses, or to adopt the correct method. The former will usually be more convenient but if the amounts of input tax are large, it may be preferable to use the method set down in the *Lennartz* decision.

Second step: what does the business input tax relate to?

Once one has determined the taxpayer has suffered input tax one must then determine whether it relates to an exempt onward output supply or another business activity other than the making of taxable supplies. If all the output tax relates to an onward taxable supply the total input tax can be reclaimed provided there is a direct and immediate link between the input and the onward taxable supply. In *The Commissioners v Redrow Group plc* [1997] STC 1053 a developer agreed to pay the estate agency costs of prospective purchasers who bought homes from the developer and who had to sell their existing homes. Estate agency fees were incurred in respect of the disposal of the existing homes which were owned by the prospective purchasers. Customs argued that the input tax charged by the estate agents could thus not be reclaimed by the developer (*see* Figure 7.1).

The true test required two things:

(1) Before the input tax could be reclaimed there had to be a direct and immediate link between the estate agents' costs and the supplies by the developer (*BLP Group plc v The Commissioners* [1995] STC 424).

(2) It is not permissible to take a global view of transactions in the chain of supplies; each transaction in the chain must be examined separately to ascertain objectively what output tax is payable and what input tax is deductible (*The Commissioners v Robert Gordon's College* [1995] STC 1093, especially Lord Hoffman at 1099).

Figure 7.1: TFM (trouble free move) schemes

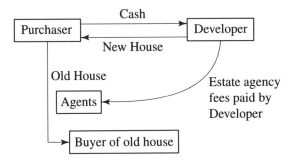

The Court of Appeal held that on dissecting the transaction the estate agents must have made the supplies to the prospective purchaser and not the developer as it was the houses of the prospective purchasers which were sold by the estate agents.

At 1060 Peter Gibson LJ stated:

In the present case there were two transactions involved each time Redrow (the developer) became liable to pay the estate agent: one was the sale by the prospective purchaser of his house and one was the sale by Redrow of its new house. It is in connection with the latter sale that Redrow is claiming as input tax the VAT on the supply by the estate agent of his services. But those services were the services which an estate agent ordinarily supplies when a house is to be sold and objectively they can be seen to be directly attributable to the sale by the prospective purchaser of his own house and not the sale by Redrow of a new house, even though the estate agents' supply benefits by facilitating Redrow's sale . . . the supply by the estate agent of his services does not have 'a direct and immediate link' with the sale by Redrow and is not 'objectively linked' to that taxable transaction.

PARTIAL EXEMPTION

The general position with respect to the reclaim of input tax is governed by the 1995 Regulations, regs 99–111. The general rule is that a taxpayer can reclaim input tax which is attributable to taxable supplies which he intends to make. Thus, if a taxpayer buys a building and is charged VAT, and he intends to make a vatable supply of that building, the VAT can be reclaimed. The regulations set out the requirements which must be satisfied before the VAT can be reclaimed.

Standard method

The standard method contained in reg 101 involves the taxpayer in a number of steps:

(1) The taxpayer's prescribed accounting period, generally a three-month period (reg 25), shall first be determined.

(2) The goods or services supplied to the taxpayer in that period are then determined (reg 101(2)(*a*)).

(3) There is then attributed to taxable supplies the whole of the input tax on the supply of goods and services made to the taxpayer as are used or are to be used by him exclusively in making taxable supplies (reg 101(2)(*b*)). Such an attribution means the input tax can be reclaimed (VATA 1994, s 26(1) and (2)(*a*)).

(4) Input tax is not attributed to taxable supplies to the extent that the goods and services supplied to the taxpayer are to be used exclusively in making exempt supplies, or in carrying on any activity other than the making of taxable supplies (reg 101(2)(*c*)).

(5) If a supply of goods or services to the taxpayer is not to be used exclusively by him in making taxable supplies, then one nevertheless assumes that the taxpayer will use the goods and services in making taxable supplies with respect to such a proportion of the input tax as bears the same ratio to the total of such input tax as the value of taxable supplies made by him bears to the value of all supplies made by him in the period (reg 101(2)(*d*)).

(6) In calculating that ratio the following are excluded:

(a) any sum receivable by the taxable person in respect of the supply of capital goods used by him for the purposes of his business; and

(b) any sum receivable by the taxable person in respect of certain supplies set out in reg 101(3)(*b*) where such supplies are incidental to the taxpayer's activities.

Other methods

It is possible, however, for taxpayers to use other methods to reclaim input tax. These must be agreed with Customs and, once agreed, they have the force of law by virtue of reg 102.

Customs may direct that a special method be used if they have reasonable grounds so to do, eg they believe the method in use produces an unfair result. Examples of 'special methods' are the use of individual profit centres, eg properties, companies, departments/divisions or head counts, management accounts and costs allocations.

The method largely favoured by property investors with little or no development under way or planned is a method which couples direct attribution to both specific transactions and individual properties/sites, with a residual recovery which is based on turnover.

Property companies which are carrying out developments, on the other hand, will not want to rely on a turnover basis of apportionment as it will not be truly indicative of the way in which general expenditure is incurred. To reflect VAT on development costs being incurred on *future* taxable and exempt activities, the residual calculation may be based upon input tax attribution.

Ignoring certain exempt supplies

Certain supplies made to the taxpayer on which VAT has been charged are treated as attributable to taxable supplies. The list is set out in reg 105. These include, for example, the grant of any lease or any tenancy of or any licence to occupy any land where in any longer period (generally a period of a year: reg 99(3)) the input tax attributable to all such supplies by the grantor is less than £1,000 and no exempt input tax (ie input tax on supplies which are not to be used for a taxable purpose) is incurred by the grantor in respect of any exempt supply, other than a supply of a description which is treated as ignored under reg 105.

Small value exempt supplies

There is a further *de minimis* rule in reg 106. It states that where, in any pre-scribed accounting period or in any longer period, the exempt input tax of any taxable person does not amount to more than £625 per month on average and does not exceed one-half of all his input tax for the period concerned, all such input tax in the VAT period shall be treated as attributable to taxable supplies.

Attribution under reg 101 only provisional

Regulation 101 enables the taxpayer to reclaim input tax only provisionally, as it is subject to what may be termed an annual adjustment under reg 107.

Basically, the taxpayer must determine what his longer period is (generally a year) and ascertain whether, overall, taking into account the prescribed accounting periods in that longer period, he has overdeclared or under-declared his input tax (reg 107(1)(*b*)).

If he has claimed back too much input tax, then he must repay that to Customs. If he has claimed back too little, then Customs will repay the input tax to him.

A 'longer period' is generally a period of 12 months commencing on the first day of April, May or June, according to the prescribed accounting periods allocated to the taxpayer (reg 99(1)(*d*) and (3)).

Anti-avoidance regulations

There are two anti-avoidance provisions in regs 108 and 109.

It will be noted from reg 101(2)(*b*) that a taxpayer can reclaim input tax if he can show that the goods and services supplied to him are used or are *to be used* by him exclusively in making taxable supplies.

It may be that the taxpayer has deducted input tax because he intended such a use but, during a period of six years commencing on the first day of the pre-scribed accounting period in which the attribution was determined, and before he actually uses the goods or services supplied in making a taxable supply, he uses or forms an intention to use the goods and services concerned in making exempt supplies or in making both taxable and exempt supplies.

In such a case, unless Customs otherwise allow, the taxable person shall, on the return for the prescribed accounting period in which the use occurs or the intention is formed, account for an amount equal to the input tax which has ceased to be attributable to the taxable supply.

For the purposes of this regulation, any questions about the nature of any supply are determined in accordance with the provisions of the Act and any regulations or orders made thereunder in force at the time when the input tax was first attributed (reg 108(3)).

Thus, if a taxpayer intends to use goods and services in making a future taxable supply, and four years later, when he makes that supply, the law has changed so that such a supply becomes an exempt supply, nevertheless the taxpayer does not have to repay the input tax.

Regulation 109 deals with the situation where the taxpayer was not able to reclaim any input tax because he intended to use the goods and services supplied to him in, for example, making an exempt supply. If, during the period of six years commencing on the first day of the prescribed accounting period in which the attribution was determined and before the intention to make the exempt supply was fulfilled, he uses or forms an intention to use the goods in making, for example, taxable supplies, then he is able to reclaim back the VAT (reg 109(1) and (2)).

Once again, there is a provision—reg 109(3)—which requires an examination of the law at the time when the input tax was first attributed. Thus if the taxpayer intends to use a supply in making an exempt supply, and three or four years later the law has changed so that the supply he actually always intended to make and did make becomes vatable, he still is not able to reclaim the input tax.

Problems with 'pre-registration input tax'

Exceptional claims for relief for input tax are dealt with in reg 111.

Customs may authorise a taxable person to reclaim VAT charged to him where the supply was made to the taxable person before the date with effect from which he was or was required to be registered, or the VAT was paid by him before that date for the purposes of a business which either was carried on or was to be carried on by him at the time of such supply or payment (reg 111(1)(*a*)).

However, no tax may be treated as input tax (which can be reclaimed) under this provision in respect of goods or services which had been sold on by the taxpayer, or, in respect of goods consumed by the taxpayer, before the date with effect from which the taxable person was or was required to be registered unless the Customs allow the reclaim.

Further, tax in respect of services which had been supplied to the taxable person may not be reclaimed if the supply to him was made more than six months before the date of the taxable person's registration.

Thus, there can be problems if a taxpayer, for instance, receives supplies and is not registered for VAT, and has consumed or sold the supplies before he registers, or, in the case of a supply of services, the six-month period elapses.

CAPITAL GOODS PROVISIONS: CLAW-BACK

These provisions, contained in the 1995 Regulations, regs 112–116, may well affect the ability of the taxpayer to reclaim input tax and indeed retain input tax which has been reclaimed where construction works have been carried out or property has been purchased and on which VAT has been charged. These provisions require the position of the taxpayer to be looked at over a period of, possibly, ten years, to determine whether input tax can be reclaimed or whether any input tax which has already been reclaimed must be paid back to Customs. The provisions are dealt with in detail in Chapter 22.

BLOCKED INPUT TAX

Certain supplies of goods and services made to a taxpayer can give rise to 'blocked' input tax, ie, the taxpayer cannot reclaim the input tax even though he may use the goods or services in making an onward vatable supply. The restrictions apply to various situations including business entertainment, supplies of works of art, antiques and collectors' pieces and motor cars, but the most significant one concerning land is found in the Value Added Tax (Input Tax) (Amendment) Order 1995 (SI No 281) (which adds art 6 to the Value Added Tax (Input Tax) Order 1992 (SI No 3222)), which prevents developers who make zero-rated supplies of, for example, new domestic buildings, from reclaiming input tax on goods incorporated into the dwelling houses etc which do not fall within the definition of 'building materials' (*see* Figure 7.2).

'Building materials' is defined in Note (22) to Group 5 of Sched 8, which states that, in relation to any description of building, 'building materials' means goods of a description ordinarily incorporated by builders in a building of that description (or its site) but it does not include:

(a) finished or prefabricated furniture, other than furniture designed to be fitted in kitchens;

(b) materials for the construction of fitted furniture, other than kitchen furniture;

(c) electrical or gas appliances, unless the appliance is an appliance which is—

   (i) designed to heat space or water (or both) or to provide ventilation, air or dust extraction; or

   (ii) intended for use in a building designed as a number of dwellings and is a door/entry system, waste disposal unit or a machine for compacting waste; or

   (iii) a burglar alarm, a fire alarm, or fire safety equipment or designed solely for the purpose of enabling aid to be summoned in an emergency; or

   (iv) a lift or hoist.

(d) carpets or carpeting material.

For the purposes of that Note the incorporation of goods in a building includes their installation as fittings. That Note also applies to Group 6, the protected buildings group (*see* Sched 8, Group 6, Note (3)).

Figure 7.2:

Builder ⟶ Developer ⟶ Purchaser of new building

Non-building materials (VAT charged) — Zero-rated supply

Developer cannot claim the VAT back on the non-building materials supplied to him. They are 'blocked inputs'.

PART II

TRANSACTIONS TAXABLE AT THE STANDARD RATE

Chapter 8

Grants of land rights and facilities

INTRODUCTION

VATA 1994, s 1(1) and (2) provides that VAT shall be charged on the supply of goods or services in the UK, and that tax shall be the liability of the person who makes the supply.

Supplies which are not zero-rated or exempt supplies and which are not expressly disregarded for VAT purposes or outside the scope of VAT will be chargeable to VAT at the standard rate.

The grant of any interest in or right over land or of any licence to occupy land is in general exempt (VATA 1994, Sched 9, Group 1 Item 1). One difficult question is the definition of an interest in or right over land. At first sight, the expression 'the grant of any interest in or right over land or of any licence to occupy land' should have an extremely wide meaning. Anything vaguely connected with land should come within the heading.

Commenting on the structure of the section the VAT tribunal in *Rochdale Hornets Football Club Co Ltd v The Commissioners* (1975) VATTR 71 at 83 stated:

1   The words 'right over land' appear together with the words 'interest in land' to make one composite expression 'any interest in or right over land' whereas 'any licence to occupy land' appears in isolation.

2   Only licences 'to occupy land' are expressly exempted and not other licences in respect of, or relating to, land.

3   There is excluded from the exemption the provision of certain accommodation and the granting of certain facilities, which suggest that, in certain circumstances, such supplies would otherwise fall within the exemption.

Also at p 83 the tribunal stated:

> The expression clearly covers inter alia legal estates and fee simples, terms
> of years absolute and also interests such as profits a prendre recognised as
> such by the law, that is to say rights of pasture, piscary, turbary and
> estovers, some of which interests are clearly recognised as otherwise
> falling within the exemptions by the exceptions in (certain of the para-
> graphs of Item 1).

Thus a licence to watch a rugby football match may be a licence to go on
the premises but it would not be a licence to occupy the premises.

In *Trewby v The Commissioners* [1976] STC 122 Geoffrey Lane LJ at 127
stated that:

> In our judgment, in order to make sense of this part . . . the words 'any inter-
> est in or right over land' must be confined to a legal or equitable interest in
> land in the sense used by Lord Upjohn in *National Provincial Bank Ltd v
> Ainsworth* (1965) AC 1175 at 1237. 'Interest' and 'right' are treated together
> as practically synonymous. Licence to occupy is in a contrasting category.

Thus rights granted to club members to use facilities including tennis
courts, croquet lawns and the gardens belonging to the club are not rights
over land. They are licences. The only type of licence which will provide
exemption is a licence to occupy land. *Expressum facit cessare tacitum.*
Such a licence to enter the premises is not a licence to occupy any part of
the club's premises.

In *National Provincial Bank Ltd v Ainsworth* (1965) Lord Upjohn said:

> To create a right over land of another that right, apart from statue, must
> create a burden on the land, ie an equitable estate or interest in the land. All
> this was pointed out in a closely analogous case on restrictive covenants of
> Farwell J in *Re Nesbett & Potts' Contract* [1905] 1 Ch 391, in a very full
> judgment dealing with the earlier authorities which, though at first instance,
> has always been accepted as authoritatively stating the law. So in principle,
> in my opinion, to create a right over land of another that right must in con-
> templation of law be such that it creates a legal or equitable estate or inter-
> est in that land, and notice of something though relating to land which falls
> short of an estate or interest is insufficient.

THE BROAD PICTURE

It is thus necessary to distinguish between interests in land and other interests
and determine whether particular licences are licensees to occupy land or not
(*see* Figure 8.1).

Some formal land interests can be ignored for VAT purposes (*see* p 99) and
the tax courts may also ignore conveyancing mechanics.

Figure 8.1: The broad picture

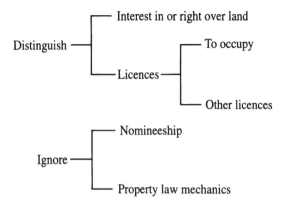

CONTRACTS FOR SALE—INTERESTS IN LAND

It seems clear enough that if A contracts to sell a legal estate to B with completion in four weeks B has an interest in land which could be registered as a Class C(iv) estate contract under the Land Charges Act 1972, s 2. If B sub-sells under contract or sells (ie assigns) his contract an interest in land will be disposed of by B (*see* Figure 8.2).

Figure 8.2: Contracts for sale

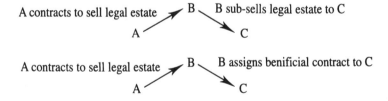

SUB-SALES—INTERESTS IN LAND

In *Kwik Save Group plc v The Commissioners* (MAN/93/11 Decision 12749) X contracted to sell property to Y who sub-sold it to Z (legal completion took place by X vesting the legal estate in Z). It was held that X had made a supply to Y who had made a supply to Z. The going concern relief was not available as Y had not used the property—retail stores—for the same business purposes as X: Y had sub-sold the land.

At p 6 the chairman stated:

> If A agrees with B to sell specific assets to B for £x and B agrees with C to
> sell those assets to C for £y (which may or may not be the same amount as
> £x) and, by the direction of B, the assets are transferred by A direct to C, in
> my judgement it is too clear for argument that two supplies and not one are
> made, namely a supply by A to B for £x and a supply by B to C for £y. If the
> assets are transferred by A to B and then by B to C, the case is even clearer.
> I am dealing here with a true sub-sale, of which the instant case is an example
> in relation to the Tates (C's) foodstores; I am not dealing with the case of
> novation of the original agreements whereby C steps into B's shoes; in such
> a case there would unquestionably be one supply only, namely by A to C.

JOINT OWNERSHIP—IGNORE CONVEYANCING MECHANICS

If freehold land is held by A and B as joint tenants beneficially or as tenants in
common beneficially they will have interests in land. It is felt that any technical arguments which may be raised that what A and B have is rights in the proceeds of sale because of the existence of the power of sale (which under the
doctrine of conversion treats a beneficiary as having rights in the proceeds of
sale (cash)) will fail under any 'reality' test. It is felt that a reasonable substance
approach can be adopted to, in effect, ignore the consequences of the trust for
sale (*see*, for example, *Kidson v MacDonald* (1974) 49 TC 503 and *Harthan v
Mason* [1980] STC 94: in the latter case Fox J stated at p 97 that 'One looks
straight through the trust for sale and finds two persons . . . as co-owners of the
property'). (Both cases are capital gains tax cases: the underlying principle of
looking to the substance derives from *Sargaison v Roberts* (1969) 45 TC
612 which was a sound decision, although not necessarily always bound to be
applicable (*Stokes v Costain Property Investments Ltd* (1984) 57 TC 688)).

Note that the doctrine of conversion has now generally been abolished by
the Trusts of Land and Appointment of Trustees Act 1996, s 3 but the general
principle that the courts in taxing matters will generally ignore conveyancing mechanics remains extant.

THE RIGHT TO CALL FOR CERTAIN RIGHTS ARE VATABLE

The grant of any right including:

   (a) an equitable right;

(b) a right under an option or a right of pre-emption; or

(c) in relation to Scotland a personal right,

to call for or be granted an interest or right which would fall within any of paras (*a*) or (*c*) to (*m*) of Sched 9, Group 1, Item 1 is not an exempt land supply (*see* Sched 9, Group 1, Item 1(*n*)).

Example: Contract to sell freehold

X has the freehold of a new commercial building. He enters into a contract to sell the building to Z. Z thus has an equitable right to a grant of the fee simple. The entry into the contract would be a vatable transaction because of Sched 9, Group 1, Item 1(*a*) and (*n*).

Example: Grant of options/pre-emption rights are freehold

A Ltd has the freehold of a new commercial building. It grants B Ltd an option or a right of pre-emption to acquire the freehold. Such an option grant or pre-emption right grant is within the ambit of Sched 9, Group 1, Item 1(*a*), because of Item 1(*n*) and a VAT charge can arise in an appropriate case.

The wording of Sched 9, Group 1, Item 1(*n*) is restrictive and it may not catch a present option to acquire a new commercial freehold after the three-year period has elapsed (after the three-year period the freehold will no longer be 'new'—see VATA 1994, Sched 9, Group 1, Item 1(*a*) and Note (4)).

LICENCES—DISTINGUISH LICENCES TO OCCUPY FROM OTHER LICENCES

Market and antique stalls

In *Wendy Fair Market Club* (LON/77/400 Decision 679) the taxpayer set up a company which ran markets and fairs under the name Wendy Fairs. The issue was whether certain receipts by the club, linked with rental payments from the traders for sites provided by the company, were taxable or exempt. The tribunal held that the company granted a licence to occupy and the supplies were exempt.

In the case of *Tameside Metropolitan Borough Council* (1979) VATTR 93, the taxpayer borough council made short-term lettings of two stores in one of its markets. The lettings were for one day only, and under the relevant bye-laws the market was open for trading from 9 am to 5.30 pm, and the stall-holder could not bring his goods on to the market before 8.15 am or leave them there after 6.15 pm. Customs considered that the short duration of the letting prevented it from qualifying as a licence to occupy land. The tribunal held that there was a licence to occupy land and that the short duration of user did not prevent there being such a licence to occupy. The taxpayer 'had exclusive occupation of the said stalls during the measurable period of each day for which he was in occupation thereof, . . . such interest was not *de minimis* and . . . it constitutes a licence to occupy land . . .' (p 113).

Thus, it seems clear enough that if X, the taxpayer, owns a site and charges various stallholders monies for allowing them to use the site on, say, Saturdays to put up their stalls and sell their wares, the monies paid to X will be monies paid in connection with the licence granted to occupy land and will be exempt.

However, in *Mrs W B Enever* (LON/83/220) the taxpayer organised and promoted antique fairs which were held in hotels or public houses. The appellant hired a room for a specific date. She arranged for the antique fair to take place and charged antique traders for space in that room during the fair. Each trader had a mobile table on which to put the antiques he wanted to sell. Members of the public were charged an admittance fee. The tribunal held that the provision of tables in hotel rooms did not amount to the grant of an interest in or right over land or any licence to occupy land. Accordingly, such services are vatable.

Shops and offices

A right to occupy two shops at an airport terminal amounted to exempt licences to occupy (*British Airports Authority v The Commissioners* [1997] STC 36) and the hire out of a furnished suite in a business centre was held to comprise an exempt supply in *Business Enterprises (UK) Ltd v The Commissioners* (1988) VATTR 160.

It is important, however, to structure transactions carefully. In *Ultimate Advisory Services Ltd* (MAN/91/1448 Decision 9523) [1993] STI 345 the appellant company received payments from an associated company. Both companies were wholly owned by the same individual and carried on financial advisory businesses from premises owned by the appellant. The appellant claimed that the payments made by the associated company were rent for its use of the premises and were therefore exempt from VAT. However, there was no evidence of an agreement between the parties for the use of any specific part of the premises. The associated company which paid the monies did not in fact have exclusive possession of any part of them. The tribunal concluded that there was no agreement which created a licence for the associated company to occupy any part of the premises. The assessment for VAT was therefore upheld.

FEES AS A PORTION OF RENT COLLECTED

In the case of *Peter Anthony Estate Ltd* (Decision 13250) the landlord granted an agent the right to manage the property of the landlord. The agent agreed to pay the landlord an agreed sum each week by way of 'rent'. The agent retained the difference between that sum and the amounts actually charged to the tenants for the accommodation as its fee.

It was held that the agent did not have an interest in land; its fee was therefore vatable. It was the landlord who granted the leases—shorthold tenancies—to the occupational tenants (page 2, line 35 of the Decision). The agent did not grant any leases (*see* Figure 8.3 *below*).

Figure 8.3:   Fees as a portion of rent collected

Of course if the landlord had granted a lease to the agent who sublet the same to the occupational tenants and kept the 'turn' on the rents (ie the £10 in the above example) the VAT liability on the agent may have been avoided.

NOMINEES

It also seems clear enough from the case of *Bird Semple & Crawford Herron v The Commissioners* (1986) VATTR 218 that the interests of a nominee would be ignored. In that case X Ltd held a lease as nominee for a partnership and it was held that supplies made by consultant surveyors to, on the face of it, the nominee, were really supplies made to the partnership as the beneficial owners.

The tribunal, at p 220F, held:

> The reality of the matter was that (the partnership) in order to simplify administration of the lease and sub-leases used (the nominee) in a literally nominal way. No supply was made to (the nominee) and indeed it had no business to which such a supply could be made. In our opinion the supply was made by (the consultant surveyors) to the (partnership), on their instructions and at their expense.

FIXTURES AND FITTINGS

No special VAT problems should arise with respect to fixtures and fittings. These should 'flow with' the land, ie take on the nature of the land interest to which they are affixed.

The position of Customs is set out in Notice 742, para 7.9 of which reads as follows:

> When fixtures are included with a building or land they are not to be treated as separate supplies for VAT purposes. This means that their liability is the same as that of the land or building with which they are being supplied.

The situation may arise where X plc owns the building. Y plc may purchase fixtures and fittings such as internal partitions or semi-structural items such as wall cladding and let them to X plc. Y plc may seek to charge VAT on the letting of the items: this would enable Y plc to reclaim the VAT charged to it. As a precaution Y plc should make an election with regard to the building in case it is found that the rental payments derived from the grant of an interest etc in land.

ASSIGNMENT OF A BUILDING LICENCE

T has a licence to enter land and construct a building thereon and then call for a lease from L. He sells his rights to T2. That is very likely to be an exempt supply with the election to waive exemption being available.

Figure 8.4:

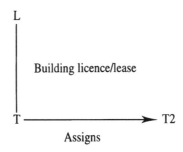

LAND CONTRACTS UNDER SCOTTISH LAW

Under Scottish law, if X enters into a contract (a missive) to purchase land X has only a personal right under the contract (*Gibson v Hunter Home Designs Ltd* (1976) SC 23 27). X does not have an interest in land.

In *Margrie Holdings Ltd v The Commissioners* [1991] STC 80 Margrie entered into a contract to acquire land from Murfield and effectively sub-sold the land by entering into another contract with the ultimate purchaser Boland. Boland took the disposition direct from Murfield (*see* Figure 8.4, *above*).

The Court of Session held that Margrie had only a personal right in the land and therefore did not have an interest in the land and therefore could not make an exempt land supply. The irresistible conclusion is that the supply by Margrie must have been a vatable one (in England and Wales the supply will have been an exempt supply because it will have been the grant of an interest in a right over land, albeit a supply of an equitable interest in land).

To ensure that such supplies are now exempt, the then Sched 6, Group 1, Item 1 was amended by the Value Added Tax (Buildings and Land) Order 1991 (SI No 2569) art 2(*a*). The relevant provision is now in Sched 9, Group 1, Item 1, which reads:

> The grant of any interest in or right over land or of any licence to occupy land, or, in relation to land in Scotland, any personal right to call for or be granted any such interest or right . . . (shall be exempt subject to exceptions).

Before the amendment made by that Order the provision simply read, 'The grant of any interest in or right over land or of any licence to occupy land . . . (shall be exempt subject to exceptions)'.

Figure 8.5:

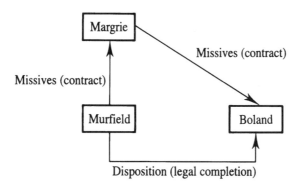

EXPRESS EXCLUSIONS FROM EXEMPTION

The following are specifically excluded from exemption in Sched 9, Group 1 and it is very unlikely that any of these can be brought within the zero-rated item in Sched 8, Group 5. They are important vatable heads and should not be overlooked.

1   Fish and game

Schedule 9, Group 1, Item 1(*c*) provides that the grant of any interest, right or licence consisting of a right to take game or fish shall comprise a vatable supply (unless at the time of the grant the grantor grants to the grantee the fee simple of the land over which the right to take game or fish is exercisable).

Note (8) to that group provides that where a grant of an interest in, right over or licence to occupy land includes a 'valuable' right to take game or fish, an apportionment shall be made to determine the supply falling outside the group by virtue of Item 1(*c*).

The Customs have agreed with the Country Landowners' Association that the sporting right is 'valuable' if its rental value exceeds 10 per cent of the total rent charged under the lease (Customs' Press Notice No 59/91, 5 August 1991).

It was (but is no longer) an open question whether the disposal of a freehold or the equivalent interest in Scotland with sporting rights attached thereto could give rise to a vatable charge—*see The Commissioners v Parkinson* [1989] STC 51, VAT (Buildings and Land) Order 1991, art 2(*c*) and now Sched 9, Group 1, Item 1(*c*). Such supplies are now clearly exempt.

2   Hotels, etc

The provision in a hotel, inn, boarding house or similar establishment of sleeping accommodation or of accommodation in rooms which are provided in conjunction with sleeping accommodation or for the purpose of a supply of catering (Item 1(*d*)) is vatable.

'Similar establishment' includes premises in which there is provided furnished sleeping accommodation, whether with or without the provision of board or facilities for the preparation of food, which are used by or held out as being suitable for use by visitors or travellers. *See* Item 1, Note (9).

In *RI McGrath v The Commissioners* (MAN/88/87 Decision 4368), it was held that the fact that the local authority may have considered accommodation which clearly fell within the above definition—it was a guest house—to be a house in multiple occupation for the purposes of certain local government housing regulations did not prevent it being a hotel, inn, boarding house or similar establishment for VAT purposes.

Simple grant of hotel leases

If L plc lets a hotel to T plc and T plc is to run its hotel business from the premises, L plc makes an exempt grant. T plc will make the vatable supply of hotel accommodation (*see* Figure 8.6).

Figure 8.6:

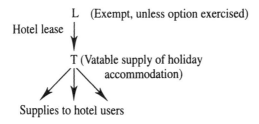

Complex situations and hotels

It can sometimes be difficult to distinguish between different types of supplies made in complex commercial transactions.

X plc may, for instance, own a hotel. If the employees of X plc run the hotel there is no problem: X plc is providing the hotel services and supplies will be made to hotel users by X plc and X plc will be assessed to VAT.

The same would apply if X plc, through its agent, supplies services to members of the public, although if the agent supplies services in its own name, Customs do have a discretion to determine that supplies have been made to the agent and then by the agent to the public. Obviously the matter would need to be taken up with Customs. If Customs do not make such a direction then, as a matter of general law, X plc will be treated as the person making a supply to the public (*see* VATA 1994, s 47(2A) and (3)).

Interestingly, the agent may have a VAT registration number in its own name. As far as the outside world is concerned they would use that VAT registration number in all transactions. Customs practice, however, appears to be that the transactions which are carried out by the agent as agent for X plc (although they have the agent's VAT registration number on the invoices) can be dealt with for VAT purposes as if X plc was making all the VAT reclaims and any VAT supplies. In other words, X plc may have a separate VAT number, but it will be able to use the invoices of the agent in settling its VAT position.

Needless to say, expressly or impliedly, the agent must have some sort of licence to enter the hotel and do the work. No licence fee will be charged to the agent in the normal course of events and the author would not expect Customs to attempt, nor does he feel that they would be successful if they did attempt, to somehow attribute a figure to the user of the premises. It is normal practice not to charge in such circumstances, just as a company does not charge its auditors rent for entering the company's premises to carry out its audit.

The agent, however, clearly has a licence to occupy but as that licence is merely a use of the premises by X plc through its agent it does not seem likely that any special problems can arise.

Of course the position may be more provocative if a formal lease is granted to the agent to carry out the works. This is because if X plc carries out no actual functions other than allowing the agent to get on with the work, Customs may be tempted to argue that the amount paid to X plc is merely rent; a formal lease is being granted and, properly analysed, any amount paid by the agent to the landlord is rent.

3   Holiday accommodation

The grant of any interest in, right over or licence to occupy holiday accommodation is vatable (Item 1(*e*)).

'Holiday accommodation' includes any accommodation in a building, hut (including a beach hut or chalet), caravan, houseboat or tent which is advertised or held out as holiday accommodation or as suitable for holiday or leisure use but excluding accommodation within 2 *above* (ie hotels etc).

The Holiday Accommodation Rules before 1 February 1991

Under the pre-1 February 1991 holiday accommodation rules, the provision of holiday accommodation in a house, flat, caravan, houseboat or tent was vatable at the standard rate (Sched 6, Group 1, Item 1(*d*) of VATA 1983). Holiday accommodation included any accommodation advertised or held out as such.

Problems arose with respect to the *Parkinson* case: could the grant of a long lease or the disposal of a freehold be treated as a supply of holiday accommodation? The wording of Item 1(*d*) of VATA 1983, namely the provision of holiday accommodation, contrasted with the wording of Item 1(*b*) of VATA 1983 (now VATA 1994, Sched 9, Group 1, Item 1(*c*)), which referred to the grant of any interest right or licence (the latter could cover a freehold sale or the grant of a long lease, but the former, following the *Parkinson* decision, would not).

Matters came to a head in the decision of *Haven Leisure Ltd* (LON/90/503Z). Haven Leisure Ltd, in 1989, decided to sell long leases of some of its holiday chalets. It granted a 40-year lease on one of them. Customs claimed that the premium was vatable at the standard rate, saying that it related to the provision of holiday accommodation within VATA 1983, Sched 6, Group 1, Item 1. The tribunal decided that the premium was exempt. What was offered was the opportunity of owning a luxury villa by the sea. It could be used to provide holiday accommodation or it could be used as a second home. It was not, however, correct for Customs to say that what had been provided was holiday accommodation. As a result of that decision, Customs, rather than appealing, had the law changed—*see* the Value Added Tax (Construction of Dwellings and Land) Order 1990 (SI No 2553).

The Holiday Accommodation Rules after 31 January 1991

The provisions relating to holiday accommodation, as a result of the *Haven Leisure Ltd* decision, were radically altered by the Value Added Tax (Construction of Dwellings and Land) Order 1990.

From 1 February 1991, it was provided, in art 3(*a*) of the Order, that the grant of any interest in, right over or licence to occupy holiday accommodation is vatable at the standard rate. This change was made by inserting a new (*d*) in Item 1 of Group 1 in Sched 6 to VATA 1983, replacing the old wording which charged the standard rate of VAT on 'the provision of holiday accommodation in a house, flat, caravan, houseboat or tent'. The relevant provision is now VATA 1994, Sched 9, Group 1, Item 1(*e*). Obviously, Customs felt that by adopting wording similar to that in Sched 6, Group 1, Item 1(*b*) (now VATA 1994, Sched 9, Group 1, Item 1(*c*)) major land interests such as long leases and freeholds would come within the new legislation. The same query which applies to freeholds and long leasehold disposals of rights to take fish and game will apply here, ie are the changes *intra vires* the Sixth Directive? It is assumed that they are for the purposes of the points made *below*, but *see* p 108–9, and the case of *Barbara A Ashworth* (LON/94/221 Decision 12924), which raises a question about the validity of much of this legislation.

Under the pre-1 February 1991 rules, holiday accommodation in Note (10) to Item 1, Group 1, Sched 6 was stated to include any accommodation advertised or held out as such. That Note has been replaced by a new Note (10) (now VATA 1994, Sched 9, Group 1, Item 1, Note (11)) which states that the grant of any interest in, right over or licence to occupy holiday accommodation includes:

(1) any grant excluded from Item 1 of Group 5 of Sched 8 to VATA by Note (13) in that Group; and

(2) any supply made pursuant to a tenancy, lease or licence under which the grantee is or has been permitted to erect and occupy holiday accommodation.

In addition, Note (12) in Sched 9, Group 1, Item 1, VATA 1994 provides that the grant of any interest in, right over or licence to occupy holiday accommodation does not include a grant in respect of a building or part of a building which is not a new building (*see* Sched 9, Group 1, Note (4)) of:

(1) the fee simple; or

(2) a tenancy, lease or licence to the extent that the grant is made for a consideration in the form of a premium.

Note (13) in Sched 9, Group 1, Item 1, VATA 1994 states that holiday accommodation includes any accommodation in a building, hut (including a beach hut or chalet), caravan, houseboat or tent which is advertised or held out as holiday accommodation or is suitable for holiday or leisure use, but excludes any accommodation within para (*d*) (which states that the provision in a hotel, inn, boarding house or similar establishment of sleeping accommodation or of accommodation in rooms which are provided in conjunction with sleeping accommodation or for the purpose of a supply of catering is excluded from exemption, ie is vatable).

It is noted *above* that any grant excluded from Item 1 of Group 5 of Sched 8 to the Act by Note (13) in that group is included within the definition of holiday accommodation and is thus vatable at the standard rate, 17.5 per cent.

VATA 1994, Sched 8, Group 5 Note (7) reads as follows:

The grant of an interest in, or in any part of—

1   a building designed as a dwelling or a number of dwellings; or

2   the site of such a building,

is not within Item 1 (ie it is not zero-rated) if:

(a) the interest granted is such that the grantee is not entitled to reside in the building, or part, throughout the year or;

(b) residence there throughout the year, or the use of the building or part as the grantee's principal private residence, is prevented by the terms of a covenant, statutory planning consent or similar permission.

The above changes came into force on 1 February 1991. Their conse-quences are, first, as already mentioned, the grant of any interest in, right over or licence to occupy holiday accommodation is vatable at the standard rate. Where such language is used, Customs *prima facie* consider that the disposal of the freehold or a long leasehold interest would come within the definition.

Second, holiday accommodation includes any accommodation in a build-ing, hut (including a beach hut or chalet), caravan, houseboat or tent which is advertised or held out as holiday accommodation or is suitable for holiday or leisure use. There is, however, precluded from the definition the provi-sion in a hotel, inn, boarding house or similar establishment of sleeping accommodation or of accommodation in rooms which are provided in con-junction with sleeping accommodation or for the purpose of a supply of catering. In the definition of holiday accommodation importance is still attached to the advertising or the holding out of particular property for holiday purposes. Thus the tribunal cases which held that accommodation amounted to holiday accommodation because it was advertised as such are still relevant—see, for instance, *Sheppard v The Commissioners* (1977) VATTR 272 where two flats were let on short leases and, mainly to ensure that the tenancies would not be controlled, the lessors registered with the English Tourist Board and the London Tourist Board, and printed for distri-bution cards with the words 'fully furnished holiday accommodation'. The VAT tribunal held that the accommodation was holiday accommodation advertised or held out as such.

Third, it is clear that any supply made pursuant to a tenancy, lease or licence under which the grantee is or has been permitted to erect and occupy holiday accommodation, including a beach hut, will comprise the supply of holiday accommodation within Item 1(*d*). In *Poole Borough Council* (LON/91/1072 Decision 7180) the tribunal held that the letting of beach huts and hut sites on which the licensees were required to erect huts was charge-able to VAT at the standard rate by virtue of VATA 1983, Sched 6, Group 1, Item 1(*d*) (*see* now VATA 1994, Sched 9, Group 1, Item 1 (*e*)). The hut licence agreement provided that the hut was not to be occupied overnight and was not to be used as living accommodation; the hut was to be used for pleasure only. The licensee was responsible for the interior decoration of the hut. The tri-bunal held that holiday accommodation in this context (VATA 1983, Sched 6, Group 1, Item 1(*d*), Note (10)(*b*) (now VATA 1994, Sched 9, Group 1, Item 1(*e*), Note 11(*b*)) was not confined to living accommodation. With regard to the site licences, these permitted the grantees to erect a beach hut on the site and the site lettings were therefore excluded from exemption for the same reasons.

Example

> L grants T a lease or licence of land. Under the terms of the lease or licence T is permitted to erect a beach hut on the land. The supply by L to T is vatable at 17.5 per cent.

Fourth, it seems that the grant of a freehold or a lease of over 21 years by the person constructing a new building, if the building is designed as a dwelling or a number of dwellings or the site of such a building, may be in certain cases vatable at the standard rate if the grantee is not entitled to reside in the building or part of the building throughout the year, or residence there throughout the year, or the use of the building or part of the building as the grantee's principal private residence, is prevented by the terms of a covenant, statutory planning consent or similar permission. If the freehold grant by the developer is not of a new building (within VATA 1994, Sched 9, Group 1, Note (4): broadly it is three or more years old) it will be an exempt grant. If the letting is not of a new building then the supply is exempt to the extent the consideration is in the form of a premium. If the freehold grant by the developer is of a new building, or the lease of over 21 years is of a new building, the supply is vatable at 17.5 per cent (*see* VATA 1994, Sched 9, Group 1, Notes (11) and (12), and Sched 8, Group 5, Item 1, Note (13)). These are very difficult provisions but this is the way the author reads them.

The Barbara A Ashworth decision

In *Barbara A Ashworth* (LON/94/221 Decision 12924), the appellant taxpayer jointly owned a long lease in a waterside lodge at a marina.

> The lease prohibited occupancy of the lodge during the month of February. Nevertheless the appellant occupied the lodge as her home for the rest of the year, and went to stay with her daughter each February. She appealed against a decision by the Commissioners in January 1994 that ground rents and service charges payable by her for the year to October 1993 were liable to VAT at the standard rate. The Commissioners did not suggest that the marina had the attributes of a holiday site, but argued that the appellant's leasehold interest was nevertheless excluded from exemption because she was not entitled to reside in the lodge throughout the year (VATA 1983, Sched 6, Group 1, Item 1(*d*), Note 10(*a*), Sched 5, Group 8, Note (7), as amended by VAT (Construction of Dwellings and Land) Order [1990 (SI No 2553), art 3, now VATA 1994, Sched 9, Group 1, Item 1(*e*), Note (11)(*a*) and Sched 8, Group 5, Note (13)]). The tribunal agreed that the restriction in the lease meant that the appellant was not entitled to reside in the lodge throughout the year. Consequently, although the appellant occupied the lodge as her home and

not as holiday accommodation, under UK law the supplies to her were not exempt from VAT (VATA 1983, Sched 5, Group 8, Note (7), [now VATA 1994, Sched 8, Group 5, Note 7(i)]). This gave rise to inequality of treatment as between the appellant and others who occupied leased property as their homes. The Commissioners contended that this treatment was objectively justified by the EC legislation (EC Sixth Directive, art 13B(*b*)) which expressly allowed member states to apply further exclusions to the scope of the exemption. The tribunal held that as the exclusion applied in the appellant's case was not confined to accommodation in the hotel sector or sectors with a similar function, it was outside the class of supplies covered by the EC provision (EC Sixth Directive, art 13B(*b*)(1)). The UK exclusion (VATA 1983, Sched 6, Group 1, Note 10(*a*) [now VATA 1994, Sched 9, Group 1, Note (11)(*a*)]) went beyond the exclusion of supplies by reference to their function (EC Sixth Directive, art 13B(*b*)(1)–(4)). The discontinuous nature of the appellant's leasehold interest did not place it in the same category as hotel or similar accommodation. The tribunal could not accept that the discriminatory effect of the UK exclusion was objectively justifiable. The purported exclusion of interests where the grantee was not entitled to reside in the property throughout the year was therefore ineffective to exclude the appellant's interest from exemption.

The taxpayer's appeal was allowed.

Customs' view

The Custom's view is set out in Leaflet 709/3/93, paras 11 and 12, and reads as follows:

Sales and leases of holiday accommodation

11 If you sell or lease a house, flat or other accommodation in the course or furtherance of any business, it is **generally** standard-rated as holiday accommodation if the property is 'new' and cannot be occupied throughout the year or used as a principal private residence because of a covenant, planning restriction or similar constraint.

A property is considered to be new, for these purposes, for three years from the date on which a certificate of practical completion is issued in relation to it, or it is first fully occupied, whichever is the earlier. You must account for VAT on the initial charge, and on any periodic charges such as ground rent and service or other charges.

If you sell or lease accommodation which is **no longer 'new'**, any payment for the freehold, or premium paid under a lease, is **exempt**. However, any periodic charges, including rent and service or other charges, are standard-rated.

However, the sale or lease of a flat or house which can be used as a person's principal private residence but which cannot be occupied throughout the year due to a time related restriction on occupancy is exempt, **if** the **development** on which it is situated is not a holiday development and it is not advertised or held out as such. This also applies to any periodic charges, such as rent and service charges.

Sites for holiday accommodation

12   If you provide the site for holiday accommodation under a tenancy, lease or licence, your supply is standard-rated even if the person to whom you provide the site is responsible for erecting the accommodation on it. A sale of the freehold interest in a site which is merely bare land is exempt unless you have elected to waive exemption.

4   Caravans

The provision of seasonal pitches for caravans, and the grant of the facilities at sites to persons for whom such pitches are provided (Item 1(*f*)).

A 'seasonal pitch' is a pitch: (a) which is provided for less than a year; or, (b) which is provided for a year or longer, but the person to whom it is provided is prevented by the terms of any consent, statutory planning consent or other permission from occupying it by living in a caravan at all times throughout the period for which the pitch is provided.

5   Tents

The provision of pitches for tents or camping facilities (Item 1(*g*)).

6   Car parks

The grant of facilities for parking a vehicle (Item 1(*h*)). This would include (within the requirements of the Sixth Directive) the letting or the licensing of open parking spaces and enclosed garages and the lease of parking spaces which formed part of a single transaction of letting the main building (*Skatteministeriet v Morten Henriksen ECJ* (Case C-173/88 13 July 1989)).

Freehold sales and car parking

After the Finance Act 1989, the question arose whether VAT is chargeable on the sale of a freehold which provides parking facilities.

The grants of certain freeholds are included in the list of items excluded from exemption in the new Sched 9, Group 1.

The exclusions to the exemption (Item 1) would, on the face of it, appear to apply not only to leases and licences of, for instance, parking facilities, but also to sales of fee simples. This is because Item 1(*a*) refers to the grant of the fee simple, and clearly the word 'grant' in the introductory words of Item 1 will include the grant of the fee simple. Hence, it may be argued that the word 'grant' in Item 1(*h*) (parking facilities), for example, would also include a situation where the taxpayer sells the fee simple in a parcel of land which is used as a car park.

The author, however, does not feel that the disposal of the fee simple would be within Item 1(*h*). This is because that item is one of those referred to in art 13(B)(*b*) of the Sixth Directive and those items deal with 'the leasing or letting' of immovable property. The sale of a freehold is not the leasing or letting of immovable property. That wording contrasts with the wording used in art 13(B)(*g*) and (*h*) which refers to supplies of land and buildings: certainly a freehold could be covered by such language, but that is not the relevant language when dealing with Item 1(*h*) in VATA 1994, Sched 9, Group 1.

The history of the provision must also be examined. Initially Item 1(*a*) was not included in the group of exclusions from exemption, and it is in fact a curious place to find exclusion (*a*). There should have been a separate provision simply stating that the grants of certain fee simples should give rise to vatable supplies. The origin of those supplies being vatable is in fact to be found in the Sixth Directive, arts 13(B)(*g*) and (*h*) and 4(3)(*a*) and (*b*), and not in art 13(B)(*b*) which is where all the other vatable items in Item 1(*c*)–(*m*) have their origin: and that provision is concerned only with the leasing or letting of immovable property.

The critical case in this area is *The Commissioners v Parkinson* [1989] STC 51 where the taxpayer sold the freehold of property, which also passed unexclusive rights to fish in the rivers covered by the freehold sale.

Harman J in the High Court stated that none of the exclusions from exemption (grant of facilities for parking vehicles, fishing rights etc as then existed in Group 1 in Sched 9) extended to the sale of freeholds.

At p 57h he stated that:

> . . . the Schedule must be read as not applying to the outright sale of freehold interests. It seems to me that the phrases are easily construed as applying only to transfers of interests less than a freehold and that they have ample scope for operation and would naturally be expected to attach to such transactions far more easily than they could ever be expected to attach to conveyances on sale of freehold interests, which on the face of it are not the probable subject of these exclusions, being primarily within the exemption in Item 1.

Rent charges and car parking

It may be prudent in certain cases not to charge rentcharges on the sales of freeholds of parking spaces.

It is possible, in certain circumstances, for a freehold to be sold with the vendor retaining a rentcharge. This is useful if he wants covenants to be clearly binding on the purchaser.

In *The Commissioners v Parkinson* [1989] STC 51 Harman J in the High Court clearly held that 'the *outright sale* of freehold interests' will be excluded from being compulsorily vatable under certain headings in Group 1, Item 1 (the exclusions from exemption). It may be that if a rentcharge is reserved, there may not be an outright sale of the freehold. However, it might be that the sale will nevertheless be exempt as the judge indicated that the grant of long leases may be exempt and outside most of the headings comprising exclusions from exemptions in Item 1, Group 1. Nevertheless, it is prudent in an appropriate case not to reserve a rentcharge especially if it is a significant sum.

Leases and licences and car parking

Harman J in *The Commissioners v Parkinson* [1989] STC 51, at p 56f, indicated that perhaps long leasehold interests (he had in mind leases of over 21 years perhaps) as well as freeholds would not fall within the then exceptions in Item 1. The reference to long leaseholds must be *obiter* and the relevant extract reads as follows:

> ... If we look at them again, first of all there is hotel accommodation: would anybody think that the sale of a freehold or long leasehold of hotel buildings would be naturally called a 'provision of accommodation in a hotel'? I hardly think that the English language can be stretched so far, even for value added tax purposes. Yet, if it be not right, the sale by a hotel group— and let us think of Trusthouse Forte—of a major hotel, for example, the Grosvenor Hotel in Park Lane, to another person would be, perhaps, excluded from this exemption because the purchaser would be getting the provision of accommodation in the Grosvenor House Hotel. It seems a strange and improbable concept. Then (*b*) [now Item 1(*g*)] 'the granting of facilities for camping': it is hardly likely that the camper in a tent is going to be buying the freehold or taking a term of years of the patch of land on which he pegs in his guy ropes. It is almost certain that at the most he will have a short licence. I suppose he might just possibly have a short lease. The same comment applies to (*c*) [now Item 1(*h*)], 'the granting of facilities for parking a vehicle'. (*e*) [now Item (*j*)] is 'the granting of any right to fell and remove standing timber'. Such a right is exactly the contrary of any right to

own the land. It is essentially the grant by an estate owner to another person of a right to enter on the land, not to occupy it, but to fell on it and take from it the trees. At (*f*) [now Item (*k*)] is 'the granting of facilities for housing, or storage of, an aircraft or for mooring a ship'. Again, the sale of a hangar freehold would not normally be thought as the grant of facilities for storage of an aircraft. Finally, (*g*) [no longer extant], the provision to an exhibitor of a site at an exhibition. Essentially, it seems to me, that that is something that could only be the grant by the landowner of a licence to somebody to set up a stall at, for example, the Antiques Fair held every year in London.

It is probably safest for practitioners to assume that VAT is chargeable on the grant of a lease, of whatever length, of parking facilities.

Taxpayers must remember to charge VAT in leases and licences where 'parking facilities' are provided. 'Parking facilities' has a wide meaning (*The Commissioners v Trinity Factoring Services Ltd* [1994] STC 504). The omission of a VAT charging clause in a long lease in cases where VAT is chargeable could be most unfortunate.

Customs' views on car parking

Customs' views are set out in Leaflet No 701/24/92, 'Parking facilitites', and the relevant parts, in paras 1–8 of that leaflet, are set out *below*:

General
1   The provision of parking facilities for vehicles is normally standard-rated. This leaflet explains what is meant by parking facilities; which supplies are standard-rated; and which are exceptions to the general rule.

Standard-rated parking facilities
2   There is normally a standard-rated supply of parking facilities if a specific and distinguishable grant is made and the facilities are designed for, or provided specifically for the purpose of, parking vehicles. 'Grant' includes letting, leasing or licensing. Some examples of such grants are:

• the letting or licensing of garages or designated parking bays or spaces;

• the provision of rights to park vehicles (including any accompanying trailers) in, for example, car parks or commercial garages;

• the letting or licensing of land specifically for the construction of a garage or for use solely for parking a vehicle;

• the letting or licensing of a purpose-built car park, eg to a car park operator;

• the letting of taxi ranks;

• the provision of bicycle storage.

The letting of garages is standard-rated even if they are used other than for garaging a vehicle, eg for storage of goods.

Other supplies

3   The grant or assignment of an interest in, or right over, or licence to occupy land in the following circumstances is exempt and not regarded as the provision of standard-rated parking facilities:

- the letting of land or buildings (but not lock-up or other garages) where the conveyance or contract makes no specific reference to use for parking vehicles;

- the letting of land or buildings where any reference to parking a vehicle is incidental to the main use (but see paragraph 5);

- the letting of land or buildings to a motor dealer for storing stock-in-trade;

- the letting of land or buildings to a vehicle transportation firm, to a vehicle distributor or to a vehicle auctioneer for use in the course of their business;

- the letting of land, including land used at other times as a car park, for purposes such as holding a market or a car boot sale (this also includes the charge to the car owners selling their goods at a car boot sale);

- the letting of land for the exhibition of vehicles;

- the letting of land to a travelling fair or circus (and the incidental parking of vehicles).

The above supplies are, however, standard-rated if you have elected to waive exemption for ('opted to tax') the land or buildings.

Garages or other parking facilities provided in conjunction with the sale of new dwellings

4   The sale of a new dwelling together with a garage or parking space by the person constructing that dwelling is normally zero-rated, unless it is standard-rated holiday accommodation.

Garaging or other parking facilities provided in conjunction with the letting of dwellings

5   The letting of garages or parking spaces in conjunction with the letting of dwellings for permanent residential use is exempt provided:

- the garage or parking space is reasonably near to the dwelling and;

- the letting is by the same landlord to the same tenant, whether under a single agreement or separate agreements. (Landlord here includes ground landlord, so that if the tenant pays ground rent for both the dwelling and the garage, or pays ground rent for the dwelling and rents the garage, the provision of the parking facility qualifies for exemption.)

Once a dwelling is owned freehold, however, the letting of a garage or parking space to the owner of the dwelling cannot continue to be exempt from VAT, and it must therefore be taxed at the standard rate.

Freehold sales of new or partly completed garages, car parks or car parking facilities other than in conjunction with sales of new dwellings
6   These are standard-rated. Buildings or civil engineering works are 'new' for three years from the date on which they are completed. The grant of an option or personal right to buy the freehold of a new garage or other parking facility is also standard-rated.

Freehold sales of garages, car parks or parking facilities which are not new
7   These are exempt (with the option to tax), whether for subsequent taxable letting or for the purchaser's own use.

Garages or other parking facilities provided in conjunction with the letting of commercial premises
8   The supply of the parking facilities and the commercial premises is treated as a single supply of the commercial premises, provided:
either
  • the facilities are within or on the property or reasonably near to it;
or
  • the facilities are within a complex (eg an industrial park made up of separate units with a 'communal' car park for the use of the tenants of the units or their visitors);
and
  • both lettings are to the same tenant by the same landlord.
Therefore if the rents from the commercial premises are exempt, the parking facilities will also be exempt. However, in any other circumstances the provision of parking facilities in conjunction with commercial property is a separate standard-rated supply.

Car park let in conjunction with flats

If the lessor (L) of flats is different from the lessor/licensor (L2) of the parking spaces problems can arise, as para 5 of the Customs' leaflet reproduced *above* will be breached. VAT in this case must be charged on the parking licence fees charged by L2.

   It is felt that if L charges T an all-inclusive rent covering a building (an office building) and spaces to be used for car parking (exclusively) the rent will not be vatable as a matter of law in whole or part (unless the election to waive exemption has been exercised), because of the composite supply doctrine (*see* Chapter 2). Even if the rent were apportioned under a single lease to the car spaces and the offices the author would argue the application of the

Figure 8.7:

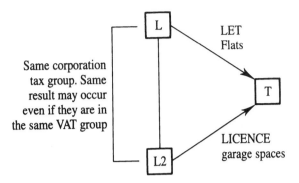

composite supply doctrine, depending on the particular facts. For the Customs' view *see* p 113 above.

7   Timber

The grant of any right to fell and remove standing timber (Item 1(*j*)).

8   Aircraft and ships

The grant of any facilities for housing, or storage of, an aircraft or for mooring, or storage of, a ship, boat or other vessel (Item 1(*k*)).

'Mooring' includes anchoring or berthing.

9   Theatres, etc

The grant of any right to occupy a box, seat or other accommodation at a sports ground, theatre, concert hall or other place of entertainment (Item 1(*l*)).

10   Sports facilities

The grant of facilities for playing any sport or participating in any physical recreation (Item 1(*m*)).

This head will not apply where the grant of the facilities is for:

(1) A continuous period of use exceeding 24 hours, or,

(2) A series of ten or more periods, whether or not exceeding 24 hours in total, where the following conditions are satisfied:

(a) each period is in respect of the same activity carried on at the same place;

(b) the interval between each period is not less than one day and not more than 14 days;

(c) consideration is paid by reference to the whole series and is evidenced by written agreement;

(d) the grantee has exclusive use of the facilities; and,

(e) the grantee is a school, a club, an association or an organisation representing affiliated clubs or constituent associations.

THE EXCEPTIONS AND THE SIXTH DIRECTIVE

The basis of the above vatable heads is to be found in the EC Sixth Directive, art 13B(*b*). Heads 2, 3, 4 and 5 implement art 13B(*b*)(1). Head 6 implements art 13B(*b*)(2) which provides that 'the letting of premises and sites for parking vehicles' is vatable (at the standard rate). It may be that the granting of car parking facilities which do not amount to a letting or leasing of immovable property do not and cannot fall within this vatable head (so that the supply should be exempt unless the art 13C option (ie the option to waive exception) can be exercised).

Note also that under art 13B the UK can (it is optional) add other heads to the four listed in art 13B(*b*), and heads 1, 7, 8, 9 and 10 *above* have been so added. Note also that under art 13B(*b*)(2) and (3) lettings of permanently installed equipment and machinery and the hire of safes comprise vatable (at the standard rate) supplies. It is clear that art 13B(*b*) is not well drafted; it relates only to the leasing or letting of immovable property but it excludes from its ambit the hire (which may be different from leasing and letting) of safes (which are unlikely to be immovable property unless the word is to have a very wide meaning).

Overlooking the specific standard-rated categories

It is easy to overlook the excluded items in Sched 9, Group 1, Item 1.

X sells a commercial building and land for £1m (assume this is an exempt supply), plus mooring facilities for £200,000. On the face of it, VAT is chargeable at 17.5 per cent with respect to the £200,000 (Sched 9, Group 1, Item 1(*k*)) and X may have forgotten to do this.

To overcome the problem the taxpayer may argue that the composite supply doctrine applies (*see* Chapter 2). Alternatively, he may try to persuade the purchaser to allow VAT to be charged on top of the £200,000: he will succeed only if the purchaser:

(a) agrees to allow VAT to be charged; and

(b) can reclaim the VAT.

The taxpayer may avoid a charge on a Sixth Directive basis. The case of *The Commissioners v Parkinson* [1989] STC 51 indicates that if a taxpayer, for instance, sells the freehold in or assigns a long lease of mooring facilities, VAT cannot be charged as there is no leasing or letting of the property; any attempt to charge VAT in this case would be in breach of art 13B of the Sixth Directive.

Customs sought to argue, in the case of *The Commissioners v Parkinson* [1989] STC 51 (High Court), that fishing rights were in effect disposed of when the freehold was disposed of. In the High Court it was held that the particular provisions, which relate to fishing rights in Group 1, Item 1 in Sched 6 (now Group 1, Item 1(*c*) in Sched 9), did not cover the sale of freeholds (now *see* p 112).

That is clearly the correct interpretation of the law and is perfectly consistent with the governing legislation in the EC Sixth Directive 77/388, art 13B(*b*) which states that the 'leasing and letting' of certain property is vatable. The sale of a freehold, and, it is felt, possibly, the assignment of a long lease, would not amount to the leasing or letting of property.

LICENCE TO OCCUPY—LAW UNDER REVIEW

Generally the tribunals have indicated that if a person can occupy exclusively an area of property he will have a licence to occupy the land (*Paul James Lamb t/a Footloose* (M/96/1232)). However, the exclusivity test was put into doubt in *Abbotsley Golf and Squash Club Ltd* (LON/96/148). The customs are reviewing the law in this area with a view possibly to defining what 'a licence to occupy' means (see Business Brief 25/97 (10 November 1997)).

Chapter 9

Exempt supplies of accommodation (education)

Supplies of accommodation may be exempt from VAT under the heading of education in Sched 9, Group 6.

That group, *inter alia*, exempts the provision of education, research and vocational training by an eligible body such as a UK university. It also exempts the supply of any goods or services which are closely related to a supply of a description falling within the above head, ie education, research or vocational training provided by an eligible body. The exemption is extended to such closely related supplies provided the goods or services are for the direct use of a pupil, student or trainee receiving the supply of education, research or vocational training.

It is necessary to identify what sort of supplies are 'closely related' to the supply of education etc.

Formerly, Group 6, Item 4 referred to the supplies having to be 'incidental' to the provision of education rather than 'closely related'. The latter words were inserted to bring the UK legislation more into line with the requirements of the EC Sixth Directive, art 13A(1)(*i*) and (*j*) which exempted:

> children's or young persons' education, school or university education, vocational training or re-training, including the supply of services and of goods closely related thereto, provided by bodies governed by public law having such as their aim or by other organisations defined by the Member State concerned as having similar objects and tuition given privately by teachers and covering school or university education.

It is felt, however, that the change of wording (from 'incidental' to 'closely related') does not significantly affect the law.

In *Joseph McMurray, a Governor of Allen Hall v The Commissioners* (1973) 1 VATTR 161 the appellant, as well as providing board and lodging for men students, exercised a degree of control over the students providing resident tutors for their assistance and encouraged the creation of a corporate as opposed to an individual existence.

It was held that the appellants were not carrying on business as a hotel, inn or boarding house or similar establishment. The appellants were not excluded from exemption under what is now Sched 9, Group 1. Furthermore, the provision by the appellant of catering and accommodation for students was an exempt supply under the heading of education as being a supply incidental to the provision of education by Manchester University.

Again, in the case of *Ralph Arthur Archer v The Commissioners (No 2)* (1975) VATTR 1, Essex University provided a number of car parks in its grounds and it was contended that the supply was incidental to the provision of education by the university. The London tribunal held that the supply was incidental to the provision of education by the university and was therefore exempt.

Chapter 10

Sales of certain commercial freeholds

The general rule is that the grant of any interest in or right over land or of any licence to occupy land is exempt. 'Grant' includes an assignment or surrender. There are some cases where the grants are zero-rated. Some supplies may also be vatable by virtue of the exercise of the option to waive exemption. In addition, Sched 9, Group 1 contains the list of items which are to be specifically excluded from exemption, ie they are vatable supplies (*see* Chapter 8).

As well as those items dealt with in Chapter 8, grants of the fee simple in the following types of property are, by virtue of Sched 9, Group 1, Item 1(*a*), vatable at the standard rate:

(a) a commercial building (excluding as a matter of strict law the land on which it stands) which has not been completed;

(b) a new commercial building (excluding as a matter of strict law the land on which it stands);

(c) a civil engineering work (eg sewers and roads) which has not been completed (the land surrounding it is excluded);

(d) a new civil engineering work (excluding the land surrounding it).

COMPLETION

A building is taken to be completed when an architect issues a certificate of practical completion or it is first fully occupied, whichever happens first (Sched 9, Group 1, Note (2)).

Completion may be delayed if the architect does not issue a certificate *and* some part of the property is left unoccupied. This may give rise to the 'vacant VAT room' in the building if the taxpayer wants to delay completion.

Figure 10.1:   Vacant VAT room

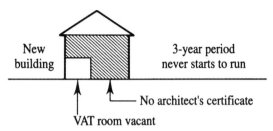

A civil engineering work is taken to be completed when an engineer issues a certificate of completion in relation to it or it is first fully used, whichever happens first. A sewer is probably first used when waste is first flushed through it.

Example (sale of bare land)

X plc has bare freehold land worth £1m. It constructs sewers therein which are valued at £100,000. It sells the land immediately thereafter for £1.1m. VAT is chargeable, in the author's view, on the £0.1m. The same applies if, instead, an office had been built and sold for £0.1m along with the land (for £1m). VAT is chargeable only on the sale price referable to the building (ie £0.1m), although it is arguable (the argument, however, is not particularly convincing) that in an appropriate case the composite supply doctrine should apply and so treat the entire sale price as exempt (assuming the election to waive exemption has not been exercised).

Customs treat any bare land which is ancillary to a civil engineering work as part of the work.

MEANING OF 'NEW'

A building or civil engineering work is new if it was completed less than three years before the grant. That is the general rule. Also, generally, if a building or civil engineering work was completed before 1 April 1989 it will not be new.

If a newly constructed freehold commercial building was completed before 1 April 1989 and is sold on or after 1 April 1989, the general rule is that VAT will not be chargeable (Sched 9, Group 1, Note (5)). However, VAT would be chargeable in those circumstances on the *first* sale of the fee simple on or after 1 April 1989 if the property was not *fully* occupied (or in the case of a civil engineering work, fully used) before 1 April 1989 (Sched 9, Group 1, Note (6)).

Example—First sale vatable

Mr X completes a new building before 1 April 1989 with the architect's certificate being issued before that date. The property is unoccupied on 1 April 1989 and is sold to Mr Y on 1 July 1989. The transaction is a freehold sale. VAT is chargeable on Mr X. If Mr Y then sells the property he will make an exempt supply although, if he exercises his option on or after 1 August 1989 in respect of the property then sold, VAT will be chargeable on the sale.

Example—First sale exempt

Mr A may have completed a building before 1 April 1989 with the architect's certificate having been issued before that date. The property was occupied (fully occupied) before 1 April 1989. The property is sold to Mr B without the election to waive exemption having been exercised. That will be an exempt land sale. If Mr B sold the property he would make an exempt supply (unless he exercised the election to waive exemption).

Example—VAT charge on multiple sales within three years

Alfa Ltd completed the construction of a building on or after 1 August 1989 with the architect's certificate being issued on or after 1 August 1989. If the property is then sold within the three-year period VAT must be charged with respect thereto. The VAT charge is not limited to the first sale.

MEANING OF 'FULLY OCCUPIED'

To make use of the transitional provisions under Sched 9, Group 1, Note (6) the building must have been 'fully occupied' before 1 April 1989.

'Fully' means 100 per cent although presumably if the building is 98 per cent occupied the remaining 2 per cent may not be relevant under the *de minimis* rule (*de minimis no curat lex*—'the law does not regard trifles').

Occupation must be of a nature relevant to the building. An office building will be occupied if the relevant rooms are used for office purposes. The toilets, cleaning cupboards, storage spaces, etc will be occupied according to usual user.

APPORTIONMENTS

If freehold land is sold with a new civil engineering work which has been built on it, an apportionment of the sale price may have to be made. Customs' practice is set out in Notice 742, para 3.2:

> Usually, unless the 'option to tax' is exercised, the freehold sale of land containing new civil engineering works will give rise to a mixed supply, exempt and standard-rated, and a suitable apportionment should be made. Your apportionment may be made on any objective basis which can be seen to give a fair and reasonable result. An apportionment according to cost may often be appropriate. The cost of the civil engineering work must reflect the cost of the land covered by the work (nil usually if the work is underground—a drain or sewer, for example) and the cost of installing or constructing the civil engineering work itself. An example of this type of transaction would be building land on which roads have been built and pipes laid for connection to mains services.

SUB-SALES OF NEW BUILDINGS OR WORKS

X contracts to buy freehold land from Y for cash. New civil engineering works (say) have been commenced on the land. X is immediately to sub-sell the land to Z (*see* Figure 10.2). The parties agree that VAT can be added to the sale considerations if properly chargeable.

Figure 10.2:   Sub-sales of new civil engineering work

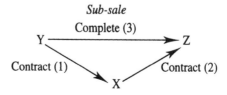

X should only pay Y monies to cover Y's VAT (as a matter of strict law and subject to the composite supply doctrine) on the apportioned amount of the purchase price—appropriately apportioned on exchange (deposit) and completion (balance)—referable to the value of the actual civil engineering works which have been carried out on the legal completion date. This excludes in strictness the land on or under which the civil engineering work has been done. This implication derives from Sched 9, Group 1, Item 1(*a*).

If there is a sub-sale, X will be making another vatable supply with regard to the civil engineering works (when it sells to Z) and should charge monies to cover the VAT for which X will be liable.

GRANT OF LEASE

If, instead of selling the freehold in a new commercial building, the taxpayer grants a lease at a premium (eg 100 years at a peppercorn rent and for a premium) the provisions which require VAT to be charged will not be applicable. They apply only to the grant of freeholds.

LONG LEASE AND OPTION

The long lease and option arrangement may prove satisfactory in practice.

X may wish to sell a new commercial freehold building to Y. It may be that a long lease without the right to enfranchise (ie call for the freehold under the property law legislation) could be granted to Y, with the parent company (preferably not in the same VAT group) of Y having the option to acquire the freehold after the necessary three-year period.

This would overcome the compulsory VAT charge situation (*see* Figure 10.3).

Figure 10.3:   Long lease and option

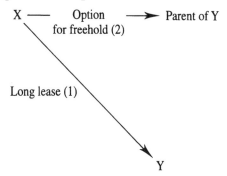

CIVIL ENGINEERING WORKS

The term 'civil engineering work' as used in VATA 1994, Sched 9, Group 1, Item 1(a)(iii) and (iv) is not defined. The *Shorter Oxford Dictionary* refers to a civil engineer as one who designs and constructs works of public utility. A work may nevertheless be a work of civil engineering even though it does not serve a public purpose. For instance, works with respect to domestic land and accommodation are not excluded from being civil engineering works just because they serve a particular house.

Civil engineering tends to involve a significant amount of removal of earth and construction of such works as bridges, roads, canals, railways, harbours, drainage, gas and water works. The term has a very wide meaning although it would not include the installation of plant and machinery (*Re GKN Dirwelco* (1983) VATTR 128).

The author feels that importance, but not decisive importance, should be attached to whether or not members of the civil engineering profession would say that the particular works amount to works of civil engineering (*En-tout-cas Ltd v The Commissioners* (1973) VATTR 101, *UFD Ltd v The Commissioners* (1981) VATTR 199 and *GKN Birwelco Ltd v The Commissioners* (1983) VATTR 128).

Perhaps the correct test is what conclusion the informed ordinary man would reach having heard expert evidence as to what constitutes a work of civil engineering. A shopping precinct comprising a number of shopping units with a covered archway is not a work of civil engineering. It is not similar to the items listed earlier—bridges, roads, canals, railways, harbours, etc. It does not have any additional function akin to that of a bridge, a road, a canal or a railway, etc. A shopping precinct is more akin to a building than a work of civil engineering although it may be that some works of civil engineering amount to buildings so that there is a degree of overlap. The definitions are not necessarily mutually exclusive.

In *En-tout-cas* (1973) VATTR 101 the taxpayer constructed tennis courts, an open air swimming pool, a running track for a college and a sports ground for a factory, and it was held that the works comprised civil engineering works (note now Sched 5, Group 8, Note 2(B)).

In *St Aubyn's School (Woodford Green) Trust Ltd* (LON/82/260 Decision 1361) construction of a playing field comprised civil engineering works.

In *Wrotham Park Settled Estates* (LON/81/93 Decision 115A) it was held that a swimming pool was a civil engineering work.

In *G P Murray* (LON/74/122 Decision 126) it was held that a new septic tank was a civil engineering work.

On the other hand the erection of railings in the front garden of a house (*Roskill v The Commissioners* (1981) VATTR 199) and the construction of a pavement crossing (*Rawlins Davy & Wells* (LON/77/251) are not such as to result in works of civil engineering.

There are many other cases on civil engineering works but it would seem that if a golf course is constructed then this is very likely to amount to a civil engineering work. Thus if a new golf course is sold within VATA 1994, Sched 9, Group 1, Item 1(*a*) the taxpayer must remember to charge VAT.

Chapter 11

Project managers, development partnerships, joint ventures, employees and nominees

This chapter looks at the VAT positions of certain *dramatis personae* involved in development projects.

PROJECT MANAGERS

Project managers usually bear VAT on their fees at 17.5 per cent. It is possible for them to avoid the charge to VAT by entering into a partnership with the other parties involved in the project rather than taking a fee.

For example, X, a developer, owns Blackacre. He employs Y to act as project manager, paying him a fee. When the project is completed and the land sold, X pays Y that fee and VAT at the standard rate must be charged. However, if X and Y had entered into partnership, VAT would not be charged on the profit taken by Y.

A partnership is a relationship which subsists between persons carrying on a business in common with a view to profit. To ensure that a partnership is created, the parties should enter into a partnership deed. There should be a sharing of net profits and, if possible, losses; there should be joint accounts; the parties should be registered as a partnership for VAT purposes; and they must work together to produce the ultimate profit.

A one-off transaction may amount to a joint venture without necessarily being a partnership (*see Theatres Consolidated Ltd v Commissioners of Customs and Excise* (1975) VATTR 13 and *Greater London Council v Commissioners of Customs and Excise* (1982) VATTR 94). The author understands that Customs will not generally register a joint venture unless it amounts to a partnership, although there have been cases where joint ventures not amounting to partnerships have been registered, but the circumstances were exceptional.

In *Strathearn Gordon Associates Ltd v Commissioners of Customs and Excise* (1985) VATTR 79, X acted as project manager for Z, a developer. The property was developed and sold, and Z paid X a project management fee. Customs wanted VAT on that fee. X sought to argue that because he was taking a share of net profits as a project management fee he was in partnership with Z. The tribunal held that merely taking net profits was not sufficient to make the parties partners. They were not carrying on the business together; X was merely supervising the carrying out of works on Z's property. Additionally there was a clause in the contract declaring the parties were not partners.

In *Five Grange Ltd* (LON/89/163 Decision 5538) X was a property consultant and was entitled to 5 per cent of the net proceeds on the sale of a project carried out on land owned by an investment company. X argued that the 5 per cent payment represented the share of profits to which it was entitled as a partner in a joint venture and was therefore outside the scope of VAT. However, the agreement expressly stated that X was not to be a partner of the investment company and the investment company was solely responsible for the management and control of the project. The investment company was the sole owner of the property. X was not to bear a share of any of the losses which might have arisen. There was thus no partnership. X was therefore liable to account for output tax on the payment in consideration for supplies and services and his appeal before the tribunal was dismissed.

In *Keydon Estates* (LON/88/1225 Decision 4471) [1990] STI 178, X purchased land and decided to have it redeveloped for residential purposes. But instead of developing it, X sold it, having previously agreed that Y would carry out the development works. X paid Y £125,000 in respect of the profits arising from the disposal of the site. Y argued that this sum represented a share of the profits under a partnership between itself and X. The tribunal held that no partnership existed. The development of the land was not a business carried out jointly between the two companies because X owned the land and made all the decisions relating to the development and sale. Y had not previously held itself out as being a partner and would not have borne a share of any liabilities or losses which might have arisen. The sum paid to Y, therefore, had to be treated as consideration for a supply of services on which Y was required to account for VAT at the standard rate.

It is clear from the cases (although the general VAT position must be considered) that if the parties could get into partnership VAT would not have been charged on the project manager's fee.

Figure 11.1:   Project manager

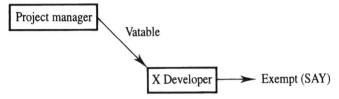

Development partnership

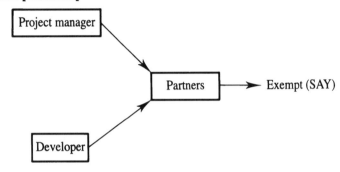

DEVELOPMENT PARTNERSHIPS

Nature of a partnership

The question arises whether, for VAT purposes, a partnership comprises a single person or a number of persons. This can be important when a partnership is first created, although the 'going concern' relief will normally apply.

No problems should arise if there are changes in the partnership members.

The principal case law in the area comprises *The Commissioners v Evans* [1982] STC 342, *The Commisioners v Glassborow* [1975] 1 QB 465 and *The Carlton Lodge Club v The Commissioners* [1974] STC 507.

The decisions are difficult to reconcile but the following points can be made:

(1) VAT is payable by persons or by a person.

(2) VATA 1994, s 45 indicates that persons carrying on a business in partnership comprise one person for VAT purposes.

(3) Section 45 allows the registration of such a body to be in the firm's name. The implication is if there were no such provision there would still be a single registration, although not in the firm's name.

(4) Clearly the partners carry on one business: each partner does not carry on his own separate business.

It may be argued for VAT purposes that where there is a partnership there are separate persons and each partner should be taxed and treated separately. Indeed, in the *Evans* decision, Glidewell J stated at 348:

> The scheme of the Act, in my view, in relation to a partnership, is that there is no more than a group of taxable persons trading jointly and thus under a joint tax liability arising out of their partnership enterprise. *The partnership itself in my view, is not a person within the meaning of the Act.* (Author's italics)

The above conclusion is correct with respect to the point under discussion in that particular case, namely whether a partner who had left the partnership could be liable for VAT which arose after he left the partnership.

In the *Glassborow* decision May J stated, at p 473:

> With this concept in mind it was conceded by Mr Slynn on behalf of the Commissioners, and I think rightly conceded, that *A carrying on business on his own account is for the purposes of the Act a different 'person' from A and B carrying on business in partnership.* Similarly the *person* comprising A and B and C trading in partnership is different from that comprising A, B, and D so trading, because the two bodies of persons are different: they consist of different individuals. (Author's italics)

The *Carlton Lodge Club* case also indicates that a partnership is a person for VAT purposes, although Glidewell J in the *Evans* case felt the decision was dealing with a different matter. At p 509 of the *Carlton Lodge Club* case Milmo J stated:

> The Act throughout refers to 'the person supplying the goods or services' and *for the purpose of this Act one has to look to the Interpretation Act s19 which provides that, unless the contrary intention shall appear, the expression person shall include any body of persons corporate or unincorporate.* The word 'person' in this context would therefore cover an unincorporated club such as The Carlton Lodge Club. (Author's italics)

The strongest case in favour of the argument that a partnership comprises a number of persons is *Evans*. However, that has to be reconciled with *Glassborow* and the fact that the judge in *Evans* considered the statements in *Glassborow* to be wholly correct.

It is likely the courts will find that a partnership is a separate person for VAT purposes, but nevertheless for certain purposes one must look through the partnership entity to find who the particular individuals are: this is particularly relevant if an assessment is made. One can only assess a particular partner with regard to supplies if he was a partner at the relevant time. That conclusion can be arrived at on a simple reading of s 45(1) of the Act which indicates that each partner retains his separate identity but that the partnership is a person for VAT purposes; that conclusion is arrived at by implication. It also produces a fairly consistent system of VAT. In addition, Customs can simply quote the Divisional Court decision in *Glassborow*, and the decision of that court is binding on Glidewell J in *Evans*, as indeed he acknowledged at p 348h.

That said, the decisions are confusing and there are statements within the same judgments which contradict each other. It may be that the statements can be confined to the particular VAT administrative point in issue—dealing with assessments and the like—leaving intact the basic point that the implication from s 45(1) is that persons carrying on a business in partnership must have one registration number (and at the discretion of Customs can be registered in the name of the firm). It is not felt that the implication can be drawn from s 45(1) that each partner must have a separate registration. That is the only alternative implication.

This point comes to a head if, say, A and B want to go into partnership to ensure that A could not be treated as having made a supply to B, with B in turn making the main supply to an outside person, which supply would be exempt.

Thus X may be a developer and landowner. It may employ Y as project manager. If the ultimate land supply is exempt then the VAT charged by Y to X would not be reclaimable. However, if X and Y went into partnership (which was not registered for VAT), rearranging the deal so that they supplied to the ultimate purchaser, for instance, the particular developed land (which is exempt in the particular case), then on what basis is Y's share of the project non-vatable? If the partnership comprises a separate single person for VAT purposes there will be no charge to VAT on the sharing of the profits because the partnership will comprise one body, and that body will make the supply to the ultimate purchaser: the partners will not make supplies to each other.

Purchase by partners

X and Y may be the partners in a firm of solicitors. They wish to buy a property and the vendor has elected to charge VAT on the sale. X and Y could buy the property and let it to themselves as partners in the solicitors' business, or they could, in their capacity as partners in the solicitors' business, buy the property. What should they do? (*See* Figure 11.2.)

Figure 11.2:

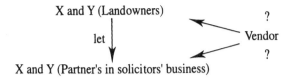

Persons rather than businesses register for VAT and thus it is not technically possible for the two partners to register a separate business and acquire the freehold property and let it to the solicitors' partnership.

It may be that Customs could be persuaded to register the land-holding partnership separately and indeed they would effectively be forced to do so if, for instance, the wives of the two partners also acquired a very small interest in the property as tenants in common.

If such a route is adopted the land-holding partnership would have to elect to charge VAT with respect to the property, which would mean it would have to charge VAT on the rents it charges to the solicitors' partnership and, unless it sold the business as a going concern to another person who elected with respect to the building, it would also have to charge VAT on the disposal of the freehold. However, it may not be necessary to pursue such a route.

No special advantage will arise from adopting the procedure described above and the solicitors' partnership itself should purchase the freehold. It is assumed the completion of the freehold construction (construction of the new building) did not take place within the last three years.

If the solicitors' partnership makes fully taxable supplies of legal services, eg, it charges VAT at 17.5 per cent with respect to all its services, then it should have no difficulty in reclaiming the VAT charged to it by the vendor. There is no reason in principle why that VAT should not be repaid within approximately one month after the end of the quarter in which the VAT is paid (to the vendor) and the VAT invoice handed over to the partnership by the vendor. It is also customary, when the invoice is handed over, for the purchaser or purchasers to be given sight of the notice to Customs by the vendor of the election to waive exemption and Custom's reply (VATA 1994, Sched 10, paras 2 and 3). The parties may provide for this in the contract.

If the solicitors' partnership subsequently sells the property within a period of ten years of acquisition, and the partnership does not elect to waive exemption then the situation will fall within the capital goods provisions in the 1995 Regulations, and this will cause the partnership to repay some of the VAT it reclaimed.

There are many possibilities. If, for instance, the property is used for five years for the purposes of the partnership which makes fully taxable supplies of legal services and is then sold, 50 per cent—five out of ten years—of the VAT reclaimed must be repaid to Customs. Very broadly, however, that VAT need not be repaid to Customs if, before the disposal, the partnership which has, to that date, used the property entirely for its fully taxable purposes elects to waive exemption for VAT under VATA 1994, Sched 10, para 2 and charges VAT (properly) on the sale of the property.

As mentioned, the taxpayers should have no difficulty in successfully reclaiming all the VAT shortly after the end of the relevant VAT quarter: when reclaims are of a significant figure, Customs do make control visits. Ideally, of course, the solicitors should seek to complete the deal—pay the purchase price and receive the VAT invoice—as near to the end of their VAT quarter as possible (the vendor will try to arrange matters in the opposite way). The relevant provisions are VATA 1994, s 25(1), (2) and (3), the latter of which provides that if 'the amount of the credit exceeds that of the output tax . . . the amount of the excess shall be paid to the taxable person by the Commissioners'.

If the person who elected to waive exemption had made an effective election and notified Customs, the election, as far as that person is concerned, is irrevocable and subsists (subject to the three-month and 20-year revocation rights) for all time. It is not possible, for instance, to make an assignment of the interest and not charge VAT on it. One way, however, in which there can be a transfer of the interest without a VAT charge is if the property is disposed of as a going concern. Thus, for example, if property is let and the vendor has exercised the election to waive exemption and disposes of the property to a purchaser who continues to let the property, and the purchaser exercises the election to waive exemption, then VAT need not be charged on this sale. But there are some very complex adjustment requirements under the capital goods provisions, which can result in the purchaser being liable to repay VAT to Customs which VAT was repaid to the vendor when the vendor first acquired the property (the 1995 Regulations, regs 112–116).

In summary, therefore, the property should be purchased by the solicitors' partnership assuming the solicitors' partnership uses the property for the purposes of making fully taxable supplies.

Also, if the intention is to sell the property at a future date, then the VAT position at the time must be considered: any exempt sale (*prima facie* the sale would be an exempt sale) would result in the partnership having to repay some of the VAT it reclaimed. If, instead of making an exempt sale, the partnership elected to waive exemption, then it would charge VAT on the sale proceeds and would not have to repay any of the VAT it reclaimed. Whether that proposition is practical depends on who the purchaser is: a bank, for instance, or a finance house may not wish to proceed with the deal if it has to be charged

VAT which it may not be able to reclaim. On the other hand, if the premises are sold to another firm of solicitors there should be no difficulty, as that firm could no doubt reclaim the whole, or virtually the whole, of the VAT charged to it. At that time it would also be necessary to see whether the sale as a going concern relief may apply, in which case VAT would not have to be charged on the sale. The exempt land provisions in Chapter 19 must be noted.

Sales of partnership interests

Some difficult points arise with respect to partnerships and going concern reliefs where the election to waive exemption has been exercised.

A and B may be in partnership. A may have a 1 per cent interest in the partnership and B may have the remaining 99 per cent interest.

If A and B sell property having exercised the election to waive exemption they may have to charge VAT, or the going concern relief may be available in an appropriate case.

If the going concern relief is not available it seems open to B to sell his 99 per cent interest to C provided this amounts to no more than a change in the persons carrying on the partnership.

VATA 1994, s 45(1) provides:

> The registration under this Act of persons—
>
> (a) carrying on a business in partnership, or
> (b) carrying on in partnership any other activities in the course or furtherance of which they acquire goods from other member States,
>
> may be in the name of the firm; and no account shall be taken, in determining for any purpose of this Act whether goods or services are supplied to or by such persons or are acquired by such persons from another member State, of any change in the partnership.

Does a partnership exist?

In any joint development project taxpayers should always consider whether they may be found to be in partnership.

If a partnership exists this can affect not only the tax consequences of the transaction but also the commercial liabilities of the parties.

Many joint land projects may amount to partnerships without the parties even considering the point.

There have been many VAT tribunal cases dealing with whether or not a partnership exists. The tribunals have generally accepted the definition is s 1 of the Partnership Act 1890 that a partnership is a relationship which exists between persons carrying on a business in common with a view to a profit (*Pollingford Farms v CCE* LON/76/103 and *see also* the cases of *CCE v Glassborow (trading as Bertram & Co)* [1974] STC 142 and *CCE v The Grape Escape Wine Bar* [1982] STC 342).

However, the meaning of 'business' under the Partnership Act 1890 is not necessarily the same as the meaning of 'business' for the purposes of VAT (*see Three H Aircraft Hire v CCE* [1982] STC 653).

Even though parties may not have expressly entered into a partnership it may be that the partnership exists. This all depends on the facts. In *Cooper v The Commissioners* (LON/81/325) there was held to be no partnership. In *Morrison and Wade v Finance Board* (MAN/85/273) a partnership was found to exist. The parties had entered into joint and several obligations with regard to a bank guarantee and mortgage and hire purchase agreement. Profits were shared equally and so were losses, and the two individuals in question were, in the sense of the words of one of them, 'doing it like everything else, together'.

There is set out *below* some guidance as to whether, under general law, in particular circumstances a partnership is likely to be found to exist.

Partnership Act 1890

In determining whether a partnership exists the Partnership Act 1890, s 2(1) provides some assistance. Joint tenancy or tenancy in common does not of itself create a partnership as to anything so held or owned, whether or not the tenants or owners share any profits made by the use thereof.

The sharing of gross returns does not of itself create a partnership (Partnership Act 1890, s 2(2)).

The receipt by a person of a share of profits of a business is *prima facie* evidence that he is a partner in the business but receipt of such a share does not of itself make him a partner (Partnership Act 1890, s 2).

A contract for the remuneration of a servant or agent of a person engaged in a business by a share of the profits of the business does not of itself make the servant or agent a partner in the business or liable as such (Partnership Act 1890, s 2(3)(*b*)).

The advance of money by way of loan to a person engaged or about to be engaged in a business under a contract with that person that the lender shall receive a rate of interest varying with the profits, or shall receive a share of the profits arising from the carrying on of the business, does not of itself make the lender a partner with the person or persons carrying on the business or liable as such, provided the contract is in writing and signed by or on behalf of all the parties (Partnership Act 1890, s 2(3)(*d*)).

Joint tenancy/tenancy in common

If A and B own Blackacre as tenants in common and receive the gross rents and divide them between themselves then there should be no partnership. It is just possible that if the gross returns are put into a common account and monies are taken from the account to bear expenses, with the net profits then being divided, a partnership may exist with regard to those profits but not with regard to the property which yields the profits.

Joining together of expertise, land and money

In *Fenston v Johnstone* (1940) 23 TC 28, X wished to buy and develop land in Kent but lacked the finance. It was arranged for Y to raise the money to buy the land and this was done. X was to be paid one-half of the profits. X was also to be responsible for one-half of the losses. The agreement stated that it was not to constitute a partnership. Wrottesley J held that there was a very strong presumption in favour of a partnership where a person had agreed to share profits and losses, and accordingly held that a partnership existed. The fact that parties work together towards a common purpose tends to indicate the existence of a partnership.

Development agreement construed as a partnership agreement

In *Walker West Developments Ltd v Emmett Ltd* (1979) 252 EG 1171 a builder sold land to a developer and the developer employed the builder to construct buildings on the land.

When the buildings had been constructed they were sold and the profits were shared between the developer and the builder. Losses were not to be shared and the parties clearly did not have in mind the creation of a partnership. The Court of Appeal construed the development agreement between the parties as a partnership agreement. The parties worked together in respect of the project. They referred to the project in the document as being a 'joint project'. The Court of Appeal held there were not two separate businesses but 'one business carried on in common as a joint venture with a view to profit'. The scheme was advertised as a joint project between the parties.

Insufficient sharing or working together

In the case of *London Financial Association v Kelk* (1884) 26 ChD 107 it was held that where a company (X) entered into an agreement with Y for Y to acquire an estate in common with X, for Y to carry out construction works and for X to raise money to acquire materials, that did not make the parties partners in the venture. Each held its separate share in the property and paid for the shares on separate accounts. There was not a sufficient working together or sharing of property rights to enable a partnership to be found.

Exempt funds

In the common situation where an exempt fund may pre-let property to a property investor who in turn lets it to an occupying tenant, with the property investor employing a developer to carry out the works, it is unlikely that the fund could be found to be in partnership with the developer. Its return will normally be gross rents and its functions would not be those of a person taking part in a joint venture but would merely involve the exempt fund in carrying out the normal precautionary steps which one would expect a freehold investor to take to ensure that its property is being developed. In *Hulme Educational Foundation v The Commissioners* (1978) VATTR 179 the taxpayer sought to argue that a freehold landowner had entered into a joint venture with a tenant who employed a builder to construct a building on the land. The VAT tribunal held that there was no joint venture. Each party was merely looking after its particular separate land interest and there was not a sufficient working together or mixing of funds to amount to a joint venture constituting a partnership for VAT purposes.

Project manager

In the situation, however, where X (the landowner and developer) owns Blackacre and he employs Y as a project manager, and Y is obliged to obtain planning permission, arrange for the acquisition of subsidiary parcels of land and deal with the sale of the completed development, a partnership could be found to exist if Y is given a share of the net profits. This is the case even though Y may not share the losses. A partnership is also more likely if there is a reference to a joint venture in the 'project management agreement' and the parties advertise the arrangement as a joint venture between them. The position, however, would be very much on the borderline (*see* p 117).

Action to show there is no partnership

It may be possible to reduce the chances of partnership by the parties having separate bank accounts and as little sharing of debts as possible. The sharing of profits and losses is virtually, but not quite, disastrous. If possible the parties should not share losses. If they must share profits the documents should be very carefully drafted, and there should be no references to a 'joint project' or 'joint venture' in the document or in any advertisements.

Statement of non-partnership

Parties often have included in a development agreement a statement that they are not partners. This in one sense may be detrimental because it shows that the parties had a partnership in mind. On the other hand, it may show that the parties have been properly advised and decided that they did not want to enter into a partnership. The author, however, finds himself swayed by the words of Cozen-Hardy MR in *Weiner v Harris* [1910] 1 KB 285 at 290 where he stated: 'Two parties enter into a transaction and they say "it is hereby declared that there is no partnership between us". The court pays no regard to that.'

LIMITED PARTNERSHIP AND VAT

The Limited Partnerships Act 1907 authorises the formation of limited partnerships. The Act enables a person to become a partner upon terms that its liability to the creditors of the partnership shall be strictly limited, like that of a shareholder in a limited liability company. A limited partner is in the position of a sleeping partner with limited liability.

There must in addition be a general partner (which can be a limited liability company) who will be liable for the debts and obligations of the partnership. Its profit share can be minimal and it can be owned (with care) by the limited partners.

A limited partner is a person who, on entering into the partnership, contributes a sum or sums as capital and who is not liable for any of the firm's debts or obligations beyond that amount. A body corporate may be a limited partner (Limited Partnerships Act 1907, s 4(4)). Local authorities, it is felt, could be limited partners (see *Jones v Secretary of State for Wales* (1974) 28 P & CR 280).

A limited partner may at any time inspect the books of the partnership and examine the state and prospects of the partnership business and may advise with the other partners thereon, but he must not take any part in the management of the business and he has no power to bind the firm.

The implications of limited partnership for VAT purposes must be clearly understood if error is to be avoided. It is fundamental to VAT that, for supplies to be within the charge to tax, they must be made in the course of a business carried on by the person concerned. A limited partner, by definition, cannot take part in the management of the partnership business, and this has implications for VAT.

In *Saunders & Sorrell* (1980) VATTR 53, two individuals had separate practices as patent agents, each being separately registered for VAT. In order to protect their practices in the event of either of them dying or being incapacitated, they entered into separate arrangements under which each formed a partnership with the other as a limited partner. The limited partner contributed £250 as capital but drew no profits and took no part in the management of the practice. The partnership was to terminate on the death or incapacity of the general partner, but the limited partner was then required to offer his services to the business for up to six months to preserve the goodwill pending sale. Customs required the two businesses to be covered by the same VAT registration, and left it up to the individuals to decide which name it should be registered in. The individuals' appeal against this decision was allowed. The Tribunal took the view that as each limited partner took no part in the management of the firm of which he was a limited partner, the supplies made in the course of the business of that firm were not supplies made by the limited partner 'in the course of a business carried on by him' as required by the VAT legislation. Accordingly each limited partner was not liable for tax on the supplies made by the limited partnership, nor was he under any obligation in relation to the submission of returns in respect of those supplies.

In addition the Tribunal said that, in each case, the limited partner was not carrying on the business of the firm concerned in partnership with the general partner within the meaning and intent of what is now VATA 1994, s 45(1).

This clearly offers both planning opportunities and potential pitfalls for limited partners.

JOINT VENTURES

Special care is needed with joint ventures. For tax purposes joint ventures beg the question of the real tax status of the entity—partnership or just two people working on a particular project who must charge VAT separately according to their separate supplies: if they make supplies to each other they must charge each other VAT in an appropriate case. X may arrange for Y to buy property. X may agree with Y to do all the necessary work and employ all the professionals to ensure that a building is put up on the property. When the building is put up the net profits may be shared between the parties as to say 25 per cent for X and 75 per cent for Y. If there are any losses the losses may be shared in the same proportions. For commercial reasons, the parties may also require that the project be publicised as a joint project between X and Y. What is the nature of such joint action?

The following tax points should be noted:

(a) the parties will almost certainly be found to be in partnership;

(b) a clause such as: 'The parties hereto each respectively hereby agree that this agreement shall not constitute a partnership' will not protect them from the ravages of partnership;

(c) if there is a clause denying partnership that may work against them, at the VAT tribunal level, at least, in the sense that if they have denied that there is a partnership they may find it difficult to claim effectively that there is a partnership if it is in their interests for VAT purposes;

(d) if the parties are registered for VAT under a single number then supplies cannot be made between them;

(e) if they are not registered for VAT as a single partnership but they are nevertheless in partnership then it is arguable that they are not making supplies to each other but are working together with a view to making supplies to other parties. Much depends on the particular facts of the case. The point is critical because if they are not making supplies to each other they should be able to share the ultimate profit from, for example, the disposal of an exempt refurbished building without having to charge VAT on the division of the profits (this would not help with regard to any payments to the outside builders or professionals: the VAT on their charges could not be reclaimed).

It has been suggested *obiter* by a tribunal chairman that persons in business as co-adventurers are liable to be registered in precisely the same way as partners (*Good v The Commissioners* (1974) VATTR 256 at 260). It is difficult to see how this proposition can be correct.

Finder's fee

X may own a parcel of land, say, farm land, which he wants to sell. Y may agree to obtain planning permission on the land in consideration of receiving 20 per cent of the sale proceeds. What is the VAT position?

Y may seek to argue that the supply (the ultimate sale) is exempt and under VATA 1994, Sched 10, para 8 his 20 per cent of the sale proceeds is also exempt.

The danger of course is that he has simply been paid a fee as project manager, estate agent or finder of planning permission, which is vatable at

17.5 per cent. It may be, if X registers for VAT, that Y could charge X VAT and X would be in a position to reclaim it. The purchaser of the land from X may be able to reclaim the VAT because, for instance, he intends to make zero-rated supplies (eg grant major interests in new residential buildings), or he has elected, or is going to put up a new supermarket for himself and would be making zero-rated or vatable supplies therefrom and will be in a position to reclaim any VAT on the new construction works subject to the possible application of the capital goods provisions.

Figure 11.3:

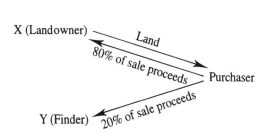

Another approach may be for X to transfer a share in the land to Y. This means that when the land is ultimately sold to the purchaser it will be beneficially sold by X and Y (assuming X keeps the legal estate and vests only the beneficial interest in the land in Y). The danger is that the transfer of the land, if it is made late in the day, may be valuable consideration paid to Y for the works he has done to date. However, if the land transfer is made early it may be in consideration of services of very little value. In other words, if Y had virtually secured the planning permission and found the purchaser when X transfers the 20 per cent land interest to Y, then the transfer of the land interest may be consideration for the provision of services by Y to X. However, if the 20 per cent land interest is transferred before any applications are made or any purchasers known then the transferred interest may have very little value. No doubt it will be part and parcel of the deal that if the permission is not obtained or a purchaser not found, then the land will revert without consideration to X in its totality.

Share of net profits

A joint venturer may be able to call on VATA 1994, Sched 10, para 8 to assist him if he finds himself in in a tight corner. Sched 10, para 8 reads:

> Where the benefit of the consideration for the grant of an interest in, right over or licence to occupy land accrues to a person but that person is not the person making the grant—

(a) the person to whom the benefit accrues shall for the purposes of this Act be treated as the person making the grant and

(b) to the extent that any input tax of the person actually making the grant is attributable to the grant it shall be treated as input tax of the person to whom the benefit accrues.

A forerunner of that paragraph which dealt with a narrower area in VATA 1983, Sched 5, Group 8 was Note (1) to that group. It read thus:

Where the benefit of the consideration for the grant of a major interest as described in item 1 accrues to the person constructing the building but that person is not the grantor, he shall for the purposes of that item be treated as the person making the grant.

The relevant Customs' comment on the ambit of the provision is to be found in VAT Notice 742, para 7.1, p 9 (now replaced by VAT Notice 742 where there is no comment on the point) which reads thus:

For VAT purposes, the person directly receiving the benefit of the proceeds from selling, leasing or letting property is deemed to be the person selling, leasing or letting that property. This is the case even though that person may not be the legal owner of that property. An example of this is a bare trust. Although the trustees are the legal owner of the property, if the benefit of the income accruing from property passes to the beneficiaries it is they who are treated as the person making the grant and, subject to the normal rules, the person who can claim any input tax which arises.

Schedule 10, Note (8) refers to the benefit of the consideration accruing to the relevant person. It is felt the Interpretation Act 1978, s 6 (gender and number) should ensure that the term 'person' can be construed as including 'persons'. The section reads:

In any Act, unless the contrary intention appears,—(c) words in the singular include the plural and words in the plural include the singular.

It seems clear enough therefore that if there is a partnership, even though it may not be a registered partnership for VAT, and the property is vested in the name of a nominee or in a name of one or other of the partners for the partners, Sched 10, para 8 will apply.

Also if X is the beneficial owner of the land and he happens to have vested the property in the name of a nominee for him (so that the nominee makes the formal legal grant), the paragraph will apply; for VAT purposes X will be the person who made the grant.

It also seems clear that if A and B are joint venturers who agree to take half the disposal proceeds each, with the formal title being vested in A, Sched 10, para 8 will apply. This is because the benefit of the consideration (the consideration being the sale proceeds) will clearly go to A and B. Some difficult points arise with respect to part (*b*) of para 8, Sched 10 but it is felt the above conclusion is correct.

The question then arises as to the position if the benefit of the consideration goes to one party indirectly as a result of a net profit sharing formula. In this case the actual sale consideration cannot be directly attributed to a particular party.

If Sched 10, para 8 does apply to a situation where there is a sharing of net profits with the formal legal disposal being made by one of the joint venturers, then it can have a very wide meaning. It is felt, however, that the courts, are likely to restrict it to cases where the amount paid to each of the beneficial owners bears some relationship to the consideration received on the making of the grant. The situation is clear if the parties are entitled to, for instance, 50 per cent of the gross disposal consideration. It is felt that the paragraph covers the case where the party is entitled to a share of the disposal consideration after the deduction of appropriate expenses. The deduction of appropriate expenses is no more than a calculation of how much of the consideration the party is entitled to; it cannot be denied that he is entitled to benefit from the consideration. If no disposal consideration is received then the party receives nothing. This will distinguish the case from say, lawyers, who may have provided legal services to the joint venturers: they would be paid regardless of what consideration is received.

Thus it is felt that if, for instance, the property is vested in X and there is a joint venture between X and Y where Y will be entitled to a percentage of the disposal proceeds after the deduction of the expenses of the project, relief under Sched 10, para 8 will be applicable so that both X and Y will be making the grant.

A curious point which arises, however, is whether Y in that case can elect with regard to the building. Furthermore, what would be the position if Y elected with regard to the building and X did not. Customs will encourage X and Y to register as a partnership; otherwise it is arguable, in strict law, that VAT must be charged on part of the disposal consideration (the part to which Y's election relates). This would certainly confuse a purchaser. Customs may well refuse to accept that the election has effect at all in such a case.

Ownership retained by one of joint venturers

AB may enter into a joint venture with CD, CD retaining the ownership of the land (*see* Figure 11.4). This situation can be handled in one of three ways.

No land interest—nominee

Ideally one should obtain the agreement of Customs that:

(a) CD will issue the VAT invoice to the purchaser in CD's name;

(b) CD and AB will both exercise the election to waive exemption with regard to the property;

(c) AB will account for half the VAT on the sale and will be able to reclaim half the VAT paid to the builder and the professional parties even though AB does not issue a VAT invoice.

This route is based on the nomineeship principle.

The attraction in this arrangement is that AB will not have to take an interest in land and technically it will be relying on the deemed land ownership provision in VATA 1994, Sched 10, para 8.

It is suggested that if AB stated in the agreement that it was not a partner and the agreement was drafted along the lines that the parties did not want to create a partnership that would not affect the likelihood of Customs accepting the above position as it is based on Sched 10, para 8, not on there being a partnership.

Land interest—nominee

Under the second route CD will vest half the beneficial interest in the property in AB under a declaration of trust (although that may attract stamp duty), or under a contract for sale with the completion date being overrun. In the later case, stamp duty may be avoided.

Under this route:

(1) CD will issue the VAT invoice in its name but Customs will agree that with respect to half the invoice figure the invoice was issued as nominee for AB.

(2) AB will be obliged to account for half the output tax on the sale.

(3) The builder's costs and professional fees will be paid as to half by CD as nominee for AB, and AB will be able to reclaim half the VAT even though the invoice will have been issued to CD.

If this route is to be adopted then once again the approval of Customs would have to be sought. AB and CD would have to elect to waive exemption.

Land interest—strict position

If the land is jointly owned beneficially the position in strict law is, it is suggested, as set out *below*.

Both CD and AB would elect to waive exemption and CD would hold the legal estate in the land. However, half the beneficial interest in the land (either by way of a declaration of trust or by way of the disposal of the equitable interest under contract with completion date being overrun) will vest in AB.

In strict law, two invoices would have to be issued to the purchaser, one by CD and one by AB, under which the entire proceeds would be vatable.

CD alone will employ the builder and the professionals so that the input tax referable to monies paid to them can be recoverable by CD only. However, CD will have made a supply to AB on which VAT is chargeable. Thus, when receiving its half share reimbursement, CD will charge VAT on the reimbursement to AB, for which it must account to Customs, but AB will be able to reclaim that VAT as input tax referable to the taxable output supply, namely the disposal of its interest in the property.

Customs may not like two invoices being issued on the output tax and thus the taxpayer may be wise to obtain their agreement to the issue of the invoices by CD exclusively, but with AB being able to charge, and actually charging, CD VAT on its supply for which it receives half the disposal consideration and on which it charges output tax: AB must account to Customs for the output tax, but CD can reclaim the VAT as input tax.

Figure 11.4:

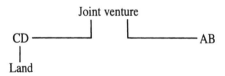

Possible changes to Sched 10, para 8

It is proposed, from a date to be determined, to add two new subparagraphs to Sched 8, para 8, so that para 8 as it presently reads will become para 8(1) (*see* Finance Act 1995 s 26(2)). The full effects of these changes to para 8 (which becomes para 8(1), (2) and (3)) are set out *below*.

VATA 1994 Sched 10, para 8(1) will state, as mentioned *above*, that where the benefit of the consideration for the grant of an interest in, right over or licence to occupy land accrues to a person but that person is not the person making the grant:

(a) the person to whom the benefit accrues shall, for the purposes of the VAT legislation, be treated as the person making the grant; and

(b) to the extent that any input tax of the person actually making the grant is attributable to the grant, it shall be treated as input tax of the person to whom the benefit accrues.

Thus if property is vested in a nominee for the benefit of X and the nominee sells the property, it may well be argued that it is the nominee which makes the grant. Paragraph 8(1) (subject to para 8(2), dealt with *below*) ensures that for all VAT purposes, X, the beneficial owner, being the person to whom the benefit accrues on the sale (ie the sale consideration accrues for the benefit of the beneficial owner), is the person treated as making the grant and is also the person who is able to reclaim any input tax with respect to the grant.

The same would apply where property is jointly owned.

The property may be legally owned by X and Y as joint tenants for the benefit of X and Y beneficially, and in that event once again, para 8(1) makes it absolutely clear (but subject to para 8(2)) that it is the beneficial owners who are relevant for the purposes of VAT, ie the consideration is deemed to accrue to them and they can reclaim the input tax. In that case there are few problems because the legal and beneficial owners are the same. However, if the property were vested in A, B, C and D legally for the benefit of A, B, C, D, E and F then it may be that A, B, C and D have made the grant, but there will be little difficulty in ensuring that for VAT purposes A, B, C, D, E and F will be treated as having made the grant, and as having received the sale consideration, and as entitled to reclaim any input tax with respect to the property.

The above situations are relatively straightforward.

Sched 10, para 8(2)

Paragraph 8(2) seeks to deal with a more complex situation, and in certain respects restricts the ambit of the above.

It provides that where the consideration for the grant of an interest in, right over or licence to occupy land is such that payment of the consideration is enforceable primarily:

(a) by the person who, as owner of an interest or right in or over that land, actually made the grant; or

(b) by another person in his capacity as the owner for the time being of that interest or right or of any other interest or right in or over the land, that person, and not any other person to whom a benefit accrues by virtue of being a beneficiary under a trust relating to the land, or the proceeds of sale of any land, shall be taken for the purposes of the legislation as the person to whom the benefit accrues.

Sched 10, para 8(3)

That provision does not apply to the extent that the Commissioners, on an application made in the prescribed manner jointly by:

(a) the person who would be taken to be the person to whom the benefit of the consideration accrues; and

(b) all the persons for the time being in existence who, as beneficiaries under such a trust, are persons who have or may become entitled to or to a share of the consideration, or for whose benefit any of it is to be or may be applied,

may direct that the benefit of the consideration is to be treated for the purposes of this paragraph as a benefit accruing to the beneficial owners rather than to the person who has the enforceable rights in respect of the sale to the sale consideration.

Effective date

The new provisions in para 8(2) and (3) are to come into force on such date as the Commissioners of Customs and Excise may by order or by statutory instrument appoint. It is possible these provisions will never be brought into effect.

Effects of the new provisions

Under the new provisions it is necessary to identify the person who can primarily enforce the payment of the consideration.

It seems clear enough that para 8(2) cuts down the ambit of para 8(1). In many cases where there is a grant of an interest, the person who makes the grant is the person who, primarily, can ensure that the consideration is paid.

Thus, the four legal owners—A, B, C and D in the *above* example—will be the people who make the grant provided they can primarily enforce the purchaser to pay the consideration to them on the sale of the property (which is very likely to be the case).

Clearly where there is a trust beneficiary under, say, a discretionary trust or a trust where property is held for A for life and then for B absolutely, the trustees will be the persons who make the grant. Trust beneficiaries will merely have equitable interests and cannot fetter the ability of the trustees to sell property and receive the consideration unless there are extraordinary provisions in the trust documentation.

The election provisions in para 8(3) may therefore be very helpful in certain cases. If there are four legal owners and six beneficial owners, the election would certainly be made and that would ensure that the six beneficial owners would be the persons making the grant. If no election is made, and if the four legal owners can primarily enforce the payment of the consideration on the sale of the property, they (the four legal owners) will be the people treated as having made the grant. This procedure may also be available in a standard trust where property is held for A for life and for B absolutely, provided all the persons under the trust are persons who have or may become entitled to a share of the consideration, or for whose benefit any of it is to be or may be applied. If A and B have all the beneficial interests under the trust then they could make such an election. If, though, there are contingent beneficiaries, eg children not yet born, then the election could not be made. Thus, in a normal discretionary trust, unless it is for a closed class where all the potential beneficiaries are included within that class, then an election cannot be made. In the normal family trust situation, one would expect the supply to be made by the trustees, and that clearly is the case if no election is made: the likelihood is that in most family trust situations, the election will be incapable of being made.

If the election could *prima facie* be made by the beneficiaries it is likely to have VAT relevance only if they are carrying on a business, and that may well not be the case (merely having a life or reversionary interest under a family trust is unlikely to amount to the carrying on of a business).

It should be noted that with respect to strict settlements (Settled Land Act 1925 settlements) the legal estate is vested in the tenant for life (usually) and the trustees are entitled to receive only the proceeds of sale and hold that on trust.

CO-OWNERS

One of the problems which the 1989 changes to the VAT regime did not fully resolve was how the VAT rules would apply if, for example, a freehold was owned by X and Y, and a premium or rent was received. In many cases the position may be academic because neither party has elected to waive exemption and the premium and rent would be exempt for VAT purposes.

However, problems would arise if A elects to waive exemption and B does not. A would make a vatable supply and B would make an exempt supply.

Customs sought, and still seek, to deal with that situation by persuading the parties to register as a partnership so that the entire supply made by the partnership is either exempt or vatable—one or the other. That of course is not a satisfactory solution where the parties are not partners and do not wish to register as partners. Technically VAT must be charged to the tenant on a proportion of the rent, for example, on that part supplied by A because he has elected to waive exemption, and not on the proportion supplied by B because he has made an exempt supply.

The new s 51A, inserted in VATA 1994 by s 26 of the Finance Act 1995 seeks to cater for this situation. The section applies to a supply consisting in the grant, assignment or surrender of any interest or right over land or licence to occupy land or, in relation to land in Scotland, a personal right to call for or be granted any interest or right in or over land, where there is more than one person making the grant, assignment or surrender.

Thus if, for example, five people own a lease and they surrender it, the provision applies. Equally it applies, for example, on the sale of a freehold, the assignment of a lease, the grant of a licence to occupy land or, in relation to Scotland, the grant of a personal right to call for or be granted any interest or right in or over property. The provision is therefore all-embracing.

Section 51A(2) provides that the grantors (called the 'property owner') are treated as a single person for VAT purposes, and that person is distinct from each of the grantors individually.

Registration of the property owner for VAT purposes is to be in the name of the grantors acting together as a property owner.

Thus the five property owners may have their separate VAT numbers, but when they come together with respect to a particular parcel of land over which they are to make a grant etc, they have a separate registration. A new person has been created for VAT purposes. All the grantors are jointly and severally liable with respect to any VAT obligations falling on the property owner. Thus Customs could sue one of the grantors for any unpaid VAT of the property owner, or they could sue all of them.

Section 51A(5) envisages the property owner having a name in which it is registered: 'the X joint venture', perhaps. If any notice or assessment is served on any of the members of the joint venture then that notice shall be treated for the purposes of VAT as served on the property owner, ie all the joint venturers.

The new provisions clearly eliminate the dangers of one grant by a number of joint owners, eg of a lease, being treated as partly exempt and partly vatable at the standard rate because one or other of the parties had elected to waive exemption. However, the new provisions ensure that each joint venturer can now be liable for the unpaid VAT of his co-joint adventurers.

Problems can of course arise if one of the joint venturers disposes of his share to a new party. For example, there may be three joint venturers, A, B and C and C may sell his share to D who becomes a new joint venturer.

It is provided in s 51A(6)(*a*) that such a change shall be disregarded for the purposes of that section in relation to any prescribed accounting period beginning before the change is notified in the prescribed manner to Customs.

The other consequence of the change is that any assessment or other notice issued by Customs, which is served at any time after the change has been notified to Customs, to the property owner for the time being, shall, so far as it relates to, or to any matter arising in, such a period, be treated as served on whoever was the property owner in that period (ie the retired co-owner is free of future VAT problems).

It is provided in s 51(A)(3) that this section shall come into effect on such day as the Commissioners of Customs and Excise may by order made by statutory instrument appoint.

EMPLOYEES

Employees do not charge their employers VAT

Under the Sixth Directive, art 4.4 there are excluded from the people who can be charged to VAT, persons who are employed and other persons in so far as they are bound to an employer by a contract of employment or by any other legal ties creating the relationship of employer and employee as regards working conditions, remuneration and the employer's liability.

Figure 11.5:

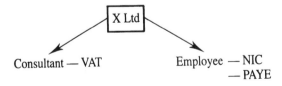

Thus VAT may be mitigated by a developer taking a project manager 'on to the staff' as an employee, although the National Insurance and PAYE provisions must be taken into account if that is to be done.

It should be noted, however, that under the Consultative Document of 21 June 1989, this so-called abuse was recognised:

Self-supply of building services

It is proposed that there will be a value added tax charge on businesses doing their own building work. This will be effected by an Order made under s 3(6), Value Added Tax Act 1983 [now VATA 1994, s 5(6)]. This is an anti-avoidance measure designed to prevent exempt or partly exempt businesses avoiding value added tax on the salary, labour and profit element of the building process.

The Order was passed into law with effect from 1 April 1989—*see* Chapter 21, but there is £100,000 *de minimis* limit.

NOMINEES

The use of nominee companies to take leases should not give rise to problems in practice. In *Bird Semple & Crawford Herron v The Commissioners* (1986) VATTR 218, a firm of lawyers took a lease from the landlord in the name of their nominee company. The nominee sublet parts of the land which were not required by the lawyers and the balance was used by the lawyers. Consultant surveyors who carried out negotiations with respect to the leases sent a fee note to the lawyers, and the VAT thereon was reclaimed. Customs claimed that the supply had been made to the nominee company. The tribunal held that the supply had not been made to the nominee company but to the lawyers. The supply had been made on their instructions and at their expense and for the purposes of their business. The VAT could therefore be reclaimed.

Figure 11.6:

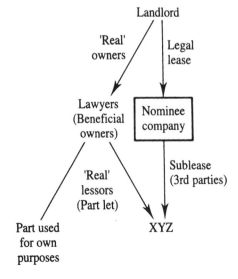

In *Glass Bros v The Commissioners* (1989) VATTR 143, supplies were made to X, Y and Z (who held the land to which the supplies related jointly), with Z in essence acting as nominee for X and Y. X and Y were carrying out a business in partnership. It was held the supply had been made to X and Y.

It is important, however, that if the necessary nomineeship situation is to be created—for example, if X is to give land to Y and hold the land as Y's nominee—that the necessary legal formalities are complied with; it is not enough to have unsigned board minutes to that effect (*see Veale* (Decision 14637)).

AGENCY

If a taxpayer receives a supply as agent for another, Customs' powers over agency situations in VATA 1994, s 47 may come into play.

Under VATA 1994, s 47(3) where *services* are supplied through an agent who acts in his own name, Customs can treat the supply as both a supply to the agent and as a supply by the agent (*Metropolitan Borough of Wirral v The Commissioners* [1995] STI 308) Thus, the general rule is that a supply of services by an agent of X is a supply by X but that rule can be overridden by s 47(3).

In respect of a supply of *goods*, VATA 1994, s 47(2A) provides that where the goods are supplied through an agent who acts in his own name, the supply is treated both as a supply to the agent by the principal, and as a supply by the agent to the customer. If the agent does not act in his own name the supplies will be made by the principal direct.

RENT COLLECTION AGENT

A rent collection agent who is allowed to keep part of the profit rent as his fee has to pay VAT thereon (*Peter Anthony Estates Ltd* (MAN/94/653 Decision 13250)).

Chapter 12

Damages and compensation

The payment of damages can give rise to a charge to VAT. X may supply furniture to Y for £100,000 plus VAT. Y may refuse to pay and X may sue for damages. VAT would be chargeable on the damages. If that were not the case a coach and horses would be driven through the legislation.

SETTLEMENTS IN GENERAL

In 1987, Customs reviewed their policy on the VAT treatment of payments made under out-of-court settlements of disputes after proceedings commenced by service of originating process (or appointment of an arbitrator) (News Release No 82/87).

They take the view that, where such payments are in essence compensatory and do not relate directly to supplies of goods or services, they are outside the scope of VAT. This will be so even if the settlement is expressed in terms that the payment is consideration for the plaintiff's agreement to abandon his rights to bring legal proceedings. But payments will remain taxable if, and to the extent that, they are the consideration for specific taxable supplies by the plaintiff, eg where the dispute concerns payment for an earlier supply, or where the plaintiff grants future rights to exploit copyright material under the settlement.

These changes of policy were applied from 19 November 1987. Customs had previously taken the view that payments under out-of-court settlements were generally taxable. The revised view brings the VAT treatment of out-of-court settlements into line with the VAT treatment of payments under court orders.

In *Cooper Chasney Ltd v The Commissioners* (LON/82/1409 Decision 4898), the taxpayer in effect received 'damages' of £30,000 from X over a dispute concerning the use of the name 'Info-link'. Under the agreement to settle the matter, the taxpayer gave up the use of the name (there was thus a supply). It was held by the tribunal that the taxpayer had 'done something' within VATA 1983, s 3(2)(*b*) (now VATA 1994, s 5(2)(*b*)) and the sum was vatable.

In a meeting with Customs on 23 October 1991, The Law Society took up a number of points in respect of Customs' practice in this area. A note of the meeting, which was published in *VAT Intelligence*, March 1993, pp 1012–1014, is set out *below. See* also De Voil, F8.736.

VAT: Settlement of disputes
Meeting at H M Customs and Excise on 23 October 1991

Introduction
The Law Society said that the tribunal decision in *Cooper Chasney Ltd v CCE* (LON/89/1409Z) had generated comment and correspondence within the VAT Sub-Committee of the Law Society's Revenue Law Committee on the basis that it might be understood as throwing doubt on the guidance contained in Customs' press notice of 19 November 1987. An approach was therefore made to Customs, who had replied that they did not consider the decision to be in conflict with the press notice. The Law Society, however, felt that were several aspects of the settlement of disputes where VAT treatment is not straightforward and that further clarification was necessary. It was important that solicitors should be applying the correct principles, and assurance from Customs with a view to giving agreed guidance to the profession would be welcome.

Customs' original approach
Customs' original approach had been that giving up a right to sue somebody in return for payment was a taxable supply and it satisfied s 3(2)(*b*) VATA 1983, which provides that anything which is not a supply of goods but is done for a consideration (including, if so done, the granting, assignment *or surrender of any right*) is a supply of services (if done in the course or furtherance of a business).

There had never been any question that if a payment by way of compensation was made pursuant to a court order this was outside the scope. However, given that basic principle and the uncertainty surrounding out-of-court settlements prior to the issue of the press notice, it had seemed that Customs were forcing taxpayers to go all the way through the courts and not to enter any settlement by way of compromise, in order to guarantee that any payment would not attract VAT. Customs had reviewed their policy in the light of the decision in *Whites Metal Co v CCE* (LON/86/686Z) where the VAT tribunal had held that services were not supplied by a plaintiff to a defendant in reaching a settlement of an action in tort.

Press Notice 82/87
The press notice had been issued with the object of restricting its application to genuine disputes only. If a settlement agreement was worded in terms that the plaintiff

was giving up rights to sue the defendant in exchange for a sum of money, this was not a supply. If the agreement not to sue and to settle out of court confirmed a previously agreed price, or confirmed a reduction to a previously agreed price, VAT would be adjusted, using the credit note mechanism, by reference to the price finally agreed. The situation when payment was made subject to a court order remained unchanged.

Since the press notice had been issued, very few cases had been brought to VAT headquarters. *Cooper Chasney* and *Edenroc* were notable exceptions. Customs believed that both these decisions were in accordance with the press notice. Local offices had been dealing with queries. However, it was the Law Society's view that the lack of cases which had been brought could indicate unawareness of the potential traps where elements of a settlement could attract a VAT liability.

Customs had considered, when drafting the press notice, the particular example of royalties when there had been an inadvertent breach of copyright. If payment was partly to compensate for a past breach and partly for permission to use in the future the material subject to copyright, there should be a reasonable apportionment. A distinction needed to be drawn. Payment by way of compensation in respect of a *past transgression was outside the scope, but payment in consideration of allowing the future use of the copyright material* was in respect of a taxable supply.

Cooper Chasney Ltd v CCE (LON/89/14092)

In the Law Society's view the facts of *Cooper Chasney* were perhaps more straightforward than difficulties which could be experienced in practice. In that case the plaintiff had expressly allowed the defendant to use the name 'Infolink' in the future (a name which the plaintiff had previously used in his business), but the terms of the settlement were that in return for payment to the plaintiff by the defendant of an agreed sum the plaintiff reverted to his own name (Cooper Chasney Ltd) and agreed to discontinue proceeding against the defendant. It was clear that the elements of the agreement went beyond breaches which had occurred in the past and giving up a right to sue.

Customs said that in deciding what the payment in the settlement of a dispute was for, they look carefully at the words used by the parties (as in *Cooper Chasney*, where an agreement had been entered into which had been set out in the decision) and tax the parties accordingly.

Practical consequences

The Law Society asked if Customs were happy that Press Notice 82/87 was correct, and they confirmed that they were satisfied with the general approach and did not think it should be extended, for example on the basis of the decisions in *Neville Russell v CCE* (1987) VATTR 194 and *Gleneagles Hotel plc v CCE* (1986) VATTR 196, to indicate that anything done in exchange for consideration is a supply.

Customs did not consider that a person had an intrinsic right to sue so that, by not suing, a person was not necessarily giving up any right. Customs thought the position could be analysed by saying that a person was really exercising an option not to enforce an alleged wrong rather than giving up any right. The acceptance of an offer not to sue is taken because the reason for wanting to sue in the first place is settled on receipt of payment.

Customs agreed that if VAT was never mentioned in negotiating a settlement the plaintiff could suddenly find that the amount of cash he received in his settlement was reduced by VAT. There was a suggestion that this could be avoided by adding to the agreement for settlements the words 'VAT will be added [to the agreed sum] if applicable'. However, it would obviously be preferable to issue clear guidance to avoid the necessity of requiring such terms automatically to be added to settlement wordings.

The Law Society asked if Customs agreed that liquidated damages paid under contracts were also outside the scope, and Customs confirmed this. Such cases would not involve litigation but were within the spirit of the press notice. If a contract contained provisions for damages in respect of a breach this would generally be within the press notice, but if a plaintiff was giving up a separate right—for example, the right to receive notice—this could be a taxable supply.

Customs have agreed a joint statement of practice (JSP) with the principal leasing association in order to avoid contractual arguments and any ambiguity over the correct VAT treatment of termination payments and rebates/refunds of rentals arising under equipment leases. The object of the JSP is to establish a common treatment which provides as follows:

(a) All lease termination payments may be treated as being in respect of taxable supplies (ie of the right to terminate). Here the termination payment is usually calculated by reference to the amount of rental payments outstanding under the primary lease period.

(b) Where, on expiry or termination of an equipment lease, the lessee receives from the lessor a rebate or refund of rentals, no adjustment for VAT previously charged need be made. However, credit notes should be endorsed with the words 'This is not a credit note for VAT purposes'.

Importantly, the JSP does not override any contractual arrangements in force. If the lessors wish to revert to the terms of their original agreements they may do so. For example, lease termination payments may arise on default by a lessee which are by way of liquidated damages and therefore outside the scope of VAT.

Taxpayers who were not within the major leasing associations could rely on this agreement but they would not necessarily be aware of it. It was confirmed that local VAT offices had knowledge of it.

Specific examples
The Law Society's letter of 18 June to the Solicitor's Office at Customs had listed examples of where the Law Society had sought Customs' guidance on specific issues. These were raised for discussion and the following answers given:

(a) Customs confirmed that Press Notice 82/87 covered only payments made *after proceedings had commenced*. If it was clear that payments had been made before proceedings had been commenced, but such payments would not be within [s 5(3)(*b*), Customs would extend outside-the-scope treatment to such payments.

(b) In the area of involuntary supplies (eg a dispute concerning right of light for which damages are awarded), Customs confirmed that *only damages in respect of past infringements would be outside the scope*. Where a settlement covered past infringements, and also permission to continue in the future the conduct which gave rise to those infringements, Customs would accept a reasonable apportionment. The Law Society asked about the case where the court required a party to give up a right (eg a right of light or an intellectual property right) in exchange for a payment from the other party. Customs said that this was a difficult point which they would need to consider further. Article 6(1) of the Sixth Directive was relevant where it referred to 'tolerating an act or situation' as a possible supply for VAT purposes. Questions concerning rights of light can cause problems. Much depends on whether a payment is made in return for the right to take someone else's light or whether it is compensation for the loss of light subsequent to an adjacent building being constructed. It could be argued in exceptional circumstances that the court is deciding what level of consideration is due in return for the granting of the right. However, it is thought that in the majority of cases the payment will be damages imposed upon the payer by the court and therefore outside the scope of VAT. For example, in cases where the court decides that light may be taken and that compensation is payable this will be seen as outside the scope of VAT—there is no consensual element.

(c) Where litigation has involved a supply on which VAT had already been accounted for (but the price was not paid) and the result is a reduction in the price paid for the supply, it may be necessary for a supplier to issue a credit note in order to recover part of the VAT which he had previously accounted for and which he had not received. Customs confirmed that in such a case the credit note could be accepted as valid and it would *prima facie* be necessary for the recipient of the supply to repay to Customs the tax which he had already claimed back.

(d) By way of clarification as to when damages were considered to be compensatory and when such payments would constitute consideration for taxable supplies, Customs offered the example of a local authority digging up a pavement in front of a parade of shops. Compensation paid by the local authority to a shopkeeper for loss of trade suffered as a result of such action would not be regarded as a taxable supply. However, if a shopkeeper was paid by the local authority to allow the latter to work on his land the payment would be consideration for a taxable supply.

Customs said that they would want to consider in greater detail the question of warranty claims. For example, in a standard-rated property transaction, where a warranty had understated the rent and contract provided for a reduction in the purchase price in such a situation, the procedure set out in (c) above would apply and the vendor would have to issue a credit note to recover that part of the VAT previously accounted for. The example of net assets of a business having been overstated in warranties given on sale was not so relevant since if it was a question of shares it would be in the realm of exempt supplies anyway. Compensation in these circumstances would be regarded as outside the scope unless the agreement provided for a reduction in price.

(e) Where the settlement involved cross-supplies (other than the mere surrender of the right of action) tax would be payable by each party, without netting-off, according to the nature of the supply. The situation may arise that there may be a consideration paid in return for a party agreeing to enter into an agreement. For example, in the property industry, reverse premiums may be paid to a potential tenant in consideration of the tenant agreeing to enter into a property lease or for agreeing to carry out building, refurbishment or demolition works, *viz Neville Russell* and *Battersea Leisure.*

If the supply under the agreement was, for example, free services, VAT would not be due.

(f) Customs confirmed that interest on damages is outside the scope of VAT. It has been confirmed in the European decision in *BAZ Bausystem A G v Finanzamt München für Korperschaften* [1982] ECR 2527 that interest would not increase consideration for a supply.

If an international breach had occurred the same basic principles should be followed. For example, Sched 3, VATA 1983 [now Sched 3 of VATA 1994] should not apply to a cross-border giving-up of rights. Apparently the Dutch and the Germans had had bilateral discussions and had confirmed that they would apply outside-the-scope treatment on the same basis as in the UK.

DAMAGES FOR BREACH OF COVENANT

In *Elite Investments Ltd v T I Bainbridge Silencers Ltd (No 2)* the plaintiff landlord claimed a sum in respect of VAT at 15 per cent of the amount awarded in an earlier action (*Elite Investments Ltd v T I Bainbridge Silencers Ltd* [1986] 2 EGLR 43), representing the cost of repairs to premises which the defendant tenant had failed to carry out. The plaintiff company was not registered for VAT and would not have been able to recover the tax incurred (on payment to the builder) if it undertook the repairs directly. That company was the assignee of the claim of the original landlord entitled to the benefit of the tenant's covenants. The original company was not registered for VAT as it had been ordered to be wound up in 1985.

In the earlier case of *Drummond v S & U Stores Ltd* (1980) 258 EG 1293 Glidewell J decided that an individual landlord was entitled to recover, in addition to the cost of repairs, an amount equal to the VAT, if any of the options open to the landlord involved incurring such tax in circumstances in which it could not be recovered. This would be the case if the landlord was not registered for VAT (and, under present law, assuming he would not exercise the election to waive exemption).

The defendant argued that the landlord, although not registered for VAT, could, for example, require the repairs to be carried out by a new tenant who was registered and could therefore recover the tax incurred.

Judge Paul Baker QC held that an amount could be claimed in respect of VAT if, looking at the evidence as a whole, there was some realistic option open to the landlord for repairing the premises which would throw the burden of the VAT in respect of the cost of those repairs on to the landlord. The option which gave this result need not be the landlord's only or probable choice; the court would not assess the likelihood of the burden falling on the landlord and discount the amount to allow for the possibility of the tax being recovered. However, in the present case, several months had elapsed since the compensation had been paid and no repairs had been carried out. In the absence of evidence of the plaintiff's intentions, the carrying out of the repairs by the plaintiff directly was not apparently being considered as a realistic option. Accordingly this was not a case where a further amount in respect of VAT could be added to the amount claimed.

To summarise, if it can be shown that a landlord who is suing a tenant for breach of a repairing covenant will be imposing, or is likely to be imposing, the obligation to do the works on a new tenant (by, for instance, giving an appropriate rent reduction), and that new tenant can claim back any VAT charged by the repairer (or presumably it was reasonable to assume the landlord would exercise the election to waive exemption), the landlord may not be able to add a sum equal to the VAT to his compensation entitlement. This is because any VAT charged to the landlord could be assumed to be recovered. If the landlord will be bearing, or is likely to be bearing, the repair expenditure, and he cannot reclaim or will not be reclaiming the VAT charged thereon by the repairer, then a sum equal to the VAT may be added to the compensation figure.

The cases mentioned *above* give the critical guidance as to which side of the line a case is likely to fall, although they were decided before the election to waive exemption was introduced.

DILAPIDATIONS

Customs treat dilapidations claims as outside the scope of VAT. Their position is set out in Notice 742, para 4.12 and reads thus:

The terms of a lease may provide for the landlord to recover from tenants, at or near the termination of the lease, an amount to cover the cost of restoring the property to its original condition. The amount is often agreed between the parties and may be based on a surveyor's or contractor's estimate.

Dilapidations represent a claim for damages by the landlord against the tenant's 'wants of repair'. Consequently the payment involved is not the consideration for a supply for VAT purposes and is outside the scope of VAT.

COMPENSATION

If a tenant is given notice to quit and complies, he will be entitled to compensation under the Landlord and Tenant Act 1954 or the Agricultural Tenancies Act 1986, as the case may be. That compensation is outside the scope of VAT entirely and thus is not vatable.

However, if the landlord pays an additional amount over and above the statutory entitlement of the tenant, because, for instance, the tenant is vacating the property earlier than is allowed by the period of grace given in the notice to quit, then that additional payment will be consideration for the tenant's surrendering the lease, and will be exempt, unless the tenant had exercised the election to waive exemption (*see* Notice 742, para 4.9).

Compensation paid by a local authority for revoking a planning permission probably derives from an interest in land.

COMPULSORY PURCHASE COMPENSATION

Customs' view on compulsory purchase compensation is set out in Notice 742, para 7.4 and reads as follows:

> If you are obliged to dispose of property under a compulsory purchase order you are making a supply for VAT purposes.
>
> The liability will be exempt if
>
> - it is the purchase of bare land; or
> - it is the purchase of buildings that are not 'new',
>
> but it will be standard-rated if
>
> - the building/civil engineering work is 'new'; or
> - the election to waive exemption has been made; or
> - it is the sale of holiday accommodation less than 3 years old.
>
> If at the time of supply you do not know how much compensation you are to receive, there will be a tax point each time you receive any payment for the purchase.

Chapter 13

Place of supply of services

GENERAL RULE

The basic rule for determining where a supply of services is made for VAT purposes is by reference to where the supplier belongs. If the supplier belongs in the UK, the supply of services will be made in the UK.

However, that general rule is overridden by special 'place of supply' rules (VATA 1994, s 7(10) and (11)). The basic material is found in art 9 of the EC Sixth Directive, and art 9(2)(*a*) refers to:

> services connected with immovable property, including the services of estate agents and experts, and of services for preparing and coordinating construction works, such as the services of architects and of firms providing on-site supervision.

In the case of services falling within the above definition the supply takes place where the property is situated, regardless of where the supplier belongs.

That rule is implemented into UK law by art 5 of the Value Added Tax (Place of Supply of Services) Order 1992 (SI No 3121). Services included within that order are grants, assignments and surrenders of interests in or rights over land and of licences to occupy land, works of construction, demolition, conversion, reconstruction, alteration, enlargement, repair or maintenance of a building or civil engineering work and services of agents, auctioneers, architects, surveyors and others involved in matters related to land (*see Aspen Advisory Services Ltd* (LON/94/2773 Decision 13489).

Thus, if a German firm carries out demolition and reconstruction work for a UK individual, and the works relate to UK land, the supply takes place in the UK because the land is situated in the UK. If appropriate, the supplier must register for VAT in the UK.

These rules interact with the reverse charge provisions in VATA 1994, Sched 5 and s 8.

If the recipient of such services is VAT registered in the UK and the services are not within Sched 5, paras 1–7, the place of supply is deemed to be in the UK. However, the recipient must account for VAT under the reverse charge provisions under Sched 5, paras 9 and 10. That is the rule, in spite of the fact that the supply is treated as being made in the UK.

Another area of difficulty is art 16 of the Place of Supply of Services Order and Sched 5, which deems certain services to be supplied where received.

If a UK supplier supplies Sched 5 services to a German client, the UK supplier does not charge VAT, but the German client must account for VAT under the German version of the reverse charge provisions. If, however, a German supplies Sched 5 services to a UK recipient, then the German supplier does not charge VAT, but the UK recipient has to account for VAT under the UK reverse charge legislation.

Paragraph 3 of Sched 5 covers services of consultants, engineers, consultancy bureaux, lawyers, accountants and other similar services; data processing and provision of information (but excluding any services relating to land).

Thus, in the above examples, if the services relate to land, then on the face of it the supplies are wholly outside the reverse charge provisions in Sched 5. Thus if the UK supplier supplies services to the German client, and these relate to land in the UK, the UK supplier must charge VAT and the German reverse charge provisions do not apply. Again, if the German supplier supplies services to the UK recipient and the services relate to land in Germany, then the German supplier must charge German VAT. If the land is in the UK the reverse charge is inapplicable and the German supplier must revert to art 5 of the Value Added Tax (Place of Supply of Services) Order 1992 and register for UK VAT.

CUSTOMS' PRACTICE

The supply of services by lawyers could come within Sched 5, para 3. If, however, they relate to land, then they are excluded from Sched 5 and will clearly fall within art 5 of the Place of Supply Order.

In Notice 741, Customs consider legal services such as conveyancing and dealing with applications for planning permission as services relating to land.

The relevant paragraphs of Notice 741 relating to legal services and supplies connected to land read as set out below:

3.1 Place of supply of services relating to land and property

If you supply certain services relating to land, the place of supply of those services is where the *land itself* is located, irrespective of where you or your customer belongs.

This rule applies only to services which relate *directly* to a specific site(s) of land. It does not apply if there is only an indirect connection with land, or if the land-related service is only an incidental component of a more comprehensive service.

'Land' includes land generally, growing crops, buildings, walls, fences or other structures fixed permanently to the land or sea bed; or plant, machinery or equipment which is an installation or edifice in its own right, for example, a refinery or fixed production platform. Machinery installed in buildings other than as a fixture is normally not regarded as 'land' but as 'goods'.

3.2   Examples of services relating directly to land

(a) Services supplied in the course of construction, alteration, demolition, repair or maintenance (including painting and decorating) of any building or civil engineering work on land.

(b) Services of estate agents, auctioneers, architects, surveyors, engineers and similar professional people relating to land, buildings or civil engineering works. This includes the management, conveyancing, survey or valuation of property by a solicitor, surveyor or loss adjuster. (If you are an estate agent, you should read VAT Leaflet 700/28 *Estate agents*.)

(c) The supply of plant or machinery, *together with an operator*, for work on a construction site.

(d) Seismic surveying and associated data processing services on land.

(e) The supply of hotel accommodation.

(f) Legal services such as conveyancing, dealing with applications for planning permission.

3.3   Examples of services not relating directly to land (or where the land element is incidental)

(a) The legal administration of a deceased person's estate which may include property;

(b) Repair and maintenance of permanently installed machinery;

(c) Advice or information relating to land or property markets;

(d) Insurance of property;

(e) The hiring out of civil engineering plant on its own; or the secondment of staff to a building site;

(f) Feasibility studies assessing the potential of particular businesses or business potential in a particular geographic area.

3.4 Customers receiving services relating to land

From 1 November 1993, the reverse charge principle of accounting for UK VAT was extended to all types of services, which, although provided by overseas suppliers, are deemed to be UK supplies and are therefore subject to UK VAT.

If you are a UK VAT registered recipient of services relating to land or property in the UK—*other than* the supply of land or property itself—you will be required to account for VAT under the 'reverse charge' procedure if the supplier belongs overseas.

3.5 When you are a non-UK supplier

If you are a supplier who does not belong in the UK, and your customer is not registered for VAT, you, as the supplier, are responsible for accounting for the VAT in the UK where your supply is made. If you are not already registered in the UK, you will be liable to register subject to the current threshold—see paragraph 1.8.

Customs guidance printed in the *Law Society's Gazette* of 1 February 1978, p 92, is still referred to, but Customs do not consider themselves bound by that statement and appear to be taking a wider view of what services relate to land in the UK and which are therefore vatable, as opposed to supplies which are outside the scope of VAT (formerly zero-rated). The statement reads as follows:

VAT—international services—land

1   A note appeared in The Law Society's *Gazette* on 1 February 1978 at p 92 summarising the rules which apply after 1 January 1978 to the export of legal and other services and indicating that the supply of services relating to land situated in the UK for overseas clients could not, after that date, be zero-rated.

2   The zero-rating provisions are found in FA 1972, Sched 4, Group 9, as amended, [now Value Added Tax (Place of Supply of Services) Order 1992] and the three relevant items (which should be read subject to the notes in Group 9) are:

'*Item 1*—The supply of services relating to land situated outside the UK and the Isle of Man.

'*Item 5*—The supply to a person in his business capacity . . . who as such belongs in a country, other than the UK, which is a Member State of the European Economic Community, of any service comprised in Sched 2A, paras 1–7 to this Act [now art 16 of the Order].

'*Item 6*—The supply to a person who belongs in a country, other than the Isle of Man, which is not a Member State of the European Economic Community of:

'(*a*)–any service (other than insurance and re-insurance services described in Sched 5, Group 2 [now *see* VATA 1994, Sched 5, para 5 and art 16 of the Order] to this Act) comprised in Sched 2A, paras 1–7 to this Act . . .'.

3   The result of the above provisions is broadly to zero-rate:

(*a*) all supplies of services relating to land outside the UK; and

(*b*) all the supplies mentioned in FA 1972, Sched 2A as amended [now VATA 1994, Sched 5] to business clients in the EEC but outside the UK; and

(*c*) all the supplies mentioned in Sched 2A [now art 16 of the Order], other than exempt insurance or re-insurance services, to business and private clients in countries outside the EEC.

4   The supplies mentioned in Sched 2A [now art 16 of the Order] to the Act include lawyers' services but para 3 [now VATA 1994, Sched 5, para 3] specifically excludes any services relating to land. Services relating to land are deemed to be supplied in the country where the person supplying the services belongs. A solicitor belonging in the UK must therefore charge VAT at the standard rate on services which he supplies relating to land in the UK irrespective of where his client belongs. When the land is situated outside the UK the supply of services may be zero-rated under Group 9, Item 1 [now art 5 of the Order], once again irrespective of the client's location.

5   Certain difficulties have arisen as to the meaning of the phrase 'services relating to land' both in Group 9, Item 1 and in Sched 2A, para 3 [now art 5 of the Order]. The interpretation of this phrase is, of course, a matter of law but Customs have helpfully indicated their views which are set out below.

6   First, Customs have said that they consider that the expression 'services relating to land', as used in both Group 9, Item 1 and in FA 1972, Sched 2A, para 3 [now *see* arts 5 and 16 of the Order], only affects those services provided by lawyers which relate directly to the sale, disposal, transfer or surrender of an interest in or right over land or a building attached thereto. Accordingly a solicitor's services in connection with a conveyancing transaction, whether the property be freehold or leasehold, are services relating to land; on the other hand, where a solicitor acts for a client in the take-over of a company, one of whose assets might be freehold land, the services relate to the taking over of the company and are not 'services relating to land'.

7   The following are certain specific examples which illustrate Customs' views:

(*a*) A company client who belongs in the US is in the business of providing management consultancy services all over the world. It has a client in the UK and sends one of its employees on a six-month assignment in the UK to provide the management consultancy services. At the request and cost of the American company the solicitors advise on and arrange for completion of a lease of furnished residential accommodation occupied by the company's American employee while he is on his UK assignment. Are the services so rendered to the American company 'services relating to land' and therefore charged to VAT at the standard rate, even though the client belongs in the US?

  Customs have stated that they would regard the lawyer's services of advising on, and completion of, the lease as 'services relating to land', and therefore as taxable at the standard rate even though the client belonged in the US.

(*b*) In connection with the activities described in (*a*) above an executive of the American client company visits the employee in the UK; during his visit he is injured when entering the premises of a public house; he falls through a trap door in the floor negligently left open after there has been a delivery of beer. 'The injured executive (who 'belongs' in the US) seeks the advice of solicitors and asks them to institute proceedings against the owner of the public house to press a claim for damages arising from the defectiveness of the premises. Are these services considered to be 'services relating to land'?

Customs have said that they would not regard the lawyer's services as 'relating to land' in this instance: they could therefore qualify for zero-rating under Group 9, Item 6 [now art 16 of the Order].

(*c*) An American bank (with no place of business in the UK) instructs solicitors to act for it in connection with a loan to a UK company, the loan to be secured by a fixed charge on the UK company's freehold property. The work includes preparation of a loan agreement, personal guarantees and the investigation of the UK company's title to the property and registration of the client bank's mortgage against it when the loan is drawn down. Are these services 'services relating to land'? Are the solicitors required to apportion their fees as between zero-rated services rendered in connection with preparation and negotiation of the loan and loan agreement (zero-rated) and the standard-rated services in investigation of title and preparation and registration of the mortgage?

Customs have said that the work appears to involve the transfer of an equitable interest in land: however, this is only part of a package of 'services' relating to a loan agreement and they would not require apportionment of the services of investigation of title and preparation and registration of mortgage. The whole consideration for the service would therefore normally qualify for zero-rating under Item 6. If however, the solicitors of their own accord were separately to itemise investigation of title etc on their invoice and assign to those services a separate consideration tax would have to be charged.

(*d*) Based on the facts in (*c*) above, the UK borrower defaults on its obligations under the loan agreement and the solicitors are instructed by the US lender to act in connection with obtaining a court order for possession of the mortgaged real property and the subsequent sale. At the same time they are to apply for judgment against the guarantors of the loan on their personal guarantees, the guarantors refusing to honour the guarantees by paying the UK company's debt. Are the solicitors to standard-rate their work on the litigation relating to the application for the possession order but zero-rate the work done in relation to enforcing the guarantees?

Customs have said that in these circumstances the same considerations would apply as for (*c*) above.

(*e*) Based on the facts in (*c*) above, a third party offers to purchase from the US client the benefit of the UK company's indebtedness under the loan agreement together with the benefit of the mortgage on the UK company's property. Must the solicitors apportion their services in acting for the UK company on the sale, as between work on the sale of the loan agreement (zero-rated) and work on the transfer of the mortgage (standard-rated)? Is it relevant that the transaction is completed by execution of a single sale document, rather than separate documents for sale of loan and transfer of mortgage?

Customs have said that the same considerations would apply as for (c) above.

(f)   An American company with no place of business in the UK sends a solicitor some tender documents with instructions to 'review and give legal advice'. The documents are for procuring the construction of a factory on land in the UK and the contract when issued will be a Royal Institute of British Architects' contract. Is this a 'service relating to land'?

Customs have said that they consider that any request by a client to 'review and give legal advice' on documents which themselves relate to land in the UK, either directly or indirectly, is too far removed from any direct relationship with land for services to be expected from Sched 2A, para 3 [now art 16 of the Order] as 'services relating to land'. The services therefore fall within Sched 2A and zero-rating might apply under the provisions of Group 9, Item 6 [now *see* the Order].

(g)   A German company is drafting a contract binding two parties (one English and one German) to the completion of a construction project on land outside the UK. The solicitors are asked to review the tender documents. Is this a 'service relating to land'?

Customs have said that they consider that any request by a client to 'review and give legal advice' on documents which themselves relate to land outside the UK, whether directly or indirectly, is too far removed from any direct relationship with land for the services to be excepted from Sched 2A, para 3 as 'services relating to land'. The services therefore fall within Sched 2A [now art 16 of the Order] and zero-rating might apply [now 'outside the scope'] under the provisions of Group 9, Item 5 [now *see* the Order].

8   Any member of the profession who is uncertain as to the application of the legislation to the facts in any particular case may obtain the views of Customs by writing to:
VAT Administration Directorate, HM Customs and Excise, King's Beam House, Mark Lane, London EC3R 7HE.

Note: The updated legislation referred to in the square brackets *above* does not precisely relate to the old legislation because of the many changes in this area since 1978. The Statement can thus only be of the most general guidance.

Furthermore, zero-rated supplies are now replaced by supplies which are outside the scope of VAT, but the supplier can still reclaim his input tax as if he had made a 'zero-rated' supply. VATA 1994, s 26(2)(b) enables a taxpayer to reclaim input tax if it relates to 'supplies outside the United Kingdom which would be taxable supplies if made in the United Kingdom'.

Example

X, a solicitor in the UK, makes a supply to a client which is treated as made where the client belongs (Value Added Tax (Place of Supply of Services) Order 1992 (SI No 3121), art 16). The supplies are technically outside the scope of VAT (VATA 1994, ss 4(1), 7(10) and (11) and Part 16 of the said Order), but VATA 1994, s 26(2)(*b*) enables the input tax referable to the supply to be reclaimed.

PART III

DOMESTIC BUILDINGS

Chapter 14

Zero-rating

VATA 1994, Group 5, Sched 8, as substituted by the Value Added Tax (Construction and Buildings) Order 1995 (SI No 280) which came into force on 1 March 1995, zero rates four separate transactions relating to domestic accommodation.

ZERO-RATED TRANSACTIONS

Sales and leases of new and newly converted dwellings, etc

The first grant, by a person constructing a building (ie a developer) designed as a dwelling or a number of dwellings, or intended for use solely for a relevant residential or a relevant charitable purpose, of a major interest (ie a freehold or a lease of over 21 years) in or in any part of the building, the dwelling or its site, is zero-rated.

Example

Y plc constructs a block of flats. It grants to tenants leases of over 21 years for premiums and rent. Y plc is a person constructing the building. It will have constructed a new building designed as a dwelling and will have granted a major interest. A zero-rated supply will have resulted. This means that any input tax in connection with the development which Y plc will have paid (eg payments for the professional services of architects, engineers, surveyors, solicitors, estate agents, valuers, consultants and other persons supplying supervisory services, site security payments, site investigation payments, payments for catering, the cleaning of site offices and workmen's huts, temporary lighting, transport and haulage to and from the site, certain plant hire services, hire of scaffolding services etc) will be reclaimable. For reasons mentioned below the builder employed by Y plc will not have charged VAT on his construction services.

Also, the grant by a person converting a non-residential building or a non-residential part of a building into a building designed as a dwelling or a number of dwellings, or into a building intended for use solely for a relevant residential purpose, of a major interest in or in any part of the building, dwelling or its site, is zero-rated (Sched 8, Group 5, Item 1).

Supply of new construction services

The supply, in the course of the construction of a building designed as a dwelling or number of dwellings or intended for use solely for a relevant residential purpose or a relevant charitable purpose, of any services related to the construction, other than the services of an architect, surveyor or any person acting as a consultant or in a supervisory capacity, is zero-rated (Item 2).

Example

A plc is a builder. B plc owns the freehold of Blackacre. B plc employs A plc to build a home providing residential accommodation for children on Blackacre (such a use is a relevant residential use). When A plc charges B plc for the construction works it will not have to charge VAT. The supply will be zero-rated.

Furthermore, the supply in the course of the construction of a civil engineering work necessary for the development of a permanent park for residential caravans, or any services relating to the construction other than the services of an architect, surveyor or other person acting as a consultant or in a supervisory capacity, is zero-rated.

Thus, a builder who provides services and normal materials for the construction of any civil engineering work necessary for the development of a permanent park for residential caravans would make zero-rated supplies. This would not include the installing of a foul drainage system and services to a natural water basin for use by residential houseboats *see The Littlehampton Houseboat Association* (LON/90/44 Decision 5420).

Supply to housing associations

The supply, to a registered housing association, in the course of conversion of a non-residential building or a non-residential part of a building into:

(a) a building or part of a building designed as a dwelling or a number of dwellings; or

(b) a building or part of a building intended for use solely for a relevant residential purpose,

of any services related to the conversion, other than the services of an architect, surveyor or any person acting as a consultant or in a supervisory capacity, is zero-rated (Item 3).

Supply of materials

Finally, the supply of building materials to a person to whom the supplier is supplying services within Items 2 or 3 of Group 5 which include the incorporation of the materials into the building, or its site, is zero-rated (Item 4).

DEFINITIONS, ETC

'Grant'

Note (1) to Group 5 provides that a grant includes an assignment or surrender.

'Designed as a dwelling'

A building is designed as a dwelling or a number of dwellings where, in relation to each dwelling, the following conditions are satisfied:

(a) the dwelling consists of self-contained living accommodation;

(b) there is no provision for direct internal access from the dwelling to any other dwelling or part of a dwelling;

(c) the separate use or disposal of the dwelling is not prohibited by the terms of any covenant, statutory planning consent or similar provision; and

(d) statutory planning consent has been granted in respect of that dwelling and its construction or conversion has been carried out in accordance with that consent.

Garages

The construction of, or conversion of a non-residential building to, a building designed as a dwelling or a number of dwellings includes the construction of, or conversion of a non-residential building to, a garage, provided that:

(a) the dwelling and the garage are constructed or converted at the same time; and

(b) the garage is intended to be occupied with the dwelling or one of the dwellings.

'Relevant residential purpose'

'Relevant residential purpose' means:

(a) a home or other institution providing residential accommodation for children;

(b) a home or other institution providing residential accommodation with personal care for persons in need of personal care by reason of old age, disablement, past or present dependence on alcohol or drugs or past or present mental disorder;

(c) a hospice;

(d) residential accommodation for students or school pupils;

(e) residential accommodation for members of any of the armed forces;

(f) a monastery, nunnery or similar establishment; or

(g) an institution which is the sole or main residence of at least 90 per cent of its residents,

except use as a hospital, prison or similar institution or a hotel, inn or similar establishment.

Where a number of buildings are:

(a) constructed at the same time and on the same site; and

(b) are intended to be used together as a unit solely for a relevant residential purpose;

then each of those buildings, to the extent that they would not be so regarded, are to be treated as intended for use solely for a relevant residential purpose.

'Relevant charitable purpose' (Note (6))

Use for a relevant charitable purpose means use by a charity in either or both the followng ways, namely:

(a) otherwise than in the course or furtherance of a business;

(b) as a village hall or similarly in providing social or recreational facilities for a local community.

'Non-residential' (Note (7))

Subject to Note (9) *below*, 'non-residential', in relation to a building or part of a building, means:

(a) neither designed nor adapted for use as a dwelling or number of dwellings nor for a relevant residential purpose; or

(b) if so designed or adapted, was constructed before, and has not been used as a dwelling or number of dwellings or for a relevant purpose since, 1 April 1973.

References to a non-residential building or a non-residential part of a building do not include a reference to a garage occupied together with a dwelling (Note (8)).

Conversion (Note (9))

The conversion, other than to a building designed for a relevant residential purpose, of a non-residential part of a building which already contains a residential part is not included within Items 1(*b*) or 3 unless the result of that conversion is to create an additional dwelling or dwellings.

Apportionment (Note (10))

Note (10) applies to cases where:

(a) part of a building that is constructed is designed as a dwelling or number of dwellings or is intended for use solely for a relevant residential purpose or relevant charitable purpose (and part is not); or

(b) part of a building that is converted is designed as a dwelling or number of dwellings or is used solely for a relevant residential purpose (and part is not).

In these cases:

(a) a grant or other supply relating only to the part so designed or intended for that use (or its site) shall be treated as relating to a building so designed or intended for such use;

(b) a grant or other supply relating only to the part neither so designed nor intended for such use (or its site) shall not be so treated; and

(c) any other grant or other supply relating to, or to any part of, the building (or its site), requires an apportionment to be made to determine the extent to which it is to be so treated.

Where, a service falling within the description in Items 2 or 3 is supplied in part in relation to the construction or conversion of a building, and in part for other purposes, an apportionment may be made to determine the extent to which the supply is to be treated as falling within Items 2 or 3.

Certificate (Note (12))

Where all or part of a building is intended for use solely for a relevant residential purpose or a relevant charitable purpose:

(a) a supply relating to the building (or any part of it) shall not be taken for the purposes of Items 2 and 4 as relating to a building intended for such use unless it is made to a person who intends to use the building (or part) for such a purpose; and

(b) a grant or other supply relating to the building (or any part of it) shall not be taken as relating to a building intended for such use unless, before it is made, the person to whom it is made has given to the person making it a certificate in such form as may be specified in a notice published by the Commissioners stating that the grant or other supply (or specified part of it) so relates.

With respect to the issue of certificates, there must be an intention, on the part of the recipient of the supplies, that the building is to be used for a relevant residential purpose or a relevant charitable purpose. For the purposes of that requirement, it is not necessary that the recipient itself will use the building for the relevant purpose; it is sufficient that it may, for instance, let the property to a person who will so use it. This first hurdle is important and must be satisfied.

The second hurdle is to make sure that, although the taxpayer may have that intention, the legislation does not deem otherwise. There are two ways in which the intention may effectively be cancelled for the purposes of VAT.

First, in the case of a builder supplying construction services and material (within Items 2 and 4 (not within Item 1), Sched 8, Group 5, the intention will be deemed not to exist unless the supplies of services and materials are 'made to a person who intends to use the building (or part) for such a purpose'. It is felt that this means that the recipient of the services must actually use the property for the relevant residential or charitable purpose. Thus, if the supplies are made to X charity, which will use the property for its relevant charitable purposes, then the relief will be available. However, if the supplies (of services and materials) are made to X, a property developer, who intends to let the property to a charity, it is felt that the condition in Note (12)(*a*) will not be satisfied.

The second condition applicable to Items 1, 2 and 4 of Sched 8, Group 5 is that the recipient must be able to provide a certificate stating that the supplies made to it are to be used for such charitable purposes.

Figure 14.1:

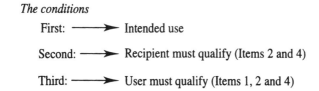

The conditions

First: ⟶ Intended use

Second: ⟶ Recipient must qualify (Items 2 and 4)

Third: ⟶ User must qualify (Items 1, 2 and 4)

The consequence of this is as follows:

(1) In all cases the recipient must be able to show that the building is intended for use for a relevant residential purpose or a relevant charitable purpose, either because the recipient will so use it itself or because it intends to make it available, by, for example, a letting, to someone who will so use it.

(2) If the *above* condition is satisfied, any builder providing services and goods in the course of the construction of such a building must ensure that the supplies are made to a person who intends to use the building (or part) for the qualifying purpose. It is felt that making it available for someone else to use it for a qualifying purpose is not sufficient.

(3) In addition, the recipient must provide a certificate stating that it intends to use the supply for a qualifying purpose.

If the intention is to sell the completed building to a person, and that person provides a certificate—which he can if he shows that he will use the building himself for the charitable or residential purpose, or that it is to be used by, for instance, letting it for a charitable or residential purpose—then the relief will be available.

Figure 14.2:

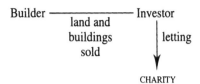

If the residential accommodation, for instance, for students, comprises dwellings, there is no need for a builder's certificate. This is because VATA 1994, Sched 8, Group 5, Note 12(*b*) applies only to a building 'intended for use solely for a relevant residential purpose or a relevant charitable purpose'.

Restricted user (Note (13))

The grant of an interest in, or in any part of:

(a) a building designed as a dwelling or number of dwellings; or

(b) the site of such a building,

is not within Item 1 if:

(a) the interest granted is such that the grantee is not entitled to reside in the building or part, throughout the year; or

(b) residence there throughout the year, or the use of the building or part as the grantee's principal private residence, is prevented by the terms of a covenant, statutory planning consent or similar permission (see p 106).

Lease premiums (Note (14))

Where the major interest referred to in Item 1 is a tenancy or lease:

(a) if a premium is payable, the grant falls within that item only to the extent that it is made for consideration in the form of the premium; and

(b) if a premium is not payable, the grant falls within that item only to the extent that it is made for consideration in the form of the first payment of rent due under the tenancy or lease.

Civil engineering (Note (15))

The reference in Item 2(*b*) of this Group to the construction of a civil engineering work does not include the conversion, reconstruction, alteration or enlargement of such a work.

Construction of building (Note (16))

For the purpose of this Group, the construction of a building does not include:

(a) the conversion, reconstruction or alteration of an existing building; or

(b) any enlargement of, or extension to, an existing building except to the extent that the enlargement or extension creates an additional dwelling or dwellings; or

(c) subject to Note (17) (*see below*), the construction of an annexe to an existing building.

Annexes (Note (17))

Note 16(c) *above* does not apply where an annexe is intended for use solely for a relevant charitable purpose and:

(a) is capable of functioning independently from the existing building; and

(b) the only access or, where there is more than one means of access, the main access, to:

(i) the annexe is not via the existing building; and
(ii) the existing building is not via the annexe.

Ceasing to be an existing building (Note (18))

A building ceases to be an existing building only when:

(a) it is demolished completely to ground level; or

(b) the part remaining above ground level consists of no more than a single façade or, where a corner site, a double façade, the retention of which is a condition or requirement of statutory planning consent or similar permission.

Caravans (Note (19))

A caravan is not a residential caravan if residence in it throughout the year is prevented by the terms of a covenant, statutory planning consent or similar permission.

Services (Note (20))

Item 2 and Item 3 do not include the supply of services described in para 1(1) or 5(4) of Sched 4.

Registered housing associations (Note (21))

In Item 3, 'registered housing association' means a registered housing association within the meaning of the Housing Association Act 1985 or Part II of the Housing (Northern Ireland) Order 1992.

'Building materials' (Note (22))

'Building materials', in relation to any description of building, means goods of a description ordinarily incorporated by builders in a building of that description, (or its site), but do not include:

(a) finished or prefabricated furniture, other than furniture designed to be fitted in kitchens;

(b) materials for the construction of fitted furniture, other than kitchen furniture;

(c) electrical or gas applicances, unless the appliance is an appliance which is—

   (i) designed to heat space or water (or both) or to provide ventilation, air cooling, air purification, or dust extraction; or

   (ii) intended for use in a building designed as a number of dwellings and is a door-entry system, a waste disposal unit or a machine for compacting waste; or

   (iii) a burglar alarm, a fire alarm, or fire safety equipment or designed solely for the purpose of enabling aid to be summoned in an emergency; or

(iv) a lift or hoist;

(d) carpets or carpeting material.

Where a taxable person constructing or effecting any works to a building, in either case for the purpose of making a grant of a major interest in or in any part of it or its site which is of a description in Sched 8, incorporates goods other than 'building materials' (as defined *above*) in any part of the building or its site, input tax on the acquisition of the goods is excluded from credit (Value Added Tax (Input Tax) (Amendment) Order 1995 (SI No 281) and Figure 14.4, *below*).

It is clear that VAT must be charged by the builder on goods which are not 'building materials' as defined, and the *above* statutory instrument ensures that such input tax cannot be reclaimed; it is 'blocked' input tax.

For the purposes of Note (22), the incorporation of goods in a building includes their installation as fittings (Note (23)).

'Major interest'

In order to make a zero-rated supply under Item 1, it is necessary for the person who constructed or converted the building to grant a major interest in that building; anything less is not sufficient.

A major interest in relation to land means a fee simple or a tenancy for a term certain exceeding 21 years.

In the case of *American Real Estate (Scotland) Ltd v The Commissioners* (1980) VATTR 88, X Ltd purchased land and erected a number of houses thereon. It then sold rights to occupy the houses for specified weeks each year for holiday purposes. It issued certificates to the purchasers, each granting to the holder the right to occupy a particular house on the estate for a particular week or weeks in perpetuity. The tribunal held that the issue of such certificates did not confer on the holder any heritable right in the house concerned, and accordingly there was no grant of a major interest in the house. Additionally, the issue of a certificate amounted to the provision of holiday accommodation. The supply was therefore vatable. The tribunal held that the holiday accommodation item (in Sched 9, Group 1, Item 1(*e*)) was not confined to short-term arrangements.

In *Isacc* (Decision 14656) the developer granted a lease for 21 years. It was thus not a major interest. However, he entered into a deed of rectification which extended the terms. It had been held in *Eades the Blaney* (1977) 247 EG 211, CA that negligence by a solicitor did not bar rectification. It was held a major interest had been granted.

Customs generally take the view that only a formal grant of the legal lease can be a major interest. Thus if a taxpayer enters into an agreement for a lease for over 21 years but never grants a formal lease, the supplies may be exempt, even though the taxpayer may have constructed the building (dwelling). Nevertheless the law in this area is not clear cut.

Major interest schemes

If a taxpayer wants to grant a major interest but the tenant only wants, say, a four-year lease, the taxpayer could:

(a) grant a lease of over 21 years (say, 22 years) to a company which then grants the four-year lease; or

(b) grant a lease of over 21 years (say, 22 years) to the tenant but give him an option to leave after four years (one could possibly have put and call options) (*see* Figure 14.3).

Figure 14.3:

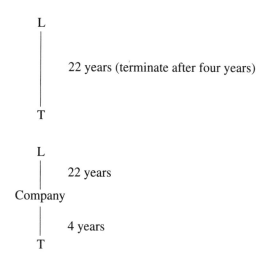

CLAW-BACK ON CHANGE OF USE

There are provisions in Sched 10, para 1 designed to ensure that if a taxpayer has received zero-rated supplies which relate to a building intended for use solely for a relevant residential purpose or a relevant charitable purpose, the benefit of that treatment is counteracted if that intention changes. These 'claw-back' provisions apply if within a period of ten years beginning with the date on which the building is completed:

Figure 14.4:   How zero-rating works on a typical domestic building development

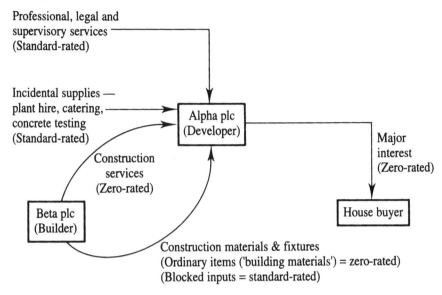

Note:
Alpha plc can claim back all the VAT charged to it except the VAT on the blocked inputs supplied to it by Beta plc.

(a) the property is let and is not intended to be used solely for a relevant residential purpose or a relevant charitable purpose any more; or

(b) the taxpayer who has received the zero-rated supplies uses a building or any part of it for a purpose which is neither a relevant residential purpose nor a relevant charitable purpose.

In the first situation, where the property is let, the supply, instead of being an exempt or zero-rated supply, would be a taxable supply and charged at the standard rate.

In the second situation ((b) *above*), there is a deemed disposal of the building for VAT purposes when the taxpayer first uses it for a purpose which is neither a relevant residential purpose nor a relevant charitable purpose.

There are two extraordinary aspects of this deemed supply. The first is that it relates only to a change of user with respect to 'relevant residential purpose' buildings and 'relevant charitable purpose' buildings. It does not apply to buildings designed as dwellings or a number of dwellings.

Second, the claw-back does not apply to a situation within Sched 8, Group

6. Thus, if a taxpayer receives a supply in the course of an approved alteration of a protected building which is zero-rated, and at the time when the supplies were received he intended the building to be used solely for a relevant charitable purpose or a relevant residential purpose after the works were carried out, then there will be no claw-back of the zero-rated treatment under Sched 10, para 1 if subsequently, for example, the taxpayer changes his mind.

Example

> X University builds an extension and this is an approved alteration under Sched 8, Group 6, Item 2. This is because the protected building which is extended is intended to be used solely for relevant residential purposes. If in later years the university decides to use the property not for relevant residential purposes (for example it may have been used for student accommodation but it may then be let to outsiders, eg delegates attending business conferences), then there is no mechanism to claw-back the zero-rating. It is difficult to see how the capital goods provisions, or the general regulation which enables claw-back after six years could be made to apply to such a situation. (See the 1995 Regulations, regs 99–111.)

TIME AT WHICH A GRANT IS MADE

There is no clear answer to the question of when a grant takes place for the purposes of Sched 8, Group 5, Item 1. On a simple reading of the legislation, the requirement is that there be a grant of the fee simple or a tenancy for a term certain exceeding 21 years, and thus a contract to sell the freehold is a contract to grant and not the grant itself. Again, a contract to grant a lease is a contract to make a grant and not the grant itself.

In the author's experience Customs have tended to look at the position in this simple fashion, and probably that is the correct position in law. The alternative argument is that, for many land law purposes, an agreement to grant a lease is as good as a grant and thus a taxpayer who enters into an agreement for a lease of over 21 years should be entitled to make a zero-rated grant even though a formal lease has not been executed.

Some support for Customs' view is to be found in *Margrie Holdings v The Commissioners* [1991] STC 80 where A contracted to sell land in Scotland to B who then sold to C. At p 85 the Lord President (Hope) stated:

> . . . there was no divestiture by (A) of their major interest in the land until they delivered the disposition (conveyance) to (C) and there never was a disposition of that interest at any stage in favour of (B).

'IN THE COURSE OF THE CONSTRUCTION'

To be zero-rated, supplies must be made in the course of the construction of a building.

Generally, Customs seem to take the view that a building can be completely constructed for these purposes when the owner or a lessee or licensee occupies it (*see*, however, p 190).

In the case of *Gazzard v The Commissioners* (LON/89/1391Y Decision 6029) the taxpayer had to carry out remedial works to a completed building. The tribunal chairman, Mr R H Widdows, at pp 5 and 6, stated:

> The (relevant work) was done as part of the construction of a new house in that (the builder) was called in to remedy some incomplete or defective work which should have been completed before the purchasers moved in. The fact that it was done afterwards, to meet a complaint, does not, in my opinion, prevent it from forming part of the work of the construction.

The author would tend to the view that if the construction of a new building has not been completed and there is a fire and a substantial amount of the building is destroyed, or indeed any part of the building is destroyed by the fire, the further works which have to be done to remedy the damage and complete the building would be zero-rated.

When does construction start?

If a person constructing a dwelling sells his freehold interest or grants a lease of over 21 years in or in any part of the building or its site the supply will be zero-rated.

On the other hand, if a taxpayer merely disposes of land which he has not developed, the supply will virtually always be an exempt supply subject to the election to waive exemption provisions.

If a developer starts the construction of the dwelling and disposes of it before completing construction, the disposal of the building and the site will constitute a zero-rated supply.

In the case of *Stapenhill Developments Ltd* (MAN/82/229) the taxpayer had dug a trench to contain the foundations of some houses, but had dug it in the wrong place and abandoned the project. The taxpayer had not even commenced the construction of a building. The tribunal held that to obtain zero-rating it was not necessary to complete the building. The tribunal, at p 16 stated that 'The operative word is "constructing" and not "a person who has constructed"'. The question is to be decided as a matter of substance and degree whether or not, on the facts of the case, what had been done on the land was sufficient to bring the work within the ambit of the expression. The tribunal held that it was only necessary that the building must be seen to be under construction at the time of the disposal.

Thus if the vendor makes a *bona fide* start to the project before sale because, for instance, there is a delay in the sale but the vendor, who must be a developer or builder, wishes to start the project straightaway because 'time is money', zero-rated supplies will result from the sale (*see* however *R v IRC, ex p Harrow London Borough Council* [1983] STC 246 and the *Taxation of Land Development* (Butterworths) 1985 footnote 3 on p 257).

In *LCC v Marks & Spencer Ltd* [1953] AC 536 a company, on 16 June 1938, applied to the London County Council under the Town and Country Planning (General Interim Development) Order 1933, for permission to erect certain buildings in accordance with the terms of a building agreement relating to a site on which other buildings were standing. Permission was granted, by letter dated 9 August 1938, for the erection of the buildings, subject to the condition that the work should be commenced within 18 months failing which the consent was to become void, and subject to five further conditions. No reason was ever given for imposing the conditions. In 1939 the company entered into a contract with a firm of contractors for the demolition of the existing buildings on the site. This work was completed before August 1939, but no contract for the erection of the new buildings was entered into before war broke out in September 1939. The company never abandoned the intention to erect the buildings but nothing more was done until November 1948, when it notified the council that it was proposing to proceed with their erection. The council, purporting to act under the Town and Country Planning Act 1947, refused to sanction what was described as development of the site. The company thereupon applied to the Central Land Board for exemption from the payment of development charge. The application was refused. The House of Lords held that the words:

> 'works for the erection ... of a building' in s 78(1) of the Town and Country Planning Act 1947, meant, in relation to the present case, the totality of the works on the site necessary to carry out the building project authorised in 1938, beginning with the work of demolition, and did not refer only to building operations of a constructional nature and ... that the words 'decided to the contrary' in s 10(3) of the Town and Country Planning Act 1932 means 'decided not to grant the application unconditionally'.

Accordingly, before 1 July 1948, the appointed day under the Act of 1947, the company had begun but not completed works for the erection of the building and, under s 78(1) of the Act of 1947, it was deemed to have a valid planning permission for the works, on the footing that, since no reasons for the imposition of the conditions attached to the permission of 9 August 1938 had ever been given, then, under s 10(3) of the Act of 1932, the council must be deemed to have granted unconditional permission for the completion of the works. Thus the company was entitled to complete the building without further permission of the local planning authority and without payment of a development charge.

The works, for VAT purposes, should comprise the construction of the whole or part (preferably the whole) of the foundations of the building plus some actual brick work which will comprise part of the building itself. Hence the common reference to 'VAT bricks', which bricks can in appropriate cases be worth their weight in gold especially if the developer or builder must make a zero-rated supply in order to claim back, for instance, the VAT charged on a project manager's fee, legal fees etc made to him in connection with the project and the site acquisition and sale.

Guidance on this point is to be found in the proceedings of Standing Committee G on the Finance Bill 1989, where Mr Lilley stated:

> Construction . . . commences when on the particular facts a meaningful and ongoing start has been made to the construction process. Customs will be looking for good evidence of such a start, and also evidence, for example, that planning permission has been obtained and building contracts let.

The author does not feel that trench works (where the land is held as an investment) will, in the normal course of events, result in an appropriation of the land to trading stock for Schedule D Case I purposes (*see Hudson's Bay Co Ltd v Stevens* 5 TC 424 at 437, *CH Rand v Alberni Land Co Ltd* (1920) 7 TC 629 at 638, *Pilkington v Randall* (1966) 42 TC 662 at 672 and *The Alabama Coal, Iron, Land and Colonisation Co Ltd v Mylam* (1920) 11 TC 232 at 253).

The commencement of the works may, in appropriate cases, bring the situation within TA 1988, s 776(2)(c) (*see Winterton v Edwards* [1980] STC 206 at 217d and *see* s 776(7)).

Tax planning: 'the golden brick'

When land is being disposed of by a builder or developer he should see whether this would give rise to an exempt VAT supply. If that is the case he should see whether it is possible to make a *bona fide* start on the construction of the project building and foundations prior to the disposal in order to convert the exempt supply into a zero-rated supply. The option may of course be available, but this will require VAT at 17.5 per cent to be charged.

Before entering into any such transaction to mitigate VAT, the *Ramsay* doctrine (*IRC v Ramsay* [1981] STC 174) must be carefully considered if the development transactions are entered into exclusively to avoid tax and there is a pre-ordained scheme comprising a number of steps which enable tax to be avoided (*see* Chapter 5).

Break in the works

If a taxpayer has completed a building and then does new works, the later works will be taxable as they will not have been done 'in the course of the construction' of the building. In *Total Protection (Western) Ltd* (LON/94/1838P Decision 12945) it was held that a time gap between the works of two years was fatal.

Customs' view is to be found in Leaflet 708, para 7, which read as follows:

7.1   General

It is a matter of fact when a building has been completed. This is normally when it has been finished to the original plans. In cases of doubt, a building can be regarded as still under construction up to date of the certificate of completion, or when contracts have been completed and all building regulations complied with. The date when a building is occupied may also be an indication if any of the above indicators cannot be relied on.

Where a new dwelling has been completed any further works done to the building, such as the addition of a conservatory, will be standard rated.

7.2   Staged occupation

Where a new building is occupied in stages, 'first occupation' will apply to the occupation of any part of it. For example, occupation of the ground floor of a block of flats or other qualifying building three months before the upper floors are fitted out will not prevent you from zero-rating the work on the upper floors.

Civil engineering works

In *Rannoch School Ltd* (EDN/90/217 Decision 6784) the taxpayer had been required under planning law to build a new separate sewage system for a new accommodation block which was to be built at the school. The Commissioners said that the installation comprised replacement sewage works. Thus the works were civil engineering works and zero-rating was not applicable. Zero-rating applied only to a supply made in the course of the construction of a residential building. The tribunal held that the supply of services in the course of construction of a building could include services of a civil engineering nature. The civil engineering services were supplied in the course of construction of the new block at the school. The services of the engineering contractors were supplied at the same time as, or shortly after, the block was constructed, and the block could not be occupied until the plant was installed. The Commissioners' appeal at the Court of Session was refused (*The Commissioners v Rannoch School Ltd* [1993] STC 389).

If X (developer) owns the freehold of Blackacre and commissions Y (builder) to construct a new building (dwelling) and various civil engineering works on the site, Y's supplies will be zero-rated with regard to the dwelling and vatable at 17.5 per cent with regard to the civil engineering works (unless the case comes within the *Rannoch School* decision, *above*, or Customs treat it as part and parcel of the construction of the dwelling). Works of demolition, as a matter of strict law, will generally be vatable at 17.5 per cent (but *see below*). When X sells the dwelling and its site (which would include the civil engineering works) it is arguable that it will make a zero-rated supply because X is selling a new building with its site, or the composite supply doctrine applies; there is no zero-rating as such on the sale of a civil engineering work. Such sales are in general either exempt or vatable at 17.5 per cent.

DEMOLITION

Works of demolition will always be vatable at 17.5 per cent unless done in the course of the construction of a dwelling or other qualifying building or work (Notice 708, para 9.1).

ESTATE ROADS

If the builder puts in new estate roads in a housing estate he must charge VAT unless Customs agree it is part and parcel of the construction of the zero-rated estate (*see* Notice 708, para 2.3). When the developer sells the dwellings with the rights to use the roads, the sales are likely to be zero-rated under the composite supply doctrine, or as comprising part of the site of the building, and the VAT charged (if any) on the civil engineering works (estate roads) can be reclaimed.

EXEMPTION

If the disposal of a domestic building does not qualify for zero-rating, it will be exempt. The option provisions will not be available.

Example

> X sells a dwelling which he did not construct. The supply is exempt. If he had sold an old office, the supply would be exempt but the election to waive exemption would have been available.

PRELIMINARY CIVIL ENGINEERING WORKS—NOT ENOUGH

In *Permacross Ltd* (MAN/94/878 Decision 13251) a developer carried out considerable site works preparatory to the construction of dwellings (including constructing a roadway) on his land and then sold the land. It was held the sale was an exempt supply as there was no building or part of a building on the site.

Chapter 15

Lease terms

When drafting residential leases the VAT position is simplified because the election to waive exemption cannot have the effect that VAT is charged on the rent etc.

SERVICE CHARGE

The view which Customs have consistently applied over the years is that if a service charge is imposed by the landlord on the tenants then the service charge will take on the nature of rents (*see* Notice 742, para 5.2). That rule applies to services provided for the upkeep of a building as a whole and so must extend to the external fabric and to the common parts of the building or estate.

Thus, if the landlord of a block of flats charges the tenants £100,000 rent (the rent would be exempt), plus £10,000 for repair works, plus a further £1,750 to recover the VAT charged to him by the builder who did the repairs (the builder having charged the landlord £10,000 plus £1,750 VAT), then the entire supply is exempt. The landlord does not give the tenant a VAT invoice and the landlord will not be able to reclaim the VAT charged to him by the builder.

The second arm of Customs' practice is that any services such as heating, lighting or cleaning supplied to a tenant's particular flat are regarded as supplies made to the tenant and are separate from the grant of a right to occupy the premises. VAT is therefore chargeable at an appropriate rate.

For example, a landlord has let four flats and he provides a service of cleaning the particular flat of Mr X who is one of the tenants. He must charge Mr X VAT on that cleaning service and provide Mr X with a VAT invoice (assuming the landlord is VAT registered). This is so even though the cleaning and upkeep of the common parts are exempt supplies (ie the landlord must not charge VAT on those supplies and he must not give the tenant an invoice).

In *Trustees of the Nell Gwynn House Maintenance Fund v The Commissioners* [1994] STC 995 (QBD) the tenants paid rent to the landlord and paid service charges to a separate trust which was responsible for repair work etc. It was held in the High Court that the trust had made a separate vatable supply to the tenants. It was not possible to apply the composite supply doctrine to the situation; nor could it fall within Customs' practice, then set out in para 10 of Notice 742(B). The Court of Appeal, however, [1996] STC 310 held that VAT was not chargeable under the VAT legislation on the amount of the service charge which was paid to cover staff costs; the trustees received no benefit from those reimbursements and they were non-vatable contributions (EC Sixth Directive, art 11A(3)(*c*)).

However, Customs published a valuable concession on 15 February 1994 (*Business Brief* 3/94, *see* also Notice 742, para 5.10). Under that concession they accept that the service charge supply in the case of domestic accommodation may be exempt even if the supply is made by a third party. The brief reads as follows:

Changes to Service Charges on Dwellings

An Extra-Statutory concession, effective from 1 April 1994, will exempt various mandatory service charges paid by the occupants for residential property from VAT.

The charges exempted are for the upkeep of the common areas of the estate or dwellings or blocks of flats, for the provision of a warden, superintendent, caretakers or people performing a similar function connected with the day to day running of that estate of dwellings or blocks of flats, and the general maintenance of the exterior of the block of flats of individual dwellings (eg painting and window cleaning) if the residents cannot refuse this.

Removal of anomaly
Service charges relating to the upkeep of the common areas of dwellings, or the common areas of a domestic dwelling if it is multi-occupied, are exempt from VAT under the general exemption for land, if they are paid by leasehold owners of property under the terms of the lease, or by people renting the property, and these charges are paid to the lessor or the ground landlord.

Previously service charges paid by freehold owners of domestic property, and by anyone for services which are not supplied by or under the direction of the lessor or ground landlord, have been taxable. This was because they could not be consideration for any supply of land.

This has led to an anomaly for the occupants of residential property, since the liability of the service charges they pay towards the upkeep of the common area does not depend on the services provided, but instead on the tenure of their residence and on the status of the supplier.

The new concession means that the liability of the service charge will no longer depend upon the tenure of the residence or on the status of the supplier. What will be important is whether each resident is obliged to accept the service because it is supplied to the estate of buildings or blocks of flats as a whole.

Optional services supplied personally to a resident, such as carpet cleaning and shopping continue to be taxed in their own right.

Non-domestic property and holiday accommodation
This extra-statutory concession does not affect the VAT treatment of service charges paid by the occupants of non-domestic property such as shops, offices, industrial units etc, which will continue to depend on the tenure of occupation, on the status of the supplier and on whether any landlord supplying the service has elected to waive exemption in relation to the property by taking the option to tax.

It also does not affect the VAT treatment of service charges paid in respect of holiday accommodation which remain standard rated.

SUPPLIES TO DEMISED PREMISES

If supplies are made to demised premises they should be split up.

In *Richard Haynes Associates v The Commissioners* (LON/92/2594 Decision 12300) the taxpayer built a flat and sought to reclaim input tax on the basis he would be making exempt supplies (rent) and vatable supplies of laundry, shopping and secretarial services. The tribunal held the services had to be apportioned from the rent, and the amount of input tax reclaimed had to be calculated on that basis, following *Customs and Excise Commissioners v Briararch* [1992] STC 732.

There has been a number of cases dealing with this area (*Sovereign Street Workspace Ltd* (MAN/91/403), *Clovelley Estate Co Ltd* (LON/91/1356X) and *Business Enterprises (UK) Ltd* (LON/89/90).

In *First Base Properties Ltd* (Decision 11598) the landlord let furnished office accommodation to tenants and charged £15 per square foot for rent and £40 per square foot for services (eg telephone, fax, copying, use of furniture). The tribunal held the supplies were separate: there was no composite supply.

Chapter 16

Development schemes (domestic buildings)

This chapter looks at a number of property development situations and the present VAT rules applicable thereto.

TYPES OF DEVELOPMENT SCHEME

Developers may enter into the following types of arrangement with institutions and landowners.

(1) *Buy and sell:* A developer (D Ltd) contracts (ie enters into binding contracts to purchase) and completes (ie has the freehold title vested in his name) the purchase of land from the vendor (V Ltd) and then contracts and completes the sale of the land to the ultimate purchaser (UP Ltd) without having carried out any development works. That would be an exempt transaction (Sched 9, Group 1, Item 1) although the option to waive exemption is available unless the situation falls within Sched 10, para 2(2) to (3AA).

Figure 16.1:

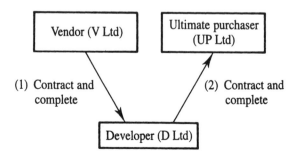

(2) *Buy and sell, then undertake work:* It may happen that the developer (D Ltd) of the land, after having disposed of the property entirely to UP Ltd—under contract and with completion—will enter into a contract undertaking to construct a building thereon. In this event, the only way the development profit to be obtained by D Ltd can be zero-rated is if it comes within Sched 8, Group 5, Items 2, 3 or 4. This it should normally do. Item 1 can have no application. The land sale by D Ltd will be exempt, although the option to waive exemption will generally be available.

Figure 16.2:

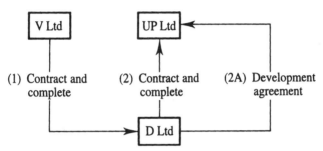

(3) *Buy, contract to sell, execute works and then complete:* Customs generally consider the date of 'grant' (for the purposes of Sched 8, Group 5, Item 1) to be the date when formal legal completion takes place. D Ltd may purchase land under contract and complete. It may unconditionally contract to dispose of the land to UP Ltd and at the same time undertake to put a domestic building on the land and to complete the sale only when the building is put up. In this case the 'grant' would take place after the building has been put up by D Ltd so that D Ltd would appear to come within Sched 8, Group 5, Item 1. The option cannot be exercised because of Sched 10, para 2(2).

Figure 16.3:

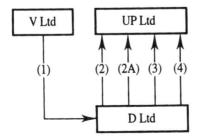

(1)   Contract and complete (to purchase)
(2)   Contract (to sell)
(2A)   Development agreement
(3)   Development completed
(4)   Complete sale of freehold

(4) *Sub-sell and then execute works:* If D Ltd were to purchase the property by way of exchange of contracts and complete in the name of UP Ltd direct, after having contracted to sell to UP Ltd, the supply of the land to UP Ltd would appear to be exempt. If completion is the relevant date, however, it appears that it may be that the land never belonged to D Ltd because it never completed the purchase in its name. In this event the transaction could be ignored for VAT purposes; the alternative and, it is felt, correct interpretation (*see* p 95), however, is that the supply is an exempt supply so affecting D Ltd's VAT recovery position. The developer's profit for putting up the domestic building could be made to be zero-rated in the usual way.

Figure 16.4:

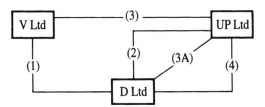

(1)   Contract to purchase
(2)   Contract to sell
(3)   Complete (legal)
(3A)   Development agreement
(4)   Development completed

VAT TRAP ON SUB-SALE?

The situation may arise where X Ltd owns freehold land. It agrees to sell the land to Y Ltd after Y Ltd has constructed a new domestic building on it. Y Ltd will be the person constructing the building for the purposes of VAT. Y Ltd, having virtually completed the works, then contracts to sell the land and the completed building to Z Ltd. When the works are completed formal legal completion takes place, with X Ltd transferring the freehold to Z Ltd.

On the face of it, it appears that no zero-rating is available. X Ltd could not obtain zero-rating because it was not the person constructing the building. Y Ltd could not obtain zero-rating because it did not grant the major interest; Customs may take the view that for there to be a grant of a major interest it is necessary for the formal legal title to be granted (eg a legal lease or the transfer of the formal freehold estate).

However, it seems from Sched 10, para 8 that if the benefit of the grant accrues to the person constructing the building, zero-rating will be available (to Y Ltd). Because the paragraph (in effect) refers to the benefit of the consideration for the grant going to the person constructing the building, it *seems* to be necessary (some may argue, although it is unlikely Customs will take any point in this respect) that the entire consideration paid by Z Ltd goes to Y Ltd, even though Y Ltd may be under a further obligation to pay the monies or part thereof to X Ltd (*see* Figure 16.5, *below*).

A similar type of situation can arise where X Ltd has vested the freehold estate of his land in Y Bank plc, or in the name of another company, with the bank or that other company being mere nominees of X Ltd. When X Ltd has constructed the building on the land and disposed of it, directing the nominee to transfer the legal estate into the name of the purchaser, zero-rating would be available to X Ltd because of para 8 of Sched 10.

Figure 16.5:

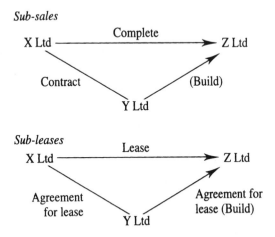

If, in the first part (sub-sales) of the example in Figure 16.5 *above*, instead of there being a deal under which the freehold is to be disposed of, X Ltd were to agree to grant a lease to Y Ltd and Y Ltd directed that X Ltd grant the formal lease to Z Ltd with Y Ltd taking a cash sum on the transfer of the rights to Z Ltd, Customs may argue that Sched 10, para 8 is not available because the benefit of the consideration has not gone to Y Ltd; only part of the consideration has gone to Y Ltd, with another part, in the form of rents, being paid to X Ltd. The paragraph requires in effect that the benefit of the consideration goes to the person constructing the building. There is nothing in the Interpretation Act to say that a reference to the whole shall include a reference to part. It is a question of construction and intent of the legislation. There is no reference in the paragraph to the whole of the consideration having to go to the person constructing the building. Clearly leases are conceived of as being within the paragraph. The author feels that there is a good case that the relevant consideration, which goes to the person constructing the building, is zero-rated even though part may go elsewhere (to X Ltd in the example, in the form of exempt rents).

Often taxpayers fall into VAT traps because negotiations over domestic property development agreements and projects extend over long periods, with variations and amendments to documents being made without the parties realising that the original structure did not give rise to VAT problems, but that the ultimate structure does.

Example: Developer relegated to supervisory role

X may want to employ Y as a developer. Draft documents are prepared, but gradually X feels concerned about the abilities of Y to do the job. Ultimately the situation is that X feels that it should do more of the work and ends up employing the builder direct, with Y (the developer) being more of a supervisor. It may be in this case that monies paid to Y are vatable, as Y is a person acting in a consultancy or supervisory capacity.

Example: Corporation tax group companies

A corporation tax group of companies (A and B) may negotiate with X (a landowner) to act as developer (company A in the group) and builder (company B in the group).

After many months of negotiation the documents are executed, with X employing both B and A direct, instead of X employing only A who in turn employs the builder. In this case A is exposed in VAT terms and would appear to be a person acting as a consultant, or at least a person acting in a supervisory capacity, hence making vatable supplies.

IDENTIFYING THE DEVELOPER

The developer's profits on the construction of a new domestic building are generally zero-rated.

It is critical that the real developer (the person constructing the building) is clearly identified and property transactions correctly analysed.

Example: VAT and the developer

> X Ltd introduces Blackacre to Y Ltd and it is agreed that Y Ltd will develop the land and dispose of it to Z, with X Ltd taking 30 per cent of the profit. Y Ltd's supplies would be zero-rated (because it is the grant of a major interest in a new building (dwelling)), but X Ltd should charge Y Ltd VAT on its 30 per cent profit as it is possibly no more than an introduction fee. (X Ltd's only chance of avoiding the VAT charge is under VATA 1994, Sched 10, para 8 (*see* p 142)). If it has omitted to provide for this in the agreement it will be treated as having charged a VAT inclusive figure. Y Ltd would normally be able to claim back the VAT charged. X Ltd will have 'lost' $\frac{7}{47}$ths per cent of its profit.

The developer is generally the person constructing a building. The Commissioners extend this to a person who commissions the construction of a building, ie a person to whom supplies of construction services are made and who exercises some measure of control over the construction of the building (Notice 708, para 15.2).

The term 'person constructing a building' does not, however, include a person who merely grants a lease or licence to another person to enter on to his land for the purposes of constructing a building.

Example

> L grants a lease to T of bare land. T constructs dwellings on the land.
> T is the person constructing the building; L is not.

The VAT tribunal, in *Hulme Educational Foundation v The Commissioners of Customs and Excise* (1978) VATTR 179 at 189, construed the words 'a person constructing a building' as follows:

> In our opinion, the normal meaning of these words means that a person must either himself construct the building in the sense of putting brick upon brick or stone upon stone, or must himself or by an agent enter into a contract or arrangement with another under which that other puts brick upon brick or

stone upon stone. In other words the construction must be physically done by the person concerned or by his servants or agents or the person concerned must himself directly enter into a contract or arrangement for another to do the physical construction works.

In *Hulme*'s case, to simplify the facts, the landlord let property to a tenant with the tenant employing the builder. The builder carried out works for the tenant and not for the landlord. The VAT tribunal held that the landlord was not the person constructing the building just because it retained certain powers to approve relevant plans and specifications or to supervise actual building works. The tribunal felt that such powers are the normal precautionary powers one would expect to see retained by a freeholder when a tenant of his was arranging for construction works to be carried out.

In the case of *Monsell Youell Developments Ltd v The Commissioners of Customs and Excise* (1978) VATTR 1, X Ltd acted as developer arranging for the construction of a building on the land of Y Ltd. Both companies were members of the same corporation tax group but were not members of the same VAT group because there was no group registration. The tribunal held that X Ltd was the developer, so that when Y Ltd disposed of the land, that was no zero-rated supply because Y Ltd was not the person constructing the building. The tribunal stated, at p 9:

> The documentary evidence, such as the invoice in respect of building costs, the contract and special conditions, the National House Building Council agreement and the specifications all emphasise the separate functions of Y Ltd (the landowning company) and X Ltd (the construction company). The invoice is issued by X Ltd, the contract provides that Y Ltd will sell the land and X Ltd will build the house, the specification refers to the contractor (X Ltd) and the house purchaser's agreement is between the registered builder, X Ltd and the purchaser.
>
> In our view, to find that the functions performed by Y Ltd that consist basically of the purchase of land, the design of the houses to be built thereon and the provision of roads and sewers are those performed 'by a person constructing a building' would be to ignore the substance and reality of the matter, and strain the ordinary use of the English language.

The reference to the documentary evidence (the invoice, etc) is important as it is clear that such matters can have great significance in determining which taxpayer was the person constructing a building for the purposes of making zero-rated supplies for VAT.

It is just possible that the courts would give a narrow meaning to the words 'person constructing a building', restricting the term to a builder as opposed to a developer, who in a sense may be said to supervise the builder. In an old bankruptcy case (*Stuart v Sloper* 1849 3 Exch Rep 701) Rolfe B, at 704, stated:

this man . . . is not a builder unless the taking of these pieces of land and employing builders to build on them makes him a builder. Now, with all deference, if it is supposed to have been laid down by the Court of Bankruptcy that, under any circumstances, that creates a man a builder, I confess I have considerable doubt on that subject. If a man gained his entire livelihood by looking out for what would be the most convenient place near London upon which to build, and purchased the ground, and then employed builders to build upon it, although that would make him a jobber and speculator in houses, I very much doubt whether it would make him a builder. The plaintiff did not become liable under the laws as a builder, because he took these lands and built upon them; for although that might make him a speculator, and bring him within the mischief intended to be remedied by the bankruptcy laws, I think it does not make him a builder, as at present advised. However, that question does not arise here, because, in this case, the jury have found that what was done was not a part of a general system. This gentleman took a lease of the land, and profitably employed that land by causing houses to be built upon it by others. It is impossible to contend that that makes him a builder, within any meaning that can be given to the bankruptcy law.

In the author's opinion it is clear that a taxpayer can be a person constructing a building for the purposes of Sched 8, Group 5, Item 1 even though he is not the person who actually puts brick upon brick. A gang foreman on a building site may not actually put brick upon brick yet it could hardly be denied that he is a person who is carrying out activities which comprise the construction of the building. It is equally clear that if a landowner merely employs a builder to construct a building on his land and does nothing except check on the builder as the works are carried out and use the end product, the landowner would not be a person constructing a building. However, a developer who supervises the builder and all the other professionals involved in arranging for the building to be constructed can be said to be a 'person constructing a building' in the author's opinion, as a matter of law, if he plays such an important role that his intervention in the building process is significant in determining the final outcome of the building programme.

For instance, if the developer (the term developer is not a term of art) is closely involved with the works carried out by the builder (visiting the site and directing how things should be done) then the developer effectively intervenes in the building process and becomes part of that process, and hence can be said to be a person constructing a building. The fact that he may be called a 'supervisor' is not disadvantageous, and indeed may prove positively advantageous because of the contrast between the wording of Items 1 and 2 of Group 5 in Sched 8.

It may be, therefore, that if X owns land and he acts as developer to develop his own land with Y the builder, then X and Y are persons constructing a building. It is sufficient that X is one of the persons constructing the building and it is not relevant that Y may also be a person constructing a building with regard to Sched 8, Group 5, Item 1: X can make a zero-rated supply if he grants a major interest in or an interest in any part of the building or its site.

Note: The express exclusions in Sched 8, Group 5, Item 2 indicate that the term 'person constructing a building' has a wide meaning in Item 1.

DEVELOPMENT AGREEMENTS

Development agreements may take many forms and it is vital that VAT is taken into account when drafting them.

In a typical situation, X (Developments) Ltd (the developer) contracts to purchase land and sub-sell it to Z for, say, £1m. At the same time the developer enters into a development agreement with Z under which the developer agrees to arrange for the construction of a residential block on the site ultimately receiving from Z, say, £3m for those works. The developer would employ the builder and all consultants and advisers to ensure that the construction of the building is completed.

On the sub-sale of the land for £1m to Z, the developer makes an exempt VAT supply, although the option to waive exemption is in general available. Stamp duty may be mitigated by virtue of the sub-sale relief provisions (Stamp Act 1891, s 58(5)).

If, instead of sub-selling the land, the developer buys it outright and gives Z an option to purchase it when the building is completed, the disposal of the land and the building would be a zero-rated supply, although substantially more stamp duty may be payable (*see* Figure 16.6).

The supplies by the builder to the developer will be zero-rated (Sched 8, Group 5, Items 2 and 4), although supplies such as consultancy and legal services will be vatable and so will be 'blocked inputs' (*see* p 88). The supplies by the developer to Z in return for the £3m should be zero-rated supplies, but the developer cannot reclaim VAT charged on the 'blocked inputs' (*see* p 88).

If the development agreement provides that the developer is to receive an extra sum if it finds tenants for the premises, the VAT position is unclear. Much depends on the precise form of the deal and how the documentation is worded. Customs may contend that the extra sum is a payment for what is, effectively, estate agency work and vatable under general principles (VATA 1994, ss 1 and 2(1)), although Customs seem now to have lost interest in this point.

Figure 16.6:

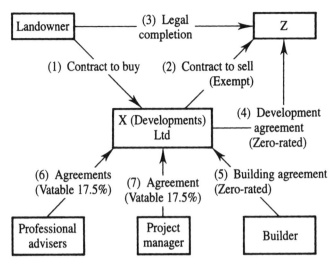

In the author's opinion, if Z and the developer simply appoint independent estate agents to find tenants, and there is no obligation on the developer to find tenants, and the additional sum is a payment for construction works payable if and only if a tenant is found, the supply is zero-rated.

If the developer is under an obligation to Z to use its best endeavours to find tenants and, as is usual, it appoints independent agents to do so on its behalf, Customs may have a case (if they sought to argue it) that the additional sum, or part thereof, is vatable.

Sometimes the payment to the developer is dependent on a successful letting. He will ultimately receive the payment, and it is often called a balancing payment. A suitable VAT clause in respect of these payments might read thus:

> 'The balancing payment' is deemed to be exclusive of any value added tax chargeable thereon or in connection therewith so that if it shall be found that value added tax shall be chargeable thereon or in connection therewith such value added tax or an amount equal thereto shall be payable by the owners to the developer in addition to the amount of the balancing payments.

In summary, the principal points for purposes of VAT planning are, therefore:

(1) The purchase of land under contract and the sub-sale of it to an investor by a developer is an exempt supply although the option to waive exemption may be available. Developers should consider retaining ownership of the land until the building is completed or is in the course of construction (*see* p 189) (having previously given the investor a call

option), so that a zero-rated supply will be made when the building is completed and the formal legal sale takes place.

(2) The normal developer's profit should be zero-rated.

(3) If the developer is, additionally, taking on the obligation to find tenants he must give careful consideration to the VAT position although this is unlikely to give rise to problems in practice.

DESIGN AND BUILD CONTRACTS

X Ltd owns Blackacre. It pays Y (Designers) Ltd £50,000 to design a domestic building to be put on the land and pays Z (Builders) Ltd £500,000 to construct it. VAT will be chargeble on the £50,000 but not on the £500,000.

What is the position if Z (Builders) Ltd simply agrees to design and build the building for X Ltd for £550,000? The legal position is determined by the composite supply doctrine (*see* p 42). Very broadly, the test is whether in substance the main thrust of the supply was that of construction services. If so, then the entire supply will be zero-rated as construction services. All the supplies which necessarily follow from that supply are also zero-rated as construction services. Thus, if a building is to be built, it must first be designed. If the above test is satisfied, the entire supply by Z Ltd will be zero-rated even though part thereof related to design works (*see* Figure 16.7).

Customs Leaflet 708, para 10.1 states thus:

> A client may obtain the necessary design work for a building project from a contractor as part of a 'Design and Build' package deal with the contractor.
>
> Where the design, workmanship and materials are supplied by a contractor to his or her client under a 'Design and Build' lump sum contract without any separate identification of the part of the lump sum relating to the design element, the VAT liability of the design element will follow that of the building work. For example, where a new building project is concerned, if the building works supplied by the contractor are zero-rated the design is also zero-rated.
>
> This also applies where, within a lump sum design and build contract, the part of the lump sum for the design element is shown separately solely for internal analysis purposes by the two contracting parties. But if there is a separate supply of design or other similar professional services to a client, it is always standard-rated.

DWELLING HOUSE EXCHANGE SCHEMES

A house developer who constructs new dwelling houses may exchange those houses for old houses owned by purchasers (householders). It may be that the

Figure 16.7:

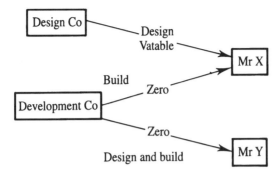

house developer would then sell the old houses to a land broker who would advance a percentage of the purchase price to the house developer and sell the houses as soon as possible. When the land broker sells the property further monies, depending on the price obtained, may be paid to the house developer.

The disposal of the old houses by the house developer to the land broker would be an exempt land supply. Also, the disposal by the land broker of each house would comprise an exempt supply. This means that the land broker could not reclaim VAT on any estate agency or other professional fees that the land broker is charged. If the land broker charged the house developer a separate fee for doing the work then, of course, he must charge VAT and any input tax on supplies made to the land broker with regard thereto could be reclaimed. However, the house developer would not be able to reclaim the VAT charged to him by the land broker because the input would have related to the exempt supply made by the house developer, ie the sale of the old houses.

Figure 16.8:

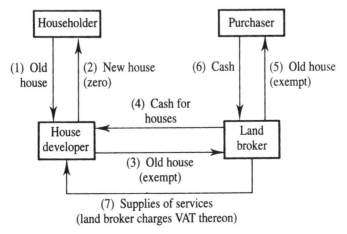

Chapter 17

Protected buildings

Special VAT reliefs apply to developers and builders in connection with protected buildings.

A new Group 6 of Sched 8 to VATA 1994 has been inserted in place of the old Group 6 by the Value Added Tax (Protected Buildings) Order 1995 (SI No 283) which came into force on 1 March 1995.

ZERO-RATED SUPPLIES

The following three supplies are zero-rated.

(1) The first grant by a person substantially reconstructing a protected building, of a major interest in, or in any part of, the building or its site.

(2) The supply, in the course of an approved alteration of a protected building, of any services other than the services of an architect, surveyor, or other person acting as consultant or in a supervisory capacity.

(3) The supply of building materials (as defined in Sched 8, Group 5, Note (22)) to a person to whom the supplier is supplying services within Item 2 of this Group which include the incorporation of the materials into the building (or its site) in question.

DEFINITIONS

Protected building

'Protected building' means a building which is designed to remain as or become a dwelling or number of dwellings, or is intended for use solely for a relevant residential purpose or a relevant charitable purpose after the reconstruction or alteration and which, in either case, is:

(a) a listed building, within the meaning of—

    (i) the Planning (Listed Buildings and Conservation Areas) Act 1990; or

    (ii) the Town and Country Planning (Scotland) Act 1972; or

    (iii) the Planning (Northern Ireland) Order 1991; or

(b) a scheduled monument, within the meaning of—

    (i) the Ancient Monuments and Archaeological Areas Act 1979; or

    (ii) the Historic Monuments Act (Northern Ireland) 1971.

Dwelling

A building is designed to remain as or become a dwelling or number of dwellings where, in relation to each dwelling, the following conditions are satisfied:

(a) the dwelling consists of self-contained living accommodation;

(b) there is no provision for direct internal access from the dwelling to any other dwelling or part of a dwelling;

(c) the separate use or disposal of the dwelling is not prohibited by the terms of any covenant, statutory planning consent or similar provision.

'Dwelling' includes a garage (occupied together with a dwelling) either constructed at the same time as the building, or, where the building has been substantially reconstructed, at the same time as that reconstruction.

Substantially reconstructed

For the purposes of Item 1, a protected building is not regarded as substantially reconstructed unless the reconstruction is such that at least one of the following conditions is fulfilled when the reconstruction is completed:

(a) that, of the works carried out to effect the reconstruction, at least three-fifths, measured by reference to cost, are of such a nature that the supply of services (other than excluded services), materials and other items to carry out the works, would, if supplied by a taxable person, be within either Item 2 or Item 3 of this Group; and

(b) that the reconstructed building incorporates no more of the original building (that is to say, the building as it was before the reconstruction began) than the external walls, together with other external features of architectural or historic interest.

In (a) *above* 'excluded services' means the services of an architect, surveyor or other person acting as consultant or in a supervisory capacity.

Where part of a protected building that is substantially reconstructed is designed to remain as or become a dwelling or a number of dwellings, or is intended for use solely for a relevant residential or relevant charitable purpose (and part is not):

(a) a grant or other supply relating only to the part so designed or intended for such use (or its site) shall be treated as relating to a building so designed or intended for such use;

(b) a grant or other supply relating only to the part neither so designed nor intended for such use (or its site) shall not be so treated; and

(c) in the case of any other grant or other supply relating to, or to any part of, the building (or its site), an apportionment shall be made to determine the extent to which it is to be so treated.

The taxpayer in *Barraclough v The Commissioners* (LON/86/699), had carried out works of alteration to listed buildings plus enlargements. The enlargements required listed building consent but the other works did not. It was held that there was no substantial reconstruction but only a minor enlargement of the building and a modernisation of its interior. To see whether the three-fifths test was satisfied one had to contrast the works of approved alterations with the total cost of reconstruction. The test was failed.

Approved alteration

'Approved alteration' means:

(a) in the case of a protected building which is an ecclesiastical building to which s 60 of the Planning (Listed Buildings and Conservation Areas) Act 1990 applies, any works of alteration; and

(b) in the case of a protected building which is a scheduled monument within the meaning of the Historic Monuments Act (Northern Ireland) 1971 and in respect of which a protection order, within the meaning of that Act, is in force, works of alteration for which consent has been given under s 10 of that Act; and

(c) in any other case, works of alteration which may not, or but for the existence of a Crown interest or Duchy interest could not, be carried out unless authorised under, or under any provision of—

    (i) Part I of the Planning (Listed Buildings and Conservation Areas) Act 1990,

    (ii) Part IV of the Town and Country Planning (Scotland) Act 1972,

    (iii) Part V of the Planning (Northern Ireland) Order 1991,

    (iv) Part I of the Ancient Monuments and Archaeological Areas Act 1979,

and for which, except in the case of a Crown interest or Duchy interest, consent has been obtained under any provision of that Part.

'Approved alteration' does not include any works of repair or maintenance, or any incidental alteration to the fabric of a building which results from the carrying out of repairs, or maintenance work.

Any works which affect the structure of a building except those of a minor nature, amount to alterations (*The Commissioners v Viva Gas Appliances Ltd* [1983] STC 819; *C N Evans* (MAN/88/587 Decision 4415). However, works of repair and maintenance will always be vatable.

Once it has been established that the works amount to works of alteration, it is then necessary to see whether listed building consent under Part I of the Planning (Listed Buildings and Conservation Areas) Act 1990 (as appropriate) is needed and, if so, to obtain it.

Thus, there is a three-point requirement:

(1) The works must amount to alterations (ie works on the structure of the building) apart from works of a minor nature and always exluding works of maintenance and repair.

(2) Listed building consent must have been required for the alterations.

(3) Listed building consent must have been obtained for the alterations.

Repainting a building would be a work of maintenance and repair. Putting in a new gas fired central heating system would be a work of alteration. Replacing a tiled roof which did not need replacing, with a new type of tiled roof, would be an alteration (*Morris v The Commissioners* (LON/83/341). Putting in new floors would be an alteration. On the other hand, if a part of the building which is in disrepair is replaced by something new which, very broadly, replicates that which was there before, that would amount to a work of maintenance and repair. In *R W Gibbs* (LON/89/1681 Decision 5596) it was held that the removal of asbestos and the replacement of pipe work in the roof of a listed building was not zero-rated. Works to stabilise a wall by inject-ing chemicals into it are not zero-rated (*B Cheeseman* (LON/90/1344 Decision 5133)).

The construction of a building separate from, but in the curtilage of, a pro-tected building does not constitute an alteration to the protected building (Group 6, Note (10)). This note reproduces a former note added to the group from 1 April 1989.

In *Bradfield* (LON/90/336 Decision 5339) (which was heard before the change in the law), X constructed a garage within the curtilage of a listed building. Listed building consent was required for the works. X argued that because the garage was within the curtilage of the listed building, its con-struction amounted to an alteration to the building.

Customs argued that the erection of the garage was not an alteration but the construction of a new building and that the grant of listed building consent by the local authority was not conclusive as to whether such consent was necessary (cf *Evans* (MAN/88/587) [1990] STI 159). The tribunal con-sidered itself bound by the High Court decision of *Cotswold District Council v Secretary of State for the Environment* (1985) 51 P & CR 139 where it was held that a free-standing structure within the curtilage of a listed building was not an alteration or extension to the building and so was not subject to listed building control. The construction of the garage was therefore outside the scope of zero-rating and the appeal of the taxpayer was dismissed.

APPORTIONMENT

Where a service is supplied in part in relation to an approved alteration of a building, and in part for other purposes, an apportionment may be made to determine the extent to which the supply is to be treated as falling within Item 2.

It has been noted that a protected building means a building which is designed to remain as or become a dwelling or a number of dwellings, or intended for use solely for a relevant residential purpose or a relevant char-itable purpose after the reconstruction or alteration (Sched 8, Group 6, Note (1)). The following example illustrates some areas requiring an apportion-ment to be made.

The example concerns a hall of residence for students. The use of res-idential accommodation by students is use for a relevant residential purpose (Sched 8, Group 5, Note (4)). The accommodation is used by students most of the time, but during the summer months it is let to visitors and other persons, so that the building could not be said to be intended for use solely for a relevant residential purpose. Let us say that the non-qualifying use is for one-tenth of the time and the qualifying use is for nine-tenths of the time.

On the face of it, the building is not a protected building and the builder must charge VAT on all the alterations whether approved alterations or not.

There are apportionment provisions in Note (6) and Note (9) to Group 6 of Sched 8 as mentioned *above*, but it is felt that they would not assist in this situation. In particular, Note (9) requires an apportionment between a service supplied in relation to an approved alteration of a building and for other purposes; this would mean non-approved alterations. The legislation nevertheless requires that the building be a protected building ie one used solely for a relevant residential purpose. Note (6), which apportions between repair or maintenance and approved alterations once again does not assist as it assumes the building is used solely for a relevant residential purpose.

Under the protected buildings provisions contained in VATA 1994, before the Value Added Tax (Protected Buildings) Order 1995 (SI No 283) came into effect on 1 March 1995, there was a specific reference in Note (2) (to the then Group 6) to Note (6) to the then Group 5 of Sched 8 to VATA 1994 (the then Group 5 has been replaced by the new Group 5 with effect from 1 March 1995 by the Value Added Tax (Construction of Buildings) Order 1995 (SI No 280)). The then Group (6) allowed an apportionment where part of a building was used for a non-qualifying purpose and the rest was used for a qualifying purpose. The new protected buildings provisions make no such reference to the relevant Note in Sched 8, Group 5; but they contain their own similar apportionment provision in VATA 1994, Sched 8, Group 6, Note (5), such that it is felt no apportionment problems will arise in this area. Note (5) of Group 6 reads as follows:

> (5) Where part of a protected building that is substantially reconstructed is designed to remain as or become a dwelling or a number of dwellings or is intended for use solely for a relevant residential or relevant charitable purpose (and part is not)—
>
> (a) a grant or other supply relating only to the part so designed or intended for purchase;
> (b) a grant or other supply relating only to the part neither so designed nor intended for such use (or its site) shall not be so treated; and
> (c) in the case of any other grant or other supply relating to, or to any part of, the building (or its site), an apportionment shall be made to determine the extent to which it is to be so treated.

NOTES IN GROUP 5

The following Notes to Group 5 apply to the protected buildings provisions as they apply to Group 5, subject to any appropriate modifications:

    (1) meaning of 'grant (*see* p 175);

    (4) 'relevant residential purpose' (*see* p 176);

    (6) 'relevant charitable purposes' (*see* p 177);

  (12) intended use (*see* p 178);

  (13) restrictions on user (*see* p 180);

  (14) first premium or rent zero-rated (*see* p 180);

  (22) building materials (*see* p 182);

  (23) installation as fittings (*see* p 183);

The above definitions are incorporated into the protected building provision from the construction of building provisions in Sched 8, Group 5 by Sched 8, Group 6, Note (3).

PART IV

COMMERCIAL BUILDINGS

Chapter 18

Election to waive exemption

In general, supplies of interests in land are exempt (VATA 1994, Sched 9, Group 1, Item 1). However, a taxpayer who makes an exempt land supply can elect to waive the exempt nature of the supply.

Assuming the supply is not exempt under another head, such as finance or education, the supply will be vatable, assuming the supplier is carrying on a business and is required to register for VAT (because his supplies exceed the registration limit for the time being), or is indeed registered for VAT. Thus it is not sufficient simply to waive exemption: one must see whether a vatable supply will ensue.

The election can only have the effect of causing an otherwise exempt grant under Sched 9, Group 1, Item 1, to cease to be exempt. There must be a grant of an interest in or right over or a licence to occupy land.

Thus if X proposes to sell a freehold or grant a lease or licence to occupy land or grant an easement over the land, then the supply, which would otherwise be exempt, may be treated as vatable if the taxpayer elects to waive exemption.

The expression 'grant' in Sched 9, Group 1 includes the surrender of a lease; since the case of *Lubbock Fine* (*see* p 321) it is clear that the surrender of a lease will give rise to an exempt land supply, and Note (1) to Group 1 to Sched 9 now specifically states that. If a taxpayer wishes to make a surrender into a vatable supply, he can elect to waive exemption.

Example

X owns the freehold of property. Z is the tenant. X elects to waive exemption, and therefore must charge VAT with respect to all grants of land interests which he makes. Z has not elected to waive exemption. If Z sells his lease or grants a sublease or surrenders his lease, the supply will be exempt. However, if Z elects to waive exemption, then assigns his lease or grants a sublease or surrenders his lease, a vatable supply is made by Z.

CIRCUMSTANCES IN WHICH THE ELECTION IS NON-EFFECTIVE

Schedule 10, para 2 provides that the election will not have effect if made in relation to the grant of:

(1) *land and buildings* by a developer with the intention or expectation that the land would become exempt land: this is a critical heading introduced by the Finance Act 1997 and is dealt with in Chapter 19;

(2) *dwellings etc:* a building or part of a building intended for use as a dwelling or a number of dwellings, or solely for a relevant residential purpose. Technically the taxpayer may be able to elect with respect to a dwelling house, for example, but the effect of the election would be nullified, ie, the supply will still be exempt (Sched 10, para 2(2)(*a*));

However, if a taxpayer has elected and that election may be disapplied because of the purchaser's intended use of the land for residential purposes, the supply will stay vatable if the following conditions under FA 1997, s 36(1) are satisfied:

(a) that an agreement in writing made, at or before the time of the grant, between:

(i) the person making the grant, and
(ii) the person to whom it is made,

declares that the election is to apply in relation to the grant; and

(b) that the person to whom the supply is made intends, at the time when it is made, to use the land for the purpose only of making a supply which is zero-rated under Sched 8, Group 5, Item 1(*b*).

(3) *charitable property:* a building or part of a building intended for use solely for a relevant charitable purpose, other than as an office (Sched 10, para 2(2)(*b*));

(4) *caravan pitch:* a pitch for a residential caravan (Sched 10, para 2(2)(*c*));

(5) *residential houseboat:* facilities for mooring a residential houseboat (Sched 10, para 2(2)(*d*)). 'Houseboat' means a houseboat within the

meaning of Group 9 of Sched 8 (Sched 10, para 3(7A)). A houseboat is not a residential houseboat if residence in it throughout the year is prevented by the terms of a covenant, statutory planning consent or similar permission (Sched 10, para 3(7A));

(6) *housing associations:* to a registered housing association where the association has given to the grantor a certificate stating that the land is to be used (after any necessary demolition work) for the construction of a building or buildings intended for use as a dwelling or number of dwellings or solely for a relevant residential purpose (Sched 10, para 2(3)(*a*)). A registered housing association means a registered housing association within the meaning of the Housing Associations Act 1985, or Part VII of the Housing (Northern Ireland) Order 1981 (Sched 10, para 3(8));

(7) *own-use dwellings:* to an individual where the land is to be used for the construction, otherwise than in the cause or furtherance of a business carried on by him, of a building intended for use by him as a dwelling (Sched 10, para 2(3)(*b*));

(8) *land and buildings to connected persons:* this restriction applies to grants made on or after 30 November 1994, but shall not have effect in relation to any supply made after 26 November 1996 (FA 1997, s 37(1)) (*see below* and pp 220–1).

The Value Added Tax (Buildings and Land) Order 1994 (SI No 3013) which came into force on 30 November 1994 inserted a new subpara (3A) into para 2 of Sched 10 to VATA 1994. The new subparagraph ensures that the election to waive exemption does not have effect with respect to certain grants made to connected persons where either of the parties—the grantor or the grantee— are not fully taxable persons.

The provision applies only to grants made on or after 30 November 1994.

Whether persons are 'connected' is determined by TA 1988, s 839. For example, under s 839(5) a company is connected with another company:

(a) if the same person has control of both, or a person has control of one and persons connected with him, or he and persons connected with him, have control of the other; or

(b) if a group of two or more persons has control of each company and the group or groups either consist of the same persons or could be regarded as consisting of the same persons by treating (in one or more cases) a member of either group as replaced by a person with whom he is connected.

Again, under s 839(6), a company is connected with another person if that person has control of it.

'Control' is determined by s 416 of TA 1988.

Finally, a person is a 'fully taxable person' if, at the end of the prescribed accounting period of his in which the grant is made, he is entitled to credit for input tax on all supplies to and acquisitions and importations by him in that period (apart from any on which input tax is excluded from credit by virtue of s 25(7) (these are specific supplies made to a taxpayer on which credit is denied by Treasury Order)).

Example

X elects to waive exemption and reclaims VAT on a major property development. X grants a lease, at market rent or less than market rent, to Y. Y is a company under the control of X and so is connected to X. Y is not a fully taxable person. The effect of the VAT (Buildings and Land) Order 1994 (VATA 1994, Sched 10, para 2(3A)) is that X has made an exempt supply and may have to repay input tax claimed on the project.

The following points should be noted in connection with this provision:

(1) It applies to all grants, whether of leases or otherwise.

(2) It applies only if the grant is made to a connected person, so it may be possible to avoid it if the parties are not technically connected within TA 1988, s 839.

(3) The provision applies only to leases granted on or after 30 November 1994 or other grants taking place on or after that date (*Business Brief* 22/94).

(4) The provision can be a dreadful trap for practitioners who may expect to make vatable supplies but end up making exempt supplies. On the other hand, it could be a saviour if a taxpayer wishes that he had never made the election, is not in a position to revoke it, and is happy to repay input tax rather than have to charge VAT on the sale.

Example

X is a land dealer. X acquires land and elects to waive exemption. X pays a small amount of VAT to various suppliers which he reclaims as input tax. He then receives an exceptional offer for the land, but the purchaser is not in a position to reclaim the VAT charged to him. It may be that X could ensure that the election is disapplied under VATA 1994, Sched 10, para 2(3A). Perhaps Customs unwittingly gave the taxpayer an option to avoid the election to waive exemption. X will have to repay his input tax unless relieved, eg under the 1995 Regulations, reg 108(3).

Note: the connected persons provisions do not apply in relation to any supply made after 26 November 1996.

EXERCISING THE ELECTION

There was a rule at one time that input tax could not be reclaimed if it related to a supply made to the taxpayer before the date the election had effect. That rule no longer applies (*see* Sched 10, para 2(4), (8)).

The present position is that no difficulties will arise if a taxpayer receives supplies and incurs input tax and intends to exercise the election to waive exemption, provided he does not make any exempt supplies before the election has effect.

If he does make exempt supplies but intends to exercise the election in the future, then the restrictions in Sched 10, para 3(9) must be considered. These provide that where a person who wishes to make an election in relation to any land has made an exempt grant out of the land before the day the election has effect, he cannot make the election unless he obtains the prior written permission of Customs.

Customs will give such permission only if they are satisfied, having regard to all the circumstances of the case, that it should be given. In particular, Customs will have regard to:

(a) the total value of the exempt grants in relation to the relevant land made or to be made before the day from which the person wishes election to take effect;

(b) the total value of grants relating to the relevant land that will be taxable were the election to have effect; and

(c) the total amount of input tax which has been incurred or is likely to be incurred in connection with the land.

Customs would then seek to secure a fair and reasonable attribution of the input tax to the grants in relation to the land which would be taxable; in so far as they are attributable to the taxable supplies the input tax can be reclaimed.

The author would anticipate that, if a taxpayer had incurred £100,000 worth of input tax and makes an exempt grant receiving rent of £10,000 and then exercises the election to waive exemption when his freehold property interest is worth £200,000, Customs would permit the election to be exercised with the taxpayer being able to claim back VAT of:

$$£100,000 \times \frac{200,000}{210,000} = £95,238$$

Customs will give 'automatic permission' if the conditions set out in a Customs Notice are satisfied. Thus if the conditions are satisfied the election will be effective even though the consent of Customs to the particular election has not been obtained.

Election now—getting back your input tax

A taxpayer may have simply refurbished a commercial building and used that building himself for an exempt purpose for a number of years. If he now exercises the election to waive exemption and lets the property, can he reclaim any of the VAT?

Part of the VAT might be reclaimable under what may be a special scheme agreed with Customs (*The Commissioners v UWCC* [1995] STC 611), but that may not produce a very satisfactory result as the exempt user rights may be taken into account. If the taxpayer makes some exempt grants, a more satisfactory result *may* be produced under Sched 10, para 3(9)—para 3(9)(*a*) refers to 'exempt grants' rather than 'exempt user'.

Recovery of input tax following election where exempt grants made and capital goods provisions apply

The High Court in *The Commissioners v R & R Pension Fund Trustees* [1996] SWTI 849 held that if a taxpayer has made exempt grants and thereafter the election to waive exemption applies and the property falls within the capital goods provisions, then the capital goods provisions are simply applied. This will require an annual adjustment of the input tax reclaim position (see p 266). One does not apply the 'fair and reasonable' formula set out in Sched 10, para 3. For the Customs' celebration of the victory see Business Brief 17/96.

Date on which election has effect

The election has effect at the beginning of the day on which it is made or on any later date specified in the election (Sched 10, para 3(1)(*a*)). Thus if the taxpayer makes the election on 1 January 1996, it will have effect on that date unless he specifies that it is to have effect on a later date, eg, 1 February 1996.

The election cannot be backdated. It can be effective only from the date allowed by the legislation (*Hi-Wire Ltd* (MAN/90/990)).

WHAT IS COVERED BY THE ELECTION

An election has effect in relation to any land specified in the election or land of the description specified in the election (Sched 10, para 3(2)).

Where an election is made in relation to any part of a building, or a building which is planned, it has effect in relation to the whole of the building, and all the land within the curtilage of the building.

Curtilage

The term 'curtilage' is difficult and vague. There are numerous cases, of varying degrees of assistance, on the meaning of the word. *See Pilbrow v Vestry of the Parish of St Leonard, Shoreditch* [1895] 1 QB 33 (Divisional Court) and 433 (Court of Appeal); *St-Martin-in-the-Fields Vestry v Bird* [1895] 1 QB 428; *Methuen-Campbell v Walters* [1979] QB 525; *Sinclair-Lockhart's Trustees v Central Land Board* 1951 SC 258; *Marson v London, Chatham and Dover Rly Co* (1868) LR 6 Eq 101; *Caledonian Rly Co v Turcan* [1898] AC 256; *Harris v Scurfield* (1904) 91 LT 536; *Weaver v Family Housing Association (York) Ltd* [1976] RA 25.

The term is not a term of art, but it is felt that the best guidance as to its likely meaning in the VAT legislation (on the basis that the term takes its meaning from the context in which it is used) can be derived from the following extract from the judgment of Buckley LJ in *Methuen-Campbell v Walters* [1979] QB 525 at 543–4:

> What then is meant by the curtilage of a property? In my judgment it is not sufficient to constitute two pieces of land parts of one and the same curtilage that they should have been conveyed or demised together, for a single conveyance or lease can comprise more than one parcel of land, neither of which need be in any sense an appurtenance of the other or within the curtilage of the other. Nor is it sufficient that they have been occupied together. Nor is the test whether the enjoyment of one is advantageous or convenient or necessary for the full enjoyment of the other. A piece of land may fall clearly within the curtilage of a parcel conveyed without its contributing in any significant way to the convenience or value of the rest of the parcel. On

the other hand, it may be very advantageous or convenient to the owner of one parcel of land also to own an enjoining parcel, although it may be clear from the facts that the two parcels are entirely distinct pieces of property. In my judgment, for one corporeal hereditament to fall within the curtilage of another, the former must be so intimately associated with the latter as to lead to the conclusion that the former in truth forms part and parcel of the latter. There can be very few houses indeed that do not have associated with them at least some few square yards of land, constituting a yard or a basement area or passageway or something of the kind, owned and enjoyed with the house, which on a reasonable view could only be regarded as part of the messuage and such small pieces of land would be held to fall within the curtilage of the messuage. This may extend to ancillary buildings, structures or areas such as outhouses, a garage, a driveway, a garden and so forth. How far it is appropriate to regard this identity as parts of one messuage or parcel of land as extending must depend on the character and circumstances of the items under consideration. To the extent that it is reasonable to regard them as constituting one messuage or parcel of land, they will be probably regarded as all falling within one curtilage; they constitute an integral whole.

Applying the above test, there would be included within a factory's curtilage all areas which enable it to function as a unit such as forecourts, parking bays and landscaped areas.

Buildings

For the purposes of this legislation, buildings linked internally or by a covered walkway, and complexes consisting of a number of units grouped around a fully enclosed concourse, are treated as a single building (Sched 10, para 3(3)).

It seems clear enough from VATA 1994, Sched 10, paras 2(1) and 3(3) that the taxpayer can elect with respect to a building or even a planned building.

For instance, a taxpayer elects with regard to building X which is situated in five acres of an industrial park (not within an enclosed concourse). If, in the future, building X is demolished, the election with regard to that building will not have any effect on the land on which it stood or on the rest of the five acres of the industrial park (Notice 742, para 8.5(b)).

But if the taxpayer elected in respect of the five acres of the industrial park, then all the land, and building X, would be incorporated in the election. In that event, if building X were demolished, the election would (in law) catch any new building and any supplies made with respect to that building, and indeed any other part of the taxpayer's land interests within the industrial park. For the Customs' practice see Notice 742, para 8.5.

NATURE OF THE ELECTION

Irrevocability

The election to waive exemption is irrevocable. That is the general rule and is contained in Sched 10, para 3(4). There are two important exceptions, however.

If less than three months have elapsed since the day on which the election had effect, the election may be revoked from the date it was made if three conditions are satisfied:

(a) no tax has become chargeable and no credit for input tax has been claimed by virtue of the election;

(b) no grant in relation to the land which is the subject matter of the election has been made which, by virtue of being a supply of the assets of a business to a person to whom the business (or part of it) is being transferred as a going concern, has been treated as neither a supply of goods nor a supply of services; and

(c) the person who made the election obtains the written consent of the Commissioners to the revocation.

The second circumstance in which the election is revocable is where 20 years have elapsed since the day on which the election had effect, and the person making the election obtains the written consent of the Commissioners to revocation. In such a case, the election is revoked from the date on which the written consent of the Commissioners is given, or such later date as they may specify in their written consent.

Personal to the elector

The election is irrevocable (subject to Sched 10, para 3(5), ie the three-month and 20-year revocation rights) with respect to the particular person who has exercised the option (Sched 10, para 3(6)) (*see Devoirs Properties Ltd* MAN/90/1061 (Decision 6646)). If he disposes of the property having exercised the election then of course he must charge VAT on the sale proceeds as well as on the rent. A purchaser, however, can look at the matter afresh. He does not have to exercise the option to charge VAT on the rents or any other supplies with respect to the building. But if he does not exercise the option then he may not be able to reclaim any VAT charged to him by the vendor.

Objection by tenant is of no avail

If the landlord elects and the tenant objects the election is still effective and irrevocable. In *Coachorse Property Management Ltd* (LON/91/1709 (Decision 7564)) the taxpayer company elected to waive exemption for specified ground-floor premises. The tenant objected to paying VAT on the rent and the company sought to revoke the election. The tribunal held that the irrevocability of an election was unqualified and it was within the powers of the EEC member states to provide that the election shall be unqualified. The election could therefore not be revoked.

NOTIFICATION

If the taxpayer makes the election, it has effect only if written notification of it is given to Customs not later than the end of the period of 30 days beginning with the day on which the election is made, or not later than the end of such longer period beginning with that day as Customs may in any particular case allow (Sched 10, para 3(6)(*b*)(i)).

In *Russell Properties (Europe) Ltd* (EDN/95/330 (Decision 14228)) the appellants purchased property from a vendor who charged VAT but had not properly elected to waive exemption and had also not notified the same to the Customs. At p 2 the tribunal chairman stated 'The procedure requires not only an election by the trader but also formal notification of that election to the Commissioners.'

Of course, if the taxpayer has made exempt supplies in connection with the land in question, he may need the consent of Customs before the election to waive exemption can be exercised (*see* p 221). Thus:

(a) the taxpayer must first make the election; and

(b) he must give written notification of it to the Commissioners within the relevant time limit.

When making the election in the first place the taxpayer must decide whether it is to have effect from the date it is made or from a future date.

The election itself is all-important. It has effect in relation to any land specified in it, or to land of a description specified in the election.

It is therefore quite clear that if the election covers Blackacre only, any notification of the election cannot extend to Blackacre and Greenacre unless the notification also has effect as an election.

Thus, if for instance X Ltd elects with regard to Blackacre and the secretary of the company notifies Customs of the election, but notifies Blackacre and Greenacre, then either the notification is treated as void because notification of the actual election made has not been given, or it is valid but only covers Blackacre. Under no circumstances can the mere notification have the effect of extending the election beyond Blackacre.

It is felt that Customs could not take the view that, because Blackacre and Greenacre have been notified, *ipso facto* the election related to Blackacre and Greenacre. If the election related to Greenacre only, then only Greenacre can be covered by the election and the notification cannot be valid at least as far as Greenacre is concerned.

However, if the notification is drafted in an extraordinary form so that it can also be construed as being an election, and it is sent by a person duly authorised, then the election and the notification may encompass both Blackacre and Greenacre.

In the case of *Devoirs Properties Ltd v The Commissioners* (MAN/90/1061 (Decision 6646)) the appellant company wrote to the VAT Office in the following terms:

> This is to inform you that from the rental quarter commencing 25th December 1989 we wish to charge VAT on our rental invoices (in respect of a particular property).

The question was whether that was an election to waive exemption.

At p 6 of the judgment, the Chairman, A Hilton, stated the following:

> The effect of this legislation is that where a taxpayer wishes to waive the VAT exemption relating to certain property he must make an election and notify the Commissioners in writing that he has done so. The Commissioners have indicated that written notice need not be given in cases where amounts involved fall below a certain figure but that is not germane to this appeal. The statutory provisions do not require the Commissioners to take any steps in order to complete the effect of the election. The only action required is that of the taxpayer.
>
> What I have to determine in this Appeal is did the taxpayer elect to waive the exemption to VAT which would normally apply, if so when was that election made and were the Commissioners informed. The statute does not require the election to be made in any particular form nor is it necessary to produce any such election to the Commissioners. They simply have to be told in writing that an election has been made. I find that the letter dated 6th November 1989 (as quoted above) . . . was notice to the Commissioners that the Appellant had elected to waive exemption relating to property and that it is also evidence of a decision to make that election. Once the Appellant had taken that step he could not resile from it and so VAT should have been charged on rents and any other outputs relating to the property concerned from the date of the election.

In *Resource Maintenance Ltd* [1995] STI 1023 a property developer wrote to the Customs stating its intention to elect that 'as from now the building is to be treated as taxable'. The letter claimed the company intended to reclaim VAT from 1 August 1989.

The taxpayer claimed the 'election' was only an 'intention' document. The tribunal held it was an effective election, especially as the company intended to reclaim VAT.

HOUSING ASSOCIATIONS

Housing associations, by providing a certificate within VATA 1994, Sched 10, para 2(3)(*a*), can prevent a taxpayer charging VAT on a supply.

A developer who has purchased land and been charged VAT, may have elected to waive exemption under Sched 10, para 2 and reclaim the VAT as input tax. If subsequently he sells the land to a housing association and the association gives the developer a certificate stating that the land is to be used for the construction of a building or buildings intended for use as a dwelling or a number of dwellings or solely for a relevant residential purpose, then the supply may be exempt. The developer will be required to repay to Customs the VAT he reclaimed, by virtue of the 1995 Regulations, reg 108; he has reclaimed input tax because he has attributed it to a taxable supply, but within the six-year period the goods or services in question, ie the land, have been used in making an exempt supply. The capital goods provisions will not be relevant because the land is trading stock—*see* reg 112(2).

One way out of this problem is if the taxpayer can make a zero-rated supply. It could be that the developer is intending to construct the relevant dwelling houses etc for the housing association.

He may contract to sell the land to the housing association, with the purchase price being paid and completion taking place after all the buildings have been put up. The housing association may well have received a grant within Sched 10, para 2(3)(*a*) when contracts are entered into, and may well provide the necessary certificate to the developer causing the grant, on the face of it, to be exempt.

However, 'grant' for the purposes of Sched 8, Group 5, Item 1 is likely to mean the date of legal completion (the contract to sell the land was merely an agreement to grant a major interest: see *Margrie Holdings v The Commissioners* [1991] STC 80 'at 85a). The documentation should be carefully drafted. Even though the grant, for the purpose of Sched 10, para 2(3)(*a*), may take place at the time the agreement was made and the housing association provided a certificate, the supply will be zero-rated so that the developer can keep the VAT charged to him when he acquired the land, and indeed he can reclaim all the other VAT charged in connection with the project (1995 Regulations, regs 101 or 102 if relevant).

Figure 18.1:   Housing Associations

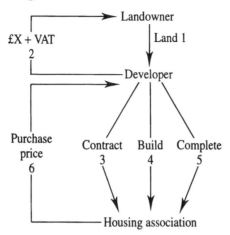

REGRETTING THE ELECTION

On many occasions taxpayers find that they have elected to waive exemption with regard to VAT and particular buildings, and come to regret having done so. When the election was made the amount of tax which could be reclaimed by virtue of the election may have been comparatively small, but the property, however, is then to be sold and VAT on the entire proceeds must be paid over to Customs.

There is one interesting route out of the election. If the person who had elected sells a building or part of a building *intended* for use as a dwelling or number of dwellings, or solely for a relevant residential purpose (eg student accommodation or a residential home for children, but not a hotel, inn or similar establishment), then VAT cannot be charged on the sale proceeds (VATA 1994, Sched 10, para 2(2)).

Thus, for example, X may have let property to Y to use as a hotel; X elected to waive exemption but now proposes to sell the property to Z. If the purchaser (Z) can show that the building or part of the building is intended to be used as a dwelling or a number of dwellings (eg he intends to convert the hotel into flats), then VAT cannot be charged on the sale proceeds. The sale will be an exempt land supply. The design of the building is not relevant; what is important is the *bona fide* intention to use it as a dwelling or a number of dwellings (*see* also p 218).

In *Watters* (LON/94/2980 Decision 13337) the election was disapplied where a public house intended to be used as dwellings was sold by a brewery.

Figure 18.2:

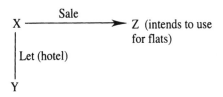

For the provisions in FA 1997, s 36 (buildings intended to be used as dwellings), which have effect from 19 March 1997, *see* p 218.

THE 'FENCING TRAP'

Taxpayers must be very careful before charging tenants or licensees VAT when they should not do so or they may find that they have inadvertently elected to waive exemption so that VAT becomes chargeable not only on the rents, but also when the property is sold (VATA 1994, Sched 10, para 2(1)).

In *Fencing Supplies Ltd v The Commissioners* (MAN/92/618 (Decision 10451)) the landlord was under the impression that he had to charge VAT as a matter of law on his rental receipts and accordingly charged it for a year or so. Subsequently, the landlord sold his reversionary interest. The VAT tribunal held that VAT was chargeable on the sale of the reversionary interest because the landlord charged VAT on the rent knowingly and with the intention of so charging; because there is nothing laid down in the legislation as to how an election can be made, such an intentional charge amounted to the exercise of the election to waive exemption (*see* Figure 18.3).

Figure 18.3:

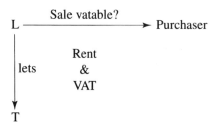

The chairman stated:

> since the Appellant (landlord) had no right to charge value added tax on the rents except by making an election . . . in my judgment by demanding and receiving value added tax on the rent, the Appellant was clearly indicating its decision that henceforth its supplies in relation to the property were no longer to be exempt from tax with the consequence, whether intended or not, that paragraph 2 (the election provision) and its associated paragraphs applied thereafter.

A decision along similar lines was reached in *Brollier Ltd* (MAN/93/556 (Decision 11966)).

It is provided in VATA 1994, Sched 10, para 3(6) that an election shall not have effect unless written notification of it is given to the Commissioners. That notification, however, can be given not later than either at the end of a 30-day period beginning with the day on which the election is made or the end of such longer period beginning with that day as the Commissioners may in any particular case allow. If the Commissioners find out about the election because VAT is charged, even though they may be so notified outside of the 30-day period, they have discretion to grant a longer period of notification.

The Customs in VAT Notice 742, para 9.6 (now withdrawn) state one must notify an election, except where the value of the supplies made with respect to the property covered by the option is expected to be less than £20,000 in the year ahead, and the taxpayer is not seeking to register for VAT on the basis of these supplies. Thus, if the taxpayer simply charged VAT (under the old practice) and his vatable supplies were less than £20,000 per annum, then he would have made an effective election and there was no need to notify and he was bound by the election. However, if a taxpayer has been charging VAT over the years without notifying the Customs of the election as such, and the supplies were £20,000 or more per annum, then the position is treated differently by the Customs.

On the basis of the *Fencing* decision above, the election will have been exercised, but the taxpayer will need to notify the Customs of that fact and request retrospective notification which the Customs may or may not grant. They will want details of the property, who it is rented to, what VAT charges have been made and what input tax has been reclaimed.

Technically the taxpayer will have made exempt supplies, and if the Customs refuse retrospective notification and the taxpayer wants to elect to waive exemption for the future, he will need the Customs' approval (which is the general rule where an election has been preceded by the making of exempt supplies).

ELECTIONS THAT BACKFIRE HORRIBLY

It is important for a company to realise that the election is made with respect, for example, to a particular building and this picks up all interests it owns or will own in that building. Thus, if X Ltd has elected to waive exemption and has a leasehold interest, supplies made in respect of that interest are vatable. If subsequently it acquires the superior leasehold interest in the same building, the supplies in connection with that superior interest will become vatable. That could prove an unpleasant trap (*see* Figure 18.4).

Figure 18.4:

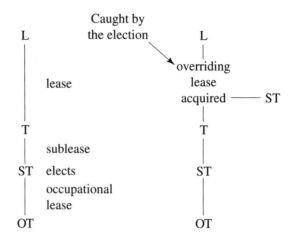

RELATIVE ASSOCIATE PROVISIONS

If a body corporate exercises an election to waive exemption with regard to a particular building, this will result in vatable supplies being made whether the building is held by the particular person who elected or by a relevant associate.

A relevant associate, in relation to a body corporate, means any body corporate which under s 43 of the Act:

(a) was treated as a member of the same group as the body corporate by which the election was made at the time when the election first had effect (Sched 10, para 3(7)(*a*));

(b) has been so treated at any later time when the body corporate by which the election was made had an interest in, right over or licence to occupy the building or land (or any part of it) (Sched 10, para 3(7)(*b*));

(c) has been treated as a member of the same group as a body corporate within para (a) or (b) *above*, at a time when the body corporate had an interest in, right over or licence to occupy the building or land (or any part of it) (Sched 10, para 3(7)(*c*)). *See* Figure 18.5.

VATA 1994, s 43 sets out the various companies which are eligible to be treated as members of a group, eg if one company controls the other. It is clear from s 43 that the expression 'group' means group for the purposes of VAT. In addition, s 43(4) states that where an application to that effect is made to the Commissioners with respect to two or more bodies corporate eligible to be treated as members of a group then from the beginning of the prescribed accounting period they shall be so treated.

It seems clear enough that if A, B and C are within the same corporation tax group but only A and B are within the same VAT group, C cannot be found to be in the same VAT group as A and B just because it is in the same corporation tax group, or just because it is eligible to be within the VAT group.

Thus, if A owned Greenacre, it is perfectly possible for A to transfer half of Greenacre to C, and for A to elect (this would catch the half interest held by A so that VAT will be chargeable on any supplies with respect thereto), but without that election in any way affecting the land interest held by C, ie any disposal of that land interest, assuming it is not a disposal of a new freehold building etc, will comprise an exempt supply for VAT purposes.

Figure 18.5a: Caught! Para 3(7)(*a*)

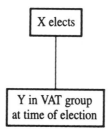

Figure 18.5b: Caught! Para 3(7)(*b*)

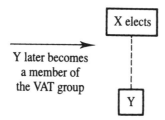

Figure 18.5c: Caught! Para 3(7)(*c*)

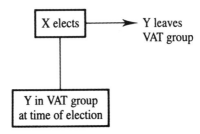

Figure 18.5d: Z is OK!

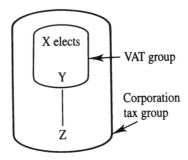

DOUBLE EXEMPTION

The exercise of the election to waive exemption only indirectly causes a VAT charge to arise. It is necessary to see if a VAT charge would arise if the exemption in VATA 1994, Sched 9, Group 1 did not exist. If so, then the effect of the waiver is to cause a VAT charge to arise under general principles—VATA 1994, ss 1 and 4. If the waiver, however, merely results in the supply being caught for exemption under another head—such as under finance or education—the election will have little relevance. The author has come across the point in connection with a students' hall of residence.

Special rules apply to residential accommodation for students. Under VATA 1994, Sched 8, Group 5, Note (4)(*d*), if a person constructing a building grants a major interest in residential accommodation for students then the supply may be zero-rated if the grant is *solely* for such use.

If it is not zero-rated, it may be necessary to decide whether such accommodation falls within Sched 9, Group 1, Item 1(*d*), ie 'the provision in a hotel, inn, boarding house, or similar establishment of sleeping accommodation' (*see also* Note (9) to Group 1).

If that is the case, the supplies will be vatable at 17.5 per cent. Exemption on the face of it, would not apply.

This point arose in the case of *Joseph McMurray, a Governor of Allen Hall v The Commissioners* (1973) 1 VATTR 161, where it was held that such accommodation was not similar to a hotel, inn or boarding house because:

(a) selectivity in the choice of residents was exercised;

(b) control over the students was exercised by the college;

(c) emphasis was laid on living a corporate, as opposed to an individual, existence while in residence: the students were part of the college as a body (p 166).

At pp 166 and 167 the tribunal said it had come to the conclusion that 'although there is similarity in the bare elements of board and lodging, the additional elements (referred to *above*) are not only dissimilar, but would be entirely foreign to life in a hotel or boarding house'. Thus such a supply would be exempt.

There is, however, a trap. In the case of *Joseph McMurray* it was held that the supply also fell within the exemption relating to the provision of education. Under that group the supply of education and of goods or services incidental to the provision of education is exempt (that group has been recast but the basic principle remains the same: *see* Chapter 9). It was held that the supply of such accommodation would also be exempt. The trap is that if the taxpayer exercises the election to waive exemption with respect to such accommodation in order to reclaim input tax he may find he has waived the Sched 9, Group 1 (land) exemption but the Sched 9, Group 6 (education) exemption still remains: the taxpayer should always formally check the situation, especially as there have been changes in the legislation since the *Joseph McMurray* decision.

ADDING VAT TO RENTS ON EXERCISE OF THE ELECTION

If the option is exercised the landlord can charge VAT on the rents otherwise payable (VATA 1994, s 89). If the property is let to, say, a finance house or a bank, it may be worth the tenant's while to pay a sum to the landlord so that he and his successors will not exercise the option. This is the 'bank's ransom' (or some may say 'a bank robbery'). The writer feels that it is unprecedented that the government has given one taxpayer (A) the right to impose tax on another (B), where in many cases no real detriment will arise to A if the tax is not imposed yet A can make a substantial profit from B if he agrees not to exercise the option. This is a feature of a tax system which is hardly to the credit of any government (*see* Figure 18.6).

If a bank, for instance, does pay the landlord not to exercise the option, it is critical that the obligation binds not only the landlord, but also all successors in title to him in respect of any interest in the land which he owns. If appropriate, the obligation must be made to accrue for the benefit of the bank and its assignees. It is safest to adopt a VAT inclusive clause.

Figure 18.6:   Bank ransom

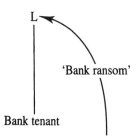

NB: The ransom payment is also vatable at 17.5 per cent.

REGISTRATION

The election is intertwined with the VAT registration provisions in VATA 1994, Sched 1. If a taxpayer elects with respect to a property, then any grant in relation to it (be it a sale or the grant of a lease) which would have fallen within Group 1 of Sched 9 to the Act, does not fall within that group (VATA 1994, Sched 10, para 2(1)).

Thus, if the taxpayer elects and the amount of his rentals, for example, does not put him above the registration limit in Sched 1, para 1, then he may not be required to register for VAT. Indeed if the taxpayer has registered he may even be able to cancel his registration under Sched 1, para 13.

Schedule 1, para 1(1) states that a person who makes taxable supplies but is not registered under the Act becomes liable to be registered at the end of any month if the value of his taxable supplies in the period of one year then ending exceeds the registration limit, or at any time if there are reasonable grounds for believing that the value of his taxable supplies in the period of 30 days then beginning will exceed the registration limit.

Paragraph 1(2) provides that where a business carried on by a taxable person is transferred to another person as a going concern, and the transferee is not registered at the time of the transfer, then the transferee becomes liable to be registered at that time if the value of his taxable supplies for the period of one year ending at the time of the transfer has exceeded the registration limit, or if there are reasonable grounds for believing that the value of his taxable supplies in the period of 30 days beginning at the time of the transfer will exceed the registration limit.

If the taxpayer manages to cancel his registration or cease to be liable to be registered because of the amount of his outputs, this will still not help him if, ultimately, he sells the elected property for an amount above the then registration limit because he will be liable to re-register (VATA 1994, Sched 1, para 1(1)(*b*); *see also* Sched 1, paras 1(7) and (8) and 4, especially 4(3) and (4), and para 13).

INPUT TAX ON PRE-1 AUGUST 1989 REFURBISHMENTS

In *Newcourt Property Fund* (LON/90/1029 Decision 5825), the taxpayer incurred input tax in connection with refurbishment works carried out before 1 August 1989. It exercised the election to waive exemption in respect of the building with effect from 1 August 1989 (VATA 1983, Sched 6A, para 2; now VATA 1994, Sched 10, para 2). UK legislation makes it clear that such input tax cannot be reclaimed, but the taxpayer contended that the UK legislation was in breach of the principles laid out in the EC Sixth Directive (77/388), art 17(1) and (2). The Commissioners contended that art 13(C), which permitted member states to restrict the scope of the election and set out the necessary details for the use of the election, gave the UK Parliament all the necessary powers to pass the relevant legislation. The tribunal held that the word 'scope' as used in that Article clearly permitted member states to limit the option to tax by providing that it could not have effect before 1 August 1989. The question remained whether limiting the input tax which could be reclaimed to input tax charged on supplies on or after that date was in breach of art 17. The right to deduct input tax became exercisable when the goods supplied were used. If at that time the person claiming the right was not a taxable person, or the goods could not be used for non-taxable purposes, he was not entitled to credit. In the absence of anything to the contrary it had to be assumed that the goods and services supplied to the taxpayer were used before 1 August 1989. They were used to refurbish the building for letting, and at the time when they were so used a letting of the building could not have been a taxable transaction. The refusal by the Commissioners of the taxpayer's claim to deduct input tax on those goods and services did not contravene EC law.

BUILDING LAND AND FIRST OCCUPATION

In *Norbury Developments Ltd v The Commissioners* (Decision 14482) the appellant, in March 1994, agreed to purchase a piece of land with the intention of selling it at a profit with the benefit of planning permission for a development of houses and a local centre. Planning permission was obtained on 26 April 1994 and three days later the appellant agreed to sell the land to a developer. The appellant's purchase and sale of the land were completed on the same day. VAT was charged by the vendor but not by the appellant. On 10 May the appellant notified the Commissioners of its election to waive exemption in respect of the land. The appellant accepted that under UK legislation its sale of the land was exempt from VAT (VATA 1983, Sched 6, Group 1, item 1) and the election to waive exemption was not retrospective (VATA 1983, Sched 6A, paras 2 and 3; *see also Pinchdean Ltd v The Commissioners* [1993] STI 386). However, it appealed against an assessment disallowing input tax claimed in connection with the sale of the land on the ground that the sale was a standard-rated supply under EC law.

The appellant contended that the UK legislation was inconsistent with EC law under which the sale of building land was exempted from exemption (EC Sixth Directive, art 13B(h)) and that the transitional period during which member states were permitted to continue to exempt supplies of building land (arts 4(3)(b) and 28(3)(b), annex F(16)) ceased to apply in 1989 when the 1977 UK provisions on exemption for, *inter alia*, building land were changed (FA 1989, s 18 and Sched 3). The Commissioners agreed that the appellant was entitled to rely on the direct effect of a provision in the EC directive even if it had not been implemented in UK law, and that exemptions to VAT had to be narrowly construed, but they argued that the EC provision (art 13B(h)) did not prevent building land being treated as exempt and, if the land was not building land, it continued to be exempted under the transitional provisions (art 28(3)(b), annex F(16)).

The tribunal observed that 'building land' was not defined for the purposes of the exception from exemption. Yet the exception could nevertheless be relied on by a person who had supplied land which on any possible definition was clearly and obviously building land (*Gemeente Emmen v Belastingdienst Grote Ondernemingen* (Case C-46893) [1996] STC 496). As the land had been sold by the appellant specifically with planning permission and formed part of a new development, it was clearly within the exception (EC Sixth Directive, art 13B(h)) and was therefore standard-rated unless exemption continued under the transitional provisions (art 28(3)(b), and annex F(16)). It has been suggested that these provisions would continue until the end of 1996 (*Belastingdienst Grote Ondernemingen, above*, at p 505). The changes in the UK provisions for exemption of supplies of land had restricted the existing exemption by introducing further qualifications. The transitional provisions were limited to exemption under conditions existing in the member state concerned. The tribunal concluded that, as the interpretation and application of the transitional provisions were not clear and free from doubt, it was necessary to refer the matter to the European Court of Justice.

VALUATION—TWO MARKETS

The question arises whether there are two markets in commercial properties: one for lessees who can reclaim all the VAT charged on rents and the other for institutions such as banks who cannot reclaim the whole of the VAT.

In a hypothetical situation, Blackacre is let to a bank or a firm of solicitors. The bank may pay a premium of £100,000 for the lease because it cannot reclaim, let us say, any of the VAT on the rents. The solicitors, however, may be more than happy to pay a £117,500 premium for the lease because it can reclaim all the VAT (the example is an over-simplification).

The following points should be noted:

(1) The bank in fact may be able to reclaim a portion of the VAT as it will be a partially exempt taxpayer.

(2) The non-reclaimable VAT on the rents will be deductible from corporation tax which is presently charged at 31 per cent, the full rate.

(3) Tax legislation in many cases assumes that one market must exist. The way this market is created is illustrated in the case of *IRC v Clay* [1914–15] All ER 882 at 887 where Cozens-Hardy MR stated:

> An open market sale of property in its then condition presupposes a knowledge of its situation with all surrounding circumstances. To say that a small farm in the middle of a wealthy landowner's estate is to be valued without reference to the fact that he will probably be willing to pay a large price but solely with reference to its ordinary agricultural value, seems to be absurd. If the landowner does not at the moment buy, landbrokers or speculators will give more than its pure agricultural value with a view to reselling it at a profit to the landowner.

Swinfen Eady LJ, at 889, stated:

> The knowledge of the special need would affect the market price, and others would join in competing for the property with a view to obtaining it at a price less than that at which the opinion will be formed that it will be worth the while of the special purchaser to purchase.

See also the cases of *IRC v Glass* 1915 SC 499 and *IRC v Crossman* [1937] AC 26.

A bank would usually know, assuming it is free to assign its lease, that it could assign the lease at full value to, say, a firm of solicitors, or any other relevant body, which could reclaim all the VAT.

In many cases this may bring the markets closer together, though presumably there will be some premises which are so stamped with, say, bank user, that a separate market in real terms will have been created.

DECISION WHETHER OR NOT TO ELECT

Many factors must be taken into account in deciding whether or not to elect to waive exemption:

(1) If the election is exercised, input tax is reclaimable.

(2) The election is irrevocable but subject to various exceptions and loopholes (*see* p 225 and Chapter 19).

(3) The election can be made on a building-by-building basis (*see* p 224).

(4) If little input tax is in point the making of the election can be postponed.

(5) Whether or not the tenant can reclaim any VAT charged to him is relevant. If he cannot, he may offer the landlord a sum not to exercise the option (*see* p 235).

(6) If the option is exercised, VAT can be charged on the rent otherwise chargeable unless the lease contains provisions to the contrary (*see* p 31).

(7) The exercise of the election may give the landlord a cash flow advantage.

(8) The exercise of the election may affect the value of the landlord's investment (p 239).

(9) If the election is exercised VAT must be charged on the rents and on any sale proceeds if the reversion is sold (unless the going concern relief applies).

(10) Increased stamp duty may be payable if the option to waive exemption is exercised (*see* p 74).

OVERSEAS LANDLORDS

If vatable construction services are provided to an overseas landlord he can reclaim the VAT provided he is in a position to charge VAT with respect to supplies he makes.

It may be that X Inc owns freehold land in the UK. X Inc may pay the developer monies to construct a new building thereon and it may also incur professional fees. It was established in *WH Payne & Co* (Decision 13668) that an overseas landlord is not to be treated as belonging in the UK as a consequence of owning UK land interests.

It is felt, however, that in the case of the grant of a major interest, ie a lease of over 21 years, there will be a supply of goods, and the goods must be located in the UK. The goods will be the land. The supply will have been made in the UK within VATA 1994, s 4 and thus the transaction will be within the scope of a UK tax charge. That being the case the option can be exercised, the company can register and the VAT on the construction and professional services can be reclaimed.

If the supply is a supply of services then one must refer to VATA 1994, s 7(10). A supply of services is treated as made in the UK if the supplier belongs in the UK.

The supplier of services is treated as belonging in a country if:

(a) he has there a business establishment or some other fixed establishment and no such establishment elsewhere; or

(b) he has no such establishment (there or elsewhere) but his usual place of residence is there; or

(c) he has such establishments both in that country and elsewhere and the establishment of his which is most directly concerned with the supply is there (VATA 1994, s 9(2)).

For the purposes of that provision (but for no other purpose) a person carrying on a business through a branch or agency in any country is treated as having a business establishment there, and the reference to the usual place of residence in relation to a body corporate means a place where it is legally constituted.

Article 9(2)(*a*) of the Sixth Directive, dealing with services connected with immovable property provides that:

> The place of the supply of services connected with immovable property, including the services of estate agents and experts, and of services for preparing and co-ordinating construction works, such as the services of architects and of firms providing on-site supervision, shall be the place where the property is situated.

It may be argued that, for instance, the grant of a short lease always results in the supply being made in the UK if the property is in the UK because of this article.

It is felt, however, that the Value Added Tax (Place of Supply of Services) Order 1992 (SI No 3121), art 5, ensures that the supply of such a service, eg grant or sale of a short lease of UK land, will result in the supply being made in the UK, and the election can thus effectively be made. That Article sets out the rules and scope of services that are treated as supplied in the UK and these are:

(1) The grant, assignment or surrender of:

- any interest in or right over land;
- a personal right to call for or be granted any interest in or right over land;
- a licence to occupy land or any other contractual right exercisable over or in relation to land.

(2) Any works of construction, demolition, conversion, reconstruction, alteration, enlargement, repair or maintenance of a building or civil engineering work.

(3) Services supplied by estate agents, auctioneers, architects, surveyors, engineers and others involved in matters relating to land.

Chapter 19

Grants by developers: exempt land

The election to waive exemption will be disapplied with respect to a supply which would otherwise be taxable if:

(a) the grant giving rise to the supply was made by a person (the grantor) who is a developer of the land; and

(b) at the time of the grant, it was the intention or expectation of:

(i) the grantor; or
(ii) a person responsible for financing the grantor's development of the land for exempt use,

that the land would become exempt land (whether immediately or eventually and whether or not by virtue of the grant) or, as the case may be, would continue for a period at least, to be such land (VATA 1994, Sched 10(2)(3AA)).

Note that the grant giving rise to the supply requires one to look at the relevant grant. If an agreement for a lease is entered into then any rents payable pursuant thereto would be referable to the agreement for lease and may be exempt. Once the grant has been entered into (ie the grant of a formal lease pursuant to the agreement for lease) then the rents payable under the grant would be referable to the formal grant.

One has to look at the intention or expectation of the relevant parties (the grantor and the financier) at the time of the grant.

Strictly, if at the time of the agreement for lease the intentions were that the land would become exempt land but at the time of the grant (whereafter—and only whereafter—rents would flow) the intentions were that the land would not be exempt land then the provisions would not be offended.

It is probably safest to assume that one should not have the intentions or expectations that the land should become exempt land both at the time of the agreement for lease and the time of the formal grant.

GRANT MADE BY A DEVELOPER OF THE LAND

The provisions can only apply to cause supplies made by the developer of the land to be exempt supplies where otherwise the developer may have expected them to be vatable at the positive rate because the election had been exercised.

A grant is made by the developer if the land or a building or part of the building on the land is an asset falling in relation to that person (ie the developer) to be treated as a capital item for the purposes of the Capital Goods Regulations and the grant was made at a time falling within the period over which such regulations allow an adjustment (normally a ten-year period).

An item is a capital good with respect to any person (referred to as 'the owner' in the regulations) if the item falls within the paragraphs *below* (the list is not exhaustive—*see* Chapter 22 for the full list).

The first is any land or a building or part of a building where the value of the interest therein supplied to the owner by way of a taxable supply which is not a zero-rated supply is not less than £250,000.

Instead of buying a building the taxpayer may build his own one. In this case the building will be a capital good where the aggregate of the value of taxable grants relating to the land on which the building is constructed and the value of all taxable supplies of goods and services, other than any that are zero-rated, made or to be made to him in connection with the construction of the building is not less than £250,000.

Example (New Building)

> X Ltd buys land on which VAT is charged and constructs a building thereon on which VAT is charged. The total costs of acquisition and building works on which VAT is charged is not less than £250,000. In the hands of X Ltd the building is a capital item and subject to the capital goods provisions.

A building which the owner alters or an extension or an annexe which he constructs is also a capital item where:

(a) additional floor area is created in the altered building, extension or annexe of not less than 10 per cent of the floor area of the building before the alteration in question is carried out, or the extension or annexe in question is constructed; and

(b) the value of all the taxable supplies of goods and services, other than any that are zero-rated, made or to be made to the owner for or in connection with the alteration, extension or annexe in question is not less than £250,000.

Example (Extension)

Y Ltd buys a building and extends the floor area by not less than 10 per cent and the value of the construction works all of which are vatable at 17.5 per cent are not less than £250,000: the building comprises a capital item in the hands of Y Ltd.

Thus if the developer holds an asset which is not a capital item the provisions cannot apply to him. If a developer buys a new property and is charged VAT and the purchase price is less than £250,000 then the disapplication of the election will not apply.

One generally (but not always) ignores rent in determining whether the £250,000 figure is reached (*see* p 260) and trading stock does not normally get caught by these provisions (*see* p 259).

Example (Rent)

X Bank constructs a new office on its freehold land for £10m. It is a capital item in the hands of the bank. The bank is a developer of the land within Sched 10, para 3A(2). A lease is granted to Z Ltd which pays the rent of £1m per annum. The item is not a capital good in the hands of Z Ltd. Although it paid £1m rent one generally excludes so much of the value as may consist of rent in determining whether in the hands of the tenant he has exceeded the £250,000 limited (see the VAT Regulations 1995 (SI No 2518), reg 113(*b*)).

Example

X Developer constructs a new office development for £20m. He develops the property with a view to selling the same at a profit. If he lets the same but receives no rent and does in fact sell the same then the capital goods provisions should not be applicable. The Customs may argue he would not have developed the property solely for the purpose of selling the same but also for the purpose of letting. However, if the letting is done and he receives no rent and then he sells the same it is felt that the better argument is that he would have developed the same solely for the purpose of selling it, and so the capital goods provisions would not apply.

Finally, with effect from 3 July 1997, certain refurbishments can cause buildings to fall within the capital goods provision; civil engineering works can also fall within the definition (*see* p 261).

FINANCIER

As well as the developer (grantor), the financier at the time of the grant must have not had the intention or expectation that the land will become exempt land. Also it is arguable that he must not have had that intention at the time when the finance is provided.

A financier is a person who has provided the finance to the grantor for the development or has entered into any arrangement, agreement or understanding whether or not legally enforceable to the grantor to carry out the development.

The financier could be said to have provided the finance for the developer for carrying out the development if he does any one of the following:

(a) directly or indirectly provided funds for meeting the whole or any part of the cost of the grantor in carrying out the development (eg X Bank lends the grantor monies to carry out the development, therefore X Bank will fall into the definition of a financier);

(b) the person has directly or indirectly procured the provision of funds to the grantor to carry out the development by another person (eg X Ltd provided security to Z Bank, whereafter Z Bank lends the money to the grantor to carry out the development);

(c) a person directly or indirectly provides funds for discharging in whole or in part any liability that has been or may be incurred by any person for or in connection with the raising of funds to meet the cost of the grantor's development of the land (eg B Ltd lends money to the grantor to carry out the development. B Ltd having borrowed from N Ltd, K Ltd discharges the liability of B Ltd to pay its lender). Any person who directly or indirectly procures that any such liability is or will be discharged in whole or in part by another.

Finally, note that the provision of funds for the purposes of this legislation includes loans, the giving of guarantees or securities, the provision of any of the consideration for the issue of any shares or securities issued wholly or partly for raising such funds, or any other transfer of assets or value as a consequence of which any such funds are made available for that purpose.

The above definition is not exclusive but it is felt that the provision of funds must generally relate to transactions of a similar nature such as the making of loans, etc. It is not felt that the payment of rent, for example, could be a provision of funds.

Example

> X Ltd carries out a £20m development and is a grantor. It grants a
> lease to Z Ltd and Z Ltd pays rent. The rent is used by the grantor to
> discharge its loan obligations to P plc, a bank. Technically the rent
> could be said to be the provision of monies to meet part of the cost of
> the grantor's development, but it is not felt that it is the provision of
> funds to do so within Sched 10, para 3(*a*)(v).

The pre-let problem

It may be argued that if a grantor enters into a pre-let which then enables him
to borrow monies to carry out the development, there will have been an agreement, arrangement or understanding (para 3A(3)(*b*)) for directly or indirectly
procuring (within para 3A(4)(*b*)) the provision of funds for meeting the
grantor's expenditure on the development.

Certainly if the tenant were active in this arrangement and, for example,
took a reverse premium to increase the rent to ensure that the relevant funding
was forthcoming, provisions would be offended. At the other end of the spec-
trum it may be argued that the tenant had no connection at all with the
grantor's borrowing arrangements and simply took a lease perhaps without
any reverse premium that he would not be a financier within this legislation.

Example

> X is the freeholder and pre-lets the property to Z. X pays Z a reverse
> premium and they both approach B Bank to fund the development to
> be carried out by X. There is a danger that Z would be a financier; X
> would be the grantor. If either had the intention or expectation that
> the land would become exempt land then the election by the grantor
> would be disapplied.

GRANTOR'S DEVELOPMENT OF THE LAND

References in the legislation to the grantor's development of the land are references to the acquisition by the grantor of the land which consist in the land
or a building or part of a building on the land and in relation to the grantor
falls to be treated as a capital item within the capital goods provisions.

An acquisition of an asset should be taken to include its construction or
reconstruction and the carrying out in relation to that asset of any other works

by reference to which it falls to be treated as a capital item under the capital goods provisions (Sched 10, para 3A(6)).

EXEMPT LAND

Land is exempt land if at any time falling within the capital goods period (usually ten years) the grantor or the financier, or a person connected with the grantor or the financier, is in occupation of the land without being in occupation of it wholly or mainly for eligible purposes. Note that the test has to be applied at the time of the grant; what actual use is made of the land is technically not relevant if the correct intentions and expectations exist at the time of the grant. The word 'mainly' is not defined.

Example

X grants a lease to Y. At the time of the grant the intention and expectation of the grantor and the financier is that the land would not become exempt land. In fact within three years it does fall within the definition of exempt land. That fact is not relevant. The election will not be disapplied.

In *Re Hatcschek's Patents, ex p Zerenner* [1909] 2 Ch 69 at p 83 Parker J held that where the word 'mainly' is used with the word 'wholly' (or 'exclusively'), 'mainly' does not just mean over 50 per cent. The disparity must be greater than a mere small percentage. He stated:

For example, if the total manufacture in the United Kingdom were 1200 and the total manufacture elsewhere was 1250, giving a total of 2450 in all, I do not think it could be said that the manufacture was mainly abroad within the meaning of [the relevant section]; to come within the subsection the disparity must, in my opinion, be greater than a mere small percentage, and, indeed, if the article be manufactured or the process be carried on within the United Kingdom, not only to a substantial extent, but to an extent as substantial as may be reasonably be expected having regard to what is done abroad.

An eligible purpose is one which results in supplies where the input tax wholly attributable to those supplies would give the supplier a credit.

Occupation by certain governmental and other bodies set out in VATA 1994, ss 33 and 41 are treated as being eligible purpose occupations (Sched 10, para 3A(10)). There are also special provisions for occupations by VAT groups (para 3A(12)).

'Connected persons' is defined by reference to TA 1988, s 839 and there are transitional provisions in para 3A(4)–(6).

Paragraph 3A(13) states that for the purposes of these provisions a person should be taken to be in occupation of any land whether he occupies it alone or together with one or more other persons and whether he occupies all of that land or any part of it.

Paragraph 3A(11) states that, for the purposes of this legislation, where land of which any person is in occupation

(a) is being held by that person in order to be put to use by him for particular purposes; and

(b) is not land of which he is in occupation for any other purpose,

that person shall be deemed during that period to be in occupation of that land for purposes of which he proposes to use it.

Example

X a firm of accountants proposes to use 55 per cent of the property for eligible purposes. The remaining 45 per cent (which would not bring the situation within the word 'mainly') is to be let. The occupation of part by the accountants is deemed to be the occupation of the whole. There is thus no problem in envisaging the complete occupation by the accountants of the property. One thus has to look to the use made by them during that occupation (the accountants moving into premises, for example, may occupy the whole but may decide with respect to parts to use the same for varying purposes). There seems to be no inconsistency between the words 'use' and 'occupation' and indeed para 3A(7) seems to envisage an occupation and a purpose; use may equate with purpose.

It may be argued that if the accountants intend to let the 45 per cent then they could be deemed to be in occupation of the property for the purposes for which they propose to use it (ie an exempt letting). It is not felt that that is the correct interpretation of the legislation. It is difficult to see one using premises if they are let. Also if the letting is to a person who is not the grantor or a financier it would be an odd interpretation of the legislation if the accountants who were, for example, the grantor or the financier had full eligible use with the exempt use being taken up by a person who is not the grantor or a financier, which use causes the election to be disapplied.

FURTHER EXAMPLES OF THE PROVISIONS IN ACTION

Example: Tenant's contribution—caught

The landlord grants a lease to the bank. The bank makes a contribution towards the fitting-out costs which the landlord has agreed to carry out. The election will be disapplied (*inter alia*) if the intention or expectation at the time of the grant is the bank will use the premises for its partly exempt purposes. Tenants' contributions must therefore be very carefully watched.

Example: City centre development—caught

L is to carry out a major development of 20 commercial units. The bank which owns part of the adjoining land transfers its land to L and takes a lease back. L borrows from a separate independent finance house giving a charge over all the property. The danger is that the bank will have made a transfer of assets in consequence of which funds are made available for the development and strictly the election is disapplied with regard to the entire project (the Customs may agree only to disapply it with regard to the particular property which was transferred and leased back by the bank but other tenants may still nevertheless argue that the election should be disapplied with respect to them; they are not bound by any Customs' decision in that area).

Example: Issue of shares—caught

X plc may issue shares or debentures to raise money for a specific project; if the bank takes up some of the shares and also takes a lease the election may be disapplied (VATA 1994, Sched 10, para 3A(5)(*c*)).

Example: Lease premium—caught

X plc carried out a development and grants a lease to the bank. X plc takes a premium on the lease. The election may be disapplied.

Example: Tenant's own expenditure—not caught

It may be that X plc is carrying out a development and the bank-tenant enters into a separate contract with the builder for the builder to carry out works direct for the bank-tenant. In this case there is no provision of funds by the tenant for the development being carried out by the landlord and the election will not be disapplied. It may even be possible for the landlord to enter into the relevant contract as nominee or agent for the tenant; in this event it is likely that the election will not be disapplied.

Example: Paying landlord's solicitor's costs

Contributions towards the landlord's costs of the development may cause a problem to arise. The grantor's development comprises not only the physical works to the property, but also the acquisition of the land, and thus contributions towards the landlord's solicitor's costs *may* cause a problem (VATA 1994, Sched 10, para 3A(6)).

Chapter 20

Abolition of the deemed property charge and the developmental lease charge

DEEMED PROPERTY CHARGE

The deemed property charge provisions are contained in VATA 1994, Sched 10, paras 5 and 6. However, this deemed charge has been abolished with respect to projects where the works started on or after 1 March 1995.

The charge could arise if a taxpayer:

(a) constructed a new commercial building or civil engineering work; or

(b) extended an existing building over new land; or

(c) extended an existing building so as to increase the gross external floor area by at least 20 per cent; or

(d) reconstructed an existing building which involved the removal of at least 80 per cent of the floor structures during the rebuilding works; or

(e) extended an existing civil engineering work to new land.

However, as mentioned, if the works commenced on or after 1 March 1995 the charge cannot apply. The time at which work began may fall to be determined. Guidance on this point can be found in the proceedings (Standing Committee G) on the Finance Bill 1989. Mr Lilley stated:

> Construction . . . commences when on the particular facts a meaningful and ongoing start has been made to the construction process. Customs will be looking for good evidence of such a start, and also evidence, for example, that planning permission has been obtained and building contracts let.

If a project is within the charge because works started before 1 March 1995, it may nevertheless still fall outside the deemed charge if the project had not been completed by 1 March 1995 and the developer makes no claim after that date to credit for input tax (entitlement to which depends on his being treated in due course as having made a taxable deemed supply under the self-supply provisions) and he has made no such claim before that date; or he accounts to Customs for a sum equal to any such credit previously claimed (*see* VATA 1994, Sched 10, para 5(3A)).

The transitional provisions in Sched 10, para 5(3A) are summarised in Customs' *Business Brief* as follows (7/95, 4 April 1995):

> However, if you meet two criteria you can elect to remove the development from the scope of the self-supply. The first is that from the 1st March 1995 you only recover input tax in accordance with your agreed partial exemption method. The second is that on the VAT return for the period ending 31st May 1995, 30th June 1995 or 31st July 1995, whichever is appropriate, you repay the balance between the input tax recovered before the 1st March 1995 and the amount of input tax you would have been permitted to recover in accordance with your intended use of the building and the normal rules of partial exemption.

If the taxpayer does not make use of this right to remove himself from the self-supply charge, and he is within the self-supply charge (because he commenced works before 1 March 1995), he will suffer the charge on the earlier of the following two dates:

(a) 1 March 1997;

(b) the first occasion during the period beginning with the day when the construction of the building or work was first planned and ending ten years after the completion of the building or works on which:

  (i) the taxpayer makes an exempt supply, eg an exempt letting; or
  (ii) the taxpayer occupies the building or uses the works or any part of it when he is not a fully taxable person (Sched 10, para 5(1)).

Example

X Ltd started the construction of a commercial building before 1 March 1995 and half of it was completed on 1 March 1995. He does not make use of the 'election' provisions to repay the input tax he has reclaimed and he is fully within the deemed charge provisions. He completes the building on 1 January 1996 and makes an exempt grant on 2 January 1996. The exempt grant will cause the self-supply charge to arise, and under Sched 10, para 6(1) it will arise on the last day of the prescribed accounting period during which the exempt grant takes place. If no exempt grant takes place before 1 March 1997, or if the taxpayer does not occupy the building when not a fully taxable person before 1 March 1997, then there will nevertheless be a self-supply charge by reference to 1 March 1997.

As the self-supply charge has now been abolished subject to the transitional provision, it is not dealt with further in this book; *see* Chapter 11 of the fifth edition.

DEVELOPMENTAL LEASE CHARGE

The developmental lease charge (introduced by the Value Added Tax (Buildings and Land) Order 1991 (SI No 2569), now found in VATA 1994, Sched 9, Group 1, Item 1(*b*) and Note (7) and Sched 10, para 7) is very much tied in with the deemed property charge and, subject to certain transitional provisions, is abolished along with the deemed property charge.

It is provided in Sched 9, Group 1, Item 1(*b*) that a supply made pursuant to a developmental tenancy, developmental lease or developmental licence is excluded from exemption and is therefore vatable, ie the rents arising from such a tenancy or lease or licence will be vatable at 17.5 per cent.

In Note (7) to Group 1 it is stated that a tenancy of, or lease of or licence to occupy a building or work is treated as becoming a developmental tenancy, developmental lease or developmental licence (as the case may be) where a tenancy of or lease of or licence to occupy a building or work is treated as being supplied to and by the developer under para 6(1) of Sched 10, except where that paragraph applies by virtue of para 5(1)(*b*) of that Schedule.

This means that if a tenant carries out a development which gives rise to a deemed property charge under Sched 10, paras 5 and 6 (because construction etc commenced before 1 March 1995 and an exempt letting for instance takes place before 1 March 1997) then the landlord will become liable for VAT on the rents charged under the lease or tenancy or licence.

However, if the deemed charge arises because a development commenced before 1 March 1995 and there is no exempt letting or user prior to 1 March 1997 (so that the deemed charge arises by reference to 1 March 1997 date) then although there is a deemed property charge the developmental lease/tenancy/licence provisions will not apply and the rents will not become chargeable to VAT.

Example

X granted a developmental lease to Y. Y commenced commercial construction works before 1 March 1995 and made an exempt letting of the property on 1 March 1996. Y suffers a deemed charge under Sched 10, para 6; the lease granted by X to Y becomes a developmental lease and VAT is chargeable on the rent. On the other hand, if there is no deemed property charge under Sched 10, para 6 prior to 1 March 1997 the developmental lease provisions will have no application, ie X's rents will be exempt, unless of course X has elected to waive exemption.

Chapter 21

Self-supply of construction services

The Value Added Tax (Self-Supply of Construction Services) Order 1989 (SI No 472), which came into force on 1 April 1989, contains provisions on self-supply which are particularly relevant to land transactions.

Under the Order, a charge to VAT arises where a person, in the course or furtherance of a business carried on by him for the purposes of that business or otherwise than for a consideration, performs the following services:

(a) the construction of a building; or

(b) the extension or other alteration, or the construction of an annexe to any building such that additional floor area of not less than 10 per cent of the floor area of the original building is created; or

(c) the construction of any civil engineering work; or

(d) in connection with any services described in (a), (b) or (c) *above*, the carrying out of any demolition work contemporaneously with or preparatory thereto.

Thus a bank or insurance company, for instance, using its in-house expertise may have a new building constructed within (a) *above*, or a building extended within (b) *above*. The bank or insurance company, in the course or furtherance of the banking or insurance business carried on by it, for the purposes of that business and otherwise than for a consideration, performs construction and extension works. Thus, the situation is subject to the self-supply charge.

The charge works on the basis that the services of construction etc are treated as supplied to the bank or insurance company (as the case may be) for the purposes of that business and in the course of furtherance of that business. The supply is treated as taking place at a value equal to the market value of the services.

The supply would appear to take place in the prescribed accounting period in which the services are performed.

This deemed charge applies only if:

(a) the value of the construction services is not less than £100,000 (presumably per project); and

(b) such services would, if supplied for a consideration in the course of furtherance of a business carried on by a taxable person, be chargeable to tax at a rate other than nil.

Construction services are not defined, but there is no reason why a normal developer's profit would not arise from construction services.

Example: VAT on developer's profit

In June 1997 the developer buys bare land (on which VAT is not charged) for £1m. It employs a builder who charges it £4m plus VAT to put up a new commercial building on the site; the developer also employs professionals who charge it £1m plus VAT. The charge the developer could have made for its own construction services had it supplied them to somebody else would have been £0.5m. The developer can suffer a deemed construction service charge when it has completed the performance of the services, ie when the building has been erected.

The jurisprudential nature of the self-supply is confusing, but if the developer has exercised the election to waive exemption it is unlikely to have any relevant effect although the capital goods provisions will have to be considered if the property is used for an exempt purpose.

In the figures *below* it is sought to illustrate the loophole which the Order may have been designed to remedy. The developer in Figure 21.1 has made a supply to the fund and will have charged the fund VAT on the £10m development fee. The developer itself would have been charged £9m plus VAT under the building contract by the builder, but the developer will reclaim that. The fund, having not exercised the election to waive exemption, will thus bear VAT on £10m.

To mitigate the VAT, the fund may set up its own in-house development section and employ the builder direct. The builder will be paid £9m plus VAT, and the 'fund-developer' will bear VAT on £9m. The 'fund developer' will have carried out its own development services to the extent of £1m and would have avoided VAT on that, but for the Value Added Tax (Self-Supply of Construction Services) Order 1989 (*see* Figure 21.2).

Figure 21.1:

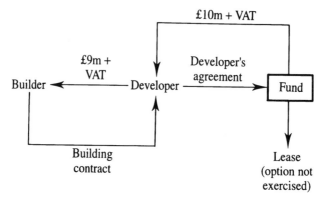

Figure 21.2:

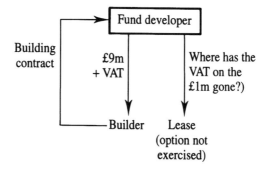

Chapter 22

Capital goods provisions

The 'capital goods provisions' are to be found in the 1995 Regulations, regs 112–116 (*see also* art 20(2) of the EC Sixth Directive). They deal with the situation where a taxpayer acquires an item such as a building, and reclaim the VAT which has been charged to him (because he intends to use the property and does use it in making taxable supplies, as when a firm of solicitors uses a building for carrying out its business), but subsequently changes the use to which the building is put.

Having reclaimed the input tax, the taxpayer may subsequently, for example, use the property in making exempt supplies, eg the firm of solicitors may let the property without electing to waive exemption.

The capital goods provisions are designed to ensure that some of the VAT which was reclaimed is repaid to Customs because of this later exempt user.

Again, a taxpayer may not be able to reclaim VAT because he has, for instance, let the property, making an exempt supply, but later uses the property for a fully taxable purpose. In this event, he may be able to reclaim some of the original VAT charged to him.

These rules apply only to capital items, and not to items which a taxpayer acquires solely for the purposes of selling (reg 112(2)).

Example

X is a land dealer and acquires land solely for the purposes of selling it at a profit. Regardless of the value of the land or the sale price, the capital goods provisions are irrelevant. The 1995 Regulations, regs 101–110 deal with the input tax in that situation (not the Capital Goods Regulations).

Assuming the property is not trading stock, the rules apply to the various items set out in reg 113. The items included within reg 113 and thus comprising capital items for the purposes of the capital goods provision are the following:

(1) Any land or building or part of a building or a civil engineering work or part of a civil engineering work where the value of the property interest therein supplied to the owner by way of a taxable supply (which is not a zero-rated supply) is not less than £250,000. When determining whether one has reached the £250,000 figure or has exceeded it, one excludes any consideration comprising rent (including charges reserved as rent) where the rent is neither payable nor paid more than 12 months in advance nor invoiced for a period in excess of 12 months (reg 113(*b*)).

(2) A building or part of a building where:

(a) the owner's interest in, right over, or licence to occupy the building or part of it is treated as supplied to him under Sched 10, para 1(5) of the Act. (This is a deemed supply which arises on the change of use from a residential or charitable building to, say, an office or other commercial use); and

(b) the value of that supply is not less than £250,000 (reg 113(*c*)).

(3) A building or part of a building where the owner's interest in, right over, or licence to occupy the building or part of it was on or before 1 March 1997 treated as supplied to him under the developer's self-supply charge provisions (that deemed supply is now abolished), as set out in Sched 10, para 6(1), and the value of that supply is not less than £250,000.

(4) Any commercial building constructed by the owner costing not less than £250,000 to construct (reg 113(*e*)).

(5) A building which the owner alters, or an extension or an annexe which he constructs, where:

(a) the additional floor area created in the altered building, extension or annexe is not less than 10 per cent of the floor area of the building before the alteration in question is carried out or the extension or annexe in question constructed; and

(b) where the extension etc costs £250,000 or more (reg 113(*f*)).

(6) A civil engineering work constructed by the owner and first brought into use by him on or after 3 July 1997 where the aggregate of the value of

(a) taxable grants relating to the land on which the civil engineering work is constructed made to the owner on or after 3 July 1997, and

(b) all the taxable supplies of goods and services, other than any that are zero-rated, made or to be made to him for or in connection with the construction of the civil engineering work on or after 3 July 1997,

is not less than £250,000 (reg 113(*g*)).

(7) A building which the owner refurbishes or fits out where the value of capital expenditure on the taxable supplies of services and of goods affixed to the building, other than any that are zero-rated, made or to be made to the owner for or in connection with the refurbishment or fitting out in question on or after 3 July 1997 is more than £250,000 (reg 113(*h*))

Example

X, Y and Z, a firm of solicitors, buy a building and land for £250,000 or more and are charged VAT at 17.5 per cent on the purchase price. They are to carry out their solicitor's profession from the building. The capital goods provisions apply to that purchase (reg 113(*b*)).

Example

X plc carries out a major refurbishment work to its office building costing not less than £250,000. That outlay relates to capital expenditure on which VAT at 17.5 per cent is charged. The building is within the capital goods provisions (reg 113(*h*)). Note that if the refurbishment expenditure is less than £250,000 then the capital goods provisions will not apply. There is therefore still scope available for planning.

INPUT TAX RECLAIMS—AVOIDING CAPITAL GOODS

It still may be possible for colleges to set up structures enabling their input tax to be reclaimed, but there are dangers which have to be looked out for. In *The Commissioners v Robert Gordon's College* [1995] STC 1093 the college, an independent school which made exempt supplies of educational services for VAT, developed some land for use as playing fields and ancilliary facilities. It granted a lease of 12 years to X Ltd in return for a premium and rent and obtained a non-exclusive licence for the use of the land from the company for an annual fee payable by the college to the company. The college and X Ltd were registered for VAT and elected to waive exemption from VAT in respect of the grants of the lease and licence.

The case, which finally ended up before the House of Lords, was basically involved with the self-supply charge, but there seemed little doubt that the input tax incurred by the college on the works was properly attributable to the grant by it of the lease and therefore a vatable supply. At p 1100d Lord Hoffman stated:

> It is true that the college did make exempt supplies, but the whole of the expenditure on the works was attributable to the taxable supply to [X Ltd] and the input tax on that expenditure was therefore as the Commissioners accept, fully deductible from the taxable supply to [X Ltd].

The House of Lords referred to *DLP Group plc v The Commissioners* [1995] STC 424 at 420 to make the point that each transaction in a chain must be examined separately to ascertain objectively what output tax is payable and what input tax is deductible.

Thus under present UK VAT law, if a school wishes to carry out an extension, and assuming the transaction is not within the capital goods provisions, it could grant, say, a 12-year lease to an associated or connected company and take a licence back.

The option will be perfectly effective but note that the option is disapplied if the building or part of the building is intended for use solely for a relevant charitable purpose; the provision may therefore have little effect if, for example, a church which is part of a school is to be refurbished and be the subject matter of this transaction. It also assumes that the school carries on an exempt business so that it does not fall within the definition of a building used for a relevant charitable purpose (see VATA 1994, Sched 10, para 2(2)(*b*)).

Under the VAT Regulations 1995, reg 108 it is provided that where a taxable person (a school) has

(a) deducted an amount of input tax which it has attributed to taxable supplies because it intended to use the refurbishment works in making taxable supplies, and

(b) during a period of six years commencing on the first day of the prescribed accounting period in which the attribution was determined and before that intention to use the refurbishment works for the making of taxable supplies is fulfilled, the school uses or forms an intention to use the refurbishment works in making both taxable and exempt supplies, the Customs can adjust the input tax position under reg 108(2). The Customs do generally tend to apply a first use rule: in Notice 706/2/90 in the Introduction (capital goods scheme) it is stated: '. . . under the normal rules recovery of input tax on all capital goods was usually determined once and for all by the first use of the goods'. If that is the case, then the arrangement should succeed without much difficulty, even though it may be collapsed after a couple of years; this is because the taxable use will have been made and the intention fulfilled within the six-year period. If one did not apply a first supply rule it is arguable on reg 108 that the taxpayer may have intended to use the refurbishment works only in making taxable supplies but he never could have wholly achieved that intention because, for example, he may use the items himself for an exempt purpose. The intention was therefore not fulfilled. Within the six-year period the refurbishment works are used for making both taxable and exempt supplies and thus the apportionment can be made.

In this respect the decision of *The Commissioners v Briararch* [1992] STC 732 is generally felt to have put an end to the first supply rule, but one can clearly see that if the school in the above example intended only to use the property for the purposes of making taxable supplies and it changed its mind after the six-year period with the lease being surrendered and with the property then owned by the school being used for exempt purposes, that regardless of the first supply rules there would be no claw-back of the input tax.

Any argument that in reality the refurbishment works should be looked upon as being attributable to the vatable supply pursuant to the exercise of the election on the grant of the lease to X Ltd and the exempt user by the school must be treated as being discredited following the *Robert Gordon's College* case.

Figure 22.1:

THE CAP ON INPUT TAX RECLAIMABLE

There is a rule with respect to the capital goods provisions that the maximum amount of input tax claimable by the taxpayer with respect to a capital item is limited to the amount of output tax chargeable by that person on a supply of the capital item. This cap on the recovery of input tax is provided in reg 12 of VAT (Amendment) (No 3) Regulations 1997 (SI No 1614), which amends reg 115 of the 1995 Regulations.

One looks at the total input tax with respect to the capital item which has been recovered by the owner on the acquisition of the item and as a result of subsequent adjustments, and the owner must make an adjustment in his account when he sells the item so that his right to retain any input tax so recovered does not exceed the output tax chargeable on the sale of the item.

The Customs Business Brief 15/97 (16 July 1997) gives an example of the type of tax avoidance situation which the cap is designed to overcome. The taxpayer may buy a new commercial freehold building as a capital item and recover the full input tax charged to him thereon on the basis that, for example, he intends to make only taxable supplies with respect to the building. The owner may subsequently make an exempt supply by, for example, granting a 999-year lease. He can then sell the freehold building which would have a very low value and account for output tax on the sale of the freehold. The sale of the freehold would be a compulsory vatable supply, being the sale of a new commercial building freehold. The new capping provisions ensure that the amount of input tax recovered by the taxpayer which he can keep does not exceed the small amount of output tax payable on the disposal of the freehold; the amount of output tax would be very small considering it would be encumbered by a 999-year lease. If the total input tax exceeds the output tax chargeable on the disposal the owner is required actually to pay to the Customs an amount which ensures that the two are equal.

On the face of the legislation, of course, if the taxpayer purchased a building for £10m and was charged VAT and reclaimed the same and as a result of market forces he sold the building for £½m, he would have to repay to the Customs the difference between the output tax on the sale and the input tax reclaimed. However, the new rules provide that effectively the reclaim position shall be 'save as the Commissioners may otherwise allow'.

In the Business Brief 15/97 (16 July 1997) the Customs have stated that the measure would not be applied to genuine cases where an owner has had to dispose of an item at a loss due to market conditions or for other legitimate reasons. The rules for capping will be applied where 'the value of the sale has been reduced by some artificial means in order to achieve tax mitigation or some other unintended benefit'. For this reason the provision includes a 'save as the Commissioners otherwise allow' clause so that there are powers not to apply the measure in genuine cases. So, for example, the measure would not be applied in circumstances where a capital item was sold at a loss because the item's value had depreciated due to a downturn in the market (as sometimes happens with property). *See* the Business Brief 15/97, paras 4 and 5.

TRANSFER OF A GOING CONCERN

An area of difficulty arises with respect to the capital goods provisions where there is a transfer of a business as a going concern (eg the sale of let property where the owner of the let property which comprised capital goods disposes of the same as a going concern).

Regulation 114(5A) (inserted therein by the VAT (Amendment) (No 3) Regulations 1997, reg 11(*d*)) applies if a capital item is disposed of during its adjustment period (generally ten years) and the disposal is in the course of the transfer of a business or part of a business by the owner as a going concern. In that situation the interval then applying to the owner shall, on the date of the transfer, come to an end and thereafter each subsequent interval applicable to the capital item shall end on the successive anniversaries of that date.

Note that this rule does not apply where the new owner is registered with the registration number of and in substitution for the transferor. If the new owner is registered with the registration number of and in substitution for the transferor (which is a rare occurrence), the position would be governed by reg 114(7) (as substituted by the 1997 Regulations) and basically the transferee stands in the shoes of the transferor for the purposes of the capital goods provisions with one however looking to the accounting periods of the new owner to determine the new intervals.

The effect of the new provisions is thus to keep the period of adjustment (generally ten years) very much alive so if the new owner uses the property for an exempt purpose he may find that he has to repay to the Customs some of the VAT initially reclaimed by the former owner. He therefore inherits a potentially expensive VAT position if the amount of vatable use made by him of the premises is less than that used by the transferor (*see* p 352).

Of course, if the purchaser uses a building for fully taxable purposes when prior to the acquisition if it had been wholly used or partly used for exempt purposes then he may in fact find himself in a reclaim position for the remaining adjustment periods. On the other hand, where a partially exempt business purchases a building as a going concern or as part of a going concern, there is the danger that the purchaser will have to make payments to the Customs under the scheme. Whichever way the adjustments go it is necessary for the records to be transferred to the purchaser so that he is able to calculate the amounts involved (*see* p 398 for a relevant precedent).

CALCULATING THE REPAYMENT

Regulation 114(1) provides that the proportion of the total input tax on the capital item which may be deducted under the general rules in reg 101 is subject to adjustments in accordance with the capital goods provisions, ie they override the general regulations, but where they do not override them, the general regulations apply.

The period of adjustment must first be ascertained. It is ten successive intervals, unless the interest in the land which is acquired is, say, a lease and has less than ten years to run (in that case, special rules apply) (*see* reg 114(3)(*b*)).

The first interval would generally commence on the acquisition of the capital goods. Generally each interval is one year. Adjustments are made for each interval, depending on whether the use made of the capital item in making taxable supplies is greater or less than in the first interval.

If, in the first year, there is a 100 per cent taxable use, and in the second year that taxable use decreases, the owner must pay to the Commissioners some of the VAT initially reclaimed. If the total VAT reclaimed was £100,000, and in the second year the asset is used solely for an exempt purpose, then one-tenth of the VAT initially reclaimed must be repaid to Customs.

The adjustments are made by reference to the use in the first year. A building may cost £1m plus VAT of £175,000. The recovery in the first year may be 75 per cent (because of a 75 per cent taxable user). If in the second year the taxable user increases to 80 per cent the taxpayer can reclaim £875 for that year calculated thus:

$$\frac{£175,000}{10} \times (80-75) \text{ per cent} = 875$$

In subsequent years further adjustments may have to be made depending on the user of the premises in the year (interval) in question.

If the taxpayer uses the item for the taxable purpose for five years and then sells it, making an exempt supply, then for the subsequent five years he is deemed to use the asset for an exempt purpose and he must pay five-tenths of the VAT he initially reclaimed.

Chapter 23

Development structures

This chapter looks at a number of development structures related to non-domestic buildings and their VAT consequences.

MOORGATE DEALS

The High Court decision in *Clarke v United Real (Moorgate) Ltd* [1988] STC 273 has thrown some light on how property development transactions can be structured to avoid a charge to capital gains tax on monies received by the landlord and to avoid VAT problems.

Moorgate (L) was a property investor. In 1978 it employed a builder to construct a new building on its (L's) freehold land.

The works were being completed when, in 1979, the Norwich Union Life Insurance Society (T) agreed with L to repay L's past and future cost of the development in consideration of L granting T a 99-year lease of the property on completion of the development.

The rent payable under the lease, needless to say, was calculated to take into account the fact that T repaid L's costs on the development both past and future.

L was assessed on the monies paid to it by T to corporation tax on chargeable gain on the grounds that the payments constituted a premium or a like sum within TCGA 1992, Sched 8, paras 2(1) and 277(2).

Walton J held that a premium comprised 'a sum of money paid to a landlord as consideration for the grant of a lease'. He held that the reimbursement monies comprised a premium, and if there were any doubt on that they would definitely amount to 'any like sum'.

Thus L was chargeable to capital gains tax as if he had received disposal proceeds equal to the sums paid by T. (It may be asked why L is chargeable to CGT if his expenditure is simply being reimbursed. Assume L paid nothing for the freehold. Assume his payments to the builders and the professionals amounted to 100. Assume he charges T a rent of 20 per cent of the occupational rents. Assume T reimburses the 100. L's CGT cost is only 80 (*see* TCGA 1992, Sched 8, para 2(2)). He has thus made a gain of 20 (100 (premium)—80 (CGT base cost).)

The following four types of situation (involving, say, an office develoment) should be noted.

Situation 1: Simple charge of premium

L arranges for a new building to be built on its land. The building is built and L then grants a long lease (over 50 years) to T charging T a premium.

It is quite clear in a case such as this that L can be chargeable to capital gains tax by reference to the premium (note that if the lease were for 50 years or less the lease premium provisions in TA 1988, s 34 *et seq* must be looked at: these could charge part of the premium as if it were rent). For VAT purposes the supply would be one of a land interest. The supply would be exempt, but L would have the option to charge VAT on the premium and any rents (*see* Figure 23.1).

Figure 23.1

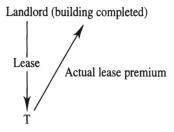

Situation 2: *Moorgate* deals

L employs a builder to construct a building and halfway through the construction T agrees to reimburse L for the past and future expenditure if L agrees to grant a lease at completion to T.

This situation is covered by the *Moorgate* decision, and the monies paid by T to L would comprise a premium for the purposes of capital gains tax. The supply would be exempt although L would have the option to charge VAT on the premium and any rents (*see* Figure 23.2).

Figure 23.2:

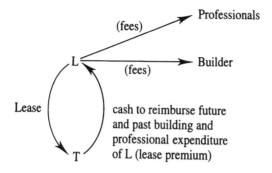

Situation 3: Classical building lease

L grants a lease to T requiring T to construct a new building on the land leased. T employs the builders and the necessary professionals to ensure that the building is properly put up. L lays out no expenditure although his rental return would reflect the value of the land.

In this case there would be no question of L's being charged to capital gains tax. L has never received a premium. At p 300f Walton J stated that in a case such as that:

> ... there would not have been any question of there having been a premium for the lease; at any rate, under present practice the Crown would not have so contended.

Thus the classical building lease structure would not give rise to any capital gains tax problems. The builder will charge VAT at 17.5 per cent on his supplies. T, when it sublets, would make an exempt supply for VAT but will have the option to charge VAT on the rents. L may also have the option to charge VAT on the rents it charges T.

Figure 23.3:

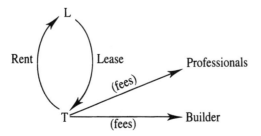

Situation 4: Landlord developer deals

L grants a lease of bare land to T. T enters into a development agreement with L under which L agrees to develop the property. L enters into a building agreement with the builder and the other professionals to ensure that the building is put up.

Under the development agreement L would have agreed with T that L would put up the building and will be paid a development fee for doing the works, in one lump sum or by stage payments.

These payments by T to L would not amount to premiums for the purposes of capital gains tax. L would be trading as a developer. The payments made to him by T under the development agreement would be trading income against which he could offset his trading expenses, such as the payments made to the builder and the other professionals.

Walton J at p 300g referred to this type of proposition and said:

> Of course, *Moorgate* (L) might have been very properly employed by the Society (T) to discharge its obligation to build, and pay proper sums for that purpose.

L must charge T VAT on the fees paid under the development agreement; the parties cannot treat this situation as if an exempt premium was being charged, with L having the option to charge VAT on the premium.

Figure 23.4:

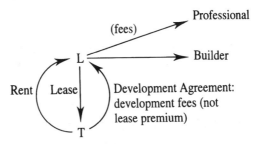

The parties should decide exactly how they wish to structure their development ie as a lease premium arrangement, a development agreement (between the tenant and the landlord) arrangement, or a building lease arrangement. They should then ensure that all the steps they take are compatible with that type of arrangement.

HIDDEN VAT

The situation may arise where a landlord has agreed to let property to a developer to develop into penthouses in return for a £1m premium. The landlord may be obliged to do some building works (vatable) for an adjoining penthouse tenant of his for £50,000. It may be agreed between the parties that the developer will do those building works and pay the landlord a reduced premium of £950,000. What VAT consequences arise from that? In addition the landlord may have to pay the adjoining tenant £40,000 to give up a right to light so enabling the developer to complete the works on his plot. What is the VAT consequences of that? (*see* Figure 23.5).

Figure 23.5: Hidden VAT

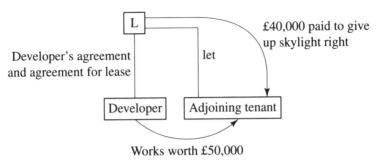

THE £40,000 PAYMENT FOR LIGHT RIGHT

One would anticipate that no VAT will be charged by the tenant on this sum paid to the tenant by the landlord. This is because:

(a) it will be an exempt surrender of a land interest and it is not possible to exercise the election to waive exemption with respect to domestic accommodation;

(b) apart from being exempt under general principles one would have thought that if the payment related to domestic accommodation the transaction would not have been carried out in the course or furtherance of a business for VAT purposes (if part is used for non-domestic purposes this position may have to be reconsidered);

(c) the figure is under the VAT registration limit (if the tenant is otherwise registered for VAT or decides to register with respect to this transaction then different considerations may apply).

THE £50,000 PAYMENT FOR WORKS

Reverse premium

The original documents must be amended to enable the price to be reduced. If one alters the basic rights the parties are in effect stating that the landlord will pass over its financial liabilities in respect of the building works to the developer in return for the 'payment' by the landlord to the developer of the premium reduction (ie the landlord is effectively saying to the tenant 'take over this obligation, I have to carry out work on the neighbouring tenant's land and I will pay you (in effect) a sum equal to the reduction in the premium'. VAT at the rate of 7 over 47 of the premium reduction will be payable by the developer to the Customs.

Original deal

One can see that if the deal was originally structured so that L granted a lease to T for a fixed premium with T being under an obligation to pay for all the building works including the works for the adjoining tenant so far as necessary, the result could well be different (*Clarke v United Real (Moorgate) Ltd* [1988] STC 273).

No bounty

However, the parties must deal with the legal position they have. No party is making a gift to the other.

EC Sixth Directive

It is not felt that anything special turns on the fact that the premium is reduced or could be said to be discounted. Certain discounts under the EC Sixth Directive, art 11A(3)(*a*) and (*b*) are not vatable considerations. Those relate to price reductions which are allowed to clients; in the case in point the price reduction is the consideration for the provision of the service by the developer for taking over the building obligations. The taxpayer is thus not assisted by those provisions.

DEVELOPER'S LAND INTEREST

A fund which owns a freehold may grant a lease to a developer, who carries out the various development obligations and then grants subleases to the occupational tenants. This is the 'dangling cherry' structure.

Normally there should be no tax problems. The developer holds his interest as trading stock and then assigns or sells it. Problems can arise, however, if he decides to 'stay in'.

A pension fund may own a parcel of land. It agrees with D Ltd (the developer) for D Ltd to arrange for a building to be constructed on the land, and for D Ltd to take a lease. D Ltd will then grant an occupational lease. Let us say that, of the £100 paid by the tenant to D Ltd, D Ltd has to pay £70 to the fund. Thus D Ltd takes its developer's profit in the form of a land interest. It is assumed that D Ltd decides to retain its land interest as an investment.

It appears that the Revenue argue that the value of D Ltd's land interest must be treated as a fee paid by the pension fund to D Ltd for carrying out development works.

The author is aware of cases where the Revenue have taken this point even though D Ltd had, at commencement, an agreement for a lease.

If the Revenue are right, it follows that D Ltd will have made a supply for VAT, though the author is only aware of one situation where Customs have taken a point such as this (*see* Figure 23.6).

Figure 23.6:

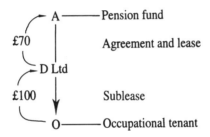

WORKS FOR LOCAL AUTHORITY

If a developer does, say, refurbishment works for a local authority the VAT position must be noted.

A developer may want land from a local authority (Green land). It may agree to refurbish a building on Blue land (owned by the local authority) in return for the Green land (*see* Figure 23.7).

A VAT charge may arise on that transaction.

Figure 23.7:

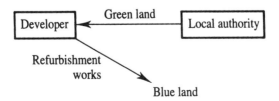

GUARANTEE FEES

The provision of finance is exempt under VATA 1994, Sched 9, Group 5.

Item 1 of Sched 9, Group 5 exempts the issue of any security for money or any note or order for the payment of money.

It may be that the parent company of a developer can issue such a security to the employer and make an exempt supply while the amounts paid to the developer would be vatable.

Figure 23.8:

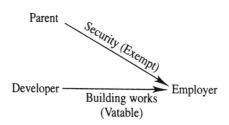

One point of warning for guarantors is they must ensure that their guarantee cannot be construed as a contract of insurance as Insurance Premium Tax (FA 1994, Pt III) of 17.5 per cent (in fact, a furtive VAT charge) may be exigible on any payments made to get the guarantee. What then is a contract of insurance? The following guidelines may prove helpful.

Labels

Labels are, of course, important although not decisive by any means. A performance bond should be called a performance bond (*Seaton v Heath* [1899] 1 QB 782 at 792; *Trade Indemnity Co v Workington Harbour and Dock Board* [1937] AC 1).

Substance

One will look to the substance of what has been created between the relevant parties (*Seaton, above*, at 792).

Link of insured to insurer

Contracts of insurance are generally matters of speculation: the person taking out the insurance (the buyer) has a good knowledge as to the risk whilst the insurer has not the same knowledge (*Seaton, above*, at 793).

The insured generally puts the risk before the insurer as a business trans-action and the insurer fixes a proper price to be remunerated for the risk to be undertaken. The insurer agrees to pay the loss incurred by the insured in the event of certain specified contingencies occurring (*Seaton, above*, at 793).

Link of surety to supplier

In the case of a guarantee there is a fundamental direct relationship between the supplier and the insured. The supplier undertakes to do some-thing and feels he can perform, but if performance fails then the surety enters into a relationship of creditor and debtor to the purchaser. There may be no direct bargain between the surety and the creditor. The risk under-taken is generally known to the surety and the circumstances generally point to the view that as between the creditor and surety it was contem-plated and intended that the surety should take upon himself to ascertain exactly what risk he was taking upon himself (*Seaton, above*, at 793). The guarantee is in the nature of a contract under which the surety agrees to answer for the debt default or misconduct of another (*Trade Indemnity, above*, at 17).

Indemnity

Thus if a builder agrees to carry out a contract for a client, the client may want a performance bond from a bank. The bond may have to be paid if the builder defaults. A very strong indication that there is no insurance would exist if the surety has a right of indemnity from the builder who did not properly perform. The same principles apply if a parent company (instead of a bank) gives a bond to a client (employer) that the parent company's subsidiary (the builder) will perform its building obligations. Sheen J in *V Zuhar K Ann v Selin* [1987] 1 Lloyd's Rep 151 stated that the existence of a counter-indemnity is wholly inconsistent with the notion of insurance.

Intention

The question will ultimately depend on the parties' intention as expressed in the relevant documentation (Lord Esher in *Dane v Mortgage Insurance* [1894] 1 QB 54 at 60).

BUILDING FOR THE LANDOWNER

If a developer carries out construction works for an exempt landowner he must ensure that he is not acting as agent (as far as the inputs of the developer are concerned) of the landowner who may ultimately make exempt supplies.

In the case of *Drexlodge Ltd v The Commissioners* (MAN/88/705 (Decision 5614)), X was a property developer. It found sites which were purchased by the Co-operative Insurance Society Ltd (the Society). X undertook to develop the sites and to find tenants for the developments when completed. All the contractual arrangements for developing the sites were made by X. It also arranged the advertising and negotiation of the lettings although the leases were granted by the Society as the landowner. X deducted input tax on all the supplies referable to the development. Customs contended that the taxpayer (X) at all times acted as agent for the Society. The Society was the undisclosed principal. The supplies were not made to X and so X could not reclaim input tax.

The tribunal held that in making the contracts with the builder and the professionals, X was acting in its own name.

X provided services to the Society to develop the sites for which it was paid the appropriate monies. The services supplied by the builder and the various professionals were made to X as a principal and not as agent for the Society.

There was no evidence that the Society interfered with the day-to-day work on the site or attended any meetings. The Society wanted a building as an investment and the arrangements with X were that X should supply the building to an agreed specification and tenanted at an agreed sum. There was no agency arrangement. The legal ownership of the land to be developed was in the hands of the Society but that did not prevent it from allowing a third party from operating a business of its own on the land. The agreements for the development operated as licences to the taxpayer (X) to occupy the land for the purposes stated in the agreements.

It was held in *Kerrott and Kerrott v FM-M* (No 73/85) CJEC (1987) BTC 5015; [1987] 2 CMLR 221 that the sale of land and the grant of contracts to build thereon was not a supply of buildings (within art 4(3)(*b*) of the Sixth Directive).

SPLICE-UP DEALS

Where a taxpayer buys land and disposes of part to a developer, with a view to the developer carrying out works on the retained part, tax problems can arise.

X may grant a lease to Y of an old building comprising two floors. Y may wish to use the first floor for the purposes of carrying out its trade of selling widgets, for example. It may not want the second floor but the landlord may insist that the entirety be taken. Y may transfer the lease to a developer in consideration of an obligation on the developer to refurbish the first floor. Y will take a leaseback from the developer of the first floor for 125 years at a peppercorn rent. The developer would employ the builder and all the other professionals. Are there any tax problems? Assume that the lease by X to Y was for 126 years for a premium at a peppercorn rent:

(1) On the assignment of the lease (by Y to the developer) there may be technically a total disposal as a matter of law for the purposes of capital gains tax, although the Revenue are unlikely to take the point.

(2) The consideration for VAT and corporation tax purposes received by the developer for the provision of development works in respect of the first floor equals the market value of the lease encumbered by the leaseback to the developer, ie, broadly, the market value of the second floor area. VAT may therefore have to be paid by the developer because he has received a land interest as a development fee. The VAT charge must be calculated with reference to VATA 1994, s 19(3).

(3) Y may be found to have dealt in the property for income tax or corporation tax purposes: *see Iswera v IRC* [1965] 1 WLR 663, *IRC v Paul* (1956) 3 SALR 335 and *Kirkham v Williams* [1989] STC 333.

(4) Stamp duty may be payable with respect to the premiums and the sale consideration and on the land exchanges.

Figure 23.9:

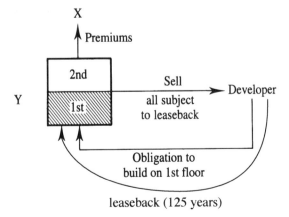

leaseback (125 years)

ASSIGNED BUILDING LEASE DEALS

L may enter into a building lease (ie an agreement under which L will grant T or T's assignees a lease when the building is constructed on the land) with T. T may assign the lease to a bank, with the bank employing T to find tenants and develop the property. The bank would fund the development.

Ultimately when the building is completed L will grant the formal legal lease to the bank, who will in turn grant the formal leases to the occupational tenants.

The tax points to bear in mind are as follows:

(1) The sale of the building lease by T to the bank should be an exempt supply although the option to charge VAT will be available. Note that the supply will be an exempt supply only if it comprises the disposal of any interest in or right over land. In *Trewby v Customs and Excise Commissioners* [1976] STC 122 Geoffrey Land LJ stated:

> Right over land must receive a restricted interpretation. If it were given the broad meaning contended for by Counsel for the taxpayer, the words which follow (that is to say all or any licence to occupy land) would be otiose. A licence of almost any description would be covered by the words 'right over land'. In our judgment in order to make sense of this part of Sched 5 the words 'any interest in or right over land' must be confined to a legal or equitable interest in the land in the sense used by Lord Upjohn in *National Provincial Bank Ltd v Ainsworth* [1965] AC 117 at 1237. Interest and right are treated together as practically synonymous. Licence to occupy is in a contrasting category.

(2) One is, therefore, required to look to general land law principles to see whether an equitable interest has been created. The position is unclear if an agreement for lease is entered into but the grant of the formal lease is conditional on the building being constructed. This is because the courts may not grant an order for specific performance if a condition has yet to be fulfilled, ie the building works must be completed. Unless the courts were at least in a position to grant specific performance then there could be problems in establishing that the interest is an interest in land. Of course, an order for specific performance is discretionary, but if the courts would not even entertain an application because the necessary condition is not fulfilled it is arguable that no right over land was created by the building lease.

(3) If that is the case then, of course, the supply would be vatable at 17.5 per cent and the option provisions would not be relevant. To the

author's knowledge such assignments in the past have always been treated by practitioners as exempt supplies and Customs have not taken any points in this respect.

(4) Stamp duty will also be payable on the sale of the agreement for lease.

(5) It is not felt that any stamp duty will be payable on the building costs. However, if the tenant had constructed the building and then sold it to the bank with the formal lease being granted direct by the landlord then duty would be payable on the amount paid by the bank to T to acquire the property. Additionally stamp duty may be payable on the grant of the lease. It should also be noted that stamp duty may have been payable on entering into the agreement for the lease in the first place.

(6) Instead of assigning the agreement to the bank the tenant may have merely mortgaged it to the bank in return for advances, with the tenant ultimately selling the interest if needs be to the bank to repay the advances.

(7) Another approach may have been for an overriding lease of little value to be granted to the bank with the tenant, when the building is completed, surrendering his interest for a premium to the bank. The bank will then become entitled to the occupational rents. The surrender may be vatable but the bank will be in a position to reclaim the VAT if it exercises the election to waive exemption. No stamp duty will be payable on the surrender of the lease by the tenant to the bank if it is done by operation of law and not preceded by an agreement.

AVOIDING VAT ON REFURBISHER'S PROFITS

A developer may agree with an exempt fund to carry out refurbishment works. The developer would employ the builder and other professionals. It is likely that any VAT which the exempt fund cannot claim back will be borne by the developer as a development expense.

If the developer has contracted to buy the land which he is to sell to the exempt fund this will in all cases be an exempt supply (assuming the option is not exercised). This is so whether or not he sub-sells the land with legal completion taking place at inception or when the building has been refurbished. The developer should contemplate legal completion after the refurbishment works have been completed, because in this event no VAT is charged by the developer to the fund (there is an exempt property sale); and although the developer may have to bear the VAT on the costs charged by the builder and the professionals no VAT need be charged with respect to the developer's profit (*note*, however, Chapter 21) (*see* Figure 23.10).

Figure 23.10:   Avoiding VAT on Refurbisher's Profits

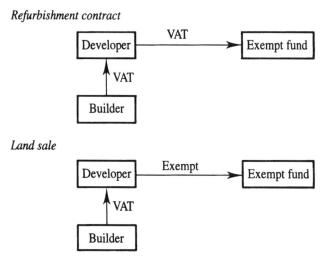

EURO HOTEL 'INTEREST' PAYMENTS

'Interest' figures in many development agreements are not really interest properly so called, according to the *Euro Hotel* case.

In *Re Euro Hotel (Belgravia) Ltd* [1975] STC 682, L granted a building lease to T who sold it to a bank for £1.5m, had an agreement to take a lease-back and received funding from the bank to carry out the development. The bank charged interest on 'the current total investment' (ie the bank's development cost outlay). It was held that there was no interest properly so called (*see* Figure 23.11).

Figure 23.11:   Euro hotel 'interest' payments

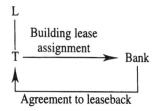

Megarry J at 691–692 stated thus:

It seems to me that running through the cases there is the concept that as a general rule two requirements must be satisfied for a payment to amount to interest, and a fortiori to amount to 'interest of money'. First, there must be a sum of money by reference to which the payment which is said to be interest is to be ascertained. Plainly, there are sums of 'money' in the present case. Second, those sums of money must be sums that are due to the person entitled to the alleged interest; and it is this latter requirement that is mainly in issue before me. I do not, of course, say that in every case these two requirements are exhaustive, or that they are inescapable. Thus I do not see why payments should not be 'interest of money' if A lends money to B and stipulates that the interest should be paid not to him but to X; yet for the ordinary case I think that they suffice.

Now in the case before me there is no question of any loan. True, the petitioning creditor has paid money to the company, but that money has been paid not as a loan but as an out-and-out payment to the company for carrying out the development and giving the petitioning creditor property rights in the development, and so on. The provision for payment of 'interest' on the current total investment when it reaches the maximum amount was doubtless intended to act as a spur to the company to complete the development economically in order to obtain the underlease, and to get the agreement for the sub-underlease made in order to increase the maximum amount.

Once the current total investment had reached £2,135,000, 'interest' on it became payable by the company to the petitioning creditor under cl 5(1)(*b*) of the sub-building agreement, unless the company had increased the 'maximum amount' under the agreement to £2,303,000, which the company could do by entering into the agreement for the sub-underlease of part of the premises in a satisfactory form: and if 'interest' became payable under this head, it continued until the 'maximum amount' was duly increased.

Further, when the current total investment reached £2,303,000, 'interest' on it was to become payable by the company to the petitioning creditor under cl 5(1)(*a*) until the underlease was granted to the company by the petitioning creditor: and this would not be done until the development was completed. The general import of the provision for 'interest' seems to be to provide an incentive to the company to hasten on both with making the agreement for the sub-underlease and with completing the development.

Such payments do not seem to me to be 'interest', and certainly not 'interest of money', within the statute. There are indeed sums of money from which the 'interest' will be ascertained, but I cannot see that those sums of money are anything more than units of calculation. What the company has to do is to make certain payments, the amount of which has to be calculated from the sums of money in question; but the payments do not seem to me to be 'interest' on those sums in any true sense of the word. The sums of money have been paid to the company once and for all, and are not due to the petitioning creditor in any way. They are not debts or obligations of the company, and they are not sums which belong to the petitioning creditor in even the most colloquial sense. The payments to be made are not payments made for the use of the money of another, but payments made because the company has not proceeded fast enough with its obligations to complete the development and enter into an agreement for the grant of the sub-underlease. The payments are not compensation for delay in payment but for delay in performance of other obligations; and the payments are not payments by time for the use of money but payments by time for non-performance for those obligations. It is not easy to think of a suitably comparable case, but there seems to be a possible analogy if a landowner were to sell part of his land, covenanting to erect a dividing wall within three months of completion, and also, if the wall was not then complete, to pay 'interest' on the purchase money paid by the purchaser until the wall was completed. Such payments do not seem to me to wear any of the guise of 'interest of money'.

This is an important case to bear in mind, as payments in property development agreements may be called interest (which would be exempt for VAT purposes) when, in fact, they may be payments for construction or for buying land.

A and B, for example, may set up a joint venture company. X, the subsidiary of A, may agree to develop land (build an office block) which is sold by B to the joint venture company for a share of the profits made by the joint venture company from the development and sale of the land. X also funds the development costs out of its own monies and charges the joint venture company notional interest. When the property is developed and sold the entire profit made by X (including the notional interest) may be a vatable construction fee—the sum paid to B would be land sale price (*see* Figure 23.12).

SELLING LAND IN CONSIDERATION OF SERVICES

It often occurs that a taxpayer owns two parcels of land and sells parcel A to the developer in consideration of a cash sum and the developer building on parcel B.

The position may be that the vendor is a charity and wishes a new village hall to be built on parcel B. It may sell parcel A to the developer for £200,000 plus an obligation taken from the developer to build the new village hall, which obligation is worth £300,000, on parcel B which is retained by the charity. The builder for its own trading purposes wishes to start constructing a new office development on parcel A immediately.

The sale of parcel A may be exempt, but its real value is £500,000. £300,000-worth of land value has been transferred to the developer in consideration of the developer constructing the new village hall on parcel B.

Figure 23.12:   Joint development company

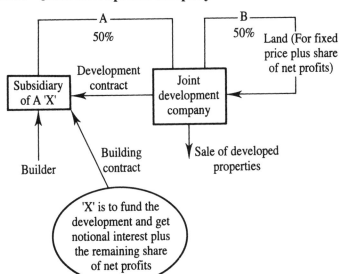

It may be that the building on parcel B is to be used for a relevant charitable purpose (*see* p 117). The charity should be able to obtain a certificate enabling the £300,000-worth of fee paid to the developer to be zero-rated (*see* p 178).

The charity, however, may wish to retain the legal estate in parcel A, with completion taking place only after the developer has completed the works on parcel B (*see* Figure 23.13).

Delaying completion may raise some difficult VAT and commercial points.

Figure 23.13:   Selling land in consideration of services

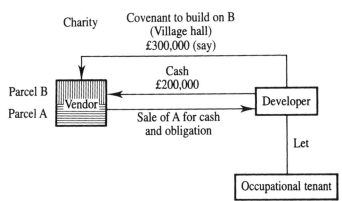

At the time of the formal grant there will be a newly constructed commercial building on parcel A and, thus, on the face of it, a vatable supply at 17.5 per cent may arise.

The charity could grant a long lease to the developer and give the developer an option to acquire the freehold when the works are completed.

An alternative may be for the vendor to sell the freehold to the developer and take a charge on the property. Yet again, the property could perhaps be put in the name of a nominee for the developer, but with the developer being unable to demand the property from the nominee until the works of putting up the village hall had been completed. The vendor will also have a charge on the land.

COMPANY SALE PLANS

VAT is not payable on the sale of a company.

X Ltd owns Y Ltd. Y Ltd has elected with respect to Greenacre. If X Ltd sells Y Ltd no VAT is chargeable (*see also* Chapter 3).

Figure 23.14:   Company sale plans

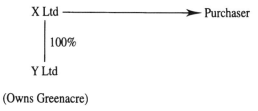

(Owns Greenacre)

SALE AND SURRENDER

It may be possible for X to sell his freehold land and retain a non-building covenant. If the purchaser obtains planning permission the covenant at the purchaser's option can be released for a cash sum (*see* Figure 23.15).

In particular, the charge to capital gains tax which will arise when the sums are received by the grantors of the restrictive covenant options (after the options have been exercised and the surrender of the particular covenant takes place) will result in disposals in the tax years in which the sums payable by the developer are received by the grantors. This is because TCGA 1992, s 22(2) provides that if a capital sum is received in return for the surrender of rights the time of disposal shall be the time when the capital sum is received (this is contrary to the general rule which takes as the time of disposal the time when unconditional contracts are entered into).

The following points should be noted.

(1) On the surrender of the covenant rights a supply for VAT purposes will be made by the grantor and he must charge VAT to the builder at 17.5 per cent on the surrender consideration, but only if he has elected to waive exemption: if he has not, the supply is an exempt surrender. No doubt the builder will register for VAT and be in a position to reclaim any VAT.

(2) It is assumed that the grantor will not be connected for capital gains purposes with the builder. For instance, they must not be in any form of partnership or otherwise connected within TCGA 1992, s 286. If they are connected the anti-avoidance provisions in s 62(5) will have to be considered.

(3) This route may mean that the purchaser can (it can be argued) avoid stamp duty on the surrendered right.

(4) Steps should be taken to ensure that the covenant is enforceable.

(5) There should be separate agreements for the sale of the land and the retention of the covenant rights assuming that that does not give rise to any land law problems.

(6) Retirement relief and roll-over relief for capital gains tax purposes within TCGA 1992, s 152 should be examined.

(7) There may not be any base cost available with respect to the monies payable under the option which causes the release of the covenant. This is because of the narrow interpretation given to the expression 'part disposal' in the case of *Berry v Warnett* (1982) 55 TC 92, but it may be that the base cost plus indexation is such that the parties are not too concerned about the point. This area of law is also unclear, and in practice it is possible that the Revenue will allow the part-disposal rules to apply.

(8) If the documentation is carefully drafted one can achieve the basic objective of ensuring that there is a disposal of the land followed by a subsequent surrender of rights: that is critical to ensuring that capital gains tax on the bulk of the consideration is payable only when the surrender of rights consideration is received and not earlier, when, say, the land is purchased. There is no reason in principle why this type of transaction set up in the way described should not be respected by the courts as a legitimate way of carrying out the transaction for tax purposes.

(9) Present tax rates are modest. It may be that when the option is exercised the rates have increased considerably. However, some risk is inevitable, and, of course, tax rates could go down at the relevant times.

Figure 23.15:   Sale and surrender

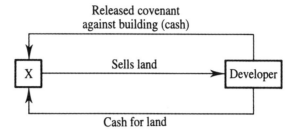

Released covenant
against building (cash)

Sells land

X   Developer

Cash for land

DEDICATIONS, s 106 AGREEMENTS AND TRANSFERS OF ROADS

Customs' views on dedications, s 106 agreements and transfers of roads to management companies are contained in Notice 742, para 7.11–7.14, set out *below*:

Dedications
7.11   (a) *Dedications of roads and sewers and transactions under planning agreements*
Agreements drawn up between developers, local authorities and water sewerage undertakers make provision for a wide variety of land, buildings and works to be provided, at the developer's expense, in connection with the granting of planning permission for the development.

(b)   *Dedications of new roads and sewers to local authorities and sewerage undertakers*
If, as a developer, you dedicate or vest, for no monetary consideration:

• a new road (under the provisions of the Highways Act 1980 or the Roads (Scotland) Act 1984); or
• a new sewer or ancillary works (under the provisions of the Water Industries Act 1991 or the Sewerage (Scotland) Act 1968),

this does not constitute a supply by you. No VAT is, therefore, chargeable to the local authority or sewerage undertaker.

Input tax you incur on the construction of such works is, however, attributable to your supplies of the development which is served by the road or sewer, ie the land or buildings (houses, shops, factory units, etc). If your supplies of the land or buildings are taxable supplies, or if you are liable for a taxable self-supply, then the input tax you incur on constructing the roads and sewers is recoverable according to the normal rules. Where, however, you make exempt supplies—of buildings or of areas of land on the development—you will not be able to recover all your input tax.

Agreements under section 106 of the Town and Country Planning Act 1990 or section 50 of the Town and Country Planning (Scotland) Act 1972

7.12   As a developer, you may provide many other types of goods and services free, or for a purely nominal charge, to the local or other authority under section 106 or other similar agreements which may loosely be described as 'planning gain agreements'.

Such goods and services may include buildings such as community centres or schools, amenity land or civil engineering works. Or they may be in the form of services such as an agreement to construct something on land already owned by the authority or a third party. Any such provision of goods or services does not constitute a supply for consideration to the local, or other, authority or to the third party. Consequently, no VAT is chargeable by you on the handing over of the land or building or the completion of the works.

The input tax you incur is attributable to your supplies of land and buildings on the development for which the planning permission was given as in paragraph 8.6.

Cash contributions made by developers

7.13   You may be required to pay sums of money, or sums of money in addition to buildings or works, to a local authority or a third party under section 106 and other similar agreements eg for the future maintenance of a building or land or as a contribution towards improvement of the infrastructure. Such sums are not consideration for taxable supplies to you by the local authority or by the third party.

Transfers of roads etc to management companies

7.14   If you are a developer of a private housing or industrial estate, you may transfer, usually for a nominal monetary consideration, the basic amenities of estate roads and footpaths, communal parking and open space to a management company which maintains them. No supply is regarded as taking place. The input tax you incur is attributable to your supplies of land and buildings, as in paragraph 7.11.

Chapter 24

Lease terms

CHECKLIST

The following points should be noted when looking at the VAT clauses or tax points in a non-domestic lease:

(1) The tenant may be liable to pay the landlord's solicitor's costs on the grant of the lease and subsequently if there are variations or licences are granted, for example. For the full VAT implications of the tenant's agreeing to this, *see* p 289.

(2) The landlord may want to insert a clause in the lease confirming, for the avoidance of doubt, that he can exercise the election to waive exemption.

(3) If VAT is chargeable on any supplies made by the landlord to the tenant the lease should provide that the VAT is added to the amounts otherwise payable.

(4) There should be a provision that any VAT charged to the landlord by third parties which the landlord cannot reclaim is passed on to the tenant.

(5) A distinction between the common parts and the demised premises should be made.

(6) Where appropriate, the composite supply doctrine is to be relied on.

(7) Any interest paid on rents which are paid late is probably an exempt supply of finance (Customs seem to take that view, or at least they do not consider the interest to be additional rent).

(8) Insurance (as such) is exempt (if T reimburses L's insurance premiums the composite supply doctrine is, however, likely to apply with the reimbursement likely to be treated as additional rent for VAT purposes).

(9) The supply of parking spaces can give rise to a vatable supply at the positive rate.

(10) The rent review clause should be considered. In deciding who is in the market one could assume that all persons can reclaim any VAT charged on the rent provided always that the clause cannot have the effect of reducing the rent otherwise obtainable by the landlord on a rent review.

(11) The definition clause in a lease often states that any reference to any Act of Parliament shall include any modification or extension or re-enactment, and any instruments, orders or regulations etc for the time being issued or given thereunder or deriving authority therefrom. In respect of VAT there should also be a provision such as 'and additionally in the case of the Value Added Tax Act 1994 shall include any directives and regulations adopted by the Council of the European Communities which relate to value added tax'.

PAYMENT OF LANDLORD'S SOLICITOR'S COSTS BY TENANT

From time to time Customs change their practice concerning the VAT position where a tenant reimburses the landlord's solicitor's costs. The Customs did, however, agree some guidance with the Law Society: this is reproduced in *Taxation* on 29 October 1992 (*see* p 291). (*See* also Notice 742, para 4.10 and De Voil, V6.190.)

Assume a situation where a landlord (an investment company) grants or has granted a lease to a tenant and has incurred £100 solicitor's costs, plus £17.50 VAT. The tenant is obliged to indemnify the landlord for those costs and does indemnify him. The tenant is a trader who is able to reclaim all the VAT charged to him. The following rules can be stated.

Rule 1: VAT at grant: election made

If, when L grants the lease to T, he has elected to waive exemption, L can reclaim the VAT charged to him by the solicitor; L issues to T a VAT invoice and charges him £100 plus £17.50 VAT. T can reclaim from Customs the £17.50 VAT (*see* Figure 24.1).

Rule 2: VAT at grant: no election

L grants a lease and has not exercised the election to waive exemption. T pays the landlord's solicitor's costs. The landlord cannot reclaim the VAT charged to him by the solicitor and he must simply charge the tenant £117.50, no part of which is VAT, and no VAT invoice must be given to the tenant. The tenant can reclaim nothing from Customs (*see* Figure 24.2).

Figure 24.1:   On grant of lease tenant agrees to pay landlord's solicitor's costs—L has elected

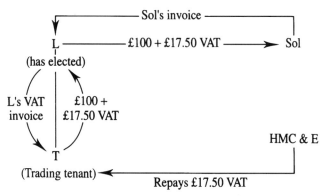

Figure 24.2:   On grant of lease tenant agrees to pay landlord's solicitor's costs—L has not elected

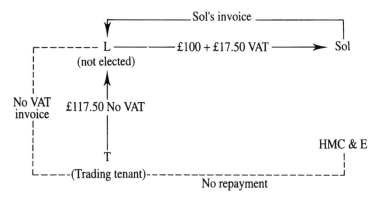

Rule 3: Lease already granted: no new rights

L has already granted the lease to T. Under the terms of the lease T is entitled to do certain things on reimbursing the landlord's costs, for example, to change user for which the landlord cannot unreasonably withhold his consent, or to change the user without needing the landlord's consent. If the landlord had elected to waive exemption, the consequences are identical to those under Rule 1 *above*. If the landlord has not waived exemption, the consequences are as under Rule 2 *above*.

Rule 4: Lease already granted: new rights

The lease has already been granted, but the landlord grants a new right to the tenant on condition that the tenant pays the landlord's solicitor's costs. For example the landlord has an absolute discretion as to whether consent is to be granted for the exercise of a right, and he agrees to exercise that discretion in consideration of T's paying L's solicitor's costs. The supply in that case would be a separate vatable supply by the landlord to the tenant unless the supply is an exempt one. For example, if the landlord has not exercised the election to waive exemption and grants the tenant the right to use the premises for a different purpose (the tenant having no rights to demand such a change of user), that would be an exempt supply (the situation would be as in Rule 2). If the landlord had exercised the election to waive exemption and granted such a new right, that would be a vatable supply (the situation would be as in Rule 1). In practical terms where a new right is granted, it is almost certain that the supply will be exempt if the landlord has not elected to waive exemption; and vatable if the landlord has exercised the election to waive exemption. That conclusion follows, *inter alia*, from the decision in *Lubbock Fine & Co v Customs and Excise Commissioners* [1993] STC 101.

Customs guidance

The guidance mentioned at p 289 *above* (reproduced in *Taxation*, 29 October 1992), is as follows:

VAT: Payment of third party costs

The Indemnity Principle
An article in the *Law Society's Gazette*, 24 October 1990, stated that when a person other than the solicitor's own client is paying the solicitor's costs, the liability of the paying party is one of indemnity only, and thus in itself outside the scope of VAT. In fact, such payment will only be regarded as outside the scope in certain circumstances, for example, as follows:

(*i*)   where following completion of litigation (or arbitration), one party is ordered to pay the other party's costs;

(*ii*)   where a party to a transaction undertakes to pay the other party's costs, and the matter does not proceed to completion, so the costs are 'abortive'.

However, there are other circumstances where the payment of costs by a third party *is* regarded as consideration for the supply for VAT purposes. One specific example of such a situation would be where a transaction obliges one party to be responsible for the costs of the other relating to that transaction, in which case payment will be regarded as part of the consideration for the supply (provided the transaction proceeds to completion).

It is worth restating the following general principles which apply when the payment is on an indemnity basis:

(*a*)   the solicitor whose costs are to be paid should deliver a tax invoice to his own client. If his client is not a registered taxable person, it is permissible to deliver a VAT inclusive bill without distinguishing the value added tax element, although this would not be common practice;

(*b*)   if the solicitor's client is a registered fully taxable person, and the supply of legal services is obtained for the purpose of the client's business, the client will be entitled to an input tax credit in which case the indemnifying party need only pay the costs exclusive of value added tax;

(*c*)   if the solicitor's client is not a registered fully taxable person and cannot obtain input tax credit, the indemnifying party is liable to pay the costs and VAT as well. However, the indemnifying party cannot recover the value added tax;

(*d*)   where the solicitor's client is a partly exempt registered taxable person, paragraph (*b*) above applies only to the extent that the client can obtain credit for input tax. Paragraph (*c*) applies to the balance;

(*e*)   *in no circumstances may a tax invoice be issued by the client's solicitor to the paying party* who is not in law entitled to receive an input tax credit as the services have not been rendered to him. The paying party should therefore receive a note of the other party's costs in such terms that the note cannot be mistaken for a tax invoice issued by the paying party.

The consideration for the supply

It is clearly stated in Customs and Excise Notice [742 (Property ownership),] at paragraph [4.10], that payment by a tenant of a landlord's costs incurred in respect of the grant of a lease or licence would be regarded as part of the consideration for the supply by the landlord to the tenant. The practical implications will depend on whether the landlord has elected to waive exemption from value added tax in relation to the property. If no election to waive exemption has been made, the landlord would not be entitled to an input tax credit on his costs, so the tenant would be required to pay the gross costs including the VAT element: there will have been no taxable supply, so the tenant will not receive a value added tax invoice and will be unable to recover as input tax the VAT he has paid to the landlord.

If the landlord has elected to waive exemption, so value added tax is payable in respect of the rent or premium, the landlord can recover the VAT element of the costs, and the tenant will only be required to pay the net amount of the landlord's costs, but to that net amount, the landlord will add a VAT charge.

In effect, the amount paid by the tenant would be the same whether or not the landlord has elected to waive exemption, but only if the landlord has done so will the tenant receive a tax invoice from the landlord, and be able to recover the value added tax element if the tenant is a registered taxable person.

Change of policy

It has recently become apparent that Customs will also regard payment of costs which have been incurred by a landlord in respect of the exercise by a tenant of an existing right under the lease or licence as constituting part of the consideration for the supply by the landlord to tenant (and thus potentially subject to value added tax as described in the paragraph above headed 'The consideration for the supply'). This represents a change from the agreed guidance published on 24 October 1990, and it has been agreed that the effective date for the new régime will be 1 December 1992. It is accepted that if, under the terms of the lease, a landlord cannot unreasonably withhold his consent to the tenant's exercising a right, or where the tenant is permitted to exercise a right without the landlord's consent, but subject to payment by the tenant of the landlord's costs, this will be regarded as an existing right. However, where the landlord has absolute discretion as to whether consent is to be granted for the exercise of a right, payment of costs incurred by the landlord is regarded as consideration for a *separate* supply, on which the landlord will charge value added tax unless the right sought to be exercised would constitute an exempt supply.

The contents of this article supersede the article which was published in the *Gazette* on 11 July 1990, entitled 'VAT and Notices of Assignment' which should now be disregarded.

Case law

In *D & K Builders & Sons (Ampthill) Ltd* (LON/88/1046 Decision 4287) X agreed to pay costs incurred by Y (Z had supplied services to Y and Y had paid, or was liable to pay, Z). The tribunal held that the costs for VAT purposes had properly been incurred by Y because the relevant supply (by Z) had been made to Y. No supply had been made by Z to X with respect to those costs. Consequently X was not entitled to deduct input tax paid in respect of the VAT on those costs.

In *Brucegate Ltd* (MAN/89/761 Decision 4903) [1990] STI 738 the taxpayer appealed against the disallowance of input tax claimed in respect of solicitors' charges paid by it pursuant to an agreement for the purchase of the share capital of another company under which the company had agreed to indemnify the vendors in respect to their legal costs. The solicitors' account was properly addressed to their clients, the vendors. The tribunal held that the solicitors' services had been supplied only to the vendors. There had not been any supply to the taxpayer for which input tax could be allowed.

In *JG & Mrs MU Potton* (LON/87/592 Decision 2882) it was held that the tenants, who had to pay the landlord's legal costs in connection with the breach of a covenant, could not reclaim the VAT on the costs as the supplies had been made to the landlord.

SERVICE CHARGES

Customs' views on service charges vary from time to time. Their present view with respect to commercial lettings is set out in Notice 742, paras 5.2–5.7, which read as follows:

General leasehold services
5.2   It is common for leases between landlords and tenants to lay down that the landlord shall provide, and the tenants shall pay for, the upkeep of the building as a whole. The lease may provide for an inclusive rental, or it may require the tenants to contribute by means of a charge additional to the basic rent. These charges are generally referred to as 'service charges', 'maintenance charges' or 'additional rent'. Providing the services fall under the criteria in paragraph 5.5 the service charge assumes the same VAT liability as the premium or rents payable under the lease or licence.

Distinction between freehold occupants and occupants under a lease or licence in commercial (non-domestic) accommodation
5.3   There is a distinction between services supplied to lease holders and those supplied to freeholders (people who purchase their property outright). Service charges raised for the upkeep and maintenance of the common areas of a development where the property is being let by the person who has raised the charges are further consideration for the supply of the property itself. As such these services will be exempt, unless:

(a)   that person has opted to tax; or

(b)   they concern the provision of a grant covered by the exceptions to the exemption; or

(c)   they are personal services.

Service charges raised where the property has been sold freehold are standard rated in their own right. You are not making a continuing supply of accommodation to occupants of property purchased freehold and therefore your provision of services must be treated for VAT purposes as separate to the supply of the property itself. This means that the services you provide will be standard rated. However a special concession applies to dwellings.

Commercial (non-domestic) accommodation—provision of services by someone other than the landlord

5.4 If you are responsible for providing services to occupants of property in which you have no interest, for example, where you are not the ground landlord who granted leases to the occupants, your services will always be standard-rated as they are not part of the supply of the accommodation itself.

Your supply may however be to the occupants of the accommodation or to the landlord (or ground landlord). This will depend on the terms of the legal agreements between you and the occupants or landlord:

(a) If you are the person legally responsible for the provision of services to occupants and your contract is to arrange for the services and to collect the service charge on the landlord's behalf as a managing agent, then your supply is to the landlord and not to the occupants. The charge you raise to the landlord, however it is calculated, is standard-rated.

(b) If you are the person legally responsible for the provision of services to occupants (but you are not the landlord), your supply is to the occupants. The service charges they pay you will normally be standard-rated.

Distinction between general services and personal services

5.5 The broad principle for both commercial and domestic service charges is that for the service to be considered as part of the supply of property itself:

(a) it must be of a nature which is connected with the external fabric or the common parts of the building or estate as opposed to the demised areas of the property of the individual occupants; and

(b) it must be paid for by all the occupants through a common service charge.

Service charges and other payments by tenants of commercial (non-domestic) property

5.6 Payments by tenants or licensees to the landlord (or ground landlord) may be:

(a) for the supply of the property and therefore exempt (or standard-rated if the landlord (or ground landlord) has exercised the option to tax); or

(b) for supplies other than of the property and therefore separately standard-rated in their own right; or

(c) disbursements and therefore outside the scope of VAT.

For example:

- *Insurance and rates*—If the landlord is the policy holder, or rateable person, any payment for insurance or rates made by the tenants is part payment for the main supply. If the tenants are the policy holders or rateable person and the landlord makes payments on their behalf, these payments should be treated as disbursements.

- *Telephones*—If the telephone account is in the landlord's name, any charge made to tenants or licensees is payment for a taxable supply by the landlord. This includes the cost of calls, installation and rental. If however the account is in the name of the tenant but the landlord in fact pays the bill, the recovery of this from the tenant is a disbursement.

- *Reception and switchboard*—If the landlord makes a charge under the terms of the lease to tenants for the use of facilities such as reception and switchboard services which form a common part of the premises, any payment received will be further consideration for the main supply of the accommodation itself.

- *Office services*—If the landlord makes a separate charge for office services, such as typing and photocopying, this is a separate standard-rated supply. However, if under the terms of the lease, there is one inclusive charge for office services and accommodation together, and the tenants are expected to pay for the services regardless of whether they actually use them, the liability of the services will follow that of the main supply of office accommodation.

- *Fixtures and fittings*—Fixtures and fittings are regarded as part of the overall supply of the property and any charges for them are normally included in the rent. When a separate charge is made by the landlord the supply is taxable.

The above list is by no means exhaustive.

Services supplied to both commercial (non-domestic) and domestic occupants
5.7   Some examples are:

- *Electricity, lighting and heating*—If the landlord makes a separate charge for unmetered supplies of gas and electricity used by occupants, it should be treated as part of the consideration for the supply of accommodation itself and thus it will assume the same VAT liability as the premium or rents payable by the occupants. However where the landlord operates a secondary credit meter, the charges to the occupants for the gas and electricity they use are consideration for separate supplies of fuel and power. These supplies will be standard-rated to occupants of non-domestic premises and subject to VAT at 8% to occupants of domestic premises.

    Furthermore where occupants have coin operated gas or electricity meters, or the landlord's agreement with them allows them to receive an identifiable supply of fuel and power for which a separate charge is made, the charge made to the occupants is also consideration for separate supplies of fuel and power.

- *Management charges*—The charge raised by a landlord to the occupants for managing the development as a whole and administering the collection of service charges etc is also consideration for the main supply of the accommodation itself.

Where a landlord leases domestic property, the management charge element of the total service charge will be exempt from VAT.

Where a landlord leases commercial property and has opted to tax the rent, the management charge will also be standard-rated.

*   *Recreational facilities*—If such facilities as a swimming pool or gymnasium are supplied to the occupants without a separate and specific extra charge being raised to them, the liability of the supply will follow that of the main supply of the accommodation, either taxable or exempt.

Any separate charge which is raised will be standard-rated.

SUPPLIES UNDER A LEASE

There is set out *below* the VAT nature of various supplies made under leases (*see* Figure 24.3).

(1) *Rent:* Exempt unless the option to waive exemption has been exercised (*see* p 216).

(2) *Common parts:* As in (1) but *see* pp 294 and 295.

(3) *Demised premises:* The supplies made by the landlord must be dissected and VAT charged according to the nature of those supplies (*see* p 295).

(4) *Interest on late rent:* Probably an exempt supply (*see* p 280).

Figure 24.3: Following the supplies

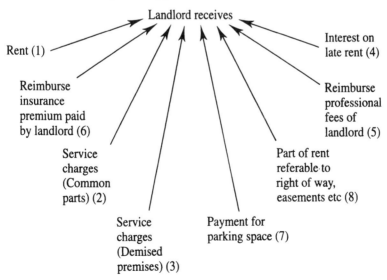

(5) *Professional fees:* This is a difficult area. For the present Customs' view *see* p 289.

(6) *Insurance:* This is an exempt supply by the landlord to the tenant under general principles, but it is likely to take on the same character as the rent under the composite supply doctrine especially if it is reserved as additional rent. In *Globe Equities Ltd v The Commissioners* (MAN/93/1449 Decision 13105) the tenant paid the landlord rent and 'insurance rent' to cover the premiums for insuring the property. It was held the amount paid to cover insurance could not be distinguished from the rest of the payment made to the landlord. The chairman, at p 13, stated:

> In my judgement the Appellant, in entering into each lease, made a single supply consisting of the grant of a legal estate in land, of which the benefit of the various obligations on the part of the Appellant contained in the lease, including those which related to insurance, was an integral part. In my judgement the provisions of the lease relating to insurance cannot realistically be extricated from the lease and considered separately: they form one part of the totality of the terms on which the Appellant was willing to grant the lease and the tenant to take it; they are closely connected with, for instance, the repairing obligations, and to treat them separately, even if they could be extricated, would, as I have said, be unreal. In this connection it is relevant that the reddendum and the proviso for re-entry respectively include the insurance rent as part of the consideration for the grant of the lease and as one of the rents which must be paid if the lease is not to be forfeited.

Note that insurance premium tax may be exigible (*see* p 274).

(7) *Parking space:* This is a vatable supply (17.5 per cent) unless the composite supply doctrine applies (*see* p 42).

(8) *Rights of way, etc:* In so far as any part of the rent ((1) *above*) is referable to the grant of rights of way over other land owned by the landlord or grants of easement etc these will be treated in the same way that the rent is treated under the composite supply doctrine.

VAT CLAUSES IN LEASE

For precedents of VAT clauses to be included in leases *see* Appendix 2, precedent 4.

PART V

MORTGAGES, DEALINGS WITH LEASES AND TRANSFERS OF BUSINESSES

Chapter 25

Mortgage transactions

This chapter deals with VAT and land mortgage transactions, in particular, the following types of transaction:

(a) creation;

(b) assignment;

(c) exercise of power of sale;

(d) taking possession by mortgagee;

(e) appointment of receiver; and

(f) discharge.

Mortgages can be legal or equitable and can be created over legal freeholds and leases and equitable interests in land.

NATURE OF THE TRANSACTIONS

The essential nature of a mortgage is that the mortgagee lends money to the mortgagor with the mortgagor mortgaging (or charging) his property to the mortgagee. The estate or other interest in the land held by the mortgagor is retained by the mortgagor. If the mortgagor defaults under the mortgage then the mortgagee can sell the mortgagor's land interest. When the mortgage is discharged all rights over the land held by the mortgagee ceases.

Creation

In *The Law of Real Property* by Sir Robert Megarry and H Wade it is stated:

> When one person lends money to another . . . he may demand some security for the payment of the money. . . . The most important kind of security is the mortgage.

The authors then state:

> The essential nature of a mortgage is that it is a conveyance of a legal or equitable interest in the property, with a provision for redemption, ie that upon repayment of a loan or the performance of some other obligation the conveyance shall become void or the interest shall be reconveyed.

When a legal mortgage of the fee simple is created the mortgagor retains the fee simple and has the equity of redemption. The mortgagee holds a lease subject to cesser on redemption. If a charge by deed expressed to be by way of legal mortgage is created the mortgagee receives no estate in the land, neither a fee simple nor a lease, but the mortgagee has 'the same protection, powers and remedies as if he had a lease for 3,000 years' (Law of Property Act (LPA) 1925, s 87(1)).

An equitable mortgage of the fee simple may also be created by, for instance, evidencing the mortgage in writing but not by deed. A mortgage (necessarily equitable) of an equitable interest may also be created.

Assignment

The lender may sell the benefit of the mortgage, so that the mortgagor will then be required to pay interest and capital to the assignee.

Exercise of power of sale

Where the fee simple has been mortgaged by the creation of a term of years absolute or by a charge by way of legal mortgage and the mortgagee sells under the statutory or express power of sale, the conveyance by him operates to vest in the purchaser the fee simple in the land (LPA 1925, s 88(1)). The mortgagee is not a trustee of the power of sale but he is a trustee of the proceeds of sale in the sense that, after taking out the monies owed to him and monies for costs etc, he must pay the balance to the mortgagor.

Where a leasehold interest has been mortgaged by the creation of another term of years absolute or by charge by way of legal mortgage and the mortgagee sells under a statutory or express power of sale, the conveyance by him operates to convey to the purchaser not only the mortgage term, if any, but also the leasehold reversion affected by the mortgage (LPA 1925, s 89(1)(a)).

When the mortgagee exercises the power of sale the purchaser will receive a good title, ie he receives the legal fee simple or the legal lease free from the mortgagor's equity of redemption. The mortgagor ceases to be able to redeem the mortgage from the time that the mortgagee enters into the contract with the purchaser for the sale of the land.

The statutory power of sale is conferred on the mortgagee only where the mortgage is made by deed. However, the mortgagee will have a right to apply to the court. The court has the power to:

(a) order a sale; or

(b) vest a legal term of years in the mortgagee, so as to give the mortgagee the power to sell the land as if he were a mortgagee under a legal mortgage.

However, in either case the mortgagee cannot sell without making an application to the court (LPA 1925, s 91(2)).

Mortgagee taking possession

Instead of exercising the power of sale or going through the foreclosure procedure, the mortgagee may take possession of the property. However, if the mortgagee does take possession and lets the property, he must ensure that a reasonable rent is fixed otherwise he is liable to the mortgagor for the difference between the rent fixed and the reasonable rent (*White v City of London Brewery Co* [1889] 42 ChD 237). Because of the risks incurred by a mortgagee if he exercises his right to take possession, in practice, a mortgagee is more likely to appoint a receiver or sell the land. But if he is to sell the land, he will only be able to do so if he can sell with vacant possession. It is by exercising his rights to take possession that he is able to oust the mortgagor and so be in a position to sell the property.

Appointment of receiver

The mortgagee could appoint a receiver to obtain the income from the land without incurring the responsibilities of taking possession. The power to appoint a receiver is conferred by LPA 1925, s 109. That section confers a power to appoint a receiver on every mortgagee under a mortgage made by deed. The Law of Property Act 1925, s 109(2) provides that the receiver is to be deemed to be the agent of the mortgagor, who is thus made solely responsible for his acts, unless the mortgage otherwise provides. The statutory power to appoint a receiver is conferred on a mortgagee under a mortgage made by deed. If a deed is not used in the creation of the mortgage, the mortgagee has no statutory power, but he may apply to the court to appoint a receiver.

Discharge of mortgage

When a mortgage is redeemed no reconveyance is now necessary because the mortgagee no longer takes the estate of the mortgagor and because of the statutory provisions relating to receipts. The only estate a mortgagee has after 1925 is a term of years (or a 'spectral' term of years if a charge is created) and on redemption this becomes a satisfied term and ceases, whether the property mortgaged is freehold or leasehold (LPA 1925, s 116).

TAXES IN GENERAL

Capital gains tax

The capital gains tax legislation deals with mortgages and charges in a way which is perfectly consistent with the essential nature of mortgage transactions.

The creation of a mortgage does not result in the disposal of the mortgagor's property. The redemption of the mortgage is ignored.

Any dealings by the mortgagee in respect of the property are treated as transacted by the mortgagee as nominee for the mortgagor: thus no problems arise on the exercise of the power of sale or indeed on foreclosure. Additionally (for the avoidance of doubt) the acts of the receiver are deemed to be the acts of the mortgagor.

There are even provisions to deal specifically with the capital gains tax repercussions which may arise if a property is purchased subject to a mortgage and sold subject to a mortgage: where the land is acquired subject to a mortgage the amount of the liability assumed by the purchaser forms part of the purchase consideration, and if property is sold subject to a mortgage the amount of the liability taken over by the ultimate purchaser is part of the sale consideration.

Development land tax

The Development Land Tax Act (DLTA) 1976, s 32 contains a similar but even more precise code (as it expressly deals with an order for foreclosure) to ensure that the acts of the mortgagee are deemed to be the acts of the mortgagor etc.

Also under that Act 'interest in land' is defined to mean any estate or interest in land, any right in or over land or affecting the use or disposition of land and any right to obtain such an estate, interest or right from another which is conditional on the other's ability to grant the estate, interest or right in question. It is expressly stated in s 46(2) that 'interest in land' does not include the interest of a creditor whose debt is secured by a mortgage or charge of any kind over land or an agreement for such a mortgage or charge; without prejudice to that, it is stated in s 46(3) that the conveyance or transfer by way of security of an interest in land (including a reconveyance or retransfer on the redemption of the security) shall not be treated for the purposes of DLTA 1976 as constituting a disposal of that interest.

Lease premium code

Under the lease premium provisions (anti-avoidance income tax legislation in Taxes Act 1988, Pt II) it is stated, in TA 1988, s 24(1), that a lease does not include a mortgage. Accordingly the creation of a mortgage will not give rise to any charge under that legislation.

Trading

Additionally it has never been suggested that if a trader mortgages his land that this results in a disposal of the land for Sched D, Case I purposes.

Capital allowances

It has never been suggested that the creation of a mortgage over property results in any balancing charge for the purposes of industrial building allowances, enterprise zone allowances etc (*see Stokes v Costain* [1984] STC 204).

Anti-avoidance

Nor has it been suggested that the creation of a mortgage could cause tax charges to arise under TA 1988, s 776 although that is an anti-avoidance section and it may be that the provision could apply if a mortgage is part of an overall tax avoidance scheme.

Stamp duty

No charge to stamp duty is leviable in respect of a mortgage deed (FA 1971, s 64(1)(*c*)).

The author's proposition is that the general scheme of the UK tax legislation in respect of mortgages is as follows:

(1) The creation of the mortgage has no tax effect on the property, ie it is not treated as disposed of.

(2) If the mortgagee exercises the power of sale the transaction which he carries out will be on behalf of the mortgagor. The same would apply with respect to a foreclosure.

(3) The discharge of the mortgage has no tax effect.

The above treatment is wholly consistent with the true nature of the mortgage.

VALUE ADDED TAX

The Sixth Council Directive (77/388) (the Sixth Directive), art 2 states that the supply of goods or services effected for consideration within the territory by a taxable person shall be subject to VAT. A taxable person, according to art 4, is any person who independently carries out in any place any economic activity (as defined). Article 5(1) states that a supply of goods means the transfer of the right to dispose of tangible property as owner. Article 6 states that a supply of services shall mean any transaction which does not comprise a supply of goods.

Article 6(4) states that where a taxable person acting in his own name but on behalf of another takes part in a supply of services, he shall be considered to have received and supplied those services himself.

VATA 1994, s 1 states that VAT shall be charged on the supply of goods and services in the UK.

Section 4(1) states that the tax shall be charged on any supply of goods or services made in the UK where it is a taxable supply made by a taxable person in the course or furtherance of any business carried on by him. A person who makes or intends to make taxable supplies is a taxable person while he is or is required to be registered under VATA 1994. A taxable supply is a supply of goods or services made in the UK other than an exempt supply.

Section 5(3)(*a*) provides that a supply includes all forms of supply, but not anything done otherwise than for a consideration. Anything which is not a supply of goods but is done for a consideration is a supply of services.

VATA 1994, s 47 states that where services are supplied through an agent who acts in his own name the Commissioners may, if they think fit, treat the supply both as a supply to the agent and as a supply by the agent. Where goods are supplied through an agent who acts in his own name the supply shall be treated both as a supply to the agent and as a supply by the agent. VATA 1994, Sched 4, para 7 states:

Where in the case of a business carried on by a taxable person, goods forming part of the assets of the business are, under any power exercisable by another person, sold by the other in or towards satisfaction of a debt owed by the taxable person, they shall be deemed to be supplied by the taxable person in the course or furtherance of his business.

Land forming part of the assets of a business are deemed to be goods forming part of the assets of the business.

Administrative provisions to give effect to that paragraph are contained in the 1995 Regulations, reg 13(2).

The Value Added Tax (Special Provisions) Order 1995 (SI No 1268), art 4 provides that the disposal of a boat by a mortgagee after he has taken possession, or of an aircraft by a mortgagee after he has taken possession under the terms of a mortgage, shall be treated as neither a supply of goods nor a supply of services by the mortgagee. That provision indicates that at least where the mortgagee takes possession the supply would otherwise be a supply by the mortgagee.

VATA 1994, Sched 9, Group 5, Item 1 provides that the issue, transfer or receipt of, or dealing with, money, any security for money or any note or order for the payment of money is exempt. Item 2 provides that the making of any advance or the grant of any credit is exempt. Item 5 provides that the making of any arrangement for any transactions within Items 1 and 2 are exempt.

Schedule 9, Group 1, Item 1 generally exempts the grant 'of any interest in or over land or of any licence to occupy land'. Note (1) to that group provides that 'grant' includes an assignment or a surrender.

Land, under the Interpretation Act 1978, includes buildings and other structures, land covered with water, and any estate, interest, easement, servitude or right in or over land.

In the author's opinion the mortgagee has an interest in land. He takes a conveyance of property subject to the right of reconveyance. There is no conveyance as such if a charge by way of legal mortgage is created but the mortgagee has the same rights and remedies as if he had had a mortgage. The author does not feel it can be seriously contended that a mortgage does not have an interest in land for the purposes of the relevant VAT provisions.

VAT ON MORTGAGE TRANSACTIONS

Creation

When the mortgagee lends money to the mortgagor under the terms of the mortgage the mortgagee is making an exempt supply for VAT purposes and thus VAT does not have to be charged on the repayment of the loan or on any interest or other payments made by the mortgagor (VATA 1994, Sched 9, Group 5, Item 2).

The mortgagor will issue a security for money within VATA 1994, Sched 9, Group 5, Item 1 and thus the mortgagor will make an exempt supply. There will be no VAT charge on, for instance, the monies received by way of loan.

The nature of the mortgage, be it legal or equitable, or by way of mortgage properly so called or by way of charge, and whether it covers a fee simple or a leasehold, is not relevant to the above conclusions.

The following points may be made on the above conclusions:

(1) It cannot be controversial that the mortgagee has made an exempt supply.

(2) In general legal parlance the creation of a mortgage involves the issue of a security for the payment of money (*see* the extract from *The Law of Real Property* on pp 267–8). There is nothing in the VAT case law to throw any doubt on that conclusion and indeed the cases support it. In *The Commissioners v Guy Butler (International) Ltd* [1976] STC 254 it was stated by Roskill LJ at 258h (when referring to Item 1) that:

> the word 'security' is itself there undefined but would appear to be used in its ordinary sense, that is to say some instrument whereby the indebtedness of the borrower to the lender is by some means 'secured'.

In *Williams & Glyn's Bank Ltd v The Commissioners* (1974) VATTR 262 at 269 it was stated that 'security for money' within Item 1 means 'charges and guarantees, and notes and orders for the payment of money'.

Assignment

If the mortgagee assigns the benefit of its loan and mortgage rights then it seems to the author that the transaction is an exempt one under VATA 1994, Sched 9, Group 5, Item 1, ie the assignment is '. . . the transfer . . . of . . . any security for money . . .'.

This applies to the assignment of a legal mortgage and an equitable mortgage whether the mortgage relates to freeholds, leaseholds or equitable interests in land.

Exercise of power of sale

Under general principles when the mortgagee exercises his power of sale, the mortgagee will make a supply for the purposes of VAT.

In particular, in the case of the sale (under the statutory or under an express power) of the freehold and leasehold the mortgagee actually makes a conveyance. The purchaser pays the vendor (mortgagee). The position is the same where an equitable mortgage is in point and a court order is obtained.

That is thus a consistent theme throughout the UK tax code; there are special provisions in the capital gains tax legislation etc to ensure that the mortgagee is treated as having made the disposal on behalf of the mortgagor.

The relevant provision which does the same thing for VAT is VATA 1994, Sched 4, para 7.

The conclusions, therefore, which follow from the above, are:

(1) If there is a mortgage of land and the mortgagee exercises its power of sale then VATA 1994, Sched 4, para 7 will apply and the mortgagor will be treated as having made the disposal.

(2) The special provisions in the 1995 regulations will have application to make sure that the appropriate administrative requirements can be complied with (*see* p 313).

(3) If the mortgagor has exercised his option to charge VAT with respect to any supplies he makes in connection with the freehold then he will be making a vatable supply (at the positive rate) even though the mortgagee is the person who sells under the power of sale.

Additionally, the agency provisions may apply; *see* p 311; and in particular the distinction between a supply of goods and a supply of services must be drawn.

Taking possession

It is not felt that the taking of possession by the mortgagee has any particular VAT significance.

Discharge

It seems clear that on the discharge of the mortgage the mortgagee's totality of rights in connection with the property are extinguished. The reality of the situation is the loan and the interest are repaid to the mortgagee and the mortgage is simply discharged without consideration. It may be that Customs simply treat the transaction as outside the scope of VAT. On the repayment of the loan and the interest, the land interests of the mortgagee became of nominal value and are 'surrendered' to the mortgagor for no consideration. VAT is thus not in point.

LPA receiver

The VAT treatment of supplies made by an LPA receiver is far from clear in either law or practice.

A receiver may be appointed with respect to a particular property in accordance with the document creating the fixed charge over that property, or under the provisions in ss 101 and 109 of the Law of Property Act 1925. The receiver is appointed by the lender before the borrower company goes into liquidation. The receiver normally acts as agent for the mortgagor, ie the borrower company.

For example, X plc defaults on its mortgage payments to Z Bank and an LPA receiver is appointed. X plc is not in liquidation and has elected to waive exemption with respect to the property.

It seems clear enough, from a combination of the general rules of agency as they apply to VAT (VATA 1994, s 47, but *see* p 311) and the special provision in VATA 1994, Sched 4, para 7 (which applies where one person, under a power which he has been given, disposes of the property of another), that, on the sale of the property, VAT must be charged by the receiver. The same applies with respect to rent; the VAT charged on the rent will be charged by the receiver as agent for the mortgagor. Any vatable costs incurred by the receiver would be incurred on behalf of the mortgagor and it can be safely assumed that the mortgagor will be in a position to reclaim that VAT. The mortgagee as such could not reclaim that VAT.

It is understood that in certain cases Customs have agreed that the receiver can elect with respect to the property so that VAT becomes chargeable with respect to the *rents*; it is the receiver who makes that supply (and the receiver issues a VAT invoice of its own), but any VAT chargeable with respect to the *sale* is a supply by the mortgagor because Sched 4, para 7 applies to a sale but not to a letting. If that is the case then any VAT incurred by the receiver in respect of the letting can be reclaimed by the receiver. However, it is not clear that Customs would adopt that procedure, especially in view of para 6 of Notice 742, referred to *below* at p 314.

The position of the receiver may change when the company goes into liquidation. From that time, Customs may allow the receiver to register separately for VAT and elect with regard to the building, so that all VAT charges which arise on the sale and letting of the building will be made by the receiver acting on his own account and not as agent for the mortgagor. This will enable VAT charged on supplies to the receiver to be reclaimed and retained by the receiver.

The property, of course, mysteriously will have been supplied for VAT purposes by the morgagor to the receiver (that will have had to have occurred if the receiver is to sell the property on his own account): what is the VAT consequence of that supply?

If the mortgagor has elected and the receiver has elected then the overwhelming likelihood is that the going concern relief will apply so that the supply will be outside the scope of VAT and no VAT need be charged.

Figure 25.1:

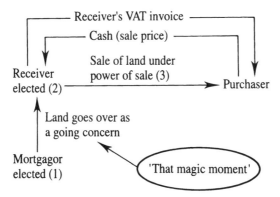

However, if the mortgagor has elected but the receiver has not, there will be a VAT charge on the transfer and the receiver may not be able to reclaim that VAT.

NEW AGENCY RULES

Under the new agency rules in VATA 1994, s 47(2A) if goods are supplied by an agent acting in his own name the supply is treated 'both as a supply to the agent and as a supply by the agent'. There are thus two supplies. There is no Customs' discretion involved in this situation. The rules apply on or after 1 May 1995. VATA 1994, Sched 4, para 7, however, states that if X sells on behalf of Y (even presumably if X is Y's agent and whether or not in his own name) the supply is treated as made by Y direct to the ultimate purchaser. Which provision prevails? The author feels that VATA 1994, Sched 4, para 7 prevails where X sells the property 'in or towards satisfaction of a debt owed by the taxable person'. Thus it is unlikely the new agency rules will have any relevant bearing on mortgagee or receivership sales but it could be a point to put to Customs to solve some of the non-reclaimable VAT problems which arise on sales by lenders or the receivers.

RECEIVERS PAYING VAT TO CUSTOMS

In *Re John Willment (Ashford) Ltd* [1979] STC 286 a bank created a floating charge over a company's undertaking. Pursuant to that charge a receiver was ultimately appointed to carry out the company's trade and the receiver made vatable supplies. It was held the VAT charged by the receivers had to be paid to Customs and not to the bank. At the time it would have been a criminal offence not to pay the monies to Customs.

In *Sargent v The Commissioners* [1994] STC 1 a bank had a fixed charge over specific assets and a receiver was appointed to collect the rents plus VAT because the company had elected to waive exemption. It was held the receiver was obliged to pay the VAT over to Customs.

HAS THE MORTGAGOR ELECTED?

Problems can arise if property is sold by an LPA receiver and the parties are uncertain whether the mortgagor elected to waive exemption.

VAT can be payable on the purchase price only if the vendor (the mortgagor, not the LPA receiver) has elected to waive exemption. The better view is that the LPA receiver does not have the power to elect to waive exemption unless, exceptionally, a power to do so was contained in the original documentation.

If the LPA receiver claims that he (the LPA receiver) has elected to waive exemption, it is important to verify that he has the authority to do so; the better view is that he does not, and in general Customs assume that an LPA receiver cannot elect.

Figure 25.2:

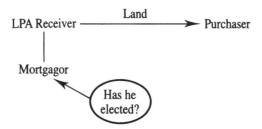

It therefore remains to determine whether the mortgagor has elected. Customs would advise the LPA receiver to see whether tenants have been charged VAT on rent over the years; whether the legal advisers or auditors to the mortgagor can assist; and whether the mortgagor himself can assist. If, after those inquiries, the LPA receiver is still uncertain, he will not avoid a VAT charge if he sells the property without charging VAT when the mortgagor had in fact elected to waive exemption.

The LPA receiver may seek to place that obligation or problem on the purchaser by a VAT inclusive clause.

If, because of the bargaining position, the VAT inclusive clause remains, then the purchaser should seek as much information as possible from the LPA receiver about what searches he has made with respect to the mortgagor and the exercise of the election to waive exemption. A commercial judgement then has to be made on the position.

FORMALITIES ON EXERCISE OF POWER OF SALE

If a mortgagee in possession sells the property under his power of sale, and the mortgagor has exercised the election to waive exemption, VAT must be charged (VATA 1994, Sched 4, para 7).

The mortgagor is deemed to have made the supply (Sched 4, para 7).

The mortgagee must provide the purchaser with the VAT invoice issued in the name of the mortgagor (the 1995 Regulations, reg 13(2)), and it must contain the particulars detailed in reg 14.

Within 21 days of the sale the mortgagee must furnish Customs with the details set out in reg 27.

Figure 25.3:

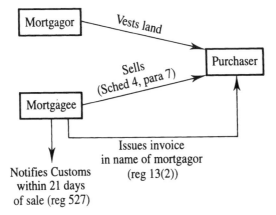

CUSTOMS' VIEWS

The present Customs' views on mortgages are contained in Notice 742, para 6, which reads as follows:

General
6.1   If you mortgage your property, as security for borrowing money, it is not regarded as a supply of the property.

Sales of repossessed property
6.2   *Sales under a power of sale*—If a financial institution, or any other person, sells land or buildings belonging to you under a power of sale in satisfaction of a debt owed by you, a supply by you takes place. If tax is due on that supply, either because you are the freehold owner of a partly constructed or new non-qualifying building or civil engineering work or because you have opted to tax the property, the person selling the property is responsible for accounting for that VAT using the procedure set out in paragraph 62 of Notice 700 *The VAT Guide.* That person cannot opt to tax the property unless it has been agreed in the mortgage deed that it has the power to opt to tax on the borrower's behalf.

   Foreclosures—If, instead of selling property under a power of sale, a person obtains a Court Order and forecloses on land or buildings belonging to you, there is a supply by you to that person of the land or building unless it is treated as an asset of a business which is transferred to them as a going concern (see VAT Leaflet 700/9 *Transfer of a business as a going concern* for further details). If the land or building is subsequently sold by the person foreclosing, who may, if they wish, opt to tax the property.

Renting out of repossessed property
6.3   If a lender repossesses land or buildings or appoints an LPA receiver without foreclosing and rents the property out to tenants, a supply by the property owner takes place if the rental income received by the lender is used to reduce a debt owed to the institution or to service interest payments due in respect of that debt. If the supply is a taxable supply, the lender may account for VAT using the procedure set out in paragraph 62 of Notice 700 *The VAT guide.*

The Customs' generous treatment on the recovery of VAT on costs incurred by lenders where land is sold under a power of sale, *Business Brief* 24/94 (8 December 1994) is reproduced *below*).

Sale of Property under a Power of Sale—Recovery of VAT on Costs Incurred by Mortgage Lenders

Customs and Excise have reconsidered the VAT treatment of costs incurred by mortgage lenders when selling property to realise their security in circumstances where a borrower has defaulted on a loan.

This Business Brief explains the reasons for this and sets out the arrangements which will apply for the future. It also sets out the position on payment of claims for past periods.

Background

Business Brief 20/93 indicated that Customs were prepared to see lenders as agents of the borrower in arranging the sale of repossessed property, and hence allow them to claim bad debt relief (BDR), where appropriate, on the VAT incurred on selling costs.

However, Customs subsequently became aware that the order of attribution of the proceeds of sale under Section 105 of the Law of Property Act 1925 might override the Bad Debt Relief Regulations. This is because under Section 105 the proceeds of sale are allocated first to costs such as those incurred in selling the property, which threw some considerable doubt over whether a bad debt was created on which relief could be claimed.

Doubts arose also about the status of lenders as agents and there was concern that some claims had included costs which went beyond the terms of the Business Brief. Customs therefore issued a further Business Brief 5/94 suspending the processing of claims, until such time as they could take legal advice and examine more fully the issues involved.

Current Position

Having taken Counsel's advice, Customs are of the view that there is a good argument that in arranging the sale of repossessed property, mortgagees act under rights conferred by the mortgage agreement, and not as agents of the borrower. However, Customs believe they can rely on the wider interpretation of 'agent' contained in the Sixth VAT Directive in maintaining their current view on agency, as laid out in Business Brief 20/93. They face more difficulty with Section 105 LPA, as it may override the order of attribution in the BDR Regulations, but again the matter is not free from doubt.

In the circumstances, Customs believe that the finely balanced nature of the legal advice allows some freedom of choice and they are re-introducing a form of easement.

New Arrangements

General

The easement is strictly for the purposes of allowing a measure of relief for VAT on bad debts and depends crucially on Customs taking a relaxed view of the supply position. Lenders must not extend this treatment more widely in accounting for VAT within their businesses.

The new arrangements will apply to BDR claims relating to supplies made on or after 1 July 1994. The overall aim is to provide relief to lenders where they suffer sticking tax on the costs of selling property in circumstances where borrowers have defaulted—in effect where the net proceeds of sale are reduced because the VAT element of the costs has not been recovered.

In principle, the easement covers costs incurred by lenders in arranging the sale of repossessed property and also to selling costs incurred when property is sold through an LPA receiver. It is emphasised that, with the single exception of build-out costs, the arrangements apply only to sale costs, and not to any incurred in relation to letting.

Although the Law of Property Act does not apply in Scotland, there are analogous provisions in Section 27 of the Conveyancing and Feudal Reform (Scotland) Act 1970. The arrangements therefore apply equally in Scotland.

Basic Principle

Under the new arrangements, lenders can be seen as agents of the borrower in relation to the costs of sale whether or not the mortgage deed specifies such a relationship. As an agent, the lender may treat the selling costs incurred as supplies made to them and by them under Section 47(3) of the VAT Act 1994. The order of attribution of the sale proceeds in the BDR regulations can then be applied and bad debt relief claimed as appropriate in accordance with normal rules.

These new arrangements apply only to costs relating directly to the sale of property, which would ordinarily have been incurred by the borrower had he arranged the sale himself. Examples of such costs include charges for professional services connected with the sale e.g. legal and estate agency fees.

The easement does not include costs incurred on services provided to, and used by, the lender as principal, even though they may be charged on to the borrower under the mortgage deed. Examples of such costs include legal fees associated with taking possession, and locksmiths' fees for securing the property. Costs incurred in pursuing claims against a valuer for negligence are also excluded.

Other Expenses

The position of certain other expenses incurred by lenders was discussed at recent meetings with trade representatives. Treatment of these under the new arrangements is outlined below.

LPA Receivers' Charges

LPA receivers' charges which relate specifically to the sale (not letting) of the property and any costs incurred by them in respect of the sale can be regarded as falling within the scope of the new arrangements, but only where the proceeds of sale received by lenders have been reduced by the VAT element of the charges. Where this happens, lenders may be regarded as acting as agents for the borrower in paying the costs.

This means that Customs are not prepared to apply this arrangement where the LPA receiver recovers the VAT incurred on behalf of a VAT registered borrower and this is reflected in the proceeds passed to the lender. This may occur, for example, where the LPA receiver has control of the borrower's VAT returns.

Build-out Costs

These are expenses incurred on completion of a partly-completed building or major refurbishment of the property before sale. Customs' legal advice is that lenders incur such costs as principals and do not make any onward supplies to the borrower even though the costs are charged on under the terms of the mortgage deed. It was argued at the recent meetings with trade representatives that strict application of this line would create a hidden VAT charge in respect of buildings whose sale is zero-rated.

Customs are sympathetic to this view and are therefore prepared, very exceptionally, to treat the onward charge of the build-out costs as a supply by the lender as principal to the borrower, where the sale of the building by the borrower is the subject of a taxable supply or the transfer of a going concern for VAT purposes. In the case of build-out costs only, Customs are also prepared to see a supply where the property is the subject of a taxable let and output tax on the rents has been accounted for to Customs.

Chapter 26

Dealings with leasehold interests

The VAT consequences of various lease transactions (whether of domestic or non-domestic accommodation) are dealt with *below*. Before VAT can be in point the supply must be made in the course or furtherance of a buisiness or a deemed business. If there is no such business then VAT is irrelevant. That is the view Customs take. In fact, strictly, the correct expression should be 'economic activity' (as opposed to 'business') as that is the wording used in art 4(1) and (2) of the EC Sixth Directive 77/388.

If Mr X surrenders the lease of his flat to his landlord for £100,000 it is unlikely that the transaction is carried out in the course of his business (Mr Lilley, Standing Committee G (p 112) '. . . surrenders of leasehold interests in dwellings will not normally be in the course of business'). It is a family or non-business transaction. On the other hand, if a firm of solicitors surrenders its business lease to its landlord that is almost certainly a transaction carried out in the course of business.

Even if a transaction is carried out in the course of a business the consideration may be of such an amount as to be below the registration limits (in this event unless the taxpayer has registered voluntarily VAT will not be in point).

It is assumed that both those requirements (ie a business is being carried on and the taxpayer is or should have been VAT registered) are satisfied in the examples *below*, but if they are not then VAT would not be in point.

Note that this whole area of law has been 'unsettled' by the *Lubbock Fine* decision (*see* p 321).

GRANTS, SURRENDERS AND VARIATIONS

The examples *below* are based on a simple case where a commercial property is let or is to be let, and the landlord and the tenant have not elected to waive exemption.

Example

A landlord grants a lease to a tenant and receives rent and a premium. The supply by the landlord is exempt and no VAT is payable on the rent or on the premium (VATA 1994, Sched 9, Group 1, Item 1). As it is the landlord who makes the supply, the tenant's VAT position is irrelevant.

Example

The tenant surrenders a lease to the landlord and the landlord pays the tenant £1m for the surrender. The supply is an exempt transaction by the tenant and no VAT is chargeable with reference to the £1m (*Lubbock Fine & Co v The Commissioners* [1994] STC 101 and EC Sixth Directive, art 13(b)). As it is the tenant who makes the supply, the landlord's VAT position is not relevant.

Example

The landlord agrees to a variation of the terms of a lease and receives £100,000 from the tenant in consideration of the variation. This will be an exempt supply by the landlord (*Lubbock Fine & Co v The Commissioners* and *Business Brief* 16/94). This would clearly cover the lifting of a restrictive covenant against the tenant, or indeed where one landowner lifts a restrictive covenant against another landowner's land, whether or not they are in a landlord and tenant relationship (*Business Brief* 17/94).

Reverse premiums

The VAT position where a tenant pays the landlord to accept a surrender of the lease was subject to great controversy, but the situation has now been settled (*see* Customs and Excise *Business Brief* 7/95 (4 April 1995), [1995] STI 629 (13 April 1995) and the Value Added Tax (Land) Order 1995 (SI No 282)). The new law has effect from 1 March 1995.

The VAT position of the landlord must be examined to determine whether VAT must be charged on the surrender monies.

It is the landlord who makes a supply—of agreeing to accept the surrender of the lease—in consideration of a payment from or under the direction of the tenant. Thus if the landlord has not elected to waive exemption and he receives a reverse premium from the tenant on or after 1 March 1995 the landlord will have made an exempt supply (*see* Figure 26.1).

Figure 26.1:   L has not elected: exempt supply by L

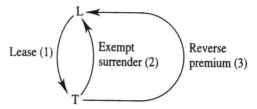

Figure 26.2:   L has elected: vatable supply by L

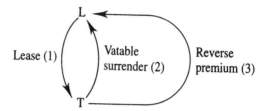

On the other hand, if the landlord has elected to waive exemption with regard to the property and he agrees to accept the surrender of the lease from the tenant in consideration of a payment from the tenant, then the supply by the landlord will be a vatable supply and the landlord must account for VAT on the consideration he receives (*see* Figure 26.2).

As it is the landlord who makes the supply for VAT, the VAT position of the tenant is not relevant.

The new law has effect from 1 March 1995; the position with respect to reverse premiums before that date is unclear, but it is felt that the better view following the *Lubbock Fine* decision is that such supplies will be exempt if the landlord has not elected to waive exemption, or vatable (at 17.5 per cent) if the landlord has elected to waive exemption, ie the new law reflects what the law was before 1 March 1995 (*see Marbourne Ltd* (LON/93/590 Decision 12670) [1994] STI 1352) and *CCC Ltd* (MAN/94/2393 Decision 13319 [1995] STI 1151).

In *Lloyds Bank Ltd v The Commissioners* (Decision 14181) L granted a lease to T for 25 years in 1974. The lease was to expire in 1999. The parties entered into a deed of variation in 1994 under which T was given the option to terminate the lease on paying L £X compensation. L had elected to waive exemption. L argued that the compensation was outside the scope of VAT.

The tribunal held that it had to look at the transaction as a whole (*BRB v The Commissioners* [1977] STC 1; but *see also* p 262) and look at the substance and reality of the situation in order to determine the real deal. At p 16.20 the tribunal stated: 'there clearly was one transaction, the entire transaction of grant and exercise on agreed terms'. The consequence was the land-lord had surrendered rights with respect to a taxable interest. The landlord had exercised the election to waive exemption with regard to its property and con-sideration it receives when altering that interest would similarly be vatable.

Article 13B of the EC Sixth Directive had been interpreted in the *Lubbock Fine* decision; in para 9 of the judgment which dealt with the ambit of art 13B(*b*) the court held as follows:

> Where a given transaction, such as a letting of immovable property, which would be taxed on the basis of rents paid, falls within the scope of an exemp-tion provided for by the Sixth Directive, a change in the contractual rela-tionship, such as the termination of the lease for consideration, must also be regarded as falling within the scope of that exemption.
>
> Consequently, the reply to be given to the National Court is that the term 'letting of immovable properties' used in Article 13B(*b*) of the Sixth Directive to define an exempt transaction covers a case where a tenant surrenders his lease and returns the immovable property to its immediate landlord.

The VAT tribunal held that it had no reason for holding that the term 'surren-der' used in that judgment was intended to have any particular narrow meaning. At p 18.20 the tribunal stated:

> It seems clear from the reasoning of the court that it seeks symmetry between the creation of an interest in property in the way of a lease and a change in that contractual relationship leading to the return of the property to the immediate landlord by surrender or termination.
>
> The tribunal considers that it has an obligation under the terms of the judgment of the European Court of Justice in the case of *Marleasing v La Commercial de Alimentacion* [1990] ECR 4135 to interpret the terms of national law in so far as possible consistent with the terms of the European legislation, as defined by the European Court, and considers therefore that here the term 'surrender of any right' used in s 5(2)(b) of the VAT Act 1994 must be read in the light of the wider definition of the term 'surrender' given to Article 13B(*b*) of the Directive.

The true effect, therefore, of the *Lubbock Fine* decision would appear to indicate that although the word 'grant' as defined in VATA 1994, Sched 9, Note (1) seems to be restricted to the surrender of, for example, a lease, in fact it would apply to any surrenders or terminations of interests for which a land-lord who has exercised the election to waive exemption receives considera-tion (in that case vatable supplies would result: if the landlord had not exercised the election to waive exemption then exempt supplies would result). It is thus important for practitioners when reading Note (1) to Group 1 of Sched 9 to VATA 1994 to read the same in the light of the *Lubbock Fine* and the *Lloyds Bank* decisions.

Finally, it is important to distinguish reverse premiums from inducement payments. If a payment is made to a proposed tenant to induce him to take on a lease, that would be a vatable supply by the proposed tenant and he must charge VAT on the inducement payment. If the landlord who paid the inducement payment elects to waive exemption he should be able to reclaim that VAT (*see* Figure 26.3).

Figure 26.3:

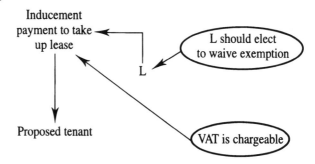

See p 335 below for 'sideways' reverse premiums and p 331 for inducements.

Assignments

Transactions involving leases can often take one of two forms and the better one, from the VAT point of view, should be considered.

L may have granted a lease to T which has 15 years left to run. L has not elected to waive exemption, nor has T. The proposition is that T will assign his lease to a new tenant (NT). He will receive £100,000 on the assignment. That will be an exempt transaction for VAT.

Alternatively, the parties may simply agree that T will surrender his lease for nothing and L will grant a new lease to NT. In that case the £100,000 paid by NT to T will not relate to the transfer of a land interest from T to NT and may be vatable under general principles (*see* Figure 26.4).

Surrender

L has granted a lease to T. T has elected to waive exemption. T surrenders his lease and L pays T £1m. Is VAT payable on the £1m? The answer is yes. The surrender is a deemed grant of an interest in land. The election eliminates the exemption, leaving the surrender vatable, assuming it is in the course or furtherance of a business.

Figure 26.4:   Assignments

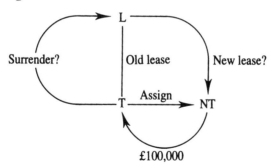

This leads to the question whether the VAT situation would be the same if the tenant has not elected to waive exemption, but the landlord has. In that case the tenant would make an exempt supply, and the fact that the landlord is registered (or has elected), or not registered (or has not elected), is wholly irrelevant. The supply is exempt and VAT is not chargeable on the £1m paid by the landlord to the tenant.

PAYMENT OF ASSIGNEE'S RENT

VAT problems arise where a tenant (original tenant) assigns a lease to a new tenant (second tenant) and the second tenant goes into receivership or liquidation; the landlord sues the original tenant for the unpaid rent, plus an amount equal to the VAT charged on the rent because the landlord exercised the election to waive exemption for VAT. It is a feature of English land law that the original tenant remains liable in such a way: this rule is not to apply to new leases granted after 31 December 1995 (Landlord and Tenant (Covenant) Act 1995) (*see* 16 PLB 25).

Customs take the view that if the rent is, say, £100 and the VAT £17.50, the supply for VAT purposes is made by the landlord to the second tenant, and the original tenant must pay the landlord £117.50.

The landlord must pay Customs VAT of £17.50 but *the original tenant cannot reclaim the VAT* of £17.50 which it paid, because the supply was not made to it (the original tenant), but to the second tenant. There is a long line of VAT cases which concentrate on who received the supply to determine whether VAT can be reclaimed. For example, if a creditor bears the receiver's fees the creditor cannot reclaim the VAT charged by the receiver, because the receiver makes supplies to the company in receivership, and not to the creditor (*see* the recent case of *M & R J Lister* (LON/92/1336 Decision 9972) [1993] STI 622).

To make sense of their approach Customs argue that this supply is a supply of the premises to the second tenant, and therefore the second tenant must receive the VAT invoice, and in an appropriate case can claim back the VAT: the original tenant is merely discharging the obligations of the second tenant.

Figure 26.5:

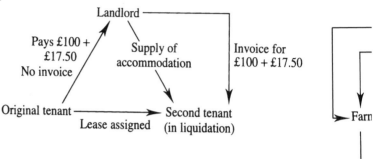

There are counter-arguments based on the 1995 Regulations and the nature of the landlord's right of recovery from the original tenant, but the problems are real and assignors of leases should take special note of the problem and advisers should counsel their clients accordingly.

The exact wording of the Customs' view is found in Notice 742, para 7.5 and reads thus:

7.5   Recovery of rent from a third party

Privity of contract—Once a tenant assigns a lease to a new tenant, the new tenant becomes liable to pay rent to the landlord. However, if the new tenant defaults and fails to pay the rent, under the law of privity of contract, the landlord can invoke the original covenant made and require the original tenant to pay the rent instead. If this happens the supply of the property is still from the landlord to the new tenant, even if the original tenant is forced to pay the rent. If the landlord has opted to tax the property any tax invoice should be issued to the new tenant and the right to recover input tax rests with the new tenant.

Sureties and Guarantors—Any rents paid by a surety or guarantor follow the liability of the original rents.

In addition the Customs have some impressive VAT Tribunal decisions in their favour in this area.

In *Vivat Holdings plc* [1995] STI 1710 a parent company *inter alia* guaranteed the obligations of its subsidiaries under leases granted to those subsidiaries. It ultimately had to pay up under the guarantee. The tribunal held the relevant supply was by the outside landlords to the tenants in the group in return for the rent. The guarantees were collateral to the real supplies and thus the parent could not recover the VAT on the rent charged by the outside landlords to the tenants.

Figure 26.6:

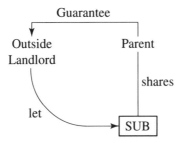

In *Kenwood Appliances Ltd* [1996] STI 691) L let to T who assigned to T1 who assigned to T2. T2 was wound up and the original surety had to pay the unpaid rent of T2 plus VAT and in turn sued T1. T1 tried to reduce the liability by claiming T could reclaim the VAT. The tribunal held that the recipient of a supply under a lease was the holder for the time being (T2). Thus when T assigned the lease, it ceased to receive supplies under it. The relevant supplies were thus not made to T and T could never recover any of the VAT. T1 could thus not reduce his liability by the VAT element.

Figure 26.7:

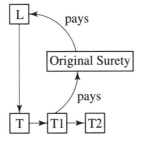

LAW OF DISTRESS AMENDMENT ACT 1908, s 6

If A lets to B and B lets to C under the above Act, A can collect rent from C if B defaults in paying rent to A (*see* Figure 26.8).

The Customs have very clear and, in the author's view, correct views in this area. In *Business Brief*, 17/93 (7 June 1993) it is stated thus:

Figure 26.8:

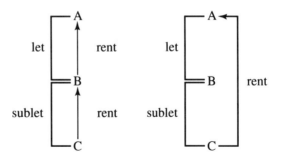

When a tenant is in default the landlord can, pursuant to the Law of Distress Amendment Act 1908 s 6, collect the arrears of rent from any sub-tenant. This is done by the service of a notice upon the sub-tenant which, until the arrears have been paid, transfers to the landlord the right to recover, receive and give a discharge for the rent. The sub-tenant can, in turn, reduce the rent payable to the defaulting tenant under the sub-lease by the amounts paid to the superior landlord.

There has been some confusion over the VAT treatment of the rental payments where an election to waive exemption (option to tax) has been exercised. Contrary to views which have been expressed, any deemed relationship between the superior landlord and the sub-tenant under the Law of Distress Amendment Act 1908 s 3 has no effect on the nature of the supplies for VAT purposes. By virtue of the lease the superior landlord continues to make a series of separate and successive supplies to the tenant; and by virtue of the sub-lease the tenant continues to make a series of separate and successive supplies to the sub-tenant.

If the superior landlord has elected to waive exemption of the property, any tax invoice should be issued to the tenant and not to the sub-tenant.

Any right to recover the VAT charged by the superior landlord rests with the tenant and not with the sub-tenant. The sub-tenant may only treat as his input tax any VAT charged by the tenant on rents payable under the sub-lease.

The above view is repeated in Notice 742, para 7.5, which reads as follows:

Law of Distress Amendment Act—If a tenant sublets a property to a sub-tenant and the tenant defaults on payment of rent to the landlord, the landlord can issue a notice under section 6 of the Law of Distress Amendment Act 1908 and collect the rent arrears from the sub-tenant. In turn the sub-tenant can reduce his rent payable to the tenant by the amount he has paid to the landlord. If this happens the supply chain remains the same; there is a supply of property from the landlord to the tenant and a supply of property from the tenant to the sub-tenant. If the landlord has opted to tax the property, any tax invoice must be issued to the tenant and any right to recover the VAT charged by the landlord as input tax rests with the tenant.

RENTAL GUARANTEES

One should bear in mind that there is more than one heading for exemption under VAT than the land exemption.

If X, the developer, sells land to Y and undertakes to pay notional rent until X finds tenants the notional rent may be a vatable reverse premium in the form of an inducement payment (*see* Figure 26.9). For the Custom's view *see* Notice 742, para 4.3. However, this whole area is in a state of flux and it is arguable the supply is exempt (*see* p 335). The author feels in law the supply is exempt.

Figure 26.9:

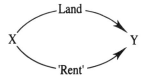

If X sells let property to Y and X guarantees that if the tenant defaults over, say, three years X will pay the defaulting sum, it seems that X has entered into a rental guarantee (which results in an exempt supply under the head of finance), giving Y a right to money which is disposed of in return for any payments made by X in the event of the guarantee being called (*see* Figure 26.10).

Figure 26.10:

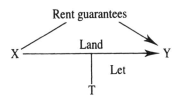

CONTRIBUTIONS BY LANDLORDS

Gleneagles case

If a landlord is proposing to make contributions towards expenditure on improvement or repair or indeed new construction, to be carried out by an incoming tenant, the VAT implications following the case of *Gleneagles Hotel plc v The Commissioners of Customs and Excise* (LON/85/473

Decision 2152) must be considered. It is likely to be the tenant who will bear the brunt of the VAT problems.

In the *Gleneagles Hotel* case, L granted a lease to T and there was an agreement that T would carry out various works to the property including repair and re-equipment, and L would contribute £1.4m towards the expenditure (anticipated to be £7.5m) (*see* Figure 26.11).

Figure 26.11:   *Gleneagles*

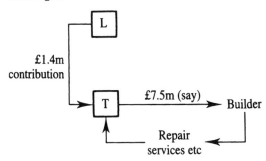

There were no provisions in the documentation for VAT, so that if VAT was chargeable the payment of £1.4m would be deemed to be VAT inclusive.

Customs argued that VAT was payable, as T provided to L the service of taking on the underlease with all its benefits and burdens.

The taxpayer argued that there was no provision of services by T, the tenant; the developer carried out the works on the property for T and L provided some of the money, but in no real sense could one say that T did anything for which he received consideration.

Lord Grantchester, the tribunal chairman, was impressed by neither argument and held that, although incapable of precise definition, effectively T agreed to provide more beneficial terms in the lease to L because of the contribution of £1.4m by L. It was unrealistic to consider otherwise because this was a commercial arrangement with neither party intending to make gifts to the other. If the contribution had not been made then the benefits provided by T to L would have been lower. Lord Grantchester stated (at p 12):

> . . . I take the view that the £1.4m was a consideration provided by the landlord for the tenant agreeing to provide more valuable benefits under the contract and the underlease (as varied by the latter) than it otherwise would have done.

The agreement providing those more valuable benefits was the provision of a service by T to L, for which consideration was received by T. Therefore VAT was chargeable.

Because there was no clause in the underlease or agreement enabling the tenant to charge VAT on the contribution, the contribution was deemed to be VAT inclusive. Therefore the tenant would have to bear the VAT and must account for it to Customs. If L could not claim back the VAT this would result in a real loss in overall VAT terms.

Clearly parties entering into arrangements where the landlord is to contribute towards the tenant's expenditure must appreciate the VAT penalty which may arise in consequence of this case.

Note to Figure 26.11:

(1) The £1.4m was vatable. The payment was VAT inclusive.

(2) The decision would have been the same whether or not VAT was chargeable on the £7.5m supply by the builder.

Neville Russell case

The second case on landlord's inducement payments was *Neville Russell v The Commissioners* (LON/86/708).

In this case the landlord, the Norwich Union Life Insurance Company, made payments to Neville Russell, a firm of chartered accountants, and gave them a period of rent reduction, in connection with Neville Russell's agreement to take a lease from the Norwich Union of 266 Bishopsgate.

The facts of the case were quite complicated because two properties were involved and there were some difficult conclusions on the facts, but from the author's understanding of the decision the following general principles can be extracted.

If a landlord makes a payment to an incoming tenant, in consideration of the tenant undertaking to ensure that necessary refurbishment and other works are carried out to the premises, then the payment is vatable.

Example: Payment to cover refurbishment expenditure

L is the freeholder of 'green' building. £100,000 of refurbishment works need to be carried out to the building. T agrees to take a lease of the building. T agrees to carry out the refurbishment works (or employ a builder or developer to do them) in consideration of L paying T £100,000. That £100,000 is vatable.

If a landlord pays monies to a potential tenant (T) to persuade T to accept a lease of 'yellow' building then that payment will be vatable.

Example: Inducement payment

L wishes to let premises to T. T is concerned that in the future his business may not be sufficiently successful to be able to afford the rent. To induce T to take the lease L pays T £200,000. That sum will be vatable. Lord Grantchester in the *Neville Russell* case at p 18 stated:

> I am left with the question of whether a payment of a sum of money by a tenant in consideration of the acceptance by him of the lease to him of the demised premises is a supply of services for tax purposes . . . In my opinion the acceptance by a tenant of the lease of the demised premises involves the execution of the counterpart lease and the acceptance of the grant. In my opinion, this is something done. Further, in my view where a sum of money is paid for that to be done as in the present case, it is the supply of services for a consideration for tax purposes. I express this opinion solely in relation to an acceptance of a lease for a monetary consideration attributed or attributable to such acceptance.

If a landlord seeks to induce a tenant to take a lease of premises by giving the tenant a rent-free period, or a period where the rent is reduced to half the market rent or to what the parties consider the market rent to be, then that reduction will *not* give rise to a vatable supply.

Example: Rent reduced period

L wishes to induce T to take a lease of 'blue' building. T is reluctant but L agrees to charge half the full rent for the first year of the lease. As a result of that T takes the lease. No VAT is charged on that rent reduction (*see* Figure 25.12 *below*).

Lord Grantchester in the *Neville Russell* case held that the rent reduction could not be vatable, following the case of *National Coal Board v The Commissioners* [1982] STC 863.

Figure 26.12:   *Neville Russell*

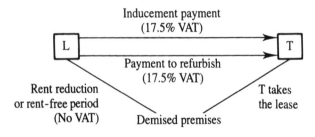

In connection with the above cases of *Gleneagles* and *Neville Russell* reference should be made to p 335 and the case of *Cantor Fitzgerald International* (Decision 15070), heard in July 1997.

BOUNTEOUS CONTRIBUTIONS

If the taxpayer is very lucky he may be able to convince the tribunal that a particular contribution was bounteous. In *Nichols* (Decision 14521) T (the tenant) employed a builder to construct a new grain store on the farm and the landlord (the trustees of the Bramham Settled Estates) contributed the major part of the cost. The Customs claimed T acted as agent for L. The tribunal held T acted as principal and the contribution was a gift.

Figure 26.13:

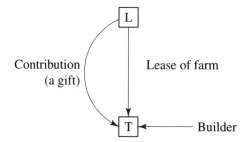

INDUCEMENT PAYMENTS—LATER CASES

Hutchinson Locke and Monk (LON/88/1028, LON/89/1763 Decision 5212) was a complicated case which raised a number of issues, but again firmly established that reverse premiums and inducement payments are chargeable to VAT. It was held that a firm of architects which was paid a sum of money by a developer to induce it to accept a lease of office premises had made a vatable supply to the developer and accordingly VAT was chargeable on the architects on the inducement payment.

In another VAT tribunal case L wanted to sell its freehold reversion. There was a letting to T. P wanted to buy the total interests and L had to pay P a sum to persuade it to buy the interests: it was held that the supply by P for the consideration was exempt 'since the entire series of transactions were concerned with the ownership of interests in land and the transfer thereof' (*Brammer plc* MAN/90/123 Decision 6420). It is not entirely easy to reconcile this case with the general run of reverse premium cases.

In *N Iliffe & DC Holloway* (1993) VATTR 439 X took a lease from a developer at a premium. X had to borrow to pay the premium and the developer agreed to pay X under a 'mortgage-capping agreement' a sum if the rates of interest on X's borrowings over a period exceeded 12.5 per cent. The payment duly had to be made and the Customs argued it was a vatable inducement payment. It was held that the 'mortgage-capping agreement' was part and parcel of the lease and the inducement payment was thus not vatable (*see* Figure 26.14).

Figure 26.14:   *N Iliffe & DC Holloway*

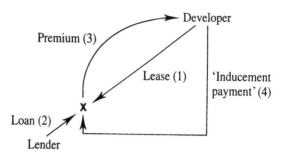

What this case demonstrates is that there is a clear possibility that a reverse premium, provided that it is structured properly and is not expressly presented as being the consideration for entering into the lease but is an intrinsic part of the overall transaction, may not be taxable at the standard rate since no supply is made. Only time and more litigation will tell.

Reference should also be made to *Cantor Fiztzgerald International* (Decision 15070), discussed at p 335.

Equalisation plans

If X Ltd is to pay Y Ltd an inducement payment to take on an onerous lease he may do this via the sale of a 'new' company.

X Ltd is to pay Y Ltd £1m to take on an onerous lease by way of assignment.

To avoid the VAT charge X Ltd funds (by way of share capital in the sum of £1m) Z Ltd (its 100 per cent subsidiary) which is in the same VAT group as itself, and then assigns the lease to Z Ltd. X Ltd then sells Z Ltd to Y for 50p (*see* Figure 26.15). Note, however, the *Cantor Fitzgerald* case (*see* p 335).

Shell and core arrangements

L has constructed the core and shell of a building with the intention that the tenant will install the necessary fixed plant and machinery. L makes a contri-

Figure 26.15:   Equalisation plans

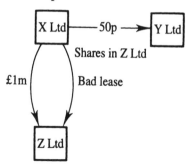

Figure 26.16:   Shell and Core Arrangements

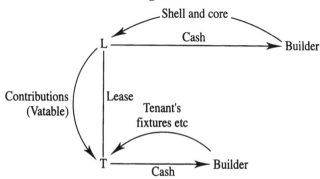

bution towards the tenant's expenditure on putting in the plant and machinery (*see* Figure 26.16).

These are common arrangements designed to ensure that capital allowances are not lost.

If, as an inducement to persuade the tenant to take on the lease in the first place, L agrees to contribute to T's expenditure on the plant and machinery then VAT is chargeable on the contribution (but *see* p 335).

If the lease is already in place and the terms are altered so that L makes a contribution, but he receives a higher rent from the tenant to reflect that contribution, then the author feels that T has surrendered his earlier rental right provisions in consideration of the contribution so that VAT is still chargeable (on T) on the contribution if T has elected to waive exemption.

Inducement to surrender

Normal surrenders are exempt, while inducement payments are vatable.

L may pay T monies to surrender his lease and take up a new lease elsewhere and render the property let under that new lease fit for its desired use (and enter into s 52 obligations). In this case, part of the supply may be exempt and part vatable. For a tribunal decision in this area *see Grantham Cricket Club v The Commissioners* (MAN/93/457 Decision 12287) (*see* Figure 26.17).

Figure 26.17:

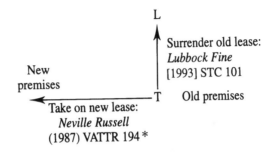

L

Surrender old lease:
Lubbock Fine
[1993] STC 101

New
premises

Old premises

Take on new lease:
Neville Russell
(1987) VATTR 194 *

* But see Cantor Fitzgerald International, discussed at p 335.

Inducement to vary—hidden supplies

The immediate landlord agrees the tenant can sublet the property. To give effect to this the landlord lifts a restrictive covenant on the land, complying with Customs' *Business Brief* 17/94, 12 September 1994.

If the immediate landlord has not elected to waive exemption, that is an exempt supply by him within the *Business Brief*. But there are further points to consider.

Whether or not the tenant is also making a supply for VAT purposes must be ascertained. Where the tenant merely pays cash there will be no difficulties: the tenant will not be making a supply. The payment of cash will be consideration for the exempt supply made by the landlord.

On the other hand, if the tenant makes a vatable supply of goods or services in consideration for the exempt supply comprising the release of the restrictive covenant, then the tenant will be making a supply and the consideration the tenant receives is the exempt release of the restrictive covenant. Thus if the tenant agrees to procure that building works be done by a builder, that is a vatable supply by the tenant in consideration for the value of the restrictive covenant which is released (*see* Figure 26.18).

In practical terms this means that if the builder charges the tenant £150,000 plus VAT, the tenant can reclaim that VAT under the direct attribution rules. But the tenant must then charge VAT to the landlord who is releasing the covenant, and the likelihood is that the market value of the apportioned part of the covenant released will be £150,000 plus VAT: the VAT must be paid to Customs. The tenant must provide the immediate landlord with a VAT invoice. In strict VAT terms, under VATA 1994, s 19(3), where a supply is for a consideration not consisting or not wholly consisting of money, its value shall be taken to be such amount in money as with the addition of the VAT chargeable is equivalent to the consideration.

Thus, the position of the taxpayer is that he pays the builder £150,000 plus VAT of £26,250; he then reclaims that £26,250 as allowable *input tax* under the 1995 Regulations. He then makes an onward supply (an 'output') of agreeing to procure building works for the immediate landlord in consideration of the release of part of the restrictive covenant; let us say that that value is also £150,000 plus VAT of £26,250; he then pays £26,250 as *output tax* and provides his immediate landlord with a VAT invoice.

The immediate landlord himself does not provide any VAT invoices because he has made exempt supplies only. The taxpayer may try to argue that the value of the restrictive covenant apportioned to the supply of procuring building works is less than £150,000 plus the VAT thereon, but in the circumstances it may be prudent for him simply to account for output tax of £26,250 and reclaim the input tax of the same amount charged to him by the builder.

Figure 26.18:

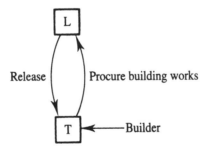

Assign a lease—assignor pays assignee reverse premium—no VAT

It has been held in the VAT Tribunal decision of *Cantor Fitzgerald International* (Decision 15070) that if a lease is assigned and the assignor pays the assignee a reverse premium to take over the lease no VAT is payable. In the case neither of the parties had elected to waive exemption with respect to the property.

The origin of the *Cantor* decision is the European Court decision of

Lubbock Fine v The Commissioners [1994] STC 101, in which it was held that if on the letting of land exempt supplies arose, then 'a change in the contractual relationship, such as the termination of the lease for consideration, must also be regarded as falling within the scope of that exemption'. Thus if the original grant was exempt a surrender of the lease will also be exempt whether the landlord pays the tenant to surrender the lease or the tenant pays the landlord to take the surrender. The earlier VAT Tribunal decision of *Central Capital Corp Ltd v The Commissioners* (Decision 13319) held that it was irrelevant whether the consideration passed from the landlord to the tenant or the tenant to the landlord.

The VAT Tribunal in *Cantor* held that the *Lubbock Fine* principle also applied to a situation where the lease was assigned. In *Cantor*, the landlord was a party to the assignment as he had to give a licence to the assignment and the assignor was not released from its obligations under the lease. If the assignment did not require the landlord's consent and after the assignment the assignor retained no liability under the lease it may be argued that there would be no change in the contractual relationship with regard to the property and the assignee merely provided a separate vatable service of taking over the onerous lease. However, it is felt, based on the *Lubbock Fine* principle, that even if the landlord's consent was not required and the assignor retained no future liabilities that the supply would nevertheless have been exempt because there would have been a change in the contractual relationship with respect to the land (ie one party was substituted for another); the supply would thus be exempt.

The Customs, however, are appealing the decision which has implications for reverse premiums and possibly (but unlikely) inducement payments (see Business Brief 28/97).

The *Cantor* decision is therefore sound authority for the proposition, assuming the relevant election to waive exemption had not been exercised, that the assignment of a negative value lease with a reverse premium being paid to the assignee by the assignor is not a vatable transaction and gives rise to an exempt land supply (*see* Figure 26.19).

Figure 26.19:   *Cantor Fitzgerald* decision—no VAT

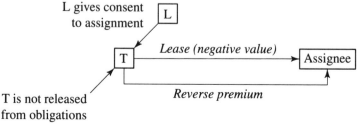

Rent-free period

The assignee of a lease may agree to the assignment in consideration of the assignor agreeing to pay, say, the rent for one year after the assignment.

It may be better for the assignor in such a case simply to pay a capital premium to the assignee rather than agree to bear the rent for one year. This is because the capital premium on assignment should be free of capital gains tax and income tax under Schedule D Case I. The question remains (although the Revenue take no point on this) whether such a payment could be chargeable to tax under Schedule D Case VI, on the basis that the assignee has provided the assignor with a one-off service of taking over the onerous lease.

If the transaction is drafted in terms that the assignor pays the rent for a year, then there is a great danger that the assignee will not be able to secure a Case I Schedule D deduction for rent (assuming the assignee is carrying on a trade or profession and uses the premises for that purpose).

The payment would also clearly be an inducement payment for the purposes of VAT and thus the assignee, assuming he is carrying on a business and the payment is above the registration limit, may be charged VAT. However, he must follow the appeals in *Cantor* to determine the final position. It is clearly arguable that if, for example, no elections have been made the supply is exempt.

If the assignor under the lease terms paid rent in advance to the landlord it is not felt that that can amount on any analysis to vatable consideration paid to the assignee for a service provided by the assignee to the assignor.

The document recording the transaction would not be chargeable to stamp duty apart from a nominal 50p.

Figure 26.20:   Rent-free period

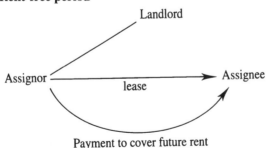

Wholly inoffensive reverse premium

'Reverse premium' is an imprecise term. Some reverse premiums may be inoffensive.

It would seem that if, for instance, the landlord says to a potential tenant 'I will put into the building extra fixtures and fittings to suit your needs, if you will take on this lease', no vatable reverse premium will be in point.

This is because the works are part and parcel of the thing on offer, in the same way that the granting of a rent-free period as an inducement is not vatable.

TAXABLE RENT-FREE PERIODS

Port Erin Hotels Ltd v The Treasury (MAN/89/722 Decision 5045) was a case where the grant of a rent-free period was found to be vatable.

A rent-free period was granted by L to the prospective tenant and was expressed to be given in consideration of the tenant undertaking to carry out works on the property which was the subject matter of the lease. The tribunal held that the tenant carried out works and the landlord paid for them in consideration of what the tribunal called 'the waiver of rent' (p 12).

In *Ridgeons Bulk Ltd v The Commissioners* [1994] STC 427, Popplewell J affirmed the substantive issue of the Tribunal Chairman, Judge Medd, that a tenant had provided services to the landlord in return for a rent-free period. The relevant linkage between the rent-free period and the construction service was found in a letter from the company to the company's solicitors which read: '. . . it has been agreed that Ridgeons Bulk Limited will undertake to carry out repairs and modifications valued £375,518 and in view of this a rent-free period of three years has been agreed. At p 444h Popplewell J stated:

> The Tribunal in the instant case took the view that the letter dated 27th January 1988 was the clearest possible indication that what Bulk was to receive for undertaking the repairs and modifications was the right to occupy the sawmill for three years without being required to pay any rent, and the benefit of the three years' rent-free was clearly directly linked to the undertaking to carry out the building works. The works were done pursuant to that agreement.

This area of law is clearly very difficult. If there is a clear link between the grant of the rent-free period and the obligation to do the works then there will be a vatable supply by the tenant of the obligation to do the works. On the other hand, if the landlord grants a lease which contains a rent-free period and at the same time, under the terms of the lease, the tenant is obliged to carry out certain works, the necessary linkage may be absent and no VAT charge will arise.

The taxpayer should take special care in this area as it is very easy to overlook the fact that a vatable supply may result in such circumstances where a rent-free period is given.

Figure 26.21a: Acceptable rent-free period

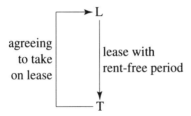

Figure 26.21b: Unacceptable rent-free period

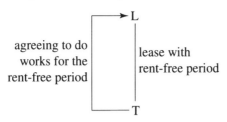

Statement in Parliament

Mr Fraser asked the Chancellor of the Exchequer (*see* [1991] STI 19) if he would review the decision of Customs to treat rent-free periods as benefits subject to VAT. Mrs Gillian Shepherd stated that it is long-standing Customs' practice that rent-free periods are outside the scope of VAT unless services are performed in return by the tenant for the landlord. As this is uncommon, in practice only a few cases will lead to VAT being charged.

It is felt that the rent-free period position is thus:

Figure 26.22:

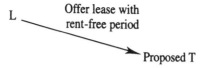

L to T: 'Take on this lease and I'll give you a rent-free period worth £1m.' No VAT problems.

L to T: 'Take on this lease and I'll give you a rent-free period worth £1m provided you spend £1m on the property from which, of course, I will benefit at the next rent review.' VAT problems.

Chapter 27

Transfer of a business as a going concern

IMPORTANCE OF IDENTIFYING A GOING CONCERN

A taxpayer may sell a business as a going concern. He may be required by the Value Added Tax (Special Provisions) Order 1995 (SI No 1268), art 5 not to charge VAT on the sale. This is not an optional matter; the vendor must not charge VAT. On the other hand, if the disposal of the business is not as a going concern the vendor must charge VAT (subject to certain exemptions) with respect to items such as plant and machinery, stock, goodwill and land in an appropriate case (eg if he has elected to waive exemption).

Omitting to charge VAT

If the taxpayer disposes of his business assets and this is a disposal of the business as a going concern then, as mentioned, he cannot and must not charge VAT.

However, should it be found that the transfer was not of the business as a going concern, then Customs will seek payment of VAT, and penalties if appropriate, with respect to the disposal of the vatable items such as plant. The amount of VAT will be deemed to be included in the sale price.

It is not possible for the vendor to obtain an extra payment from the purchaser to cover the VAT which he failed to charge unless the terms of the sale contract enable him to do so as a matter of contract law.

Incorrectly charging VAT

If, however, the vendor seeks to play safe and charges VAT on the sale price with respect to goodwill or plant and machinery etc, serious problems will arise for the purchaser if it is found that the business was sold as a going concern. This is because the purchaser can claim back, or obtain credit for, input tax only where tax was properly chargeable on the supply. Thus he cannot get credit and he will have problems recovering the monies from the vendor.

'GOING CONCERN' RELIEF

The going concern rules apply to land and buildings where the transferor has made an election to waive exemption. They also apply to new and unfinished freehold commercial buildings which give rise to a standard-rated VAT charge when they are sold whether or not the vendor exercised the election to waive exemption. It is expressly provided that if such land and buildings are disposed of and the transferee has not, before the relevant date of the supply, notified Customs that he has made an election to waive exemption with respect to the particular land or buildings, then VAT at the standard rate of 17.5 per cent must be charged (*see* Figure 27.1).

The effect of the statutory instrument is not that if the transferee exercises the election the going concern relief automatically applies: it is still necessary to look at the land and buildings in question and decide whether the business is being disposed of as a going concern. There should be no difficulty in that respect if a fully let building is disposed of. Article 5 of the Value Added Tax (Special Provisions) Order 1995 (SI No 1268) provides as follows:

> **5**—(1)   Subject to paragraph (2) below, there shall be treated as neither a supply of goods nor a supply of services the following supplies by a person of assets of his business—
>
> > (*a*)   their supply to a person to whom he transfers his business as a going concern where—
> >
> > > (i)   the assets are to be used by the transferee in carrying on the same kind of business, whether or not as part of any existing business, as that carried on by the transferor, and
> > >
> > > (ii)   in a case where the transferor is a taxable person, the transferee is already, or immediately becomes as a result of the transfer, a taxable person or a person defined as such in section 2(2) of the Manx Act;
> >
> > (*b*)   their supply to a person to whom he transfers part of his business as a going concern where—

    (i) that part is capable of separate operation,

    (ii) the assets are to be used by the transferee in carrying on the same kind of business, whether or not as part of any existing business, as that carried on by the transferor in relation to that part, and

    (iii) in a case where the transferor is a taxable person, the transferee is already, or immediately becomes as a result of the transfer, a taxable person or a person defined as such in section 2(2) of the Manx Act.

(2)   A supply of assets shall not be treated as neither a supply of goods nor a supply of services by virtue of paragraph (1) above to the extent that it consists of—

    (*a*) a grant which would, but for an election which the transferor has made, fall within item 1 of Group 1 of Schedule 6 to the Value Added Tax Act 1983 [now VATA 1994, Sched 9, Group 1, Item 1]; or

    (*b*) a grant of a fee simple which falls within paragraph (*a*) of Item 1 of Group 1 of Schedule 6 to the Value Added Tax Act 1983 [now VATA 1994, Sched 9, Group 1, Item 1(*a*)];

unless the transferee has made an election in relation to the land concerned which has effect on the relevant date and has given any written notification of the election required by paragraph 3(6) of Schedule 6A to the Value Added Tax Act 1983 [now VATA 1994, Sched 10, para 3(6)] no later than the relevant date.

(3)   In paragraph (2) of this article—

    'election' means an election having effect under paragraph 2 of Schedule 6A to the Value Added Tax Act 1983 [now VATA 1994, Sched 10, para 2];

    'relevant date' means the date upon which the grant would have been treated as having been made or, if there is more than one such date, the earliest of them;

    'transferor' and 'transferee' include a relevant associate of either respectively as defined in paragraph 3(8) of Schedule 6A to the Value Added Tax Act 1983 [now VATA 1994, Sched 10, para 3(7)].

The transfer of part of a business as a going concern will also be deemed to be a non-supply, but there is the additional requirement that the part must be capable of separate operation.

In *Michael Edmund Noble v The Commissioners* (MAN/86/168 Decision 2755) the taxpayer had two divisions in his business: one dealing with home extensions and the other with the supply of small prefabricated industrial buildings. He sold the latter division—its goodwill, plant and furniture—and it was held to comprise the sale of part of a business capable of separate operation. VAT was thus not chargeable. The tribunal stated:

Was the business capable of separate operation? In our judgement it clearly was so capable, as is demonstrated by the fact that thereafter it was so operated. Moreover, when the parties themselves have treated a business as capable of separate operation, by respectively selling it and paying for it, a tribunal does not readily hold, that they were wrong (p 7).

Figure 27.1:   Four basic scenarios

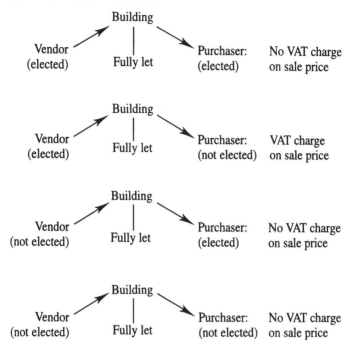

Special rules apply to the sale of the freehold of a new commercial building or one in the course of construction.

MEANING OF 'GOING CONCERN'

The wording of the contract can be important in demonstrating that a business is transferred as a going concern. Where appropriate the parties should incorporate in the contract the expression 'going concern'. An express disposal of goodwill is also a strong indication that the business as a going concern is being disposed of as well as the assets which are central to the business; these may include customer lists, know-how and specialist tools (*see Shire Equip Ltd* (MAN/83/52), *Westpark Interiors Ltd* (MAN/83/164) and *Kenmuir Ltd v Frizzell* [1968] 1 All ER 414 at 418, as well as art 5 of the Value Added Tax (Special Provisions) Order 1995, and VATA 1994, s 49).

In the *Golden Oak Partnership* (LON/90/958 Decision 7212) the appellant partnership was formed to develop a site as a business estate. It intended to make zero-rated supplies. It reclaimed its input tax with respect to planning and professional fees. It carried out road widening, installation of drainage and construction of electricity and gas stations. However, it received an unexpected offer from another developer and sold the entire property together with a building which it had used as an administrative office. Customs sought to recover the input tax which had been reclaimed because an exempt supply had been made (the 1995 Regulations, reg 108)). The partnership contended that the land and the administrative offices were sold as a going concern. The tribunal held that at the time of the sale the land was in the course of active development. The purchaser had continued the development without a break, completing the building work commenced by the partnership and granting zero-rated leases of the new buildings. The tribunal concluded 'in the particular circumstances' (p 10) that there was a transfer of the business as a going concern.

For further cases dealing with the transfer of a business as a going concern *see Conrad Systems and Engineering Ltd* (MAN/89/23 Decision 4193), *Patricia McMichael* (LON/88/968 Decision 4369), *Monitronix Services plc* (LON/88/168 Decision 4665) and *ECSG Ltd* (LON/88/580 Decision 5204) [1990] STI 873.

TRANSFER OF REGISTRATION

Where a business is transferred as a going concern it is possible for both parties in certain circumstances to elect that the transferor's VAT registration will be passed to the transferee (*see* the 1995 Regulations, reg 6).

This election will not normally be made because, although it may be convenient for the future as far as the transferee is concerned, the transferee may, in doing so, take over problems from the transferor.

VAT PLANNING

(1) Taxpayers must take special care with respect to this transfer as a going concern relief.

(2) They must clearly take a view as to whether a business is being transferred as a going concern and should draft the documentation with the point clearly in mind. In unclear cases the parties may consider leaving assets out of the sale, or adding assets in, so the transaction clearly falls within one category or the other. If it is agreed that VAT should not be added to the sale price, the purchaser may agree to

indemnify the vendor should Customs decide the VAT should have been charged.

(3) It can be catastrophic (for the purchaser) if VAT is charged when there is a transfer of a business as a going concern, or for the vendor if VAT is not charged when he is merely selling the assets of the business and not the business itself.

(4) The parties will not normally elect to transfer the transferor's VAT registration number etc to the transferee; indeed it is not always possible to make such an election even if the parties wish it.

LAND WHICH IS LET: THE VAT NIGHTMARE

X plc exercises its VAT election to waive exemption over an investment property which it owns. It charges VAT on the rents. Subsequently it sells the property to Y plc for £1m plus £175,000 VAT. Y plc has elected in respect of the property. Depending on the precise circumstances, that could be the beginning of a VAT nightmare with all parties losing, except Customs, who could win twice.

In general it is perfectly correct that if X plc exercises the election to waive exemption on the investment property, VAT must be charged not only on the rent but also on the sale proceeds.

Customs accept, and, it is felt, correctly, that the letting of property comprises a business: thus the disposal of such property to another person who exercises the election to waive exemption with regard to that property would be treated as the disposal of a business as a going concern and thus VAT must not be charged on the sale of the property by X plc to Y plc.

The nightmare begins.

Y plc, the purchaser, has been incorrectly charged VAT and so cannot reclaim it (*Northern Counties Co-operative Enterprises Ltd v The Commissioners* (1986) VATTR 250, *Chromelog Ltd* (LON/83/128 Decision 1444), *Theotrue Holdings Ltd v The Commissioners* (1983) VATTR 88, *P Howard v The Commissioners* (LON/80/157) and *T Smith v The Commissioners* (LON/80/440)). The European Court case of *Genius Holding BV v Staatssecretaris van Financiën* CJEC [1991] STC 239 confirmed that credit was not available for improperly charged VAT.

The vendor has issued a VAT invoice. To discourage people from doing such a thing a quasi-penal provision applies (VATA 1994, Sched 11, para 5). The consequence is that even though no vatable supply was made, X plc, the vendor, is liable to account to Customs for the amount of 'VAT' charged in the invoice (*see Theotrue Holdings v The Commissioners* (1983) VATTR 88) (*see* Figure 27.2).

X plc must therefore pay the monies to Customs. The purchaser may seek to sue X plc for the return of the £175,000 but he may have difficulties as it is likely that the monies will have been paid under a mistake of law and are thus not recoverable (*see Sawyer and Vincent v Windsor Brace Ltd* [1943] KB 32, *Sharp Bros and Knight v Chant* [1971] 1 KB 771 and *Ord v Ord* [1923] 2 KB 432). It may also be that there was no misrepresentation (Misrepresentation Act 1967 as amended) made to the purchaser so that all in all his chances of suing X plc are weak.

Thus Y plc, the purchaser, is left in the position of having elected with respect to the building, but is unable to claim back from Customs the £175,000. X plc has had to pay the monies to Customs and is under threat that Y plc may be able to put together some sort of contractual argument to get the money back from X plc.

The one way out of the nightmare is the credit note procedure. The vendor will admit that he has made a mistake and issue to Y plc a credit note, at the same time returning the £175,000 (*see BUS Machinery Co Ltd v The Commissioners* (1977) VATTR 187 at 192; *Lamdec Ltd* (MAN/90/1018 Decision 6078); *Re Master Stores Scotland Ltd (In Receivership)* (EDN/93/213 Decision 12522); *Creative Facility Ltd* (MAN/92/1157 Decision 10891); and *Genius Holding BV v Staatssecretaris van Financiën* (Case 342/87 [1991] STC 239)).

Figure 27.2:

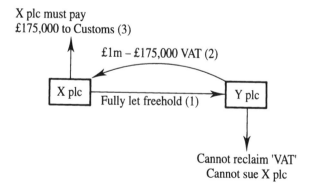

X plc must pay
£175,000 to Customs (3)

£1m – £175,000 VAT (2)

X plc — Fully let freehold (1) → Y plc

Cannot reclaim 'VAT'
Cannot sue X plc

PARTLY LET PROPERTY AND TRADING STOCK

A number of difficult questions were resolved in the case of *M J Cashmore and J D Talbot v The Commissioners* (LON/92/1291 Decision 9797).

It is clear from that decision that the disposal of let property is capable of amounting to the disposal of a business as a going concern.

Thus, in a simple case, if X (an investor) disposed of *fully let* property to Y (who continues letting the property as an investor), there will have been a disposal of a going concern. Under the original regulations in the Value Added Tax (Special Provisions) Order 1981 (SI No 1741), reg 12, it was clear that, if a taxpayer elected with regard to a particular property and disposed of the property which had been fully let, the going concern relief would apply, provided the purchaser was registered for VAT (*see Gould & Cullen* (LON/91/2439 Decision 10150) [1993] STI 913). The purchaser did not have to elect with regard to the property. The case of *Cashmore & Talbot* confirmed that that would clearly be the case. (The 1981 regulation was amended, with effect from 1 December 1991, by art 2 of the Value Added Tax (Special Provisions) (Amendment) Order 1991 (SI No 2503) and the present law is to be found in the Value Added Tax (Special Provisions) Order 1995 (SI No 1268), art 5.)

However, with effect from 1 December 1991, the going concern relief applied in such a case only if the purchaser also elected with regard to the property in question.

In the case of *Cashmore & Talbot* itself, the taxpayer had disposed of the relevant property before 1 December 1991. The tribunal held that it was not necessary for the purchaser to have elected for the going concern relief to apply, provided the purchaser was registered for VAT (although of course, had the transfer taken place on or after 1 December 1991, the purchaser will have to have elected because of the change in law).

The tribunal also held that if the vendor held the let property as trading stock, and the purchaser acquired the let property as an investment, the going concern relief could still be available: it could not be successfully argued that the businesses of the vendor and purchaser were different. They both comprise a letting of property, even though the vendor had held the property as stock and the purchaser acquired it as an investment.

A further point was raised, concerning the extent of the property which had been let at the time of the transfer.

The vendor had let the ground floor but was seeking tenants for the upper floors (therefore the property at the time of the sale was not fully let). The purchaser took over the property with the benefit of the lease of the ground floor and sought to find tenants for the upper floors. The tribunal had no difficulty in finding that the property was disposed of as a going concern within the going concern regulations. It was not necessary that the property in its entirety had been let at the time of the transfer. If the vendor was seeking tenants of the unlet part, and the purchaser continued to seek such tenants, then there will have been a disposal of a going concern or part of a going concern by the vendor.

Of course, as mentioned *above*, from 1 December 1991 if the vendor has elected (or there is a disposal of a new freehold commercial building), then in order that the going concern relief applies the purchaser must elect. In that event the case indicates that the relief will be available even though part of the property may not be let and even though the vendor may, for instance, be a land trader and the purchaser an investor.

SUB-SALES

It can be very difficult to get the going concern relief if property is subsold. The Customs' view is set out in their Notice 700/9/96, para 2.2, which reads as follows:

> There must not be a series of immediately consecutive transfers of the business. Where A sells its assets to B who immediately sells those assets on to C, B has not carried on the business. B can neither receive nor ignore its supply of the assets under the special provisions set out in this notice. In relation to property transactions such immediate transfers often occur where A contracts to sell property to B, and B 'sub-sells' the property to C with both contracts being completed by a single transfer from A to C.

PREVENTING THE RELIEF FROM APPLYING

A taxpayer may want to stop the going concern relief from applying by electing to waive exemption, say, two weeks after the legal completion of the purchase of the property. The question is whether the fact that the vendor is selling a new freehold commercial building can make a difference to that point. The answer is that it makes no difference.

Article 5(2) of the Value Added Tax (Special Provisions) Order 1995 (SI No 1268) states that a supply of assets (the freehold land) shall not be treated as outside the scope of VAT to the extent that it consists of:

(a) a grant which would, but for an election which the transferor has made, fall within Item 1 of Group 1 of Sched 9 to VATA 1994; or

(b) a grant of a fee simple which falls within para (*a*) of Item 1 of Group 1 of Sched 9 to VATA 1994,

unless the transferee has made an election in relation to the land concerned which has effect on the relevant date (broadly, the earliest tax point) and has given written notification of the election to Customs no later than the relevant date.

The effect of that regulation is that if the vendor makes, under general principles, a vatable supply either because of the sale of a new freehold (with a commercial building, etc thereon) or because of the exercise of the election to waive exemption, that supply shall not be vatable unless the purchaser makes an election in relation to the land concerned and notifies his election at the time of the earliest tax point (normally the date of legal completion).

SURRENDER OF A LEASE

If a tenant surrenders his lease to his landlord, VAT will be chargeable on the surrender proceeds if the tenant has elected to waive exemption. However, if the tenant is surrendering a lease as part of a transfer of his business as a going concern, or as part of a transfer of part of his business as a going concern, and the provisions of the Value Added Tax (Special Provisions) Order 1995, art 5 are satisfied, then VAT will not be charged on the surrender proceeds.

The tenant may run a restaurant on the leased premises. If he surrenders the lease and transfers all the business assets to his landlord then the supply will be treated as neither a supply of goods nor a supply of services if the following conditions are satisfied:

(a) he transfers the business as a going concern;

(b) the assets are to be used by the landlord in carrying on the same kind of business, whether or not as part of any existing business, as that carried on by the tenant; and

(c) an appropriate election is made (*see* p 342).

This relief also applies if the tenant transfers part of his business as a going concern—for instance, he has three restaurants but surrenders one. In this case, to qualify for relief the part surrendered must be capable of separate operation. The assets transferred must be used by the transferee (landlord) in carrying on the same kind of business, whether or not as part of any existing business, as that carried on by the transferor (the tenant) in relation to that part. Once again, for the relief to apply the transferee must make a timely election and notification.

Drafting points

Thus, VAT will not be charged on the surrender proceeds, or indeed any other proceeds of disposal, but there is the requirement that the lease is used by the landlord in carrying on the same kind of business as that carried on by the tenant.

The technical danger is that if the lease is extinguished on the surrender (usually by operation of law to avoid stamp duty), then it cannot be said that the asset—the lease—will be used by the transferee in carrying on the same kind of business as that carried on by the transferor. The asset will have disappeared.

To play safe in such circumstances, the landlord can make a declaration of non-merger which may have the effect under land law principles that the so-called surrender is really an assignment.

In addition, in the transfer documents the parties should refer to the fact that the business as a going concern, or part of the business as a going concern, is being transferred (as the case may be). The landlord should give an undertaking that the assets so transferred to him will be used by him in carrying on the same kind of business as that carried on by the tenant.

Because of the uncertainties in sales of going concerns, some practitioners seek to place the possible VAT monies in a stakeholder's account and clear the position with Customs (this should take a week or so). Typical stakeholders clauses are set out on p 396.

CUSTOMS' PRACTICE

Customs Notice 700/9/96 gives the following guidance on input tax and the capital goods provisions and examples of where the going concern relief does and does not apply.

2.5   Deduction of input tax

Although there is no supply for VAT purposes where there is a transfer of a going concern, this does not prevent the deduction of input tax on related expenses. There is, however, a distinction between the extent to which the transferor and the transferee can deduct that input tax.

From 1 June 1996, if a transferee acquires assets by way of the transfer of a going concern and the assets are used exclusively to make taxable supplies, the VAT incurred on the cost of acquiring those assets should be attributed to those taxable supplies and can be recovered in full. Conversely, if the assets of the acquired business are to be used exclusively to make exempt supplies, none of the input tax on the cost of acquiring those assets can be recovered. However, if the assets are to be used in making both taxable and exempt supplies, any input tax incurred is non-attributable and must be apportioned in accordance with the agreed VAT partial exemption method.

In the case of the transferor, the treatment of input tax is the same as before 1 June 1996. Since the sale of the business as a going concern is not a supply, the input tax incurred on the costs of selling the business cannot be attributed to any supply by the transferor. These costs are, therefore, treated as a general business expense and the input tax is residual input tax to be apportioned as necessary by the transferor's agreed partial exemption method.

Businesses which had previously treated the costs of acquiring a business by way of a TOGC as a general overhead for VAT purposes should, from 1 June 1996, attribute the cost directly as described above.

[*Author's note:*   The Customs' treatment with respect to transfers from 1 June 1996 follows from the decision of *UBAF Bank Ltd* [1996] STC 372; reference should also be made to *Abbey National plc* (Decision 14951).]

2.6   Capital goods scheme

If—
   (i)   land or buildings of a VAT exclusive value of £250,000 or more, or
   (ii)   computers or items of computer equipment of a VAT exclusive value of £50,000 or more
are being transferred to you as part of a transfer of a going concern then you, as the new owner, assume responsibility for any adjustments of input tax required under the capital goods scheme (the 'scheme') for any remaining part of the adjustment period.

The scheme was introduced on 1 April 1990 and requires adjustments of any input tax originally incurred if, within a 10 year period (for land and buildings) or within a five year period (for computers and items of computer equipment) there is a change in the extent to which these capital items are used in making taxable supplies.

If the transferor has been fully taxable since the acquisition of the capital item and the transferee is, and remains fully taxable until the expiry of the adjustment period, then no adjustments are required under the scheme. It is only when there is a change in the extent to which the items are used in making taxable supplies, within the adjustment period, that adjustments under the scheme have to be performed.

Examples where a business can be transferred as a going concern
   1   If you own the freehold of a property which you let to a tenant and sell the freehold with the benefit of the existing lease, a business of property rental is transferred to the purchaser. This is a business transferred as a going concern even if the property is only partly tenanted. Similarly, if you own the lease of a property (which is subject to a sub-lease) and you assign your lease with the benefit of the sub-lease, this is a business transferred as a going concern.
   2   If you own a building which is being let out where there is an initial rent free period, even if the building is sold during the rent free period, you are carrying on a business of property rental.
   3   If you have granted a lease in respect of a building but the tenants are not yet in occupation, you are carrying on a property rental business.

4   If you own a property and have found a tenant but not actually entered into a lease agreement when you transfer the property to a third party (with the benefit of the prospective tenancy but before a lease has been signed), there is a property rental business capable of being transferred.

5   If you are a property developer selling a site as a package (to a single buyer) which is a mixture of let and unlet, finished or unfinished properties, and the sale of the site would otherwise have been standard rated, then subject to the purchaser electing to waive exemption for the *whole* site, the whole site can be regarded as a business transferred as a going concern.

Examples where there is not a transfer of a going concern

6   If you are a property developer and have built a building and you allow someone to occupy temporarily (without any right to occupy) after any proposed sale) or you are 'actively marketing' it in search of a tenant, there is no property rental business being carried on.

7   If you own the freehold of a property and grant a lease, even a 999-year lease, you are not transferring a business as a going concern—you are retaining your asset (the freehold) and creating a new asset (a lease). Similarly, if you own a headlease and grant a sub-lease you are not transferring your business as a going concern.

8   If you sell a property where the lease you granted is surrendered immediately before the sale, your property rental business ceases and so cannot be transferred as a going concern—even if tenants under a sub-lease remain in occupation.

9   If you sell a property to the existing tenant who leases the whole premises from you, this cannot be a transfer of a going concern because the tenant cannot carry on the same business of property rental.

VAT—BUYING PROPERTY AS A GOING CONCERN: WARNING CLIENT ABOUT CLAW-BACK

It is very important for practitioners to appreciate that if they are acting for a client who buys a property as a going concern (so that no VAT is paid on the acquisition of the property) that the client is warned that if he subsequently uses the property for exempt purposes he may have to repay to Customs some of the VAT which the vendor originally reclaimed. The Customs' practice is referred to at p 265.

The situation may arise where V Ltd has carried out a major refurbishment to a commercial building spending over £250,000 plus VAT of 17.5 per cent on the same. It elected waive exemption from VAT and reclaimed the VAT charged on the refurbishment expenditure. It then sells the same as a going concern to P Ltd.

P Ltd may be more than happy to ensure that the going concern relief provisions apply especially, as amongst other things, he would not have to pay stamp duty at potentially 2 per cent on the VAT which would otherwise be charged on the purchase.

However, note that if the property sold by V Ltd comprised 'capital goods' within the VAT legislation then P Ltd may be required to repay some of the VAT to Customs which V Ltd reclaimed on the refurbishment.

What are 'capital goods'?

The first thing is to determine whether the goods are capital goods within the VAT legislation.

Under the VAT (Amendment) (No 3) Regulations 1997 (SI No 1614), which came into force on 3 July 1997, the property would comprise capital goods in the hands of V Ltd (assuming the property had not been acquired by V Ltd solely with a view to turning the same making a dealing profit) if V Ltd had refurbished or fitted out the building and the amount of capital expenditure V Ltd had expended (and on which VAT at 17.5 per cent had been charged) was not less than £250,000.

Thus if V Ltd had spent £1m in carrying out the refurbishment the VAT reclaimed would have been £175,000.

How the claw-back works

Under the capital goods provisions broadly one looks over a ten-year period to see whether the VAT which may have been reclaimed in the first instance shall be repaid to the Customs because the taxpayer, who may have originally used the property for a fully taxable purpose, may have changed the user to an exempt use.

For example, V Ltd after the refurbishment may have for Year 1 used the property for a fully taxable purpose (eg let the property having first elected to waive exemption) and thus would have reclaimed the full £175,000. If at the end of Year 1 the property is sold to P Ltd as a going concern and P Ltd subsequently itself uses the property for an exempt purpose (eg for carrying out insurance supplies or financial activities) then, very broadly, for the next nine years P Ltd must repay to the Customs each year one-tenth of £175,000.

Warning to client

The point for practitioners to note is that when they are acting for a client on a purchase of a property as a going concern they must warn the client that VAT may not be charged on the acquisition but that any subsequent change in the user of the premises from a vatable user to an exempt user (for example, the purchaser may buy the property to let and elect to waive exemption, but after, say, two years the purchaser may decide to use the property itself in making exempt supplies) will result in monies having to repaid to the Customs. In many cases this problem may prove academic but it is felt that the client should be warned of the dangers.

The dangers are particularly important since the passing of the 1997 Regulations which include within the definition of capital goods refurbishment and refitting works and civil engineering works where the expenditure thereon was not less than £250,000 (plus VAT of 17.5 per cent) (newly constructed commercial buildings and alterations, extensions and the addition of an annexe to commercial buildings where the floor area is extended by not less than 10 per cent have always been within the capital goods provisions since they were first introduced in 1990 provided the vatable (17.5 per cent) expenditure on the works has been not less than £250,000).

The relevant provisions are to be found in the VAT Regulations 1995 (SI No 2518), regs 112–16, as amended by VAT (Amendment) (No 3) Regulations 1997 (SI No 1614), regs 10 and 11.

Precedent

When capital goods are purchased and the going concern relief applies the purchaser may want warranties etc with respect to earlier VAT reclaims, the adjustments periods, etc. Suitable clauses are set out at p 398.

EXEMPTION v NON-SUPPLY

It is felt that if X has elected to waive exemption and transfers the business as a going concern in circumstances that the election is disapplied, the going concern relief—which treats the position as if no supply took place—overrides the disapplication of the election (which treats the disposal as an exempt one). No exempt supply will thus result.

THE EXEMPT GOING CONCERN TRICK

It is possible to make an otherwise exempt transfer which falls within the going concern rules causing it to be one where neither a supply of goods nor a supply of services takes place. The aim is to reclaim input tax on related expenses.

Value Added Tax (Special Provisions) Order 1995 (SI No 1268), reg 5 states that a supply of goods or services transferred as a going concern shall be treated as a supply neither of goods nor of services if, amongst other things, the transferee uses the asset for the same kind of business as that carried on by the transferor, and where the transferor is a taxable person the transferee is already or immediately becomes as a result of the transfer of a taxable person.

VAT leaflet 700/9/96 para 2.5 states: 'Although there is no supply for VAT purposes where there is a transfer of a going concern, this does not prevent the deduction of input tax on related expenses.'

Example in practice

> X pension fund desires to sell exempt properties to Z plc. X pension fund is registered for VAT and has a good partial exemption method. It seeks to ensure that Z plc registers for VAT as a taxable person (reg 5(1)(*a*)(ii)) (there is no need to elect to waive exemption).

Note that the restrictions on the going concern relief provisions which apply where land is sold are only relevant where an election has been made (and the supplier would have been exempt but for the election) or a new freehold interest is sold (*see* reg 5(2)).

Nomineeship and precedent

It may be a purchaser of property as a going concern buys the same in the name of a nominee. The Customs' suggested from of nominee document is contained in p 398.

PART VI

TIMING OF SUPPLIES

Chapter 28

The tax point

The time when goods and services are treated as supplied—the time of supply—is referred to as the tax point. It is important to ascertain the tax point for three reasons:

(a) it determines the rate of tax to be charged on the supply;

(b) it determines the relevant prescribed accounting period of the taxpayer with respect to the supply; and

(c) it determines the nature of the supply (*see* p 379).

GENERAL RULES

The basic tax point with regard to a supply of goods is the time when they are *removed* by the customer or, if not removed, when they are made available to the customer. The basic tax point with regard to services is the time when the services are *performed*.

Thus if a building company completes property conversion work in the period ended February 1997 but the price is payable five years later, the VAT is payable by reference to the period ended February 1997. The consideration might, however, have to be valued and accordingly reduced for the delay in payment and the possibility of the final price being reduced after allowing for any defects (*Mercantile Contracts Ltd* (LON/88/786 Decision 4357, LON/88/786Y Decision 5266)). In an appropriate case, a vendor who is entitled to deferred consideration should seek to receive at the outset an amount to cover his VAT.

The basic tax points may be overridden by the issue of a tax invoice or the receipt of a payment in either of the following circumstances:

(a) where a tax invoice is issued or payment is received *before* the basic tax point, the earliest date is taken as the tax point (eg X performs a service on 1 June 1997. He was paid for this on 1 April 1997. He issued the tax invoice on 1 March 1997. The tax point was 1 March 1997); or

(b) where a tax invoice is issued within 14 days *after* the basic tax point the date of the issue of the invoice is taken as the tax point (unless (a) *above* applies by reason of payment being received before the basic tax point). Customs may, at the request of the supplier, allow longer than 14 days.

The above rules are subject to any relevant regulations, which, as far as the property industry is concerned, are the 1995 Regulations, regs 85, 89, 90 and 93.

Regulation 85 provides that where the grant of a tenancy or a lease is a supply of goods and the whole or any part of the consideration for the grant is payable periodically or from time to time, goods shall be taken as separately and successively supplied at the *earlier* of the following times:

(a) whenever a part of the consideration is received; or

(b) whenever the supplier issues a tax invoice relating to the grant.

Example

X Ltd grants a lease (for rent) to Y Ltd of over 21 years (a supply of goods will be made). The time of supply is each time X Ltd receives rent or, if earlier, when it issues the VAT invoice with respect thereto.

Regulation 93 provides that where *services*, or services together with goods, are supplied in the course of the construction, alteration, demolition, repair or maintenance of a building or of any civil engineering work under a contract which provides for payment for such supplies to be made periodically, a supply should be treated as taking place at the *earlier* of the following times:

(a) when a payment is received by the supplier where the consideration for the contract is wholly in money; or

(b) when the supplier issues a tax invoice.

Another important regulation is reg 89 which provides that where any contract for the supply of goods or services provides for the retention of any part of the consideration by one party pending full and satisfactory performance of the contract, or any part of it, by the other party, a supply is treated as taking place whenever:

(a) a payment is received in respect of it; or

(b) a tax invoice is issued by the supplier,

whichever is the earlier.

Regulation 90 provides that where *services* are supplied for a period, for a consideration the whole or part of which is determined or payable periodically or from time to time, they are treated as separately and successively supplied at the *earlier* of the following times:

(a) whenever a payment in respect of the supply is received; or

(b) whenever a supplier issues a tax invoice relating to the supply.

Example

Z Ltd grants a lease (for rent) of 21 years or less to W Ltd (this is a supply of services). The time of supply is each time Z Ltd receives rent or, if earlier, when a VAT invoice is issued with respect to the rent to be received by Z Ltd.

SPECIAL RULES

Regulation 84 deals with tax points with respect to two specific land transactions.

Compulsory purchase

The first is compulsory purchase. If under any enactment an interest in or right over land is compulsorily purchased, and at the tax point the landowner from whom it is purchased does not know the amount of the payment he is to receive, then the goods, or as the case may be, services, are treated as supplied each time the grantor receives any payment for the disposal of the property.

Example

The freehold land of X is vested in the local authority under compulsory purchase powers and at the time of vesting the amount to be paid is not ascertained. The land is treated as supplied when the landowner receives the payment.

Consideration not determinable—fee simple

The second specific situation is covered by reg 84(2). This provides where a landowner grants or assigns the fee simple in any land and at the time of the grant or assignment, the total consideration for it is not determinable, then goods shall be treated as separately and successively supplied at the following times:

(a) the time determined in accordance with s 6(2) (the time of removal, etc); or s 6(4) (earlier issue of invoice or receipt of monies); or s 6(5) (subsequent issue of invoice, generally within 14 days); or s 6(6) (a period longer than 14 days may be substituted); or s 6(9) (self-supply); or s 6(10) (Customs' direction on supplies) of VATA 1994, as the case may require, and

(b) the earlier of the following times—

  (i) whenever any part of the consideration which is not determinable at the time mentioned in (a) *above* is received by the grantor or

  (ii) when the grantor issues a tax invoice in respect of such a part.

The regulation is curiously drafted, but on a reasonable interpretation it would seem that on the sale of a fee simple, when the grant takes place all the ascertainable consideration must be brought into account. Any unascertainable consideration will be brought into account when received by the grantor or whenever an invoice is issued.

Example

X sells his freehold for £1m, payable one year after the legal completion of the sale of the freehold. The freehold is treated as supplied at the time of legal completion. Following *Mercantile Contracts Ltd v The Commissioners* (LON/88/786Y Decision 4357), it may be argued that this must be discounted for delayed payment.

Example

Y sells property and vests the legal fee simple in Z for an unascertainable consideration (eg market value of the property as and when planning permission is obtained). The relevant supply takes place when the monies are received or the invoice issued.

Example

X sells his freehold to Y for: £1m payable at the time of completion; £0.5m payable one year later; and an unascertainable figure depending on the market value of the property with planning permission obtained within two years after legal completion. The £1m must be brought into account in the prescribed accounting period in which completion took place; so must the £0.5m, duly discounted for delayed payment. The contingent figure will come into the prescribed accounting period in which the invoice for it is issued or, if earlier, when the consideration is received.

RECEIVERS

If invoices are issued before receivership this will establish the VAT liabilities even if payment is made later (VATA 1983, s 5(1), now VATA 1994, s 6(5)) and the 1995 Regulations, regs 90 and 93).

Note however, that if a self-billing scheme is in operation under reg 13(3) it is the client's invoice which may establish the VAT point and this may cause tax points to arise after the receiver has been appointed.

CONTINUOUS SUPPLIES

A taxpayer may make continuous supplies, billing the client from time to time. The question arises whether each invoice or bill gives rise to a tax point.

A tax point arises only if the document is a VAT 'invoice' within reg 90(1)(*b*) of the 1995 Regulations.

There is no definition of a VAT invoice, although reg 14(1) provides that a tax invoice must contain certain particulars. It can be assumed that if a document contains those particulars then it is a tax invoice. Under reg 29(2)(*b*) a person can reclaim input tax if he, *inter alia*, holds a document which is required to be provided under reg 13.

Technically, a document may be a tax invoice although it does not contain the information required by reg 14.

In *Ford Fuels Ltd v The Commissioners* (LON/91/20Y Decision 7213) X issued an invoice to Y. No goods had been supplied and no cash had been paid at the time of the invoice and the invoice was marked '*pro forma*'. Y reclaimed the input tax and the question was whether the document was a tax invoice. Before the VAT tribunal, Customs laid great emphasis on the fact that it was a *pro forma* invoice. Thus, input tax could not be reclaimed on it. The taxpayer argued that all the requirements set out in reg 14 were satisfied and therefore, in spite of the word '*pro forma*', there was nevertheless a tax invoice and input tax could be appropriately reclaimed.

The tribunal chairman said that he was required to 'take into account the reality of the position'. When the document was issued, no goods had been delivered and no payment had been made; and the document was referred to as a *pro forma* only. In reality, he said, it was not a tax invoice.

The taxpayer in the *Ford Fuels* case stressed that the invoice in question satisfied all the conditions of reg 14. It may be prudent, therefore, for a supplier to leave out the VAT number on the invoice. That is a critical feature, and omitting it demonstrates that the issuer does not intend the document to be an invoice, and that the parties do not treat it as an invoice, but merely as a statement informing the customer that monies should be paid.

Customs, in their Booklet 700, para 69, state that a customer cannot use an invoice as a tax invoice if it is marked 'THIS IS NOT A TAX INVOICE'. (Customs advise that the words should be 'clearly' marked; para 56.) Similar reasoning would apply in an appropriate case if the invoice is marked '*pro forma*'.

The position has here been looked at from the customer's point of view, but it would be most extraordinary if Customs were to argue that the supplier has issued a tax invoice, but the recipient has not received a tax invoice.

DEFAULT IN RENT PAYMENTS

The VAT position of the landlord when the tenant defaults in the payment of rent must be carefully noted.

The general rule is that when services are performed or goods are made available to the person to whom they are supplied (in the case of goods) the tax point will have arrived by virtue of VATA 1994, s 6. Thus if services are performed and a payment must be made for those services the tax point will have arrived when the services are performed.

If the bulk of the services are performed, but there are still a few to be carried out before the payment is made, the tax point will arrive only when all the services are performed.

In *Trustees for the Greater World Association Trust v The Commissioners* (LON/88/680 Decision 3401) estate agents provided services to a landowner with respect to the disposal of land. It was held that the tax point was when legal completion took place (and the agent was paid) because there were still some services which the agents may have had to perform right up to completion, eg handing over the keys to the premises.

However, in the case of a continuous supply of services, or where the supply relates to the grant of a tenancy for a term certain exceeding 21 years, the position is not governed by s 6 of the Act, but by the 1995 Regulations, regs 85 and 90 and VATA 1994, s 5(9) (*see Legal and Contractual Services v The Commissioners* (1984) VATTR 85 at 93). In this case the tax point is the earlier of (a) when part of the consideration is received, or (b) when the supplier issues a tax invoice relating to the supply.

Regulation 94 provides that the supply is made only to the extent of the payment or the amount covered by the tax invoice.

It thus seems clear enough that if a tenant defaults in paying his rent, the landlord will be taxed only to the extent of the rent he has received (it is assumed that the landlord has not issued invoices in advance—under reg 13(1) and (5) he should issue the invoice 30 days after the time when the supply is treated as taking place (that is felt to be the correct reading of the regulation)).

Regulations 85(2) and 90(2) refer to a special invoicing procedure, which may be useful.

The critical point is that there is no reason why the landlord should pay VAT on the rent which the tenant has failed to pay. The bad debt provisions have no special relevance here. The date of the performance of the services or the supply of the goods within s 6 is not relevant: the situations governed by the regulations and the s 6 situations are mutually exclusive.

COMPLETION OF DEVELOPMENTS

If a taxpayer gets his tax point wrong, so that for the period concerned he effectively underdeclares his tax, and the amount of the underdeclaration is, or exceeds, the lesser of £1m and 30 per cent of the tax for the period, he can suffer a 15 per cent serious misdeclaration penalty under VATA 1994, s 63.

The general position with regard to the supply of services is governed by VATA 1994, s 6(3). It states that a supply of services is treated as taking place at the time the services are performed. But if, before the services are performed, the supplier 'issues a tax invoice in respect of it or . . . he receives a payment in respect of it, the supply shall, to the extent covered by the invoice or payment, be treated as taking place at the time when the invoice is issued or the payment is received' (s 6(4)).

The case law in this area is reasonably clear. *Trustees for the Greater World Association Trust v The Commissioners* (LON/88/680Z) was one of the earliest cases on the matter, and at p 8 of the decision, it is stated:

Where the services are performed over a period of time and there is one consideration for the services as a whole, then the time when the services are performed must, I consider, mean the point of time when all the services to be supplied have been performed.

Again in *Mercantile Contracts Ltd v The Commissioners* (LON/88/786Y Decision 4357) it is stated, at p 19:

... we would construe the enactment as referring to the time when the services comprised in the supply become totally performed.

However, care is needed to ensure that there is not, in effect, a number of contracts even though there may be only one document.

For example, if X has agreed to construct a building for Y and to maintain it for five years thereafter, it is likely that there are two supplies with two tax points—one when the building works are completed and the other when the maintenance contract runs out.

Again, if X agrees to construct a building the completion of the building may end one tax point. It may be that there is a second supply to cover a defects period which will have its own independent tax point. If, in addition, there is an obligation to maintain the building for a number of years after completion, that may comprise a third separate supply with a separate tax point.

Figure 28.1:

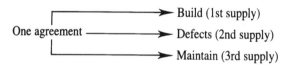

If a payment is received before the performance of the services, the tax point may be brought forward. The exact nature of the legal transaction may also need to be identified.

If, for example, X agrees with Y to construct a building on X's land and then dispose of it to Y when the building is up, that is likely to be a disposal of the land and the building (goods).

However, if X transfers the land to Y at the outset and then agrees to do works on the land for Y, X will make a supply of services and goods.

Taking into account the above factors, the VAT points in the following transactions can be identified.

D is a developer and owns Blackacre freehold. He agrees with P that he will transfer Blackacre with a completed building thereon in return for Blueacre owned by P.

The deal is therefore one of land, building works to be carried out and the finished building, in return for land.

If the parties sign up the deal, and before the buildings works are completed the land interests are exchanged with D agreeing to complete the works, then the deal is likely to be one under which there is a disposal of a freehold with a partly completed commercial building thereon, the payment (within VATA 1994, s 6(4)) being made before the completion of the development works. Thus, any attempt to delay the tax point until the works have been completed may be of little avail because the disposal of the partly completed land freehold gives rise to one tax point (part of Blueacre's value is received in return as payment) and because of the effective advance payment in the form of the rest of the land interest (in Blueacre) for the works to be completed.

Figure 28.2:

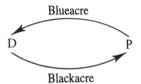

Blueacre

D   P

Blackacre

Exchanged: Blackacre is partly completed

HIDDEN SUPPLIES IN COMPLEX TRANSACTIONS

It is important to analyse particular land deals to ensure that there are no hidden VAT supplies.

A farmer who has not elected with regard to a parcel of land may sell it to a developer for £6m and a land interest. The farmer would not expect to pay VAT on the £6m or the land interest and that may be the end of the matter.

But it may be that the developer has agreed to construct a road and that the farmer has agreed to contribute, say, £300,000 towards the construction of the road. Customs may argue that the £300,000 was an inducement paid to the developer so that VAT becomes chargeable. The developer will have provided the farmer with the service of taking on the deal and thus, the £300,000 may represent the consideration for a vatable supply made by the developer to the landowner (farmer); unless there is something express or implied to the contrary enabling VAT to be added to the £300,000 it would be VAT inclusive.

In addition, the developer may agree to carry out works on land retained by the farmer. He may for instance agree to put up an expensive fence. In that case part of the land interest transferred by the farmer to the developer could be looked on as consideration for the vatable supply of putting up the fence. This will be a vatable supply by the developer, and unless there is something express or implied in the agreement to the contrary the VAT charged will fall on the developer (the consideration will be effectively VAT inclusive). Thus, if the parcel of land transferred to the developer for carrying out the works is worth £100,000, the VAT charged will be ⁷⁄₄₇ths of £100,000 (*see* Figure 28.3).

Figure 28.3:

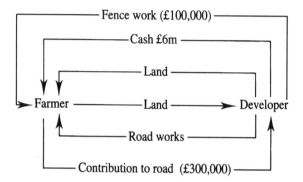

Problems may arise if the new road to be built will benefit the land of the developer and land retained by the farmer. The developer may elect to waive exemption with regard to his parcel, but the farmer may not have elected with regard to his, and he may not be using the retained land for carrying out any taxable business. If the road area is transferred to the developer and the developer carries out the works, with the local authority ultimately adopting the road for no consideration, then *prima facie*, because the developer has elected, all the VAT charged by the builder to the developer can be reclaimed (*see* Figure 28.4).

Figure 28.4:

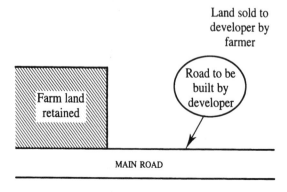

However, Customs may argue in an appropriate case that the outlay was partly for the benefit of the business of the developer, but also partly for the benefit of the land retained by the farmer. They may seek to disallow part of the input tax reclaimed.

Leasehold sale for contingent consideration, etc

It may be that when a property development is being carried out, multiple supplies are made between the parties, with consideration possibly being payable at a future date.

For example, X plc may be transferring to the council orange land, worth £10m. In return X plc is to receive red land (worth £5m); the reimbursement of future professional fees (worth £1m); the value of building works (£3m) which the council will procure Z plc (the builder) to do; and a possible equity slice in the development, which has a market value at the time of the deal of £1m but could be worth £5m in cash terms when the development is completed. It is assumed that both parties have elected with regard to VAT.

It would seem that X plc will want to charge VAT on top of the market value of the red land received by the council. It would also need to charge VAT on the market value of the covenant which the council has given to procure that the building works are carried out. The builder will not be undertaking the works for X plc for nothing. The council will in effect pay the builder, and the builder will charge the council VAT.

Indirectly, X plc has reimbursed the council for the fees which it pays the builder in the form of transferring to the council part of the orange land. *The Commissioners v Telemed Ltd* [1991] STC 89 provides some guidance as to that line of analysis.

The future payments must strictly be valued at the time of legal completion of the transfer of the leasehold of the orange land to the council. The case of *Mercantile Contracts Ltd* (LON/88/786 Decision 4357; LON/88/786Y Decision 5266) would tend to indicate that that is the correct approach.

However, it may be possible, especially with regard to the professional fees, to convince Customs to exercise their discretion under VATA 1994, s 6(6) to enable a VAT invoice to be issued when the monies actually become payable by the council, ie the monies are payable to reimburse the professional fees when these are billed and when the equity slice is payable in years to come.

If Customs cannot be persuaded to do that, on the equity slice and from the Customs booklet it is not felt that Customs envisage s 6(6) being used in such a way, then there seems to be no alternative but to value the rights, eg the right to receive future profits being the equity slice at the time of the legal completion of transfer of the leasehold.

It seems clear enough that monies (£5m) then become payable (assuming the rights were valued at £1m at the time of legal completion, but subsequently £5m is paid out). There will have been a disposal of the *chose in action*; the likelihood is that for VAT purposes either that will be ignored, or it could well amount to an exempt supply, the *chose in action* merely being a right to monies. If the orange land transferred by X plc is freehold *see* p 362.

Figure 28.5:

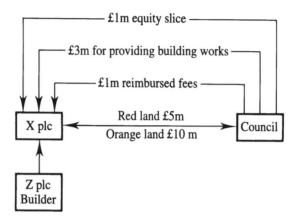

Leases, land exchanges and service charges

The tax points with respect to leases, service charges and land exchanges must be carefully taken into account.

L may grant a 125-year lease of Blackacre to T (L having elected to waive exemption). T may transfer, in exchange for the grant of the long lease, free-hold land (Greenacre) worth £1m (T not having elected to waive exemption and the freehold not comprising a new commercial building within VATA 1994, Sched 9, Group 1, Item 1(*a*)).

In addition T may agree to pay a peppercorn rent and a service charge of £30,000 per annum under the lease to him of Blackacre.

L will have made a supply for a consideration not wholly consisting of money and thus the VAT charge is equal to $\frac{7}{47}$ths of the consideration received (that is the position by virtue of VATA 1994, s 19(3)). No doubt L may wish to increase the consideration by 17.5 per cent (payable in cash) to ensure he has enough money to pay the VAT.

Thus, when he legally completes the lease in return for the freehold he will hand to T a VAT invoice referring to the £1m freehold consideration plus £175,000 to cover the VAT. T may wish to elect with respect to Blackacre in order to recover that VAT.

The tax point position of L is not covered by the general rule in VATA 1994, s 6(2), (4) which provides that goods are supplied when they are made available to the person to whom they have been supplied, or earlier if a VAT invoice is issued or payment received. Strictly, the position is covered by s 6(14) which enables regulations to be made to determine the time of supply. The relevant regulation is the 1995 Regulations, reg 85 which states that where the grant of the lease is a supply of goods (ie a major interest—the grant of the 125-year lease by L of Blackacre), and the whole or part of the consideration for that grant is payable periodically or from time to time, goods shall be treated as separately and successively supplied at the earlier of the following times:

(a) whenever part of the consideration is received; or

(b) whenever the supplier issues a tax invoice relating to the grant.

The first part of the consideration received will be the receipt of the freehold and the cash to cover the VAT, and the first invoice will be the invoice relating to the freehold and that cash. The first supply will take place at the time of legal completion, ie when the legal lease is granted and the freehold transferred and the cash handed over.

There will be subsequent supplies; VAT would be payable on the peppercorn rent if demanded and on the service charges. VAT would be payable with respect to the service charges and the peppercorn rent only as and when the monies are received each year or, if earlier, at the date when the landlord issues a VAT invoice.

THE NEW 18 MONTHS RULE

The Value Added Tax (Amendment) (No 5) Regulations 1997 (SI No 2887) came into force on 1 January 1998 and provide that when a development is completed a developer must account for the VAT on the project within 18 months unless he has already accounted for it by issuing an invoice or receiving payment (see News Release 35/97 (12 December 1997)). This is to stop developers delaying tax points. The general tax point provisions discussed above are subject to the 18 months caveat.

Chapter 29

Advance payments

In many cases it was, and still is, advantageous for a taxpayer to ensure that a particular tax point occurs before a change in the rate of VAT.

There were many cases based on the old 'alteration' provisions (alterations to buildings used to be zero-rated) showing how money can be paid in advance (or 'up-front') so that the VAT point is brought forward, so that VAT is mitigated. Taxpayers had a very high success rate in the High Court. The cases of *The Commissioners v West Yorkshire Independent Hospital (Contract Services)* [1988] STC 443, *The Commissioners v Faith Construction Ltd* [1988] STC 35 and *Dormers Builders (London) Ltd v The Commissioners* [1988] STC 735 are particularly notable. The taxpayers were equally successful in the Court of Appeal ([1989] STC 539), where the above cases and the case of *Nevisbrook v The Commissioners* [1989] STC (High Court) were all heard together.

In *Goodyear v The Commissioners* (MAN/85/316) the client paid money on special terms to the builder and obtained a bank guarantee from the builder's bank. Under the terms of the arrangement, however, the money paid to the builder before 1 June 1984 could be released only in stages over the term of the building period depending on the issue of the architect's certificates. It was held that although the client had paid the money to the builder he had not received it until after 31 May 1984 and the scheme was therefore not effective in avoiding the standard rate of VAT charge. Practitioners should also refer to *Key Kitchens v The Commissioners* (LON/85/228).

From the cases, the following arrangements to enable money to be paid in advance may be contemplated.

BANK GUARANTEE

The simplest procedure would be for the landowner/developer to employ the builder and pay him the building price securing a bank guarantee from the builder's bank.

'Fluid' guarantee

If the money paid to the builder is backed by a bank guarantee and credited to the builder's account with the bank, and there is a requirement that it should never go below a particular figure (that figure would be an amount to cover the bank's guarantee at any particular time), then there should be no problem under *Ramsay* (*see* Chapter 5), or under any specific provisions in the VAT legislation.

'Deposit funds' guarantee

The author is of the view that if that cannot be achieved, then if the landowner pays the builder in advance, and without the landowner being concerned the builder then deposits the money to back the bank guarantee given by the builder's bank to the landowner, this should succeed in its object. To be on the safe side, the VAT point should be taken as the time when the cheque is cleared by the builder.

BUILDER'S LOAN

If the builder lends the landowner the necessary money for the work and the landowner uses the money to pay for the building works in advance there should be no difficulties. As the building progresses the landowner will have to use his own money or borrowings to repay the loan made by the builder. The tax point will arise when money is actually received by the builder. It may be prudent for a zero-rated VAT invoice to be issued by the builder to the landowner at the same time, but that is not vital and it is arguable that a VAT invoice is not appropriate in a case such as that.

In the case of *The Commissioners v Faith Construction Ltd* the client borrowed money from a bank and paid it to the contractor before 1 June 1984; the contractor then lent the money back to the client who used it to repay the initial borrowing by the client. Over the term of the building programme the client then borrowed again to repay the loan made by the builder. It was held that the transaction was effective and that VAT was not chargeable. Customs raised arguments based on the *Ramsay* decision, but that doctrine was held on the facts not to apply. A similar but less provocative arrangement was also held to be successful in the case of *Dolomite Double Glazing Ltd v The Commissioners* (1985) VATTR 184.

STAKEHOLDERS

Arrangements under which money is paid to, say, an independent stakeholder and released as the development progresses must be avoided. *See Goodyear v The Commissioners* (MAN/85/316), *above*.

In *Double Shield Window Co Ltd v The Commissioners* (MAN/84/227) payments were made, before 1 June 1984, to a solicitor who held the money as stakeholder. It was held that payments were received by the contractor only after 1 June 1984 (so that VAT at 15 per cent was chargeable) as and when the solicitor received certificates of satisfaction and released the monies to the contractor (*see* Figure 29.1).

In *The Commissioners v Moonrakers' Guest House Ltd* [1992] STC 544 it was held that the payment of a refundable deposit may create a tax point.

Figure 29.1:   VAT advance payments (*Double Shield*'s case)

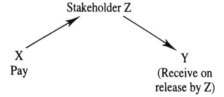

'FROZEN MONIES' ('*DORMER* ACCOUNTS')

In *Dormers' Builders (London) Ltd v The Commissioners* [1988] STC 735 a bank in effect advanced £600,000 to the client.

The client paid the money to the builder by crediting it to the builder's deposit account at the bank. However, the builder was prevented from requiring the transfer of any part of the £600,000 to its current account until presentation of architects' certificates showing that certain works had been completed. The court held that there was no sensible alternative to the conclusion that the builder was in reality the recipient of the payment when the money was credited to the deposit account. The money was placed at the disposal of the builder. The credit to the deposit account (which was made before 1 June 1984) was payment received by the builder. The payment discharged the client from a liability to pay for the building works and the builder had no right to sue the client for the sum so credited.

This is a borderline case and is barely distinguishable from cases where the money is held in a stakeholder account. Such an arrangement should therefore be used only if none of the four alternatives described *above* is possible. *See* also *S Rankin* (BEL/88/5).

Chapter 30

Bringing forward the tax point— project managers

Project managers providing services can bring forward the tax point merely by the issue of a VAT invoice.

GENERAL RULES

The time of a supply is governed by VATA 1994, s 6. The supply of services is treated as taking place at the time when the services are performed (VATA 1994, s 6(3)). The Customs, in Notice 700, state:

> If you supply services, the basic tax point is the date when the service is performed. It is normally taken as the date when all the work except invoicing is completed.

In *Trustees for the Greater World Association Trust v The Commissioners* (LON/88/6802 Decision 3401) it was held that an estate agent had fully performed his house-selling services at the time the sale was legally completed, rather than at the time when unconditional contracts to sell it were entered into. *See also W J Cooke* (MAN/84/265).

Under the provisions of s 6(4) of the Act, however, that tax point can be brought forward if payment is received or an invoice is issued. The tax point is brought forward to the extent of the figure in the invoice or the payment.

The supply referred to in the invoice or covered by the payment is treated as taking place at the time of the issue of the invoice or receipt of the payment.

The nature of the supply is determined by the law in existence at the time of the tax point—the issue of the tax invoice or the date of the payment—even if in fact the actual supply (of services) takes place at a later date.

That conclusion follows naturally from the wording of s 6, and was confirmed in *Graham (Northampton) Ltd v The Commissioners* (LON/79/332), 105 *Taxation* 452.

REGULATIONS UNDER s 6(14)

Regulations made under s 6(14) of the Act can alter the above-mentioned basic tax point rules.

The relevant regulations under s 6(14) are the Value Added Tax Regulations 1995 (SI No 2518) (the 1995 Regulations).

Regulation 90(2) can, in fact, postpone a tax point even though an invoice has been issued: the tax point would be postponed to the date of payment. However, it is relevant only if a tax invoice is issued and payments thereunder are made within 12 months, eg the invoice is issued on 1 January 1989 with payments to be made in 1989.

Regulation 89 deals with retention payments.

Regulation 91 deals with royalties and similar payments and would be relevant only if the payments could not to be ascertained when all the services have been performed and a number of payments are made thereafter (as opposed to a single payment), or a payment is to be made at the end of a particular period.

Regulation 93 deals with supplies to the construction industry and does not present problems. Regulation 84 deals with compulsory purchase and freehold sales.

These regulations should not have relevance where a project manager wants to create an early tax point by the issue of an invoice for proposed project management activities (*see* Figure 30.1).

VAT invoice properly so called

To be a tax invoice properly so called, reg 14 of the 1995 Regulations must be satisfied.

It seems to be quite clear that one can issue a VAT invoice properly so called in advance of a supply being made. Of course, if the supply is never made then the invoice will be of no effect. An invoice cannot bring into existence a vatable supply if one never actually exists (*see Howard v The Commissioners* LON/80/457).

It seems that the tax point with respect to a zero-rated supply cannot be brought forward by the issue of a tax invoice (and the same would apply to an exempt supply).

Date of 'issue' of invoice

There have been a number of cases which give guidance as to the date on which an invoice is issued (*see* for example *Woolford Motor Co Ltd v The Commissioners* [1983] STC 715), but certainly if the project manager hands over the invoice to the client the invoice will have been 'issued'. Just showing it to the customer, with the supplier keeping it, is not enough.

Figure 30.1:

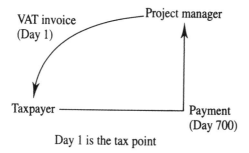

VAT invoice
(Day 1)

Project manager

Taxpayer

Payment
(Day 700)

Day 1 is the tax point

Chapter 31

Captive development companies

It may be possible to pay the developer, but not the builder, early, and mitigate VAT if there is to be an increase in the rate chargeable. This was especially relevant when the rates of VAT on many property transactions were changed from zero to 15 per cent on 1 April 1989.

X is the builder. Y is the developer. Y agrees to put up or procure that a new building be constructed on land which belongs to Z. Y and Z will enter into a development agreement. Z will pay Y and Y will receive the payment for the development works before 1 April 1989. No VAT would be charged on that development agreement payment because the supply would have been zero-rated (VATA 1983, Sched 5, Group 8, Items 2 and 3).

However, X the builder would be carrying out the building operations on and after 1 April 1989 and payments would be made to the builder on the production of VAT invoices, after 1 April 1989.

The question is whether Y can reclaim the VAT charged to it by X even though it issues no invoices and receives no payments from Z on and after 1 April 1989.

The critical provision is reg 101(2)(*b*) of the 1995 Regulations. That regulation provides that input tax on supplies 'as are used or to be used by (the taxpayer) exclusively in making taxable supplies may be deducted'. That regulation has its origins in:

(a) art 17(2) of the EEC Sixth Directive 77/388; and

(b) VATA 1983, ss 14 and 15(1) (now VATA 1994, ss 25 and 26(1));

(c) the *Rompelman* case (*see* p 18).

The supplies by X to Y are used by Y (as and when they are made to Y) in making supplies to Z. The building works organised by Y, and for which Y is responsible, are the supplies being made (by Y) for VAT purposes.

The provisions in VATA 1983, ss 4 and 5 (now VATA 1994, s 6) determine the tax point as has been seen (Chapter 28). The case of *W F Graham (Northampton) Ltd v The Commissioners* (LON/79/332) indicates that the nature of the supply is determined at the tax point. Thus is appears that a children's cut-out book would remain a book for VAT purposes if it is such a thing at the time of the tax point. If it later ceases to be a book, when the reader cuts out the various pictures and illustrations designed to be so cut out, that is not relevant. In that case the tribunal chairman stated:

> In my view, however, the critical time for value added tax purposes in judging whether the product is or is not a book is the tax point, and in the case of this product the tax point is the time at which the product is sold. Does it make any difference as at the date of the tax point that at some future time the product may change its identity and even that at the time of the sale such change of identity may have been foreseen or premeditated? If the product is a book as at the tax point it does not thereafter in my judgment cease to be a book because the reader having read the story is encouraged to cut out the figures and illustrations which are designed for that purpose.

See also GUS Catalogue Ltd v The Commissioners (MAN/87/352), *Draper v The Commissioners* (MAN/80/197).

Thus, although the actual supplies made by Y to Z seem on the face of it to have little significance for VAT purposes, that is in fact not the case. What happens is that supplies from Y to Z are deemed to take place (although they actually take place after 31 March 1989) before 1 April 1989. The rules at the time of the tax point determine the nature of the supply and thus the inputs relate to the making of that taxable supply which is deemed to take place before 1 April 1989. The outputs do not simply 'disappear' because of the earlier tax point. They are merely deemed to take place at an earlier time and their VAT character is also determined at that earlier time. It need not be argued that the inputs are used in making the *earlier* taxable supply: they are used in making the supplies which take place on or after 1 April 1989. That

Figure 31.1:

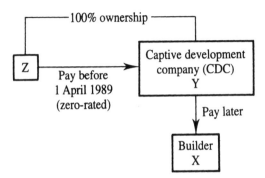

is not denied. It is simply that the supplies which take place on or after 1 April 1989 (by Y to Z) are deemed to take place, for the purposes of ascertaining the nature of those supplies and the tax points before 1 April 1989.

Y can reclaim the VAT charged to it by X even though Y is invoiced by X and pays X (and X receives payment) on or after 1 April 1989 (*see* Figure 31.1).

Although captive development companies had their heyday before 1 April 1989, they can still be useful where it is anticipated that VAT is to be charged on supplies for the first time, or the rate is to be increased. They were modified and used when VAT became chargeable on electricity and gas.

Chapter 32

Prescribed accounting periods

The timing of supplies in relation to the prescribed accounting periods (PAPs) of companies can be important.

Assume that X and Y are to be registered for VAT and they are property companies. It is envisaged that X will make a substantial supply of land which is vatable at 17.5 per cent to Y. X must account to Customs for the VAT but Y will be in a position to reclaim it. The question is whether there is any cash flow or other advantage to be obtained by seeking to ensure that the prescribed accounting periods of X and Y are different.

ADVANTAGE SOUGHT

The advantage sought is one of cash flow. If the supplier makes his vatable supply to the customer near the beginning of the supplier's PAP he will have many months (almost four in the normal case) in which to pay the VAT but the customer (if a registered taxable person) will be able to reclaim the VAT charged to him fairly quickly (possibly within a month) if the supply was made to him near the end of his PAP. On large reclaims, however, taxpayers must expect control visits from Customs.

Registration

When the applications for registration are made by X and Y, Customs will probably take the view that they have a discretion to register X and Y if, when the applications are made, X and Y have not made any supplies.

It is probable that Customs will allow registration because there is an intention to make supplies in the course of a business so that they will exercise their discretionary powers under VATA 1994, Sched 1, para 9, although in reality these powers are very restricted (*see* p 18). In general, the accounting period will be three months, although for the first period, starting with the registration date, it may be less than three months.

PLANNING

It may be that if the companies have different financial years for the purposes of corporation tax that Customs could be persuaded to allow different prescribed accounting periods which could be worked to the benefit of the taxpayer.

Thus if Y has an accounting period ending on 1 April 1997 and X has an accounting period ending on 1 June 1997, then if X bills Y and receives payment from Y on (say) 31 March 1997, then Y could reclaim the tax as soon as possible after 1 April 1997 (reg 29(1)) and X would not have to pay the tax until (possibly, depending on what is agreed with Customs) 1 July 1997 (regs 25(1) and 40(1)(*b*)).

PART VII

GIFTS, SALES AT UNDERVALUE AND DEATH

Chapter 33

Gifts and sales at undervalue: substitution of market value

In the normal case where a taxpayer makes a supply, he will receive a cash consideration and will know what the VAT charge is, ie 7/47ths of the consideration he receives.

If the consideration is not in money or not entirely in money then VATA 1994, s 19(3) requires that the consideration received be valued, and the taxpayer will pay 7/47ths of that to Customs.

Example

> X makes a supply of services to Y who transfers as consideration for the supply of the services £1m worth of land. X pays VAT of 7/47ths of the £1m.

A further general principle is found in VATA 1994, s 5(2) which states that a supply includes all forms of supply, but not anything done otherwise than for a consideration. However, anything which is not a supply of goods but is done for a consideration (including the granting, assignment or surrender of any right) is a supply of services.

Thus the general rule is that if services are provided for no consideration, subject to exceptions, VAT cannot be charged as there is no supply. The existence of a supply is a prerequisite to a VAT charge. However, if goods are transferred for no consideration, that still comprises a supply.

Bearing in mind the above basic rules, the following specific rules should be noted.

TAKING GOODS OUT OF THE BUSINESS

VATA 1994, Sched 4, para 5(1) states that where goods forming part of the assets of a business are transferred or disposed of, by or under the directions of the person carrying on the business, so as no longer to form part of those assets, whether or not for a consideration, that is a supply by him of goods (there are certain exceptions for very small gifts and supplies of samples).

Where there is a supply of goods by virtue of that provision, the value shall be taken to be:

(a) such consideration in money as would be payable by the person making the supply if he were, at the time of the supply, to purchase goods identical in every respect (including age and condition) to the goods concerned; or

(b) where the value cannot be ascertained in accordance with para (a) *above*, such consideration in money as would be payable by that person if he were, at that time, to purchase goods similar to, and of the same age and condition as, the goods concerned; or

(c) where the value can be ascertained in accordance with neither para (a) nor (b) *above*, the costs of producing the goods concerned if they were produced at that time (VATA 1994, Sched 6, para 6).

Note also that where there is a supply of goods in the situation mentioned *above* the supply is treated as taking place when the goods are transferred or disposed of so as no longer to form part of the assets of the business (VATA 1994, s 6(12)).

SERVICES NOT USED FOR BUSINESS PURPOSES

It is provided in Sched 4, para 5(4) that where, by or under the directions of a person carrying on a business, goods held or used for the purposes of the business are put to any private use or are used, or made available to any person for use, for any purpose other than a purpose of the business, whether or not for a consideration, that is a supply of services.

Thus if X makes available the free use of business goods to his son who uses them for a private purpose, although no consideration is received, there is deemed to be a supply of services and thus market value can be substituted as the consideration.

Schedule 6, para 7 states that where there is such a supply of services made otherwise than for a consideration, the value of the supply shall be taken to be the full cost to the taxable person of providing the services (except in certain cases where supplies are made by an employer to an employee).

Where there is such a supply of services, the supply is treated as taking place when the goods are appropriated to the private use (s 6(13)).

CONNECTED PERSONS

Under Sched 6, para 1, where:

(a) the value of the supply made by a taxable person for a consideration in money (the provision is restricted to cases where the monetary consideration is less than the open market value of the goods or services, eg goods worth £1m are sold for £250,000); and

(b) the person making the supply and the person to whom the supply is made are connected; and

(c) if the supply is a taxable supply, the person to whom the supply is made is not entitled to credit for all the VAT on the supply,

the Commissioners may direct that the value of the supply shall be taken to be its open market value.

The open market value of the supply shall be taken to be the amount that would fall to be taken as its value if the supply were made for such a consideration in money as would be payable by a person standing in no such relationship with any person as would affect the consideration, ie what would be paid in the market including VAT (*see* s 19(2) and (5) of VATA 1994).

Whether persons are connected is determined by ICTA 1988, s 839.

A direction shall be given by notice in writing to the person making the supply, but no direction may be given more than three years after the time of the supply.

Example

X has constructed a new commercial building. It is worth £1m but he sells it to his son for £100,000. The son cannot reclaim the VAT as he is not registered for VAT. The father (the transferor) and the son are connected within TA 1988, s 839 and the consideration paid by the son for the land is less than the open market value. Furthermore, the supply is a taxable supply as it relates to the sale of a new commercial building. Thus the Commissioners, within three years after the time of the supply, can give a direction determining that the supply shall be treated as having taken place at open market value.

CESSATION OF BUSINESS

Under Sched 4, para 8, where a person ceases to be a taxable person, any goods then forming part of the assets of a business carried on by him are deemed to be supplied by him in the course or furtherance of his business immediately before he ceases to be a taxable person, unless the business is transferred as a going concern to another taxable person or the business is transferred to, say, personal representatives in the event of a death (*see* p 391) or the VAT on the deemed supply would not be more than £250.

This paragraph does not, however, apply to any goods where the taxable person can prove to the satisfaction of the Commissioners:

(a) that no credit for input tax has been allowed to him in respect of the supply of the goods; or

(b) that the goods did not become his as part of the assets of a business which was transferred to him as a going concern by another taxable person.

It is quite clear, for instance, that if a taxpayer registers for VAT and elects to waive exemption with respect to let property and then ceases to be a taxable person, the property will be deemed to be disposed of by him in the course or furtherance of his business immediately before he ceases to be a taxable person unless he disposes of the property as a going concern or no credit for input tax was allowed to him with respect to the property.

Note that this provision applies only to goods forming part of the assets of the business. With regard to whether land comprises goods *see* p 13.

Where there is a deemed supply on the cessation of the business the value of the supply is determined by the rules in para 6 of Sched 6; these are the same as those which apply where goods forming part of a business are transferred or disposed of so as no longer to form assets to the business (*see* p 386).

For the special effects of a taxpayer deregistering for VAT, having already elected to waive exemption *see* p 236, *above*.

GIFTS WHICH TRIGGER IMMEDIATE VAT CHARGES

VAT is not normally a great concern in estate planning, but there are one or two potential traps.

The taxpayer may have elected to waive exemption with respect to a free-hold building. If he gives that property to a trust, then he will have made a supply of goods within VATA 1994, Sched 4, para 5(1). By virtue of Sched 6, para 6 (assuming the transfer is otherwise than for a consideration, whether in cash or in kind) something akin to market value may be substituted, for VAT purposes, on the gift.

If the supply is for a consideration in money, eg a nominal £1 (the consideration has to be in money: the provision would not apply if the consideration was a box of baked beans), then Sched 6, para 6 will not apply, but market value may be substituted under VATA 1994, Sched 6, para 1(1).

If the consideration for the supply is not money, only the consideration is valued (VATA 1994, s 19(3)). There is thus a major gap in the legislation.

The other possible problem when VAT has been reclaimed and a gift of the asset is subsequently made, is that Customs may argue that the goods were never acquired for business purposes and that the original input tax was not properly reclaimable.

Figure 33.1:

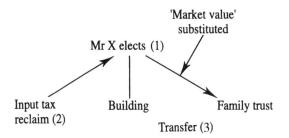

Finally, in an appropriate case the sale of a going concern relief may be available.

GIFT ELEMENTS IN A SUPPLY

In *Customs and Excise Commissioners v Tron Theatre Ltd* [1994] STC 117, a charitable trust, in return for a minimum payment of £150, provided donors with a personalised brass plaque displayed on a theatre seat, acknowledgment of the donation in the theatre foyer, priority booking for two gala evenings and a commemorative limited edition print of the brochure setting out the donation proposals. It was agreed that those benefits had a nominal value of around £5 and thus there was a substantial gift in the region of £145 per donor. It was argued that the gift element was outside the scope of VAT, but Customs argued that under what is not s 19(2) there had been a supply of vatable items worth £5 and the value of that supply must be taken to be such amount as, with the addition of the VAT chargeable, is equal to the consideration.

The taxpayer argued that under what is now s 19(4) there must be an apportionment: the part of the consideration not related to the supply of any goods or services must be treated as outside the scope of VAT.

Lord President Hope at 181H stated that the essence of a donation is that no consideration is expected for it in return. He said that in order to obtain the benefits the donors had to pay £150. The provision of the benefits was a supply and in such a case the amount vatable was equal to the consideration paid.

To avoid the problem, the charity should have sold the items for £5 and hoped to receive a gift of £145, which gift would have been outside the scope of VAT. That is often easier said than done in practice.

Chapter 34

Death of a taxpayer

A taxpayer may have elected to waive exemption with respect to a particular property, and then dies.

VATA 1994, Sched 4, para 8 provides that where a person ceases to be a taxable person any goods then forming part of the assets of a business carried on by him shall be deemed to be supplied by him in the course or furtherance of his business immediately before he ceases to be a taxable person unless:

(a) the business is transferred as a going concern to another taxable person; or

(b) the business is carried on by another person who, under regulations made under s 46(4), is treated as a taxable person; or

(c) the VAT on the deemed supply would not be more than £250.

However, this deemed supply provision does not apply to any goods where the taxable person can show to the satisfaction of Customs:

(a) that no credit for input tax has been allowed to him in respect of the supply of the goods;

(b) that the goods did not become his as part of the assets of a business which was transferred to him as a going concern by another taxable person.

Section 46(4) referred to *above* provides that the Commissioners may make regulations applying to persons who carry on the business of a taxable person who has died for securing the continuity of the application of the VAT Act. The relevant regulation is reg 9 of the 1995 Regulations, which provides that if a taxable person dies, Customs may, from the date on which he died until some other taxable person is registered in respect of the taxable supplies made, or intended to be made by that taxable person in the course or furtherance of his business, treat as a taxable person, any persons carrying on that business. This would include a personal representative or a legatee.

Any person carrying on such business must, within 21 days of commencing to do so, inform the Commissioners in writing of that fact.

Example

> Mr X has elected with regard to Blackacre. Mr X dies and so is no longer a taxable person. The personal representative carries on the business. Under reg 9, the Commissioners may, from the date of death, treat the personal representative as a taxable person and the provisions of the VAT legislation and any regulations made thereunder will apply to that person as though he were a registered person. The personal representative is required, within 21 days of commencing the business, to inform the Commissioners in writing of that fact and of the date of death.

Appendix 1

Commercial and industrial properties

Transaction	VAT consequences	Authority VATA 1994
Freehold sale of new building	17.5% VAT (no option)	Sched 9, Group 1, Item 1(*a*)(ii)
Freehold sale of new building not yet completed	17.5% VAT (no option)	Sched 9, Group 1, Item 1(*a*)(i)
Freehold sale of new civil engineering work	17.5% VAT (no option)	Sched 9, Group 1, Item 1(*a*)(iv)
Freehold sale of new civil engineering work not yet completed	17.5% VAT (no option)	Sched 9, Group 1, Item 1(*a*)(iii)
Grant of facilities for parking a vehicle, playing sports or housing aircraft and the like	17.5% VAT (no option)	Sched 9, Group 1, Item 1(*h*), (*m*) and (*k*)
Grants of certain rights in respect of hotels etc, holiday accommodation, boxes at the theatre, caravans and camping facilities, the right to take game, fish and timber, mooring rights and sports facilities	17.5 % VAT (no option)	Sched 9, Group 1, Item 1(*c*)–(*g*) and (*j*)–(*l*)

Transaction	*VAT consequences*	*Authority VATA 1994*
Sale of leasehold of new building or building not yet completed or new civil engineering work or civil engineering work not yet completed	Exempt (option available)	Sched 9, Group 1, Item 1
Grant of lease for premium (whether new building, building not yet completed or otherwise)	Exempt (option available)	Sched 9, Group 1, Item 1
Freehold sale of new building or building not yet completed preceded by a letting	17.5% VAT	Sched 9, Group 1, Item 1
Any leasehold assignment preceded by exercised option	17.5% VAT	Sched 10, para 2
Any leasehold sale where option not exercised	Exempt (option available)	Sched 9, Group 1, Item 1
Payment of premium by landlord to proposed tenant to induce him to take up lease	17.5% VAT	*See* p 327
Payment by tenant to landlord to accept surrender of the tenant's lease	Exempt (unless landlord has opted)	Sched 9, Group 1, Item 1 and Note (1)
Payment by X to Y for Y to release restrictive covenant over X's land	Exempt (unless supplier (Y) has opted)	Sched 9, Group 1, Item 1
Creation and discharge of mortgage	Exempt	Sched 9, Group 5
Exercise of power of sale by mortgagee (whether or not mortgagor has exercised option over mortgaged land)	Acts of mortgagee deemed to be those of mortgagor	Sched 4, para 7
Payment by assignor to assignee to take over negative value lease	Exempt (option available)	*See* 335

Transaction	VAT consequences	Authority VATA 1994
Payment by landlord to tenant to surrender lease	Exempt (unless tenant has opted)	Sched 9, Group 1
Guarantee fee paid to bank or other person	Exempt	Sched 9, Group 5
Sale of old buildings (freehold or leasehold)	Exempt (option available)	Sched 9, Group 1

1   If the taxpayer does not carry on a 'business' or, more strictly, an 'economic activity', he is not liable to VAT. Also there will be no charge if he is below the VAT exemption limits unless he has registered voluntarily.

2   Statutory references are to VATA 1994 unless stated otherwise.

3   A new building is one completed less than three years before the sale (Sched 9, Group 1, Note (4)).

4   In an appropriate case, the 'going concern' relief may be available (*see* 340).

5   The election may be disapplied in certain circumstances (*see* p 218).

6   The position of a payment by an assignor to an assignee to take over a negative value lease is in a state of flux following the decision of *Cantor Fitzgerald International* (Decision 15070). The Customs are appealing the decision (Business Brief 28/97, 12 December 1997).

Appendix 2

Precedents

This appendix contains a number of precedents applicable to common land transactions. The precedents are:

Precedent 1: Going concern relief—holding the monies until the problem is resolved (*see* p 349 *et seq*).
Precedent 2: Warranties etc when capital goods are purchased as a going concern.
Precedent 3: Customs' recommended form of nomineeship document where property is bought as a going concern and put into the name of a nominee for the purchaser.
Precedent 4: VAT clauses in commercial leases.
Precedent 5: Clauses for inclusion in land sale contracts.
Precedent 6: VAT chargeable on part of sale price on sale of commercial building.

1   GOING CONCERN RELIEF—HOLDING THE MONIES UNTIL THE PROBLEM IS RESOLVED (*see* p 349 *et seq*)

It may well happen that a taxpayer selling a property is uncertain about the application of the VAT going concern relief.

If the going concern relief applies he need not charge VAT on the sale proceeds because of the Value Added Tax (Special Provisions) Order 1995 (SI No 1268). However, if it does not apply, then he must charge VAT. The parties will often only be happy with going ahead if the agreement of Customs to the manner in which the transaction is to be dealt with is obtained.

A precedent along the lines set out *below* may be suitable. It should be contained in the contract for sale. It effectively requires the VAT to be held by the solicitors for the vendor (after completion) as stakeholder until the VAT position is clarified with HM Customs and Excise. The clause must be carefully considered and adapted to the particular circumstances, bearing in mind that the tax point generally arises on the earliest of the date of completion, the VAT invoice and the payment of monies to the vendor (although a payment of monies to a stakeholder does not give rise to a tax point until the monies are released to the vendor):

Clause in contract

VALUE ADDED TAX

X.1 The Vendor confirms that prior to the date of this Agreement it has exercised or procured the exercise of an election to waive exemption with respect to the Property pursuant to the provisions of para 2 of Sched 10 to the Value Added Tax Act 1994.

X.2 The Vendor shall not raise or issue a VAT invoice in respect of the sale of the Property or any part of it until requested so to do by the Purchaser or the Purchaser's Solicitors or upon completion. The Vendor shall ensure or use its best endeavours to ensure that at all times it is in a position to legally issue or procure the issue of such an invoice when requested by the Purchaser.

X.3 The Vendor and the Purchaser shall endeavour to obtain as soon as possible rulings or confirmations from HM Customs and Excise that VAT is not chargeable on the sale of the Property whether in whole or in part by virtue of Art 5 of the Value Added Tax (Special Provisions) Order 1995 (SI No 1268) (Art 5) and they shall work and co-operate with each other in this respect as necessary.

X.4 If HM Customs and Excise rule or confirm that the sale of the Property or any part is not within Art 5, VAT shall be payable on the Purchase Price (being an amount equal to 17.5 per cent (or other relevant rate of VAT for the time being) of the Purchase Price) subject to the Vendor issuing or procuring the issue of a VAT invoice in due form at the time of payment.

X.5 If HM Customs and Excise rule or confirm that the sale of the Property or any part is within Art 5 then no VAT shall be payable in respect of the whole or such part of the Property to which the ruling or confirmation relates and such fair and reasonable apportionments shall be made to give effect to the provisions of this clause.

X.6 If at the date of completion HM Customs and Excise have not given the Vendor and the Purchaser any ruling with respect to the application of Art 5, the Purchaser shall pay an amount equal to the Value Added Tax on the Purchase Price (being an amount equal to 17.5 per cent (or other relevant rate of VAT for the time being) of the Purchase Price) in addition to the amount of the consideration payable hereunder on the completion date but such sum shall be held by the Vendor's Solicitors as stakeholders, and the Vendor's Solicitors shall hold the said sum pending receipt of a ruling from HM Customs and Excise, and if HM Customs and Excise shall thereafter rule that the sale of the Property does fall within the provisions of Art 5, the Vendor's Solicitors shall immediately repay the said sum to the Purchaser together with all interest which shall have accrued thereon but if HM Customs and Excise shall rule that the sale of the Property does not fall within the provisions of Art 5 then the Vendor's Solicitors shall release the said sum to the Vendor with all interest which shall have accrued thereon and the Vendor shall forthwith provide the Purchaser with a receipted Value Added Tax invoice with respect thereto.

2   WARRANTIES ETC WHEN CAPITAL GOODS ARE PURCHASED AS A GOING CONCERN (*see* p 354)

X.1   The seller warrants that

—the Capital Goods Scheme will apply to the Property at completion;

—at completion, the seller will supply the Buyer with details of
   (i)   the date of commencement of the adjustment period and any intervals which have commenced or will commence prior to completion;
   (ii) the total input tax attributable to the Property, whether recovered or not, which is subject to adjustment in accordance with Part XV of the VAT Regulations 1995 and the amount of such input tax recovered by the Seller or any person previously responsible for making adjustments under the Capital Goods Scheme in relation to the Property during the current period of adjustment ('Predecessors'); and
   (iii) any adjustments to the input tax recovered in relation to the Property by the Seller and Predecessors in accordance with Part XV of the VAT Regulations 1995;

—all adjustments, declarations and returns made to Customs in connection with the operation of the Capital Goods Scheme in relation to the Property during the current period of adjustment have been made accurately and correctly.

Definitions

'Capital Goods Scheme' shall mean the mechanism for adjustments to the deduction of input tax on capital items as set out in Part XV of the VAT Regulations 1995 and all expressions used in clause X.1 above shall have the meanings ascribed to them in those regulations.

3   CUSTOMS' RECOMMENDED FORM OF NOMINEESHIP DOCUMENT WHERE PROPERTY IS BOUGHT AS A GOING CONCERN AND PUT INTO THE NAME OF A NOMINEE FOR THE PURCHASER (*see* p 355)

The Customs have issued a Business Brief under which the going concern relief for VAT will apply even though let property is transferred to a nominee who takes the property for the real beneficial owner. The author is not entirely sure that such new concessionary treatment is necessary, but taxpayers should prudently ensure that if they are in such a circumstance, the below mentioned requirements in the business brief are satisfied.

Business Brief 10/96 (5 June 1996)

Statement of practice on transfer of a property letting business as a going concern

This statement of practice about nominee purchasers acquiring legal title is optional and may only be applied by persons transferring an interest in land to a person who is a nominee for a named beneficial owner. The option is not available if the nominee is acting for an undisclosed beneficial owner.

Where the legal title in land is to be held by a nominee for a named beneficial owner, Customs & Excise will, for the purpose of establishing the transfer of a property letting business as a going concern, from 1 June 1996, consider the named beneficial owner of the land and not the nominee acquiring legal title to be the transferee.

The new optional practice allows a person transferring an interest in land to a nominee for a named beneficial owner, with the agreement of that nominee and beneficial owner, to treat the named beneficial owner as the transferee for the purposes of establishing whether there has been a transfer of a going concern. This Business Brief contains an example format that the parties can use to record agreement if they so wish.

Persons transferring an interest in land to a person who is a nominee for a named beneficial owner will be expected to check the VAT registration and where necessary the VAT elections made by the beneficial owner.

Examples of where a nominee might exist to hold the legal title in property for a beneficial owner are—where the legal title is held by four or fewer persons on trust for a partnership; where the legal title is held on trust for an unincorporated association; and where the legal title is held on trust for a pension fund.

Background
Customs & Excise have reviewed their policy whereby the passing of title in property between legal owners solely determined whether the VAT (Special Provisions) Order, SI 1995/1268 applied in the circumstances above.

Strictly, a transfer of a going concern cannot occur where the transferee is a nominee for a beneficial owner because the beneficial owner will be the person carrying on the business not the nominee. The optional treatment above does not disturb any transactions prior to 1 June 1996, but from that date allows a more relaxed approach to be adopted. It is deregulatory and should reduce business costs in the circumstances described.

The option does not need to apply to transactions where the nominee is the transferor of the legal title. In these cases, VATA 1994 Sch 10 para 8 deems the beneficial owner to be the transferor.

The above principles, which are based upon English land law, may also be applied to similar transactions in Scotland and Northern Ireland as necessary

Suggested format of Notice of Agreement
The following Notice of Agreement is optional and other clear written evidence of agreement will be accepted by Customs & Excise. The transferor, transferee beneficial owner and nominee should each retain a copy of any written evidence.

Notice of agreement to adopt statement of practice

Property: (Address)

Transferor/vendor: (X)

Nominee/purchaser: (Y)

Future Beneficial Owner: (Z)

X, Y and Z confirm that they have agreed to adopt the optional practice set out in Custom's Business Brief 10/96 in relation to the purchase of the property pursuant to an agreement dated _____ between X and Y.

Following the transfer of the property Y will hold the legal title as nominee for Z, the beneficial owner.

SIGNED for and on behalf of X:

SIGNED for and on behalf of Y:

SIGNED for and on behalf of Z:

DATE:

For further information traders and their advisers should contact their local VAT Advice Centre listed under Customs & Excise in the telephone book.

Note: The above business brief is also reproduced in Appendix D to Customs Notice 700/9/96 'Transfer of a Business as a Going Concern'.

4   VAT CLAUSES IN COMMERCIAL LEASES (*see* p 298)

I   VAT lease clauses (general)

To pay to the landlord amounts equal to any value added tax at the rate for the time being in force as shall be chargeable (whether or not as a result of the exercise of any option or the making of any election by the landlord) on or in respect of or by reference to or as a result of:

(a)   any rents and other consideration payable to the landlord under this lease; or

(b)   any supply made by the landlord to the tenant under the terms of or in connection with this lease

and the payments to be made to the landlord hereunder if the said value added tax shall be chargeable by reference to the rents and other consideration so payable under this lease shall be made at the like times as such rents and other consideration is payable but otherwise when the supply which gives rise to the charge to value added tax is treated as taking place for the purposes of value added tax and (for the avoidance of doubt) it is confirmed that where in any part of this lease or in the Schedule to this lease the tenant agrees to pay an amount of money (or other consideration) such amount (or other consideration) shall be regarded as exclusive of any value added tax which may from time to time be chargeable thereon or with respect thereto or by reference thereto or as a result of any supply made by the landlord to the tenant under the terms of or in connection with this lease.

Without prejudice to any statutory rights which the landlord has in this respect it is confirmed that the landlord reserves the right in its absolute discretion from time to time to exercise or not as the case may be any election to waive exemption in respect of any supply made by the landlord and nothing in this lease or otherwise shall create any implication as to how the landlord may exercise that discretion from time to time.

Where under this lease the tenant agrees to pay or contribute to (or indemnify the landlord or any other person in respect of) any costs fees expenses outgoings or other liability of whatsoever nature whether of the landlord or any third party reference to such costs fees expenses outgoings and other liability shall (for the avoidance of doubt) be taken to be increased by such a sum as to include any value added tax (or any similar tax or taxes whether in substitution thereof or in addition thereto) charged in relation thereto except to the extent and only to the extent that the landlord obtains a credit for the same as allowable input tax.

In the statutory re-enactment clause the following may be added: 'and additionally in the case of the Value Added Tax Act 1994 shall include any directives and regulations adopted by the Council of the European Communities and which related to value added tax'.

In the definitions clause the following may be added: 'value added tax shall have its meaning as in the Value Added Tax Act 1994 and shall include any similar tax whether in substitution for or in addition to it'.

In respect of the rent review clause for valuation purposes it may be assumed that the tenant is able to recover in full any VAT charged on the rent or which may be charged on the rent but one must disregard any depreciatory effect on the rent of the fact that VAT is charged or may be charged on the rent.

II   VAT lease clauses ('freezer clause')

In an appropriate case the parties may consider a clause in the following form. It is designed, *inter alia*, to give the tenant what is in effect a ten-year 'freeze' on the election to waive exemption.

VALUE ADDED TAX

(1) Subject to sub-clause (2) below if value added tax shall be chargeable in connection with or by reference to the *rents and other sums*[1] *payable by the tenant to the landlord*[2] under any of the other clauses in this lease (whether or not the value added tax is chargeable in consequence of the exercise of an election to waive exemption) the tenant shall pay in addition to the rents and those other sums (and at the like times as the rents and those other sums are payable) *an amount equal to*[3] *17.5 per cent or other the relevant rate of value added tax for the time being*[4] of the rents and those other sums.

(2) Notwithstanding sub-clause (1) above all rents payable under this lease in respect of any period before the tenth anniversary of the date of this lease (such rents being apportioned pro rata on a day to day basis where necessary) and all other sums (payable under any other clause of this lease) payable before that anniversary shall be inclusive of all value added tax provided that if as a result of any enactment:

  (a) Value added tax is chargeable by reference to the rents (otherwise than by virtue of the exercise of an election to waive exemption); or

    (b) Value added tax would have been chargeable by reference to the rents if an election to waive exemption had not been made

then the tenant shall pay to the landlord in addition to the rents and other sums payable under other clauses of this lease an amount equal to any value added tax so chargeable by reference to the rent the other sums payable under any other clause of this lease *and the sums payable by virtue of this sub-clause.*[5]

(3) Notwithstanding anything in this lease the tenant shall not be liable to pay any amount in respect of value added tax unless the landlord shall have delivered to the tenant *reasonable evidence*[6] to show that the value added tax is properly chargeable.

(4) Where under the terms of this lease the tenant is obliged:
    (a) to make a payment to the landlord (including without limitation by way of service charge indemnity or reimbursement) by reference to any amount expended or which will or may be expended by the landlord; or
    (b) otherwise to meet all or part of the consideration for a supply for value added tax purposes made to the landlord

then (for the avoidance of doubt) the obligation shall include an obligation to pay an amount equal to any value added tax charged in respect of that amount or supply except to the extent (if any) that the landlord (or any person treated as a member of the same group as the landlord for value added tax purposes) obtains a credit for the same as allowable input tax.

(5) Not later than 30 days before the first time when for value added tax purposes a supply by the landlord giving rise to a charge to value added tax by reference to the rents generally and arising in consequence of an election to waive exemption is treated as made (the first 'tax point') the landlord shall give notice to the tenant that value added tax is chargeable with effect from that time and without limiting any further rights and remedies of the tenant in respect of any breach of this clause in the event of a breach of this clause:
    (a) the tenant shall be entitled to set off against any rents or other payments to the landlord any value added tax charged by the landlord of which the tax point falls before the end of the period of 30 days commencing on the date when the landlord does give notice as set out above to the extent that by reason of the tenant not having made an election to waive exemption or not having made a claim in due time (or otherwise by reason of the notice not being duly given) that value added tax is not recoverable by the tenant as input tax; and
    (b) any failure by the tenant to pay an amount in respect of value added tax earlier than 30 days after the notice shall not give rise to interest or to any default under this lease.

(6) References in this clause to 'election to waive exemption' are references to the election to waive exemption contained in the Value Added Tax Act 1994.

Note: The definition of 'enactment' in the definition clause can read thus:

'enactment' includes every Act of Parliament now or hereinafter enacted and every instrument directive regulation and bye-law and every order notice or direction and licence consent or permission made or given under it or pursuant to it (for the avoidance of doubt in the case of the Value Added Tax Act 1994 this shall include any directives and regulations adopted by the Council of the European Communities and which relate to value added tax) and any reference to an Act of Parliament shall include any amendment extension or re-enactment thereof for the time being in force.

Notes

(1) Actual and deemed supplies are not dealt with: only deemed supplies, ie receipts (that is all that is necessary as the law presently stands because of the special timing provisions which apply to leases). This is similar in structure to that used in the Encyclopaedia of Forms and Precedents. The author in general prefers that the actual and deemed supplies be dealt with in the clause (*see* clause I above and III below).

(2) This restriction should be noted and the lease terms referred to.

(3) The tenant does not pay the landlord's VAT as such.

(4) It is useful to refer to the 17.5 per cent but not necessary.

(5) *See* VATA 1994, s 19(2) and (3).

(6) Customs may not provide a letter confirming that the election is valid.

III   VAT lease clause (freezer clause until assignment)

VALUE ADDED TAX

(1) To pay to the landlord amounts equal to any value added tax at the rate for the time being in force as shall be chargeable (whether or not as a result of the exercise of any option or the making of any election by the landlord) on or in respect of or by reference to or as a result of:
   (a) any rents and other consideration payable under this lease; or
   (b) any supply made to the tenant under the terms of or in connection with this lease

and the payments to be made to the landlord hereunder if the said value added tax shall be chargeable by reference to the rents and other consideration so payable under this lease shall be made at the like times as such rents and other consideration is payable but otherwise when the supply which gives rise to the charge to value added tax is treated as taking place for the purposes of value added tax and (for the avoidance of doubt) it is confirmed that where in any part of this lease or in the schedule to this lease the tenant agrees to pay an amount of money (or other consideration) such amount (or other consideration) is exclusive of any value added tax which may from time to time be chargeable thereon or with respect thereto or by reference thereto or as a result of any supply made by the landlord to the tenant under the terms of or in connection with this lease.

(2) Notwithstanding sub-clause (1) above all rents and all other sums (such rents or other sums being apportioned pro rata on a day-to-day basis where necessary) payable under this lease in respect of the period commencing from the date hereof and ending on the earlier of:
   (a) the tenth anniversary of the date of this lease; and
   (b) the date this lease shall first be assigned in whole or in part to a person who it is reasonable to assume looking at the position at the date of the assignment

will obtain a credit at any time within a period of three years from the date of the assignment for any value added tax which is charged or would be charged assuming value added tax was chargeable on or in respect of or by reference to or as a result of any rents or other consideration payable under this lease or any supply made to the tenant under the terms of or in connection with this lease

shall be inclusive of all value added tax provided that if as a result of any enactment (whenever passed into law):

(i) value added tax is chargeable by reference to the rents (otherwise than by virtue of the exercise of the election to waive exemption); or

(ii) value added tax would have been chargeable by reference to the rents if an election to waive exemption had not been made

then the tenant shall pay to the landlord in addition to the rents and other sums payable under this lease an amount equal to any value added tax so chargeable by reference to the said rent and the other sums payable under this lease.

(3)   Where under the terms of this lease the tenant is obliged:

(a) to make a payment to the landlord (including without limitation by way of service charge indemnity or reimbursement) by reference to any amount expended or which will or may be expended by the landlord; or

(b) otherwise to meet all or part of the consideration for a supply for value added tax purposes made to the landlord

then (for the avoidance of doubt) the obligation shall include an obligation to pay an amount equal to any value added tax charged in respect of that amount or supply except to the extent (if any) that the landlord (or any person treated as a member of the same group as the landlord for value added tax purposes) obtains a credit for the same as allowable input tax.

(4)   References in this clause to 'election to waive exemption' are references to the election to waive exemption contained in the Value Added Tax Act 1994.

5   LAND SALE CONTRACTS (*see* p 31 *et seq*)

The first clause is a VAT inclusive clause and seeks to provide that the vendor will not be able to increase the price or any other sums payable under the contract on the exercise of the option and that if, for some reason, it is charged, then the VAT will be included in the price or other sums stipulated in the contract so that, effectively, the consideration cannot be increased.

The second clause is designed to preserve the rights of the vendor to charge VAT on a sale and indeed if he exercises his option to waive exemption.

VAT inclusive clause

To be used when a price has been agreed and that amount is not to be increased on account of the vendor being chargeable to VAT whether in consequence of the exercise of the option by him to waive exemption or otherwise.

CLAUSE X (VALUE ADDED TAX)

The price and any other sums herein stipulated to be payable by the purchaser shall be inclusive of any value added tax chargeable thereon or by reference thereto or by reference to the making of any supply by the vendor which relates to the property and the vendor will not exercise any option or make any election which will cause valued added tax to be chargeable on or by reference to the price or any other sum stipulated herein or any part or parts thereof or by reference to the making of any supply by the vendor which relates to the property.

VAT exclusive clause

This clause can be used by the vendor if he wants to ensure that the price or other sums payable under the contract can be increased to take into account any liability for value added tax which he may have with respect to the disposal of the land.

CLAUSE Y (VALUE ADDED TAX)

In addition to the price and any other sums stipulated as being payable by the purchaser in the other clauses in this agreement the purchaser shall pay to the vendor on the completion date the sum of £X (alternatively the clause could refer to the rate of VAT chargeable at the time and provide for an adjustment if the rate changes) to cover the value added tax which the vendor will be liable for or be charged to on or by reference to the price and the other said sums and the sums payable under this clause or as a result of any supply made by the vendor in connection with the property.

6   VAT CHARGEABLE ON PART OF THE SALE PRICE ON SALE OF COMMERCIAL BUILDING (*see* p 218 *et seq*)

The taxpayer may have elected to waive exemption with respect to a building but, say, two-thirds of the building may comprise dwelling house use with the remaining third comprising commercial offices. In this case, assuming the Customs have agreed that apportionment, VAT on the sale of the building will be charged on one-third of the sale price. It cannot be chargeable on the remaining two-thirds. The supply with respect to this two-thirds will be exempt.

The parties may take a bona fide view that that is the correct apportionment, but it is possible the Customs will take a different view on the matter.

In this case one approach may be to charge VAT with respect to the one-third and provide that in the event of the Customs taking a different view on the vatable portion the parties will issue a credit note or a further VAT invoice as the case may be.

For example, if the vatable portion is only a fifth according to the Customs' decision, then a repayment would be made of part of the VAT and a credit note issued; if the vatable portion is, in accordance with the Customs' decision, 50 per cent then a further invoice will be issued by the vendor and the purchaser must pay further monies.

Clauses in the sale contract along the lines below may be considered appropriate by the parties.

Draft clauses

DEFINITIONS

'Deposit' means the sum of Two Million Pounds (£2,000,000.00) plus a further amount equal to the Value Added Tax chargeable on the Vatable Portion (that further amount being £116,666.66).

'VAT Supply' means the supply of the freehold of the Property made hereunder or pursuant hereto or on completion of this Agreement and any other supply within the VAT Act.

'Vatable Portion' means the part of the supply of the freehold of the Property which is a taxable supply for the purposes of Value Added Tax and the parties agree that this part is equal to one-third of the value of the property and of the Purchase Price.

'Exempt Portion' means that part of the supply of the freehold of the Property which is an exempt supply for the purposes of Value Added Tax and the parties agree that this part is equal to two-thirds of the value of the property and of the Purchase Price.

SALE PURCHASE DEPOSIT AND PURCHASE PRICE

1. The Vendor will sell and the Purchaser will purchase the Property in consideration of the Purchase Price upon the terms and conditions set out herein.
2. The sale and purchase hereby agreed should be completed on the Completion Date.
3. The Purchase Price shall be Twenty Million Pounds (£20,000,000.00) plus a further amount equal to the Value Added Tax chargeable on the Vatable Portion (if the applicable rate of Value Added Tax shall be 17.5% this further amount shall be (£1,166,666.66).
4. On exchange of contracts the Purchaser shall pay the Deposit to the Vendor's solicitors as agent for the Vendor.
5. On completion the Purchaser shall pay to the Vendor the sum of Eighteen Million Pounds (£18,000,000.00) plus a further amount equal to the Value Added Tax chargeable on the Vatable Portion (if the applicable rate of the Value Added Tax shall be 17.5% this further amount shall be £1,050,000.00).
6. In the event that H.M. Customs and Excise shall make a decision in writing that the Vatable Portion shall be more or less than one-third or the Exempt Portion shall be more or less than two-thirds then the parties agree they will accept the decision and will as soon as reasonably practicable issue credit notes or further Value Added Tax invoices (as the case may be) and repay or pay the sums referable thereto as appropriate (but not so far as they relate to any interest charges or surcharges or fines or penalties imposed on one or other of the parties hereto).

Appendix 3

Questions and answers

Questions

1 Can VAT be payable when a tenant surrenders his lease for a consideration paid by the landlord?

2 Must a builder charge VAT if he constructs civil engineering works such as an estate road where the development is a residential development?

3 If the developer sells a bare site to a person who intends to develop it for residential purposes, can he exercise the option and charge VAT on the disposal consideration?

4 If the owner of land exercises the election to waive exemption and then contracts to sell his land can he add an amount to cover the VAT to the sale price?

5 When did the capital goods provisions come into operation?

6 When were refurbishments added to the definition of capital goods?

7 What is the bank's ransom?

Answers

1 Yes but only if the tenant has elected to waive exemption (*see* p 320).

2 Strictly yes in law, but no in practice (*see* p 191).

3 Yes, unless, exceptionally, the case comes within any of the seven heads in Sched 10, paras 2(2)(a), 2(2)(b), 2(2)(c), 2(2)(d), 2(3)(a), 2(3)(b) and 2(3A) (*see* p 000).

4 Yes, provided there is an express or implicit term in the contract which enables him to do so.

5 They came into operation on 1 April 1990.

6 On 3rd July 1997 (*see* p 261).

7 This is a payment made by a tenant to persuade the landlord not to exercise his option to charge VAT on the rents (*see* p 235).

8 Is it true that stamp duty can be payable on VAT where, for instance, property is sold by X to Y and X is obliged to charge VAT, or exercises his option to charge VAT?

8 Yes (*see* p 75).

9 Can an overseas landlord exercise the option to charge VAT with respect to UK land?

9 He should be able to exercise the option in all cases (*see* p 240).

10 Is it important to distinguish between a licence and a licence to occupy land?

10 Yes, a licence to occupy land is exempt unless the option is exercised. A licence which does not amount to a licence to occupy land is vatable unless, exceptionally, it amounts to an interest in a right over land.

11 For the purposes of the option provisions, is an industrial complex grouped around a fully enclosed concourse a single building?

11 The industrial complex will comprise a building (*see* p 224).

12 If I sell a freehold with a new civil engineering work constructed thereon, must VAT on the entire sale price be charged?

12 VAT must be charged only on the part of the sale price referable to the civil engineering work (*see* p 121).

13 On the sale of freehold land with old parking facilities (over three years since completion of construction) thereon, must VAT be charged if the vendor has not exercised the election to waive exemption?

13 Following the case of *The Commissioners v Parkinson* [1989] STC 51, VAT must not be charged.

14 Is the construction of new dwellings always zero-rated?

14 Yes, provided a new building is constructed (*see* p 174).

15 If X lets property and exercises the election to waive exemption must he charge VAT on the sale of his reversion?

15 Yes, unless the 'going concern' relief can apply (*see* p 340) or the election is disapplied.

16 Are local authorities within the scope of VAT?

16 Yes, *inter alia*, if they delve into the world of commercial property development and lettings (*see* Chapter 4).

17 Are payments by a tenant in satisfaction of a landlord's claim for dilapidations at the end of a lease vatable?

17 The payments are outside the scope of VAT (*see* p 160).

18 Are reverse premiums paid by the
assignor of a lease to an assignee of
the lease vatable if the election has
not been exercised?

18 The supply is exempt (*see* p 335).

Checklists

COMMON TRAPS

(1) Exercising the election to waive exemption and forgetting to tell the lawyers that when the property is sold or let VAT must be charged on the sale proceeds or letting income.

(2) Contracting to purchase property and not realising that the vendor can exercise the election to waive exemption and add VAT to the purchase price.

(3) Acquiring part of the land owned by X in consideration of carrying out building works on the remainder of the land owned by X. The builder will have been paid in kind as opposed to cash, but there is still a vatable supply.

(4) Forgetting that any sale of a new freehold commercial building, above the registration limit and done in the course of a business, within three years from completion is vatable regardless of how many sales take place within that three-year period.

(5) Not realising that the disposal of the freehold of new civil engineering works gives rise to a vatable charge within three years of completion of the building and indeed on any sale after the building works have commenced if the sale is freehold. For example, the disposal of a new golf course within three years, if the sale is a freehold sale, could give rise to a VAT charge.

(6) Falling into going concern relief traps. The disposal of a let building is the disposal of a business as a going concern but both parties may need to elect to waive exemption in an appropriate case (*see* p 342).

(7) If a lease is granted and no reference is made to VAT, then VAT can be added to the rent otherwise payable if the election to waive exemption is thereafter exercised. However, if that lease is surrendered and a regrant made on identical terms, without reserving the right to add VAT to the rent otherwise payable, the rent may become VAT inclusive.

(8) Not realising that if a rent-free period is offered to a tenant in consideration of the tenant's agreeing to carry out works that a VAT charge can arise.

(9) Overlooking the situation where the election to waive exemption is disapplied (*see* p 218).

(10) Not realising the full effects of the '*Lubbock Fine* principle' on all manner of transactions relating to leases eg surrender, reverse premiums etc (*see* p 335).

TAX PLANNING OPPORTUNITIES

(1) Exercising the election in order to reclaim VAT.

(2) Carving up the ownership of property among companies in a corporation tax group (but not in a VAT group) so that the one company can elect and another company not elect in an appropriate case.

(3) A taxpayer may have elected in order to reclaim VAT, eg the property may be constructed to be let for hotel use. Ultimately, if the property is to be used as dwelling houses then an exempt sale would be made. This could affect the input tax position, but there is a six-year cut-off rule which, in an appropriate case, can be relevant (*see* the 1995 Regulations, reg 108(1)) (for the election procedure in this situation *see* p 218).

(4) VAT chargeable on the sale of new commercial freehold buildings or civil engineering works may be avoided by the grant of a long lease.

(5) A reverse premium which is to be paid by a company to another person could be paid by transferring the negative value lease to a subsidiary of the payer, putting the cash reverse premium in the company and transferring the company for £1 to the proposed new tenant who takes on the onerous lease (*see* p 332, but note 335).

(6) The sale of going concern relief should be used wherever appropriate. If there is doubt as to its application, the parties may want to ensure for the sake of certainty that the position does not come within that relief, with the purchaser clearly being able to reclaim the VAT in an appropriate case.

(7) Taxpayers in an appropriate case should seek to rely on the composite supply doctrine (*see* p 42).

(8) In an appropriate case companies should register as a group for VAT purposes (*see* p 50).

(9) Taxpayers should take special care over tax points, and should postpone these wherever possible by issuing invoices which do not amount to VAT invoices.

(10) Payments for finance in property deals, eg for giving a performance guarantee, are exempt from VAT. Note that if in reality premiums are paid on an insurance policy, Insurance Premium Tax may be in point (*see* FA 1994, s 48 *et seq*).

(11) The restriction in reg 108(3) of the 1995 Regulations can give rise to considerable VAT savings. If a taxpayer reclaims VAT because he intends to make a
vatable supply and he ends up making an exempt supply because of a subsequent change in the law, he does not have to repay his input tax if reg 108(3)
governs the position. This can give rise to a tax windfall (*see* p 86).

Appendix 5

Flowchart

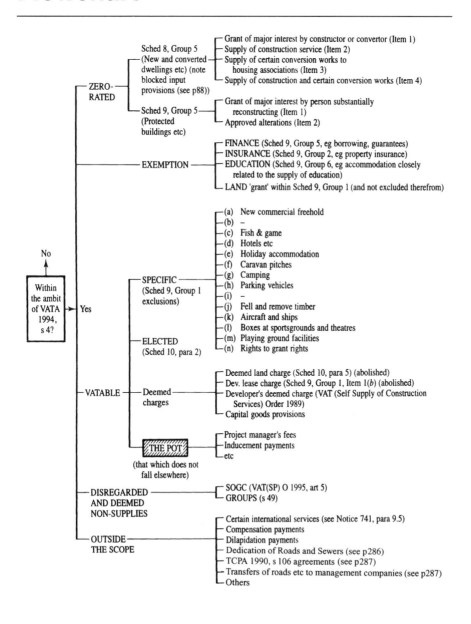

Grant of major interest by constructor or convertor (Item 1)
Supply of construction service (Item 2)
Supply of certain conversion works to housing associations (Item 3)
Supply of construction and certain conversion works (Item 4)

Sched 8, Group 5 (New and converted dwellings etc) (note blocked input provisions (see p88))

ZERO-RATED

Sched 9, Group 5 (Protected buildings etc)

Grant of major interest by person substantially reconstructing (Item 1)
Approved alterations (Item 2)

EXEMPTION

FINANCE (Sched 9, Group 5, eg borrowing, guarantees)
INSURANCE (Sched 9, Group 2, eg property insurance)
EDUCATION (Sched 9, Group 6, eg accommodation closely related to the supply of education)
LAND 'grant' within Sched 9, Group 1 (and not excluded therefrom)

No

Within the ambit of VATA 1994, s 4?

Yes

SPECIFIC (Sched 9, Group 1 exclusions)

(a) New commercial freehold
(b) –
(c) Fish & game
(d) Hotels etc
(e) Holiday accommodation
(f) Caravan pitches
(g) Camping
(h) Parking vehicles
(i) –
(j) Fell and remove timber
(k) Aircraft and ships
(l) Boxes at sportsgrounds and theatres
(m) Playing ground facilities
(n) Rights to grant rights

ELECTED (Sched 10, para 2)

VATABLE

Deemed charges

Deemed land charge (Sched 10, para 5) (abolished)
Dev. lease charge (Sched 9, Group 1, Item 1(b)) (abolished)
Developer's deemed charge (VAT (Self Supply of Construction Services) Order 1989)
Capital goods provisions

THE POT
(that which does not fall elsewhere)

Project manager's fees
Inducement payments
etc

DISREGARDED AND DEEMED NON-SUPPLIES

SOGC (VAT(SP) O 1995, art 5)
GROUPS (s 49)

OUTSIDE THE SCOPE

Certain international services (see Notice 741, para 9.5)
Compensation payments
Dilapidation payments
Dedication of Roads and Sewers (see p286)
TCPA 1990, s 106 agreements (see p287)
Transfers of roads etc to management companies (see p287)
Others

Appendix 6

Case study

The figures *below* illustrate a classical property development. The VAT questions arising are then listed, and answers provided.

Figure 1:   The initial position

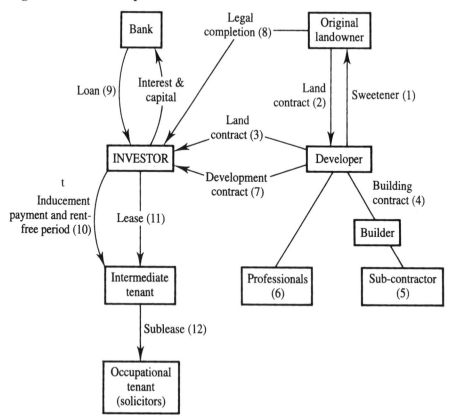

Figure 2:   Five years later

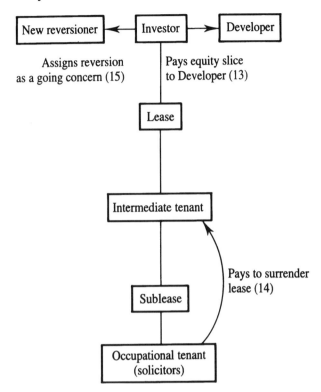

QUESTIONS

Number
on diagrams

(1) The developer seeks to persuade the original landowner, who is a farmer and who has not elected to waive exemption, to sell his land to the developer. The land is to be developed as a new office block. He pays an inducement to the landowner. Does the landowner pay VAT on the inducement?

(2) The landowner then contracts to sell the land (freehold) to the developer. Is this an exempt supply? How can VAT be chargeable on part of the sale proceeds?

(3) The developer elects to waive exemption and then contracts to sell the land to the investor. The investor elects to waive exemption. Is VAT chargeable on the sale proceeds received by the developer?

(4) The developer enters into a building contract with the builder. Would the builder charge VAT?

(5) The builder enters into a sub-contract with the sub-contractor. Would the sub-contractor charge VAT?

(6) The developer enters into a contract with the professionals for legal, accountancy project management, architectural and planning services. Would the professionals charge VAT?

(7) The developer will enter into a development contract with the investor under which he agrees to build the building for a fixed fee plus a share of the profits, depending on the ultimate rent achieved. Is the fee vatable; if so at what point?

(8) To mitigate stamp duty, legal completion takes place before any building works are started and the legal title is vested in the investor. Does this have any VAT relevance?

(9) The investor is a pension fund and borrows some money from a bank and pays interest and repays capital. Is this a vatable transaction? Does the investor suffer any deemed VAT charges?

(10) The developer has the obligation of finding a lessee and the investor agrees to pay an inducement sum to the new tenant and grant the new tenant a nine-month rent-free period. Has the intermediate tenant made two vatable supplies?

(11) The intermediate tenant succumbs and takes the lease and elects to waive exemption. Is VAT chargeable on the rents payable by the intermediate tenant? If so, can he reclaim that VAT? What is the position if the intermediate tenant agrees to pay the landlord's solicitor's costs?

(12) The tenant is a property investor and finds an occupational tenant to use the property, under a sublease, for providing legal services as a firm of solicitors. The occupational tenant does not elect to waive exemption. If the solicitors have not elected to waive exemption on what basis can they reclaim the VAT charged to them on the rent?

Five years later, the structure begins to creak . . .

(13) The investor has to pay the developer the agreed equity slice. What is the tax point?

(14) The occupational tenant is in financial difficulties and has to pay a reverse premium to the intermediate tenant to relieve himself of his sublease. Who makes the vatable supply?

(15) The investor also wishes to be free of the situation and assigns the reversion to a new reversioner who elects to waive exemption. Must VAT be charged? How do the capital goods provisions apply?

ANSWERS

(1) The inducement could be vatable (if it is above the registration limit or the farmer is VAT registered) unless it amounts to a gift or it could be shown to be part of the exempt sale proceeds.

(2) The money paid by the developer to the original landowner under the land contract would be exempt as the landowner had not elected to waive exemption. If the farmer sells a *new* civil engineering work or building freehold, VAT may be chargeable.

(3) The developer would charge VAT to the investor.

(4) The builder would charge VAT to the developer.

(5) The sub-contractor would charge VAT to the builder unless, exceptionally, he is below the registration limit and not registered for VAT.

(6) The professionals, including the project manager, would charge VAT on their fees.

(7) The amount paid by the investor to the developer would be vatable by reference to the date the services are fully performed (*see* p 359).

(8) This would simply be a formal vesting of the legal estate and would have no special consequences.

(9) This would be an exempt supply so no VAT would be charged on the interest or the repayments of capital. No deemed VAT charges should be in point.

(10) The inducement payment may be vatable (*see* p 327) but the rent-free period would not, unless, exceptionally, the intermediate tenant agrees to do works in consideration of the rent-free period.

(11) The grant of the lease would give rise to vatable rents as the investor had elected to waive exemption. In order to recover VAT on the rents, the intermediate tenant elected to waive exemption. The money paid to cover the landlord's solicitor's costs is really a vatable premium paid for the lease.

(12) The occupational tenant would be charged VAT on the rents but could reclaim it because it was using the property for a fully vatable purpose, ie as a solicitor's office.

Five years later, the structure begins to creak . . .

(13) It is very likely that the equity slice would have been charged to VAT when the developer completed his services so that there should be no further VAT payable by the developer on the receipt of the monies (*see* p 369).

(14) This is a 'reverse surrender' (*see* p 319).

(15) If the new reversioner also elects and notifies the Customs (*see* p 342) then, when the investor assigns the lease, there will be no VAT charge but the new reversioner must be careful that if the new reversioner uses the property for an exempt purpose, he may have to repay some of the VAT reclaimed by the investor on the development of the project under the ten-year capital goods provisions (*see* p 352).

Index